Internationalism and the State in the Twentieth Century

During the twentieth century, formal links between governments have become much more intense, reflecting a growing emphasis on internationalism and the world community. There has been a multi-layered transformation in the relations between states, at both a social and a diplomatic level. This has resulted in, amongst other changes, an increase in the number of international organisations and collective security arrangements and an expansion in international law.

This text examines closely the development of this phenomenon, from its roots before the founding of the League of Nations in 1919 to its present-day forms. Through her analysis of power relations, material changes and developments in ideologies, Cornelia Navari provides an accessible and student-friendly historical introduction to the changing relations between states. The subjects which she covers include long-term trends relating to war, the changing balance of power, decolonisation, the European system and the Cold War. This volume is essential reading for all those interested in the history of International Relations in the twentieth century.

Cornelia Navari is Senior Lecturer in Political Science and International Studies at the University of Birmingham.

Internationalism and the State in the Twentieth Century

Cornelia Navari

London and New York

First published 2000
by Routledge
11 New Fetter Lane, London EC4P 4EE

Simultaneously published in the USA and Canada
by Routledge
29 West 35th Street, New York, NY 10001

Routledge is an imprint of the Taylor & Francis Group

© 2000 Cornelia Navari

Typeset in Baskerville by Taylor & Francis Books Ltd
Printed and bound in Great Britain by MPG Books Ltd,
Bodmin, Cornwall

British Library Cataloguing in Publication Data
A catalogue record for this book is available from the British Library

Library of Congress Cataloging in Publication Data
Navari, Cornelia
Internationalism and the state in the twentieth century / Cornelia Navari.
Includes bibliographical references and index.
1. International organization. 2. International relations. 3.
Internationalism. I. Title.
JZ1308.N38   2000   99–42565
327.1'7–dc21   CIP

ISBN 0–415–09747–9 (hbk)
ISBN 0–415–09748–7 (pbk)

Contents

Acknowledgements

This is primarily a work of secondary scholarship and my debts are recorded in the notes. They mix general surveys with special studies, enabling the reader who wishes to go further to choose between depth and breadth. Two surveys in particular deserve special mention, however. Chapters 3 and 4 owe an enormous amount to A.G. Kenwood and A.L. Lougheed's *Growth of the International Economy*, without which they might not have been possible, and Chapter 6 draws from Colin McInnes and G.D. Sheffield's edited volume on *Warfare in the Twentieth Century*. Finally, I owe a special debt to Sir George Clark's *The Seventeenth Century*, which inspired this project and to which I referred again and again when requiring solutions to the problems of a survey.

Introduction

During the course of the twentieth century, there occurred a transformation in the relations of states so fundamental that later scholars may come to see it in terms of a revolution. For this transformation there was no single name. Some called it 'internationalisation', while others used the term 'interdependence' and still others spoke of the development of 'world community'. Nor did it have a single aspect, appearing sometimes as a social and economic movement, and at other times as a political or ideological movement. Scholars would argue as to whether it was primarily an economic transformation, or a matter of policy and political choices, or a matter of ideology and new values. But while there was no general agreement on its character, there was general agreement on its external signs.

One was the increasing density of diplomatic encounters. Even as late as the last quarter of the nineteenth century, diplomacy had been a matter for foreign offices and war councils; the entire diplomatic community as late as 1880 had consisted of perhaps no more than one hundred ambassadors in all. By the middle of the twentieth century, it had expanded to include commerce departments, health departments, treasuries and drug administrations. All the ordinary activities of the twentieth-century state, to a greater or lesser degree, came to be subjects of diplomacy. There was also the institutionalised representation of many more private groups and their intercession with state bodies. The internationalist literature of the first decade of the twentieth century proudly recorded 300 professional associations or cause groups with international links; a mid-twentieth-century manual listed more than 20,000. Instead of that thin body of official representatives of perhaps no more than a hundred altogether which had served nineteenth-century cabinet offices, twentieth-century diplomacy came to absorb hundreds of thousands of people acting on behalf of multifarious causes.

The second may be characterised as 'institutionalisation'. Steadily through the century, there developed an increasingly dense web of international organisations which linked states in permanent commitments, served by a large corps of international civil servants who actively participated in diplomacy. There was also the expansion of international law, and the development of ideas of shared or 'collective' security which were institutionalised into long-standing defence arrangements. Finally, and to some the most significant, were changes in the concept of state sovereignty. States took on obligations with regard to other states which would have been unthinkable in an earlier era. Even more significantly, they donated segments of their sovereignty to joint administration on a variety of issues which would have formerly been regarded as solely within the domestic purview of the state. Both governments and groups operated increasingly within, and by reference to, rules which distributed inter-state functions to an impressive array of inter-governmental committees and supra-national arrangements.

Indeed, so dense had relations among states become, so institutionalised in their form and so intertwined the subjects of them, that some people began to see states and national communities as constituent parts of a greater community, as subsisting within and constituting a political system that contained them all. They began to speak of the 'international system' and the 'international community' as substantive entities, with lives of their own and with determining wills.

These movements did not occur at once, nor precisely in parallel. The initiation of international organisation is generally placed in 1919, with the founding of the League of Nations. But it was not until after 1945 that the plethora of new international institutions characteristic of twentieth-century diplomacy was created. The 'new international law' was reckoned by one observer to have been born in 1911. But it jumped dramatically after the establishment of the League, and again with the establishment of the United Nations. A European movement dedicated to establishing tighter links among European states began in 1923, but it was scarcely a popular movement until after the Second World War.

Nor did its focus remain steady. During the 1930s, internationalism became associated with imperial reform, and the empire began to be thought of as a form of international organisation. It was only after the Second World War, with the onset of decolonisation, that movement turned back to linking new and old states through wider and more universal organisations.

Some have seen behind these developments the moving hand of a single principle. They have seen them as the result of late capitalism, or industrialisation, or a unilinear process of modernisation. Nor were they entirely mistaken, for changes in policy were by no means unconnected with developments in economy. But those who, like Sir George Clark, wish to 'cut the meat of reality at the joints' will not be satisfied with a vague theory that all of these things are related. They will want to know how they are related and how closely related. This book is about some of the major developments affecting the relations of states during the twentieth century, and their contribution to that transformation.

For one reason or another, not all topics have been covered. Reasons of space, for example, led to the sacrifice of any account of arms control. Equally, while the events to be considered fall generally between 1919 and the last decade of the century, some developments had their beginnings before, and some had not yet finished at its end. What I have done is to begin where the story began, paying more attention to developments than clinging to a single time frame.

The story proceeds in three parts. In the first part, I have paid attention to a number of long trends which contributed to the transformation. These were deep changes in society and social power, as well as economic developments. This section concerns internationalism as a social and economic movement. During the second part, I have outlined state policy and state choice. Internationalism was not simply produced, it was also *chosen*, and it was chosen by governments with specific political objectives in mind. Those political objectives form part of the story and deserve attention. This section concerns internationalism-as-policy. Finally, I have devoted a closing section to evaluating some of the results of internationalism. The many new diplomatic instruments created during the twentieth century largely defined internationalism; and many claims were made about the new creations. In telling that story, it seems appropriate that some attempt be made to judge the results. This section will consider internationalism-as-ideology.

The account will treat contributory ideas as well as institutions and material developments. The processes which produced internationalism were informed by conceptual categories as well as by material 'facts'. The use of statistics and the development of modern statistical runs produced many of the 'trends' which informed policy. The idea of a 'nation' informed the concepts of a 'national product', 'national power' and 'national interests', while the growing political sentiment of nationalism was one of the factors that allowed national power to be mobilised. The experience of twentieth-century wars called forth the idea of 'total war', and the idea of total war informed many subsequent developments in the use of power.

In selecting relevant ideas, I have been concerned primarily with those which had independent effects, and effects of a fairly large scale. These were ideas which significantly informed social movements, which became the major grids for the comprehension of social and economic tendencies and which affected the selection of policy instruments. They were also those which were used to judge the outcomes of internationalism. Internationalism was not only a trend or a policy, it was also an aspiration. As an aspiration, it was judged by different political and social theories which established a range of (sometimes conflicting) criteria for what it meant to be an internationalist.

These will generally be treated in the chapters to which they belong, but there is one idea which deserves to be highlighted from the beginning as it had effects across a range of developments and informed social theorising, and social ideas, more generally. This was 'holism', a substantive development in thought which rose in the second half of the nineteenth century and which had important consequences for the understanding of international relations. By holism is meant the tendency to see social formations, including states, as parts of wholes larger than themselves, as constituent parts of such wholes, and their forms, their sentiments and their evolution as directed by the development of the whole. There were various types of holism which dominated thinking about international relations from the last quarter of the nineteenth century, but by far the most influential was the Darwinian revolution, with its tendency to see an organism in relation to an environment and as changing and evolving in response to its environment.

Applied to international relations, it came in two successive and generally opposed forms. There was the 'aggressive' social Darwinism, dominant during the last decade of the nineteenth century, which pictured the real agents of international relations as nations and nations as pitted against one another in a necessary and inevitable struggle for power and survival. The French writer Renan and many in the new German national school adopted this perspective, and it was associated in the liberal mind with a selfish, inward-looking and aggressive state policy. But there were also the co-operative or 'liberal' Darwinists. According to Herbert Spencer, the main adapter of Darwinist ideas to social theory, the early antagonistic period would pass away, to be replaced by a harmonious development not only between segments of societies but between societies as a whole. These were sometimes called progressives or 'benign evolutionists'.

In its aspect as progressivism, benign evolutionism assumed that conflict was an adjustment device and that society was actually moving, some thought unilinearly, towards a higher level of social integration out of its own 'internal' developments. Sometimes the emphasis was on the growth of social needs which would require further integration for their satisfaction; sometimes the emphasis was on the moral development of individual citizens who would become increasingly aware that individual progress and individual well-being depended on social co-operation. So far as state relations were concerned, it anticipated the growth of internal connections between states, sometimes in the form of parallel institutions and laws, sometimes in the form of more co-operative tendencies among individuals and groups and the development of transnational links among 'national' social segments. It also predicted that at least some of these tendencies would be institutionalised. Spencer and the later First World War progressives, such as L.T. Hobhouse and Leonard Woolf, anticipated the growth of a variety of linking devices, including inter-governmental committees for the management of social needs and international bureaucracies with autonomous powers, as well as the growth of more legalised adjudication of conflict.

Evolutionism dominated thinking about international relations during the first part of the twentieth century, and it influenced the formation of several significant social and political programmes thereafter, such as federalism and functionalism. It was also a factor in the collection of some relevant facts: the search for 'original' nations and for the efficient secret of economic growth were both influenced by the idea that society was an organism with a potential which might be dynamised by its encounter with an environment or with environmental change. Finally, it contributed to a more general social tone which emphasised co-operation, institution-building and the inevitability of progress.

In respect of the academic study of international relations, it directed attention to 'end states' and to the interaction of parts. Thus, international law was studied, throughout the century, in terms of a movement towards 'real law', and its study was widened to include phenomena which would either promote or impede that sort of development, while the League was initially, and popularly, represented as an end-state in itself and the major focus for the study of international relations on that account. Biological holism also inclined scholars to study international institutions as social totalities whose development depended upon, variously, the development of more refined methods of interest adjudication at the 'top' level or more vigorous social movements at the 'bottom' level.

Not all of its implications for political programmes were traditionally liberal. Some progressives seized on the notion of the 'organic state' to argue for a widened remit to government and to an enhanced role for the state in promoting social progress. Evolutionism also qualified the old liberal idea of the self-determining individual, and directed attention to individuals as members of groups or to groups alone as social constituents. On the other hand, the actual exercise of authority came to be conceived in more diverse ways. The idea of the state as the main source of social regulation, prevalent in the nineteenth century, gave way under its influence to the idea that social order was an aspect of social life more generally, and that it sprang from many sources within society.

Partly in consequence, it contributed to quite new ideas of the state and to new conceptions of sovereignty. The state was increasingly conceived during the twentieth century as a residual governing agency of limited compass operating in the midst of a variety of other authorities, whose function (and not all progressives believed even this was necessary) was to co-ordinate. In respect of sovereignty, the idea that society had self-regulatory tendencies encouraged the idea that law emerged from many sources, and not merely one source. 'Legal pluralism', as this doctrine came to be known, formed the basis of a particularly intense movement in Britain during the first two decades of the century which proposed more federalised government. It would re-emerge in various forms in subsequent decades, among them integral federalism and functionalism, each of which proposed new models of international organisation. Both developed from the idea that sovereignty was not a logical necessity but rather a socially determined concept, and that it changed according to social needs and social development.

When the League of Nations was created, many in the progressive movement, influenced by the doctrine of benign evolutionism, took it for granted that the League was the 'higher order' regulatory agency, as well as the more developed form of regulation. They saw proposals for collective security and economic co-operation as evidence that states and national social orders had begun to understand the requirement of collective decision-making for their own well-being, and that the League was necessary to collective progress. Indeed, it is impossible to grasp the aura that surrounded the League, or to understand the sense of crisis that attended its failure, without reference to the belief, prevalent especially among English progressives, that regulation had to move upward, as well as more horizontally outwards, for individual societies to survive.

Evolution's progressivist associations did not outlast the rise of totalitarianism and it declined as an approach to social comprehension during the 1930s. But it was replaced by other forms of social comprehension no less 'holistic', if somewhat less optimistic in their views of future progress. The two most important were functionalism, out of anthropology, and systems analysis, developed from engineering. In the former, social movements and political institutions were analysed according to their roles in performing a range of social tasks. In the latter, they were seen from the perspective of maintaining or undercutting social and political stability, an increasing concern of social science in the age of mass politics.

The notion of a 'system' affected the understanding of internationalism. Though not completely extinguishing its organic and progressivist associations, the metaphor added a more mechanistic and more neutral aspect to the concept. By the new mechanical understanding, internationalism became associated with the idea of an 'international system' of related parts which moved rather automatically in relation to one another. There was also the doctrine of 'interdependence' – the belief that developments in one part had important consequences for developments in other parts, not all of which were necessarily benign.

While no general theory of political developments will be attempted, there are several significant sets of historical conjunctures to which attention should be drawn, as they will emerge at various points throughout the account. The first concerns the coincidence between the development of progressivist social thought and the reality of war. The First World War changed many of the presuppositions of the social theorists of the time concerning the relationship between domestic reform and international order. The second concerns the prevailing ideas which experience of the Great Depression produced with regard to economic growth, as these met the onset of the Cold War. The concern with growth was a major preoccupation of the age, and various growth formulas served to frame, and to set the path of, state policy more generally. The third concerns the globalisation of the balance of power, as this met the process of decolonisation.

War and social progress

Every age has had its philosophers who deplored war and who sought arrangements to mitigate it. But nineteenth-century progressives had a distinctive theory to account for war. They saw it as intimately connected with the social form and with the type of state engendering it. In particular, they believed war was an attribute of the pre-commercial absolutist state and an inevitable by-product of its political biases, notably its reliance on an aristocratic or warrior class and its notions of wealth-creation through seizure. Accordingly, they related the incidence of war to the refusal of absolutist states to reform, to depose their autocrats and to establish liberal constitutional orders. Albert Sorel, in a work on the diplomacy of the *ancien régime*, popularised the association, and it had become a common view during the latter part of the nineteenth century. Nineteenth-century liberal reformers also had a general belief in the inevitability of liberal reforms. Accordingly, it was believed that, as states reformed, war would simply disappear. For this reason, nineteenth-century popular peace movements spent little time addressing the problem of war directly. They simply pressed for the liberal programme.

The onset of the 'liberal empires', the popular enthusiasm for imperial ventures and for military excursions frankly in pursuit of imperial ends, such as the Boer War, might have been expected to shake liberal faith in the efficacy of their theory, and some it did: Herbert Spencer, Britain's major social theorist during the last quarter of the nineteenth century, believed imperialism threatened the liberal state and called into question the progressive reform programme. Generally, however, most liberals made their peace with the developing imperial ambitions of their governments. They saw empire as the spread of ideas of civilisation and liberalism out into the world for a period of education and advancement after which, their work done, the imperialists would gracefully withdraw. They represented it as but one phase, the external phase, in the liberalising programme, which would pass away.

Of greater concern to late nineteenth-century progressives was the social question, and the potential political responses of the newly enfranchised, the main focus of liberal theorising after the 1880s. The latter part of the nineteenth century had seen the development of decidedly illiberal movements, including illiberal nationalist movements, and the development of less-than-liberal state policies, particularly in France, Italy and Germany, which drew on the new mass politics, an integral aspect of which was a new glorification of war. In these new popular movements, an aggressive social spirit began to offer itself as the product of change, not the peaceful evolution of society which liberal progressives had predicted.

That liberal institutions might be isolated from these developments there seemed reason to hope. In France, the Dreyfus Affair, with its nationalistic anti-semitism, had left liberal parliamentarianism intact, while in Britain, the rising labour movement was gradually being transformed into a political party with the promise of incorporation into the parliamentary system. Moreover, war was held off until 1914; and some liberal progressives remained confident as late as 1915 that it would be a short campaign, settling German ambitions, and allowing social progress to proceed. With the great autumn battles of 1915, however, the last vestiges of liberal confidence were shattered.

The Great War, as it was called, distressed liberals by its internal dynamics: its scale, its destructiveness and the unexpectedness of its duration. But what disturbed them even more was its unexpected effect on the state and social policy. Everywhere, the new hesitant programmes of social reform were absorbed into the war machines. Even liberal states showed a remarkable ability to hold populations enthralled – there were few anti-war protests – and to toss them into the maw of war. There was also the changing nature of liberal institutions, including the introduction of new 'safety' measures and the internment of radicals for the war's duration, besides the use of social policy to support the war effort. That war could distort liberal institutions was an idea that the nineteenth-century liberal had never entertained, but it became a constant fear of the twentieth-century liberal. There were also the revolutions which followed the war and the economic crises engendered by it, both of which promised vast social upheaval and which appeared to be modern war's concomitant and inevitable products. 'If we do not have Peace,' wrote one progressive in 1919, 'we will not only have war, we will have social revolution and the end of any realistic hope for a new, socially just democratic order.'

In sum, the Great War, together with its immediate aftermath, caused a radical reassessment of the social programme in the progressive movement in Europe and America. Whereas before it progressives had assumed that war would be cured by social progress and the liberal programme, after it they came to believe that war had to be ameliorated in order for social progress to occur and liberalism to be assured. By 1916, a generation of progressives had changed the priorities which had dominated the nineteenth-century liberal movement. They began to see peace as the key to social progress, instead of merely its handmaiden. They turned their attention to the adjudication and arbitration of states' disputes, to war prevention and international understanding as not merely ancillary but vital parts of the liberal social programme.

Threatened liberalism informed social theorising throughout the century. In turn, fascism, nationalism and communism all came to be seen in relation to their respective threats to the liberal state, and formed between them the major entry routes for understanding the modern social condition. The different threats also produced the main fissures in liberal opinion: the political divides in the twentieth-century liberal movement largely reflected different views as to the main source of the threat to liberalism. But in whatever form the threat appeared, the liberal response was the same. Progressive opinion held steadily to the thesis that the democratic state required an external framework or legal order linking it with other states, as the condition of its own survival.

International liberalism, as this aspect might be termed, not only came to the fore in the liberal programme, it took on increasing specificity. Whereas mere participation in the League was deemed sufficient to 1919 liberals, increasing rules characterised the liberal of 1927 and firm guarantees the liberal of 1936. There were many quarrels about the content of such rules and the kinds of obligations that liberal states should undertake, but the fragility of liberalism in one country was the most common understanding of the age, and liberals moved from securing liberalism at home to defending it abroad, and to defending it by more stable legal frameworks and secure legalised international relationships.

The efficient secret of economic growth

These speculations were taking place against a background of enormous advances in material well-being and in the expansion of the social product available to the state. The great sweep of growth which had struck England in the 1850s had spread to the continent by the 1870s, and had begun to move further abroad thereafter. Steadily through the twentieth century, growth engulfed one extra-European country after another, underpinning the widened franchises of the emerging new states, and absorbing countries increasingly into international trade and exchange.

The policy responses of middle to late nineteenth-century governments had varied from freeing trade to, later, protecting it. Initially, the predominant growth theory was the theory of 'douce commerce'. Its proponents maintained that freeing trade would enhance comparative advantages, promote wealth and encourage development. They also argued that freeing trade would induce a number of other equally benign social consequences, such as more democratic social orders and more peaceful relations among states. By the end of the nineteenth century, however, the idea of growth-through-trade was demonstrably giving way to a variety of new protectionist doctrines, which argued that growth depended on some elements of closure.

The protectionist doctrines were various, and would have different consequences. One was imperial nationalism with its emphasis on empire as a protected economic zone. Imperial nationalists argued that trade followed the flag, and that imperial ventures were vital to commercial well-being and to equalising economic advantage. A movement grew in Britain during the early twentieth century to close the vast expanse of the British Empire for Britain's competitive advantage. German thinkers in the *Weltwirtschaft* movement, by contrast, developed the theory of the large, contiguous, economic space which could be closed (and defended) if economic or political development threatened economic well-being. (Growing commercial rivalries were used to justify not only economic closure but also wars to defend closure.) When the Great Depression struck in the late 1920s, countries closed their borders and controlled their exchanges to protect employment and payments balances. Where there was empire, the large imperial spaces disappeared into closed trading areas. In fascist countries, directed work programmes were established behind closed borders to raise employment.

By the late 1940s, however, elements of 'free trade' doctrine had regained the political ascendancy. Partly in response to the poor record of economic closure, as well as to aggressive fascism, the liberal powers increasingly disputed 'fascist' closure doctrines; and free trade elements increasingly worked their way into the planning, and the diplomacy, of the peace which would follow, it was hoped, the defeat of fascism.

They were aided by a growing body of professional economists concerned to evaluate the whole range of protectionist doctrines (including 'liberal' protectionism). During the late 1930s and 1940s, economic science increasingly turned against 'closure' theories of all sorts. Pure economists demonstrated that trade could not be sustained under either closed monetary zones or autarky; and their studies of the liberal economies during the depression indicated that growth could not be sustained without an increase in trade. In general, by the late 1940s, economic science had given qualified approval to conditional free trade; that is, to the idea that, all other things being equal, trade did promote growth. Political and developmental economists also demonstrated that, unless economic growth were more equal and the international economy more stable, closure would be a continuous policy temptation.

These studies not only had implications for domestic policy. They demonstrated the dependency of domestic policy on international conditions, and they influenced popular foreign policy programmes as well as official foreign policies. By the late 1930s, the 'new' liberals had expanded the peace programme to include concern with economic inequalities, with the promotion of development, and with the maintenance of open economic exchange, all of which were deemed necessary to secure peace as well as growth. Partly in consequence, the new peace programmes would include not merely decolonisation and aid, but international regulations for trade and monetary management which would help states maintain open trading relationships.

When, following 1947, the Soviet Union and China retreated to bastions of economic protectionism, they abandoned the field of international economic regulation to the construction of the liberal powers, while economic liberalism itself became one of the methods of ensuring that local and regional communisms did not disturb the political or economic structuring of the 'free world zone'. Accordingly, as the ordinary workings of the post-war international economy gradually incorporated first Japan and then South Asia into a global market structure, they increasingly entered upon modern economic exchange within an open trading regime which not only turned upon a myriad individual producers and consumers, but which was organised within a managed carapace of trade and exchange rules. When Japan joined the OECD in 1963, its first non-European member, the condition was obedience to the rules of open exchange; while the newly formed World Bank took on the task of aiding successive waves of newly released colonies, seeing them through development programmes which were designed to integrate them into Western institutions and the liberal market.

The 'globalisation' of the balance of power

The onset of globalisation is usually dated from the 1902 treaty between Japan and Britain, aimed at containing China to the east and Russia to the north. But that diplomatic initiative was itself a response to an already evident steady outward movement of Russia to colonise the great Eurasian land mass, where it would meet an already established Britain in India and a rising Japan in East Asia, adding new levels to the 'great game' of colonial espionage. The Russo-Japanese War of 1904 was a global encounter, and it was Japan's victory in that war which finally signalled the emergence of the first non-European power and made Japan a potentially valuable ally in Britain's efforts to limit Russian expansion. It was also Japan which would eventually threaten imperial hold in

South Asia and the China seas, encouraging the overthrowing of the European balance from the Asian theatre.

Equally important, however, was the emergence of the United States as an Asian as well as European power, based partly on its westward movement and partly on the development of its sea power. The United States had taken the northern half of California from Russia as early as the 1840s, and had declared itself an interested party in the Asian balance with the arrival of Admiral Perry in Japan in 1855 (with the aim of ensuring that Japan was not only 'opened' but also remained outside of the developing European imperial zones). It was already an Asian power when victory in the Spanish–American War of 1898 gave it the Philippines and Hawaii. At the same time, the United States entered into the European balance with significant effect during the First World War, throwing the balance to France and Britain, while even earlier, increasingly after 1907, Britain was allowing the United States to police the mid-Atlantic and the trade routes between Europe and Latin America.

The rise of global power encouraged subsidiary counter-movements. The European states moved during the last quarter of the nineteenth century to secure any remaining or weakly held global bastions, essentially in Africa and South East Asia, while the United States sought increasingly to 'defend' Latin America, and to prevent the incorporation of the Latin American states into the global balance on terms unfavourable to it. The first would make Africa a European dependency, while the second would determine the United States as the Western hemisphere's hegemon.

The existence of a global field of power led to disputes about the fulcrum of power. One major question was whether sea power was giving way to the power of the great land masses; another was whether it was Russia or Germany (or China or Japan) which held the key to the Eurasian land mass. In America, the central question was whether America's global role turned on keeping Asia open or on protecting the European balance against a continental hegemon; and it would produce conflicting advocacies, reflected in the struggle between the defenders of, respectively, the 'Asia-first' or 'Europe-first' strategies which troubled American strategic policy during the Second World War. The global basis of power also made the task of balancing intricate and complex. The central question of the twentieth-century continental balance following the Russian Revolution may have been who controlled Germany, but that control could only be secured by sea lanes across the North Atlantic, and by inviting in the Soviet Union to the task of German containment. Equally, maintaining the Asian balance, and the European colonial spheres in Asia, depended on the outcome of civil war in China, and on the United States preserving its position as the pre-eminent Asian sea power, with a significant role for Britain in preserving India and Burma from the Japanese onslaught.

With the gradual dissolution of the British and French empires which proceeded steadily after the Second World War, these balances became the subject of reformulation. The expected and actual release of former colonies created a new set of independent pawns upon the global board and created many new arenas of power contestation. The United States had declared itself an interested power in Arabia as early as the 1920s, when British and French imperial hold was already beginning to weaken, and it sought to curry favour with local rulers in the Arabian peninsula thereafter. It presented itself as the major protector of the new states of South Asia after the Second World War, and entered into Africa during the 1960s.

The pawns, in turn, became important regional balancers within the wider global balance. Egypt emerged as the fulcrum power of the Middle East, between a Western-backed Israel and a Soviet-backed Syria. Turkey provided the crucial bastion against the move of the Soviet Union south, particularly after the fall of Iran to Islamic fundamentalist forces and its rejection of the West. South Korea held the line against any movement of Chinese or Russian communism to the east, and Thailand to the south. After 1960, there were not only multiple boards, but multiple balancers, as formerly remote parts of the world entered into immediate functional relationships.

Within one or another of these three sets of developments will be found the causes of internationalism, in one or other of its aspects, and those aspiring after a causal theory of internationalism should pay particular attention to them. What the present volume aspires to is situating them historically and demonstrating some of the connections between them.

Part 1

The long trends

This part of the argument outlines the context within which internationalism arose and identifies some of the forces which provided its basic impetus. Both are portrayed, and identified, in terms of trends, or sets of patterns, which is the meaning of the term 'trend'. Some were material movements; others belong to the realm of compelling social movements and/or political ideas; most are mixtures of all three. In each case, each trend contributed something to the climate surrounding internationalism, and posed either a set of problems or a condition of fact with which internationalism had to deal, which it was intended to 'solve' or by reference to which internationalist policies made sense. Each will be outlined in terms of its basic movements; at the end of each chapter its contribution to internationalism will be outlined. Generally located by quantitative statistics, empirical observation and cross-boundary comparabilities, trends take the form of correlations or associative phenomena. Thus, in the case of their contributions to internationalism, war became associated with a high degree of destructiveness and with unwelcome alterations in society, while high growth rates became associated with increases in production, with trade expansion, and with new modes of industrial organisation. But they also became known by their 'causes' – by bodies of theory which tried to explain the correlations. Where appropriate, these causal theories will also be outlined.

It should be observed that the various causal theories drew on different 'causal orders' – biological and technological, social and political – and that explanations for each trend mixed elements from different causal arenas. Natural increase was understood as a social as well as a biological phenomenon, while production was shaped by technological innovation, and by the application of science to manufacturing and agriculture, as well as by natural increase. Commerce and industry were, by contrast, primarily organisational phenomena, absorbing technological change but influenced by spatial location and management techniques, which were in turn shaped by ideas of efficiency and motives of maximising economic returns, while nationalism was a social phenomena, fundamentally caused by changing ideas of social identity, but with political consequences. Finally, war was a political phenomenon, in that it had to do with the exercise of power, and was shaped by the direction and organisation of power. But it was also a technological and social phenomenon, since invention played such a large part in twentieth-century wars, and since war was fed also by social fears and social aspirations. There were many different types of causes.

If each was produced by different causes, however, all were largely unintentional so far as their additive or process aspects were concerned. Intention was not absent: parts of each process were affected by the choices of individuals – in the sense that, for example, people could choose to have children – and such individual choices, given different circumstances, were significant in driving the process as a whole. States could also choose not to go to war. But no individual choice was sufficient to control or to direct the whole trend. In particular, these processes ground their way forward irrespective of political direction or attempts at political control; and their movements constantly evaded efforts at political interference or political control. Rather, policy had to take them into account and to work around them.

They all presented, in consequence, the appearance of naturalistic phenomena. Each seemed to rise by the operations of 'rules' internal to it, and by forces or interactive processes with which rational direction could only tinker. They all presented demands of their own which had to be fed or provided for, which could be channelled, perhaps, but which could neither be dammed nor made to go away.

They could, however, to a degree be predicted. It became a truism that population would grow, and that development was inevitable to provision and to limit it. It also seemed a safe bet that economic development required political and social co-operation as well as economic resources. It became a virtual rule that war was bound to fail, and that all states participating in war were 'bound to be' losers.

Such predictions played a large part in the movement of internationalism. It was, in part, because war was understood in terms of 'bound to fail' that efforts at conflict resolution became such a prevalent part of the twentieth-century experience. It was because population was 'bound to grow' that countries sought co-operation in its management and provision. It was in part because commerce was 'bound to be interrupted' that countries sought to establish firm rules for tariffs and monetary exchange and sought to co-ordinate those rules. Internationalism-as-policy grew on the basis of social expectations and perceived 'rules' of social development; and internationalism-as-social-and-economic-movement sought to channel, or outflank, or anticipate such expectations.

1 Population

In the hierarchies of social knowledge relevant to internationalisation, few had more immediate consequences than knowledge of population. Population statistics, almost unavailable at the beginning of the twentieth century, had become general by its end, and engendered a climate of theorising which linked population profiles to large-scale social and economic changes and individual country experiences to global trends. Indeed, population growth was one of the earliest identified 'global' trends and the subject of the earliest global statistical issues.

It also engendered the most enduring international policy effort. The regulation of population became a major undertaking of the age, with greater or lesser success, and individual country efforts drew upon and were often directed by the new food and development agencies which drew upon cross-national experiences, formulated international guidelines and transferred policy from country to country, developed as well as underdeveloped. Such policies had consequences for a range of national policies, including development and notions of national capacity, and induced a range of parallel policy initiatives.

The science of counting

The application of statistics to the governing task was scarcely an invention of the twentieth century. As early as the seventeenth century, scholars and polemicists may be found who quoted numbers to support their arguments. Iceland began to collect statistics in 1703, followed by some of the Germanic states. But statistics were scarce and their application to policy was scarcely the norm. The first statistical office of any sort was the British Board of Trade, established in 1834, while the habit of collecting statistics did not become general until the very end of the nineteenth century, when a clutch of North European governments established statistical offices.[1] Even then such basic statistics as national income were not taken: calculating national income was a product of the Great Economic Depression of the 1930s.[2]

Gradually, however, as statistical offices took form and as data bases became available, the statistical element in policy became increasingly large. By the mid-century, all governments which aspired to be 'modern' had large statistical departments, and they formulated, and defended, policy by reference to statistical issues. Indeed, it became a sign of a competent state that it could present statistics, and with the rapid period of decolonisation after 1945 the 'new' states followed suit, establishing statistical offices where they could. Statistical gathering became a *sine qua non* for the new state, the sign of its determination to administer effectively, while statistical issues became as much an attribute of a new state's 'stateness' as its national airline or national flag.

The gathering of vital statistics

Nowhere was this more clear than in the area of vital statistics: births, deaths and marriages. The Ancient World aside, regular censuses only became general after the French Revolution – Britain and France set the fashion, both taking the year 1801 as their starting point. But populations were estimated, not counted. Counting of actual persons began only in the 1840s. Britain established a register for births, marriages and deaths in 1837, but it was not compulsory for citizens to register until 1874. The gathering of the first Indian census was in 1871, but again it was merely estimated by district officers, while large parts of the rest of the world remained entirely ignorant about their numbers until after decolonisation; that is, until after the 1960s and even later, since dispersed populations, widespread illiteracy and lack of skilled personnel presented at first insurmountable obstacles to the enterprise. The first 'new country' census was carried out in the Sudan in 1960, and occasioned great excitement on that account. It was also an heroic task, requiring a collaborative effort between a number of international agencies and the new Sudanese authorities, and it illustrated the problems of counting populations where illiteracy and superstition were widespread. By 1985, however, 145 of 162 states could offer population figures of some accuracy.

Traditionally, the counting of populations had been undertaken for purposes of taxation and war service, purposes which scarcely enamoured people of the census takers. During the twentieth century, however, population counting became part of the question of how to distribute resources, of giving instead of taking. Partly in consequence, peoples began to welcome it. Indeed, they began to insist on being counted. To be left out entailed exclusion from policy considerations and implied non-citizenship. Thus, whereas the nineteenth-century censuses had left out Indians in America and aboriginal peoples in Australia, these gradually came in the twentieth century to be included among 'real' peoples.

Populations were not only counted, they were divided into their differential parts. The numbers of men, women and children, age distribution, physical circumstances and intellectual characteristics began to be inquired after, making it possible to know not only the demographic profile of a nation but some of its most intimate facts. Mortality and fertility also could be calculated with some accuracy, allowing for sophisticated theory-building. If the census was a nineteenth-century development, in the twentieth century it became demography, and demography began to develop into a science. It also became an important impetus to policy-making. Once governments could know the ways in which populations were moving, physically in terrain, generationally, socially in education and qualifications, they were also thereby pushed into planning, however inadequately, for those movements.

Despite these advances, there remained enormous variation in the quality and reliability of even vital statistics. The United States could claim that it registered 99 per cent of births and deaths;[3] while population experts judged the Nigerian census of 1973, its third census, so unreliable as to be useless for even a population estimate. Nor was it the case that in all states everyone was counted, and not only for reasons of inadequate capacity. Lebanon, whose constitution was based on population ratios as between Moslems and Christians, declined to carry out censuses altogether, for fear of disturbing the delicate communal balance. Saudi Arabia, over half of whose population consisted of non-national service employees from Egypt and Palestine, also declined to make official issues, since it was not over-anxious to reveal the degree of its dependency on skilled foreign workers.

The gatherers of statistics

It was, in the main, governments who collected statistics, and the national bias was evident in census forms: the Indonesian census had many detailed questions relating to fertility, the Canadian as to French speakers, and the 1980 US census introduced a question as to Hispanic origin.[4] During the century, however, techniques were also developed for projecting large-scale results from relatively small samples, making it possible to predict national growth rates from fertility rates in a small region, town or district. There developed, in consequence, many independent survey organisations, particularly after the Second World War, which specialised in 'sample' techniques and which offered alternative sources of information.[5] The orientation of these organisations generally remained national, however. They owed their existence to the existence of stable political orders, and their informational goals tended to be set by the requirements of national marketing and national and state policy concerns. Moreover, the national census remained important for checking results.

By the mid-1950s, the United Nations was also providing recommendations for the conduct and content of national censuses, establishing a general model, and though countries continued to ask questions relevant to them, standardisation began to develop and to become widespread. The United Nations also began to publish its own monthly record of population and statistics (from 1947), and its annual *Demographic Yearbook* became a basic guide, not only to national statistics but to world population, its shape and future course.[6] The existence of world population figures induced its own consequences: after 1947, comparative population growth was increasingly noted and began to engender theories as to the role of national cultures and government policies in population growth. (Indeed, the availability and use of such figures became so widespread that the science of demography threatened to lose its autonomy as a distinct discipline and to become an aspect of economic development and other theoretical enterprises.) It also engendered thinking about the consequences of population change for the world as a whole.

Population trends

What these figures revealed was sustained and accelerating population growth. In 1960 in the *Scientific American*, Edward Deevey, an American demographer, proposed three stages in population growth over the course of human history: a bare sufficiency to guarantee survival of the species up to 8,000 BC, a second surge associated with the beginnings of settled agriculture (sometimes called the agricultural revolution), and a third surge which began with the scientific and industrial revolution of the seventeenth century.[7] The twentieth century clearly belonged to the 'third surge'. Whether twentieth-century population trends could be confined within the third surge was, however, questioned by many. By the mid-eighteenth century, world population may have reached 800 million. By 1800, it may have reached 1 billion, and by 1900 1.7 billion. The 1982 population level was, however, 4.6 billion, three times that of the turn of the century. Moreover, while population grew by 0.5 per cent per year from 1750 to 1900 and by 1 per cent per year in the first half of the twentieth century, it grew by 2 per cent per year from 1950. In 1985, the United Nations predicted stabilisation of world population in 2025, at between 8.5 and 11 billion; but even this date tended to be revised year by year.[8] The term 'population explosion' was an invention of the twentieth century and used to describe twentieth-century population growth, particularly that of its second half. Probably a fourth of all human beings ever born lived during the twentieth century.

If world population growth was accelerating, it was also the case that the rate of growth varied greatly by region and even by country. 'White' or European growth peaked in about 1930. (During the late nineteenth century, non-Europeans began to express fears of a 'white peril', as successive waves of European migration fell upon North and sub-Saharan Africa, and European colonialism spread to incorporate most of Asia.)[9] Thereafter it declined, and population growth began to accelerate in Asia, Africa and Latin America.[10] During the nineteenth century, Asia's population grew by one-third, but Europe's population more than doubled. In 1982, by contrast, the average growth rate or 'natural increase' was some 1.7 per cent for world population as a whole, but Africa's was 2.9 per cent, Latin America's 2.3 per cent and Asia's 1.9 per cent. Ghana's population grew by 43 per cent between 1970 and 1985, while in Europe and the areas of European colonisation it was much lower. In 1982, Europe had a growth rate of 0.4 per cent, North America of 0.7 per cent and the USSR of 0.8 per cent. Within areas, growth rates also varied considerably: in Africa, Kenya's population was growing at an astonishing rate of 3.9 per cent per year during the late 1970s and 1980s, while Gabon's rate was 1.2 per cent.

The distribution of population varied considerably as between states and, indeed, continents. Over half the world's population in the twentieth century lived in the Orient and half of those in China alone, while India contained 16 per cent. (India and China together provided about one-third of the world's population.) The small European littoral contained 11 per cent of the world population distributed among 23 small states, as did the great continent of Africa. As for the 'super-powers', the United States and the Soviet Union, together they totalled 11 per cent. The United States, with 232 million people in 1982, had four times the population of Britain, France or West Germany, slightly less than that of the Soviet Union, one-third that of India and less than a quarter that of China.

If a general feature of the age was growth, there were also instances of decline. Some states suffered absolute losses, notably West Germany where the rate of natural increase fell so low during the 1980s that it actually experienced 'negative' population growth. There were also significant losses in 'potential lives'. During China's famine of 1957–60, death rates doubled, fertility rates halved, and it was calculated that the famine may have claimed 30–35 million potential lives. Some demographers calculated that the Second World War resulted in the loss of 35 million lives, perhaps 20 million of which were in the Soviet Union alone, depriving it of some 60 million potential lives. These figures were, however, difficult to calculate, since hunger, war and disease tended to claim the youngest and the oldest, while women of child-bearing age tended to survive.

Malthus versus Landry

Accounting for these variations and drawing lessons from them became the major focus of the new science of demography, while the evidence of variation deeply influenced its theoretical presuppositions. Most twentieth-century demographers rejected the conclusion of their great forebear, Malthus, who in 1798 had related population drives to a constant tendency in all animated life to increase, even beyond the nourishment prepared for it. Malthus had predicted a geometric progression in population growth; his theory also implied that this geometric progression could be little influenced by either governmental policy or social change. Neither of these propositions remained untouched by twentieth-century experience. In 1920, two American demographers, Raymond Pearl and Lowell Reed, proposed, instead of a straight geometrical progression, an 'S' curve in which populations first grew along a geometric progression and then reached a 'natural' limit which caused them to drop to stable equilibria. But even this was too 'naturalistic' for most twentieth-century demographers, few of whom agreed with any purely internal theories of population growth. Most held that resources were neither so fixed as Malthus had supposed nor government policy and social change so irrelevant. They pointed not only to differential growth rates but also to the association of population change with large-scale changes in the nature of production.

In these circumstances, it is scarcely surprising that the theory which came to dominate the age was the theory of the demographic transition. First laid out by Adolph Landry in 1934, the idea of a 'demographic transition' related population changes to widescale social and economic changes, particularly to urbanisation and industrialisation.[11] Landry proposed three types of population, partly related to historical epochs: a 'pre-Malthusian' stage, characteristic of hunter-gatherer societies and societies untouched by modern civilisation, where there was both high fertility and high mortality and hence low growth overall; a transition population or 'Malthusian stage' where there was high fertility and low mortality and hence rapid population growth. (Landry associated this stage with the developing society where there was some control over death but little as yet over the tendency to multiply.) Finally, there was the 'modern' population, characteristic of fully industrial societies, where there was both low mortality and low fertility and hence very low rates of growth. Not least among the theory's virtues was its ability to explain why, whereas population growth in the nineteenth century had been largely a European affair, during the twentieth century it was developing countries which experienced high population growth.

This theory proved a useful starting point for many observations concerning the relationship between development and economic growth, although not everyone agreed with its somewhat optimistic conclusions. In 1949, a Mr Cowgill noted that Europe had had to wait a long time for the developments in medicine to control the death rate, whereas the then developing countries could 'borrow' health technology and hence increase the gap. This implied far more problems for the transition than were envisaged in Landry's theory.

Landry had also ignored geographical mobility and the distribution of population as between country and town. Mobility was an important part of the twentieth-century experience, and the gradual drift of people into the towns became a rush during the twentieth century, imposing great strains on urban life and great problems for the distribution of resources. There was also the relation between food production and population growth. By the late 1970s, a small school of what came to be known as 'neo-Malthusian' economists became increasingly concerned that marginal agricultural societies could not raise sufficient food to feed their growing populations, nor pay for food on the world market.[12]

Nonetheless, the theory of the demographic transition remained for much of the period the starting point of discussion of the causes and probable progress of population growth, and some governments eschewed population programmes entirely, out of a belief that development would in the course of time lead to a natural reduction and that no such programmes would be necessary.

Population location

The location of population as between city and country had a clearly economic aspect. As agriculture declined and industrialisation superseded it, people were drawn to centres of services and industrial production. But it was not a simple relationship. Cities had been centres of population gathering from the beginning of their existence, but the mass of populations had continued to live in the country, going to the cities and towns for services. This remained the case even after the onset of industrialisation. As late as the 1890s in Britain, probably the most industrialised country at that time, where indeed little effort had been expended on maintaining agricultural wages, there were still few towns of more than 10,000. In the twentieth century, this pattern changed; the land was virtually drained of population while twentieth-century cities became great megacentres, containing sometimes half the population of a country, and absorbing the towns and villages into them. London and New York had achieved populations of 8 million by mid-century, while Tokyo's was 12 million; and by the end of the century it was predicted that twenty-first-century populations would be overwhelmingly urban.[13] Also, in the nineteenth century it was developing and expanding economies which experienced population growth. In the twentieth century, however, it was underdeveloped countries which had population growth, countries where urban social and political structures could not in any way accommodate the large birth rates.

The decrease of hands

While it came to be widely accepted that social and political change affected population growth, it was not clear that governmental policy alone could do much to affect growth rates. This became particularly evident, since governments had policies both to encourage growth and to limit it.[14] The Germans tried population encouragement of at least certain sectors of their population during the 1930s. The French had also attempted to encourage growth from the last quarter of the nineteenth century, to achieve an equalisation effect with Germany, both, however, with little effect.

Post-war efforts to restrain population growth fared little better. India, with five decades of the most concerted effort at population control, was reckoned to have reduced the natural rate of increase by state policy scarcely at all. Only China, which entered upon efforts at population control relatively lately, was deemed to have achieved some success. It was calculated that by 2025, when population stabilised, India would have surpassed China as the world's most populous nation.

The inadequacy of such policies provided added incentive to industrialisation. Population growth was a great spur to a spate of industrialisation experiments, particularly in 'new' countries as they became independent. If new governments tried to even out their economies and to develop the range of lifestyles and expectations associated with their more developed former colonial masters, this was not only because such lifestyles and expectations were presented as the model aims for a new state, but because the theory of the demographic transition taught that it was through such social developments that populations would be led to control the numbers of children they produced.

Population and power

The uncertain outcomes of such policies altered views of the relationship between population growth and national power. During the period of relatively sustained economic development which Europe had enjoyed during the later quarter of the nineteenth century, population growth, whether through a decline in infant mortality or through migration, was generally considered a good thing. It fed an insatiable need for a work force in the great American land spaces and provided the soldiers for ambitious European governments, who could count on a continual replenishment of the infantry or colonial civil services – nineteenth-century European government regularly calculated the number of young men between the ages of 18 and 35. Indeed, no calculus of the balance of power was complete without a population calculus, and the larger the figure the more 'power' appeared to accrue to the state. After the 1950s, however, that calculus came to be questioned. If populations absorbed resources instead of freeing them, then the overall figure had to be a minus. Power, at least that part constituted by human beings, came to be seen as the ratio between population and resources, not as a simple product of adding them.

The classic device for calculating the population/resource ratio, used by the political arithmeticians calculating power balances as early as the Congress of Vienna in 1815, had been population density, the ratio between land and people, multiplied by the size of the population. This device was only useful, however, insofar as countries were more or less at similar stages of development, or at least not entirely out of reach of one another, and this was scarcely a feature of the twentieth-century experience, where some countries were not only not developing but may have been underdeveloping. Geographers continued to use density ratios through the twentieth century to predict potential wealth, all other factors being equal. But, in general, simple density ratios as methods of calculating resource availability declined.

Instead of population density, development theorists began to use the notion of 'carrying capacity'.[15] This concept sought to relate population growth, and the benefits of population increase, to the capacity of a country to carry such increases, capacity being related to such features as the ability of governments to engage in strategic planning, and of economies to earn sufficient reserves to pay for food imports and to provide employment by which food could be paid for. Calculating capacity was, however, scarcely simple, since it depended on the interaction of many factors, some of which required qualitative judgements. In the end, people tended to use per capita income times the number of heads as an indicator of capacity, or Gross Domestic Product.[16] GDP and comparative GDP became the basic indicator of growth trends and the sign that individual states were managing, or not, to provide for the 'population explosion'.

National capacity and internationalisation

The modern developments in population theory drew attention to the social and economic bases of state power and made them 'high policy' concerns. If power consisted in the ratio between a country's resources and its population trends, then these had direct strategic implications which had to be anticipated. In short, it made development not merely a 'progressive' policy but also a matter of 'realpolitik'. At the same time, rapid growth became an urgent matter of international concern, not least because of the burden that social and economic deficiencies would pose for decolonisers trying to steer fragile new countries through the decolonisation process, and for the well-being of regional allies in less developed parts of the world. If national capacity became a matter of feeding hungry mouths, transitions would be much more difficult, and alliance partners would have to divert efforts to assuring the social as well as military capacity of regional partners. Hence, 'advanced' countries became willing to finance international efforts at population regulation and, initially, to support development efforts.

The new trend in theorising also tended to treat population growth and social capacity as secular phenomena, unconnected to cultural uniqueness, except where indigenous cultural practices impeded population regulation. In that context, moreover, cultural uniqueness became an obstacle and was treated as such, with scant regard for traditional social practices. Population theorising became one of the great global rationalisers, absorbing people from very different societies into a common, and highly instrumental, discourse. Population considerations, moreover, struck at the very heart of social construction, which was family and gender relations. Population theorising thus drove notions of rationality into the heart of diverse cultural traditions and disrupted them, clearing the ground for a uniform discourse of development. The necessity of expanding the physical, social and governmental resource became one of the great 'common understandings' of the age.

Notes

1   W.O. Aydelotte, *Quantification in History* (London: Addison-Wesley, 1971).
2   On the history of attempts to estimate it, P. Studenski, *The Income of Nations* (New York: New York University Press, 1958).
3   C. Nam, *Population* (London: Prentice-Hall, 1984), p. 14.
4   Ibid., p. 8.
5   An important study of sample technique was carried out by the United Nations Department of Economic and Social Affairs and the United States National Research Council; *Indirect Techniques for Demographic Estimation* (New York: United Nations, 1984).
6   In addition to the *Yearbook*, the United Nations issued its own authoritative *Population Studies* series, which had by the end of the century issued over one hundred studies on fertility and mortality, projections, population control and rates of urbanisation and migration.
7   E. Deevey, 'The Human Population', *Scientific American*, 203, September 1960, pp. 194–8.
8   *World Population Prospects* (New York: United Nations, 1985), *Population Studies* No. 86.
9   L.G.C. Money's *The Peril of the White*, published by Collins in London in 1925, was based on the assumption that white growth was unstoppable.
10 A. Carr-Saunders, *World Population: Past Growth and Present Trends* (London: Clarendon, 1936) published the first figures.

11 M.A.A. Landry, *La révolution démographique* (Paris: Librairie de Receuil Sirey, 1934).

12 The new mood was signalled by J.H. Lowry, *World Population and Food Supply* (London: Edward Arnold, 1970); in 1975 the Sudan government held an International Symposium on the World Food Crisis in Karthoum which began to formulate the problems of marginal food producers.

13 The United Nations' *The Prospects of World Urbanisation* (New York: United Nations, 1987) reckoned that by the middle of the twenty-first century, half of the world's population would live in cities, and that half of some countries' populations would live in the capital city alone.

14 See UN Department of Economic and Social Affairs, *World Population Policies*, 3 vols (New York: United Nations, 1989).

15 Who invented the concept is not clear, but it began to influence demographic studies in the 1980s: the UN Food and Agriculture Organisation surveyed *Potential Population Supporting Capacities* in the area of food production in 1982; and in 1985, the World Bank issued *Rapid Population Growth and Human Carrying Capacity* (Washington DC: World Bank, 1985), legitimating the approach.

16 See the World Bank's annual development tables which rank countries by GDP but include also energy usage per person.

2 Production and consumption

The gross national products of most parts of the world expanded during the twentieth century, as population, and hence labour, grew. Patterns of production and consumption also changed dramatically. There were orders of increase in rates of production, and significant changes in what was produced. The balance within industrial production and between industry and agriculture changed, with consequences for patterns of trade dependence. Changing patterns of food production made formerly self-sufficient producers dependent on a global food market, while a growing mineral dependence forced rapid industrialisers increasingly onto a global mineral market. Both brought formerly remote and mutually indifferent areas of the world into immediate political contact with one another.

The pattern of growth

If population fed national product, it was noteworthy that product generally grew faster than population. Britain's gross national product grew by 2.2 per cent a year from 1900 to 1953 but its per capita income increased additionally by 1.3 per cent a year. Sweden's GNP rate was 3.6 for the same period; its per capita income increased by 2.8 per cent. Simon Kuznets, the American economist who pioneered the calculation of long-term growth rates, identified a great sweep of growth which had begun in some cases as early as 1860,[1] producing rates of growth in general of per capita incomes for most developed countries well above 10 per cent per decade since its onset. Indeed, during the twentieth century, growth passed 20 per cent per decade for some countries, including Sweden, Japan and the Soviet Union. From 1881 to 1961, the Japanese product per capita grew by almost 27 per cent per decade on average; between 1928 and 1958 the Soviet product appeared to grow by almost 44 per cent per decade.

The pattern was not universal, particularly for less developed countries where growth threatened to be eroded by particularly rapid increases in population. Egypt, for example, enjoyed a product growth of almost 12 per cent per decade during the first half of the century, but its population grew during the same period by almost 15 per cent, so that per capita income actually fell. The

Philippines' product grew by an impressive 20 per cent during the same period but its population grew by almost 25 per cent. It was only after the Second World War that the situation changed, when both countries enjoyed per capita growth of almost 30 per cent per decade, despite population increases of 27 per cent in Egypt and of 37 per cent in the Philippines. (Indeed, the overall growth in the Philippine economy from 1950 to 1970 was almost 78 per cent per decade.) India, by contrast, enjoyed absolute growth throughout the century, increasing its per capita income by 6.3 per cent per decade in the first half of the century and by 12.2 per cent per decade during the second half, despite population increases in the latter half of the century of 26 per cent, while Ghana's economy grew by well over 26 per cent per decade throughout the period to 1970.

Nor was growth a phenomenon which occurred irrespective of political conditions. Particularly in countries where civil war and famine became rife, growth prospects were radically affected by cycles of violence, particularly if development were low anyway. Between 1960 and 1980, Somalia's GNP fell by 0.2 per cent per year despite a 20 per cent growth of population, Mozambique's by 0.1 per cent, and Angola's by 2.3 per cent.

It should also be remembered that per capita growth rates were statistical calculations, not always translatable into meaningful income increases, at least not for masses of populations. Moreover, such growth as was translated downwards had to be seen in the context of what were often extremely low standards of living on the part of millions who scarcely participated in money economies. Over half the world's population in 1980 still lived in grinding poverty. Nonetheless, from such information as is available, actual incomes increased, in some cases dramatically.

European prosperity

For the majority of European countries, the second half of the twentieth century was a particularly prosperous period. Why this was so was not easy to explain, particularly given the relative evenness of growth before the First World War. Some economists attributed it to the restraint effect caused by trade barriers, established in a vain effort to ward off the effects of the Great Depression, and the dislocations caused by the war. They suggested that, when conditions returned to normal, European economies had experienced a series of small pent-up explosions. It was noted, for example, that the United States, which did not experience such differential growth between the first and second parts of the century, was the advanced country which had suffered least from trade barriers and war effects. In addition, growth in the post-war high-growth European countries had tended to fall below the 10 per cent per decade average of the inter-war period. Hence, it appeared an attractive idea that the high-growth countries had been suffering a 'restraint', and that their high post-war growth rates represented a 'catch-up' to normal. This may have been no more, however, than a statistical effect, caused by the method of calculating growth by decades, which produced a somewhat artificial mean.

There was, moreover, a proclivity on the part of growth economists, which developed with their access to growth statistics, to try to develop indices for the 'normal' growth of a developed economy, but which tended to be no more than the average growth rate over a large number of cases and years. In fact, countries grew at changing rates, not only vis-à-vis one another but in relation to their own past performances, and the notion of the 'normal' growth for the developed economy was largely an economists' chimera.

What can be said with absolute certainty about twentieth-century growth, as developed and even less developed countries displayed growth tendencies throughout its course, was that an expectation of growth became firmly established as the normal expectation in the minds of governments and peoples, and that no or low rates of growth were looked upon as puzzles which required to be explained. Moreover, no or low growth was generally attributed to extraordinary factors, such as destructive domestic or international conflicts or some social or legal inhibitions. It became widely held that there was a general human tendency to expand activity and wealth, and that, if this did not occur, it could only be attributable to some pathological condition.

The growth of government incomes

Since more people were better off, governments enjoyed an increasing surplus that could be taxed. Moreover, the pattern of taxation changed. Impossible until farmers and workers overcame pauperism, income tax had scarcely existed in the nineteenth century except towards the very end when it was a prerogative of the rich, and even then at low rates. Up to the twentieth century, indirect taxes, customs and excise taxes, and fixed class taxes were the rule wherever taxes existed. As workers and farmers came to enjoy what could actually be described as incomes, however, the income tax came into its own. It became a general, and the major, form of taxation. Moreover, tax rates tended to increase during the century. Whereas rates of 5 per cent and 6 per cent had been usual before the First World War, 25 per cent, 30 per cent and even 40 per cent became common after the Second. Government budgets, therefore, grew exponentially, and treasuries enjoyed unheard-of riches. Indeed, government income growth was as impressive as any. In 1895, the British state spent only 5 per cent of the nation's income; in 1955 it spent 40 per cent. In 1900, that government's budget was £120 million; in 1950 it was £4,150 billion.[2] In 1902, the various fiscal authorities of the United States extracted 8 per cent of the nation's wealth for government use, just over $1.5 million; in 1975 they extracted 35 per cent of a much larger pool of resources, almost $6.5 billion.[3]

The sources of growth

The cause of both growth and relative decline of per capita income was adduced to the same sources: capital inputs, better education and technical change which increased efficiency of production. Between 1909 and 1949, employed capital per man-hour in the non-farm sector of the US economy rose by 31.5 per cent. Output, influenced additionally by education and technical application of capital, rose by 105 per cent. Kuznets summarised the sources of growth more simply as 'science' or an increasing stock of tested knowledge. He observed, moreover, that the 'rate of addition to our stock of knowledge has been higher in the period between 1900 and 1950 than in 1850–1900'.[4]

Growth in agricultural production

The proportion of land devoted to settled commercial agriculture grew steadily during the first part of the century, with the result that the world's stock of potential arable land was gradually filled in by agricultural development. The Great Plains of America's West had been planted after the introduction of strains of Russian hard wheat in the 1880s: by 1914, wheat fields stretched literally from sea to sea. A spate of settler plantations was introduced into Africa after the First World War. After the Second World War, the destruction and closure in the Far East during the period of Japanese expansion led to extensive expansion of grain plantations in large areas of Latin America. The Russian Empire was the major exception; after the Revolution of 1917, and during the ferocious civil wars of 1919–23, it lost perhaps half the area under cultivation. The Soviet Union only recovered its pre-revolutionary levels in 1930. Subsequently, however, it also expanded cultivation, gradually doubling the area of land under plantation by the end of the century.

Both world wars also led to intensive cultivation by combatants of their own home fields, little of which came out of cultivation when the wars ended. By the last quarter of the twentieth century, over half of the land surface of Western Europe was under cultivation, while 10 per cent of the world's land surface was under cultivation and only about 5 per cent remained potentially cultivable (not without a massive deforestation which would, it was feared, permanently damage the world's ecology). Indeed, protests began concerning movement into the great area of the Amazonian rain forest during the 1970s, and attempts were made to dissuade the Brazilian government from licensing any further large-scale expansion into the basin.

It was not merely that more land came under cultivation; the productivity of the land was increased dramatically. The United States increased yields per acre by sixteen times during the course of the century, Canada, with greater difficulty due to climactic conditions, increased its yields by five. Rice yields in China, India and Malaya increased by three and four times.

Part of this increase was due to mechanisation which made land easier to work and which changed man-hour ratios, making farming more profitable. It was also due to education and new seed varieties which produced more yield.

Above all, it was due to intensive fertilisation and irrigation. The last three in combination produced what came to be known as the Green Revolution, developed in the laboratories of the United States to stop famine within and to produce surpluses from its Asian allies after the Second World War. As a result, rice yields in Thailand, India and other Asian producers tripled.

The application of mechanisation and wealth, combined with the political events of the age, changed the pattern of agricultural production laid down in the nineteenth century. Then, it had been the age of the great empires, informal as well as formal, where underdeveloped parts of the world were linked to the major metropolises through a series of formal and informal arrangements and where, in consequence, a certain world division of labour had taken shape. In the nineteenth and through the beginning of the twentieth century, the outreaches of the great formal and informal empires were the raw material and particularly food producers for the more industrialised metropolises; Western Europe was the only major food importer. Other parts of the world were self-sufficient and could feed themselves. With the period of decolonisation ushered in by the two great wars of the twentieth century and accomplished by the late 1960s, however, this changed. Partly because the ideology of development led them to direct scarce resources towards industrial production and to ignore agricultural development, and partly also because of a fear of resource scarcity in the old metropolises cut off from their hinterlands first by war and now by independence, agricultural development was, in fact, faster in developed than underdeveloped countries. Indeed, the age witnessed an almost revolutionary shift in the pattern of food suppliers from the 'developing' to the developed world.

If industrial countries produced more food than agricultural countries, they also did so with a much smaller labour force. This meant that in industrial countries, labour was released for industrial production. It also meant that in agricultural and developing countries, larger numbers of people had to be supported on the same amount of land and with only small-scale increases in production.

Partly in consequence, and despite the immense development in agriculture during the age, famine did not disappear. There were serious famines in Bengal in the 1940s, partly due to grain hoarding and high prices induced by the war, and in China from 1957–61; and from the 1970s onwards, famine became endemic in Central and East Africa. Moreover, its scale increased over anything known in previous centuries.[5] By the 1970s, the poorest countries of the world, comprising 10 per cent of world population, were living regularly on handouts of food through food aid programmes, while the rapid mobilisation of food surpluses for famine relief became a regular part of the late twentieth-century experience.

Industrial production

If the growth in agricultural production was dramatic in many parts of the world, the growth of other productive sectors of economies was more impressive still. Overall production in the US between 1900 and 1955 increased by 2.4 per cent per year, but industrial production grew at 3.7 per cent per year. In Western Europe, industrial growth was slower but the pattern was the same. Overall growth in the first half of the century was 1.6 per cent per year, but industrial production grew at 2.3 per cent per year.

The result was that the importance of the agricultural sector in the formation of aggregate income diminished everywhere. Particularly dramatic were: Italy, whose proportion of national income derived from agriculture dropped from 57 per cent in 1870 to 9 per cent by 1970; France, from 45 per cent in 1870 to 6 per cent in 1970; Sweden, from 63 per cent in 1870 to 4 per cent in 1970; and Russia, which owed 55 per cent of its income to agriculture in 1870 and 22 per cent in 1970.[6] At the same time, industrial production, production derived from mining, quarrying and manufacturing increased.

These changes had important implications for social profile. Everywhere, the peasantry declined or disappeared. Even where, as in Europe, there remained pockets of small farmers, most were part-time only, earning marginal incomes from farming while working in local factories for basic income.

There was also a marked shift during the century in the relative importance of the various sectors of manufacturing industry. At the beginning of the twentieth century, food and textiles together governed 47 per cent of the total manufacturing production in Western Europe and 44 per cent in the United States. By 1955, however, the two sectors represented only 21 per cent in Western Europe and 19 per cent in the United States.

As GNP increased, in particular as per capita income increased, patterns of consumption changed. People spent less of their incomes on food, fuel and housing, and they spent more on education, household goods, transport and communication. The sorts of things they consumed also changed. The Japanese were not beef-eaters in the nineteenth century; their diet consisted of rice and vegetables. By the last quarter of the twentieth century, however, they were consuming quantities of meat. Beef imports alone in 1980 were over 500 million kilograms.[7] In addition, the composition of the things people used, and hence the nature of what they consumed, also changed. The animal and plant kingdom provided a shrinking proportion of goods, and a far higher proportion of things consumed came from the mineral kingdom. Steel and cement replaced timber, artificial fibres (rayon, Dacron) replaced natural fibres, and chemicals came to make up more and more of what people consumed. Cipolla estimated that 80 per cent of twentieth-century man's needs in the developed part of the world were being provided by the chemical, metallurgical and mechanical sectors, and only 20 per cent from plants and animals.

The concepts of 'developed' and 'underdeveloped'

These respective patterns of production and consumption came to represent not only the material facts of the age. They came to be identified with the kinds of economies which produced them and formed analytical categories into which countries were classed. Thus, countries which enjoyed rapid growth, whose population was increasingly urban and industrial, whose income came increasingly from manufacturing sectors and the chemical and metallurgical parts of those sectors and whose populations consumed increasing amounts of energy and of 'processed' products with large chemical content, came to be identified as 'developed' countries. Those countries, by contrast, whose populations still lived in the majority on the land, who had low rates of agricultural productivity, who had low rates in the application of mechanisation to productive and other tasks, who used smaller amounts of energy and more natural products, came to be identified as 'underdeveloped' countries. Finally, those who seemed to be moving from the one condition to the other, whose indices of energy consumption, employment in industrial sectors and productivity in general were rising, came to be known as 'developing' countries.

Such categorisations were dependent on the availability of the statistical indices in question and owed a good deal to the statistical offices not only of the United Nations but more particularly of the World Bank, the agency established in 1944, as the war was coming to an end, to aid 'development' (this term signified the transition from one condition to the other). In the 1950s, the World Bank had begun to publish national comparisons of the trends in question, and in 1956 it began dividing country performances into the relevant categories, demonstrating the almost universal acceptance of the categorisation.[8] The common way of speaking about countries in the latter half of the twentieth century was as developed, developing or underdeveloped (sometimes, 'poorest').

The exploitation of natural resources

If mechanisation allowed, population growth demanded a more efficient and thorough-going exploitation of the earth's resources. This included not only the earth's mineral resources but also land itself, as well as water, fish and timber. Rates of deforestation were especially dramatic. The United Nations Food and Agriculture Organisation calculated that 4,100 million mha of forest or 30 per cent of the world's land area remained under various forms of forest in the second half of the twentieth century and that, of this, 10 million mha were being lost each year.[9] Territorial waters, declared at the beginning of the century to be 3 or 12 miles beyond shoreline, gradually expanded to 50 and in some cases 200 miles, so that fishing supplies could be monitored and controlled for the sake of home consumption and industry.

Above all, growth of population and economies, together with changing patterns of consumption, put a strain on mineral supplies, particularly those which provided the energy and strategic resources of countries. In all history, it has been economies that have provided for people, not resources, and the twentieth-century economy was neither a land-based economy nor even in its essence a trading economy: it was a mineral economy. Twentieth-century societies required minerals for energy, for tools, for fertilisers, as well as for the creation of the many products necessary in order to acquire them.

Growth in energy consumption, and in consumption of the mineral resources providing it, was especially dramatic. Cipolla calculates that the rate of growth of world requirements of energy, between 2 and 3 per cent during the growth spurt of early industrialisation (between 1860 and 1900), was not less than 4 and may have reached 6 per cent per year from 1900 to 1970, from 6,000 million megawatt hours electricity equivalent in 1900 to over 50,000 million in 1970. Overall, energy consumption outstripped population growth by a factor of 7. The consumption of energy was, however, not evenly spread, reflecting not only different rates of industrialisation but the fact that, as per capita income in industrial societies grew, more energy per capita was consumed by such populations. The degree of differentiation as between even industrialised countries in usage was dramatic. In 1986, the United States was consuming twice as much per capita of electricity as the United Kingdom.[10]

The foundation of the industrial civilisation of the twentieth century was coal – coal for steam and coal for smelting – and it continued to be so until the 1940s, when coal was still providing two-thirds of world energy supplies. Gradually, however, petroleum, which had begun to be exploited in Russia at the end of the nineteenth century, crept up, passing coal in the mid-1960s, to provide over half the world's energy requirements by the 1970s. Britain, whose economy had been built on coal and who remained a largely coal-based economy longer than any other industrial country, fell to oil in September 1971, when for the first time oil imports passed the total sum of coal used in the economy. Exploitation of all energy sources continued, however, and more coal continued to be mined rather than less, while wind, sun and especially water came into their own, the latter benefiting from the discovery of electric power. Cipolla recalls for us that when the great Niagara Falls project was set to work in 1896, the science of electricity transmission was so little developed that almost no potential of the great water power was released. By the third quarter of the twentieth century, however, numerous great hydro-electric systems dotted the world, providing a vital energy adjunct for those who had national water assets.

The Second World War occasioned the invention of an entirely new energy source, when the atom was split to increase the firepower of air-delivered bombs. Within several years, the potential of nuclear explosions to provide power had been conceptualised, the method of its taming had been achieved, and the first nuclear energy plants, providing electricity, had been constructed.

There were inhibitions in the use of the nuclear resource, however. Nuclear energy was dogged by questions of comparative costing and safety. There was also the ideological association with mass destruction of non-combatants: political protest could be reliably expected to surround any decision to commission a new reactor. It took strong governments with dedicated notions of state power (and also perhaps those who did not have strong lobbies attached to other forms of energy provisions) to engage in major nuclear developments. The French government, the most determined to avoid energy dependence and with few indigenous energy sources, was the only Western liberal government with a determined nuclear energy policy. By 1980, it had constructed reactors of sufficient capacity to provide the majority of its energy resource as well as an excess capacity which it delivered to European neighbours, at what some critics argued was below cost to make it competitive with other energy sources on the world market. But Japan, the Soviet Union and the United States were also major users of nuclear energy. (In fact, the United States was the world's largest producer, accounting for 28.5 per cent of world production in 1990, though nuclear energy did not form its majority energy source.)

Other mineral resources vital to developed and developing countries were the minerals of the ferrous group, the minerals needed in the production of steel. These included manganese, vital to the steel economies of the age, as well as chrome and titanium. There were also the 'war' minerals, the small specialised metals used in the production of certain very specialised forms of war material, like vanadium. Finally, there were the nitrogens and phosphates, vital to agricultural production and upon which productivity increases, and hence the economic well-being of developing countries, depended.

Demand of all these items was highest in industrialised countries. In 1939, the United States consumed 25 per cent of the world's manganese, 20 per cent of its tungsten and 50 per cent of its chrome.[11] By 1953, by which time it had become the world's largest industrial producer, it was also the largest consumer of practically all raw materials, including 65 per cent of the world's copper, 50 per cent of its zinc, and 45 per cent of its tin.[12] In 1983, it was consuming 25 per cent of the world's oil production, 19 per cent of its coal production and 32 per cent of its gas production.[13] This led to the expectation that as other countries industrialised, their consumption would also go up.

If demand was concentrated in industrial countries, supply was dispersed, and became increasingly so as the appetite of industrial society grew. The United States had ceased provisioning itself with oil in 1928, and its source of supply passed first to Mexico and then, during the 1940s, to Venezuela; by the 1960s it had become dependent on the Middle East for the provision of its shortfall. In 1973, at the time of the oil embargo, Middle East oil was providing 7 per cent of America's supply.

Strategic supply

The high ratios of incomes which derived from manufacturing industry and the cruciality of mineral supply to twentieth-century economies, combined with the increasingly dispersed location of that supply, led states to become increasingly concerned with what came to be termed 'mineral dependency', the degree to which countries were reliant on external sources of supply for fuels, fertilisers and other vital minerals. The question of mineral dependency, who had access to mineral resources, who could gain access and who could deny it, was a constant refrain in the social and political questions the age asked itself. Moreover, the provision of both energy and mineral supply came to be firmly imputed to government, with the result that concern with energy and mineral supply came to be a constant feature of the diplomacy of the twentieth-century state, particularly for those which had insufficient indigenous resources. Insufficient resources came to be known as 'strategic supplies', and it became an important function of government to provide them. Some even came to think that the denial of such supplies could constitute a *casus belli* or reasonable grounds upon which to declare a war against another state.

At first, the concern was limited to war conditions. The Great War at the beginning of the twentieth century had led to the various belligerents being cut off from some of their traditional areas of supply, and they feared being inhibited in their prosecution of the war: such goods were literally 'strategic'. It was at the end of that war that the United States government convened what was perhaps the first official study of any government's 'mineral dependence', and mineral dependence was defined as the minerals required for the sustenance of major war.

The variety of source and the accident of geographical provision, particularly of energy sources, had the effect of highlighting the 'strategic' significance of various regions and countries of the world. (Indeed, the location of strategic supply became one of the major factors in defining an area as strategic.) When coal provided the major source of energy, the strategic source for the European states was the great Ruhr heartland of Germany, access to which became for France the great object of its peace negotiations after the First World War: it was the threatened denial of coal which led it to occupy that territory in 1921. The cruciality of Ruhr coal finally led the French government to propose an internationalisation of the area after the Second World War, which was in fact accomplished. The United States, where oil was discovered in 1907, and the Soviet Union were both the major petroleum producers and world suppliers in the 1920s.

As demand outstripped supply and other areas came on stream, such areas also became the subjects of a heightened political interest. Thus, Mexico in the 1930s, Venezuela – which became a major producer and exporter during the 1940s and was the US's major external supplier until 1970 – and South Africa and Iran thereafter: each in turn became an object of special American concern. The Middle East became Europe's major supplier during the 1960s. Saudi Arabia and the Gulf States were believed to have inexhaustible supplies, and became the objects of special alliance systems, attentiveness as to their political stability and the objects of rivalry on the part of all industrial states. When, in the 1960s, oil was discovered in the North Sea, the surrounding states quickly decided on a North Sea division and rules for delineating sea beds and protecting rigs. Moreover, the notion that oil might lie off the shores of other states made their territorial waters the objects of rival states, creating an additional reason for extending territorial boundaries far into the sea. Finally, with the development of nuclear power, the location of uranium supply became a matter of urgency (it was mined originally in Canada and Australia), although, after initial fears, it had passed from lists of strategic minerals by 1970, when there was found to be greater supply than demand. (It was the terms of marketing that became the important question with regard to uranium.)

The cruciality of energy supply for the industrial civilisation of the twentieth century made governments ponder long on the mix of energy sources available to them, and the favoured mix was that which combined indigenous with secure sources. Thus, the Soviet Union favoured petroleum and coal, of which it had considerable reserves, and gas, while the Europeans, raised on coal, came to favour oil from the Middle East, where imperial ventures had established a favourable position for European oil companies. When Middle East supplies proved unstable, they generally turned to encouraging mixed sources and substitutability. They also came to prefer sources whose behaviour they could count on in the short term. Thus, despite twenty years of 'cold war' with the Soviet Union, many European governments in the late 1960s began to import natural gas from their communist antagonist, less concerned with the fact of a different social system than with the fact of a stable political regime, one whose own development objectives made the regular delivery of gas in return for needed hard currency a relative certainty. It was the Italians who first established a gas deal with the Soviet Union, in 1964, trading industrial plant and car production for a securer energy source than appeared to be offered by the unstable politics of the Middle East.

The myth of scarcity

Despite recurrent fears of scarcity, however, the scarcities which the century experienced were seldom absolute. More frequently, they were either planned scarcities or terms-of-trade scarcities. Moreover, planned scarcities were not produced by fears that goods might run out; they were induced by fears of glut. The oil cartel, the Organisation of Petroleum Exporting Countries, was formed in 1958 partly to counter low prices in a world awash with excess oil capacity. The oil producers began to plan – with the aim of restraining production and raising prices in a chaotic, over-competitive world. This may serve to explain why the oil companies which operated in those countries were so little bothered by the cartel's formation, since such induced scarcity could only raise prices of the final oil products. The great fertiliser shortage of 1974–5 was another case in point: it was induced by the major fertiliser companies who had suffered from over-capacity during the 1960s and who took advantage of the oil 'shortage' to refuse to expand production, even though there were sufficient supplies – at a price – to allow them to do so. The resultant dramatic increases in the price of fertilisers served them better than expanding supply. It was excess capacity which also induced the United States government to remove land from agricultural production after the Second World War and to release it only slowly, so as to maintain agricultural prices for American farmers. The tendency to plan production, and to relate production to market capacity – a market, moreover, of relatively high-paying consumers of sophisticated products – always produced 'shortages' when there was the smallest unexpected drop in the amount of product produced or relatively minor changes in the terms of trade.

Production, consumption and internationalisation

The changes in production and consumption drove the structure of the global economy in several directions. One basic trend was towards increasing 'product' regionalisation, as some of the largest industrial countries provided for more of their own food and hence needed developing countries' food provision less. Developing agricultural producers, in turn, had to develop products suitable for the elevated tastes of advanced consumers. This laid the foundations for a complex international market of relatively specialised agricultural producers, some of whose production depended more on marginal tastes than basic requirements.

These changes involved changes in relative power. Western consumers would enjoy more freedom to exercise consumption choices, and their consumption decisions would have greater consequences than the production decisions of developing countries, which had to take those changing tastes into account. Developing country governments would also face the problem of how to secure incomes for their producers in a situation where competitive advantage favoured more advanced countries. Providing for basic incomes became a major concern for those involved with the development task.

At the same time, the cruciality of mineral and energy supply made more advanced governments constantly alert to exploit and protect their sources of supply, which became increasingly diversified as industrial production grew. Strategic supply became increasingly global with regard to provision. At the level of production, this would give more power to the extractive industries vis-à-vis their own governments, but it would also make them no less dependent on their governments for securing and protecting their rights of access than they had been in previous periods. The significant change was at the macro level, where governments would become more concerned to secure regularity of access, particularly as decolonisation proceeded.

Notes

1 S. Kuznets, *Modern Economic Growth* (New Haven: Yale University Press, 1966).
2 A.R. Ilersic, *Government Finance and Fiscal Policy in Post-War Britain* (London: Staples Press, 1955).
3 B. Herber, *Modern Public Finance* (Homewood, Ill.: R.D. Irwin, 1979).
4 S. Kuznets, 'Sur la Croissance Economique des Nations Modernes', *Economie Appliquée*, X, 2–3 (April–September 1957), pp. 211–59.
5 L. Newman and W. Crossgrove, *Hunger in History* (Oxford: Blackwell, 1989), point to the relatively larger number of deaths in modern African food shortages, caused primarily by population pressure and the fragility of marginal food production, liable to be disrupted by relatively small population movements or civil and political unrest.
6 C.M. Cipolla, *The Economic History of World Population* (Harmondsworth: Penguin, 1962), p. 74.

7 Japan Tariff Association, *Japan Exports and Imports* (Tokyo: Japan Tourist Association, 1980).

8 In the World Bank *Annual Report* (Washington: World Bank, 1956).

9 United Nations Food and Agriculture Organisation, Forestry and Forest Products Division, *World Forest Inventory* (Rome: United Nations, 1963).

10 *The Economist, The World in Figures* (London: *The Economist*, 1987), p.13.

11 G.A. Roush, *Strategic Mineral Supplies* (New York: McGraw Hill, 1939).

12 Royal Institute of International Affairs, *World Production of Raw Materials* (Oxford: Oxford University Press, 1953) p. 8.

13 Peter Odell, *Oil and World Power* (Harmondsworth: Penguin, 1974) p. 85.

3 Commerce and finance

The expansion of production was accompanied by the expansion of trade. Trade also grew faster than product. Commerce was periodically interrupted by the wars and economic crises to which the age was prone, but the interruptions were remarkably short-lived. Despite considerable dislocation, in part caused by war itself, at each point in its closure trade growth tended to ensue. Between 1870 (when sufficiently detailed records began) and 1913, product is reckoned to have grown by 2 per cent per annum, but trade grew by 3.5 per cent per annum. The First World War caused a disruption, and the inter-war economic order suffered difficulties but, despite them, trade had recovered by 1928 to its pre-war levels. After the Second World War, yet again, notwithstanding even more severe obstacles, trade had recovered by the early 1950s, and it grew thereafter at an increasingly high rate. Only during the depression of the 1930s did international trade fall below production.[1]

These figures were significant because they indicated that 'trade dependence' was the efficient secret of the modern productive system. The high rates of trade relative to production derived from, and implied, a direct link between development, wealth and trade; in other words, trade made wealth. Trade was, at the same time, the material substance of 'interdependence' and mapped its contours. The volume and pattern of exchange – who traded with whom, and the content and intensity of their trading relations (what they traded and how much) – revealed the international division of labour in material production and who depended on whom for what. If, moreover, trade were wealth, this meant that the trade pattern also mapped the political hierarchies in the productive system. Those who traded most, and who traded the most valued goods, had 'trade power' – the ability to open markets and to determine trade rules.

Trade pattern

The high point of world trade proportion (that is, the proportion of world production that was traded) was reached in 1913, when some 30 per cent of world production crossed borders. After the interruption caused by the First World War, it climbed again, regaining the same proportion by 1928. But it never surpassed it, at least not on a world scale. For individual countries, however, the figure was higher. After the Second World War, the countries of Western Europe recorded trade proportions of sometimes 50 per cent, while Germany and the small countries of Europe's wealthy north-west triangle traded amongst themselves as much as 60 per cent or more of their domestic production.

Britain was the major trader during the nineteenth century, with a trade pattern characterised by the export of manufactures in exchange for raw materials. Britain also imported more raw materials than she exported manufactures, making up the deficit by the provision of services ('invisible earnings', as they were sometimes called). Since Britain was the first modern trading nation, this pattern came to be seen, initially at least, as the norm. Moreover, it was the prevalent pattern for most industrial countries during the first part of the twentieth century. From 1919 to 1937, trade in primary products continued to provide some 60 per cent of the total of world trade, while that of manufactures made up some 36–40 per cent.[2]

However, there were significant changes in the composition of raw materials traded during the first decades of the twentieth century. Food generally declined, but coffee, cocoa, bananas and oranges increased. Minerals also increased significantly, an increase mainly attributable to petroleum and to a lesser extent non-ferrous metals. Petroleum trade grew from nothing in 1913 to some 1,170 million barrels in 1929, and bauxite and aluminium became important traded commodities. During these years, also, the United States shifted from being an exporter to an importer of copper, lead and zinc. Europe also suffered a growing deficiency in minerals as indigenous deposits were worked out. Africa and Latin America became, in consequence, important mineral producers, and accordingly important sources of supply to the industrialising centres.[3]

The resultant stability of the primary product share of world trade, plus the shift in country of origin and the expansion of production in the non-European world, meant that primary producers, among them the underdeveloped countries, increased their share of total world export, from some 36 per cent in 1913 to just over 50 per cent in 1937. This figure grew again in 1940–52, when raw materials were much in demand to fuel war and reconstruction, making those particularly prosperous years for underdeveloped countries. Their relative share of world trade, and the demand for primary products, accordingly marked them as vital to the developing industrial society of the time.

Within the manufacturing sector, the composition of traded goods shifted significantly. Paralleling the changing pattern of production, we can already see during the inter-war period an increase in engineering products traded, as well as a slight increase in the amount of minerals traded. (The relevant value-traded figures for minerals increased significantly during the last quarter of the century, after the oil price hikes of the 1970s.) The expansion in engineering products and minerals was also accompanied by a severe decline in textile trade, that is, in the older generation of manufactures.

These changes in composition were accompanied by changes in the origin of manufactured goods traded. Britain steadily declined as a leading exporter, falling from a 30 per cent share of world exports in 1913 to 22.4 per cent in 1937. France and Germany also declined, while both the United States and Japan increased their share, especially in the manufacturing area.[4] US exports of manufactured items, which counted for 10 per cent of world total in 1913, had reached almost 20 per cent by 1937. This marked not only an important geographical shift but also an important political shift, as it brought both the United States, and eventually Japan, into the arena where the terms of trade were established and gave them a significant negotiating position within that arena.

The traditional British trading pattern had displayed a high dependency on raw materials imports, but it was not the universal pattern. North-West Europe remained an important, though declining, exporter of raw materials until the Second World War, while the United States and Canada accounted for 20 per cent of the world trade product in raw materials in 1928, marking them as significant raw material producers as well as coming manufacturing producers, and at a time when raw material product still dominated world trade.

Protectionism and the decline of trade

The slow growth in manufacturing trade during the 1920s appeared to be related to the sending of manufactures to underdeveloped countries. In the 1920s, less than half the increase in manufacturing trade was in trade between industrial countries. In the 1930s, this slow growth turned into a steep decline. This fall was accompanied by the severe trade restrictions put in place between major industrial traders. Under various protection schemes and protected currency areas, generally placed around empires, manufactured exports generally went to non-industrial parts of the world. In consequence, intra-European trade generally fell during the inter-war period, and since these were the industrial producers so too, in Europe at least, did trade in manufacturing goods fall.[5] (A significantly different pattern prevailed in North America, where there was actually an increase in the trade in manufactures between the US and Canada.)

While the trends were clear, the cause of the decline proved difficult to pin down. That it was associated with the heavy industrial and primary product protectionism which countries engaged in vis-à-vis their rivals, the protectionist retreat of the three major European countries into imperial zones for economic sanctuary, and beggar-my-neighbour policies, no one doubted. But whether these were causal factors or merely common trends became the subject of debate and theory building.

The diminishing trade thesis

The slow growth in the rise of manufacturing trade, its direction (growth within imperial zones and between more and less developed countries) and the steep fall in trade among the European industrialised powers during the 1930s, gave rise to a short-lived theory that trade expansion was a temporary phenomenon, and that trade would actually lessen over time. According to the 'trade-diminishing' thesis, as countries industrialised the factors making for trade fell in importance, leading to an overall decline in the amount of world product traded. Among such factors was, for example, the primary product share in the make-up of advanced goods. Of course, it was clear that the immediate fall of intra-European trade was due to the trade and currency restrictions put in place in response to the Great Depression. But to some economists, these seemed to be merely the immediate occasions for what they claimed was a 'natural', and long-term, trend.

The factors making for less trade were not only economic in nature. The trade-diminishing theorists identified significant political factors contributing to – and they began to plot the political conditions which might demand – trade restrictions: primarily, a decline in competitiveness vis-à-vis major rivals and the need to protect domestic earnings. The main formulator of the theory was Eli Heckscher, the great theorist of eighteenth-century mercantilism, who saw a new 'mercantilist' period in the offing after an abnormal period of trade liberalism. His theory implied that mercantilism was the normal economic condition for the modern industrial state.[6]

The post-war period did not, however, serve to confirm the thesis. After the Second World War, world trade once again overtook and grew faster than production. Between 1945 and 1960, despite trade restrictions at some periods and between some partners as severe as the trade restrictions of the 1930s, trade nonetheless grew by 6 per cent per year. When these restrictions were lifted – that is, in the decade or so after 1958 – it grew by 8.8 per cent. Between 1963 and 1970, world product grew by 123 per cent, but world trade grew by 200 per cent. During the post-war period, trade again led economic growth.

Moreover, trade composition shifted dramatically, and in the direction of manufactured products: that is, towards products produced by the more advanced countries. Steadily, trade in manufactures came to dominate world trade composition, shifting gradually to absorb some 53 per cent by 1960 and reaching a high point of 62 per cent in 1973. (Thereafter, the oil crisis of 1973 and the rise in oil prices clawed some value back to mineral raw materials, and the figure settled at some 50 per cent.) As a consequence, the shares of trade of the developing countries fell back. In effect, trade between developed countries, trading in manufacturing products and indeed in products of a similar nature, came to dominate world trade, while trade at the same time continued to grow.

The terms of trade

These changes were accompanied by a shift in the comparative prices at which goods were traded, called the 'terms of trade'. This was not a new phenomenon. During the depression, commodity prices had fallen by almost 30 per cent while manufacturing prices had tended to remain stable. But at the time this seemed an abnormal phenomenon, attributed by some to the over-production of commodities and by others to demand suppression (each theory had its adherents). In other words, the fall in commodity prices was generally attributed to the condition of depression and to the relative drop in the rate of industrial growth induced by it. It was generally believed that, when industrial production returned to normal, when indeed it increased as it did during the post-war period, a tremendous boost would be given to primary products. And such did in fact occur for about six or seven years after the war, when raw material shortages were experienced everywhere. But during the late 1950s and unevenly during the 1960s, economists doing comparative pricing began to detect signs of comparative disadvantage: that is, signs of a gradual fall in the prices of raw materials relative to the price of industrial goods.

Liberal economists attributed comparative disadvantage to the decline in the relative value of raw materials used in advanced industrial goods. They argued that, in advanced industrial goods, more of the value make-up or price was provided by research and development, services and advertising. Primary goods became, accordingly, less valuable in the overall product make-up, and their price fell accordingly.[7] To others, however, this was not a question of natural economic development at all but a question of world economic structure. These became known as 'structuralist' economists. Raul Prebisch, the Argentinian economist who later came to head the United Nations Commission on Trade and Development, claimed that the relative disadvantage for commodity producers was due to Western workers being paid more than their brethren in underdeveloped countries. Prebisch insisted that Western wage inflation was causing a rise in the prices of industrial goods relative to primary products, resulting in a relative impoverishment in developing countries. The question became intensely political, and formed one of the central issues in the great debate, which developed during the 1970s between developed and underdeveloped countries, on the need for a new international economic order. One of the major demands of underdeveloped countries during the post-war period would be international arrangements which would manage commodity prices with the aim of keeping them in line with the price of industrial goods.

Significant national patterns

The United States became the major single world trader. It also appeared less 'trade dependent' than its closest rivals: during the 1960s, imports constituted less than 10 per cent of national consumption. But, as noted previously, its expanding productive base increasingly demanded specialised raw materials from outside its territory; and it became increasingly trade dependent during the period of the Cold War, partly to balance governmental military expenditure abroad. In its exports, it remained a large commodity exporter throughout the century, as well as an industrial exporter, providing the Soviet Union with vital wheat through much of the period of the Cold War.

Other, contrasting, patterns include Canada, which was primarily a commodity exporter, and Germany, which was primarily an exporter of advanced machinery. Japan continued to export and import in a pattern which had begun in the earlier part of the century: it was a major importer of raw materials and a major exporter of finished products, products which were also, however, increasingly innovative. From the 1930s, the rest of Asia began to be major industrial exporters, but many Asian countries also remained important marginal commodity exporters.

Regions and trading zones

Trade was not evenly distributed, even after the establishment of universal trading rules following the Second World War. Colonial trade continued to show a 'colonial preference' even after the gradual decline of formal empires and the abandonment of imperial preference systems. In the case of Europe, intra-West European trade rose steadily during the 1950s and 1960s to absorb sometimes 60 per cent of the trade product, as noted above. There were also notable trade preferences within East and Central Europe, where intra-bloc trade accounted for 66 per cent of the total exports of Comecon members. (A Council for Mutual Economic Assistance was set up by the Soviet Union in 1949 to achieve co-ordinated production and national export specialisation, and to avoid competition and duplication.) Finally, Japan traded extensively with other nations of South East Asia, while the United States had particularly heavy trade ties with Canada, Mexico and Central America.

The question posed by these patterns for the nature of the late twentieth-century trading system was whether they represented 'natural preferences' or 'distorted trade'. Natural preferences were occasioned by historical ties, proximity, availability of local markets for exploitation, and cultural biases (the existence of shared languages or habits). 'Distorted' trade was produced by the imposition of political conditionalities or the existence of political dependencies. Where they were 'natural', a second question, particularly relevant with regard to internationalism, is whether they amounted to regionalism. The issue was whether there was a *natural regional* basis of trade, and whether intra-regional trade was more important than global trade.

The clearest case of distortion existed with regard to the Soviet Union and Central Europe. During the 1950s and 1960s, trade flows within the Soviet bloc were determined by a division of labour that was established by the bloc leader.[8] By 1979, following a period of only moderate liberalisation, intra-area trade among the members of Comecon had declined to 51 per cent, and it would decline drastically after 1990, with the Soviet Union's relinquishment of all controls over the countries of Central Europe. It was also notable that, during the earlier period of mild liberalisation, it was to the West that the countries of Eastern Europe turned for sources of investment and development loans.

With regard to Western Europe, the question was more difficult to determine. It is certainly the case that, after 1958, European trade grew within an albeit gradually lowering external tariff of the European Common Market. The Market was also decidedly protectionist with regard to agricultural trade. The

Common Agricultural Policy set limits on the freedom of entry of agricultural imports, through the imposition of heavy tariffs and the practice of quotas, to support European farmers. A convention was worked, initially with the former colonies of the countries of Western Europe, which allowed some Third World producers special access to the European market for their agricultural goods.[9] But they were hard-won concessions. Aside from agriculture, however, it is doubtful that the Common Market distorted trade among its members. Rather, it seems that it allowed them to exploit natural complementarities after the period of bitter economic rivalry of the inter-war period. Accordingly, the high rate of intra-European trade probably was a reflection of the natural tendency for advanced industrial countries to trade with one another, in a situation of close proximity.[10]

In other cases, political conditionalities existed but they cut across the regions. This was particularly the case with the United States' trading relations with Japan, the Philippines and South Asia, China's relations in Africa, and the Soviet Union's relations with Cuba, North Korea and Vietnam. In the case of the first, preferential trading relations were made available to America's key Asian allies in the context of the Cold War, to bolster their economies and to make them resistant to Soviet and/or Chinese influence.[11]

Where regional trade relations appeared to arise from a natural disposition, as was the case with Japan's Asian trade and the United States' Western Hemisphere trade, it was doubtful that this pattern supported a regional reading of the basic structure of world trade. Small trading nations had their natural trading partners among the larger nations within their region, to be sure, but they also traded importantly outside of their regions. What was even more striking was the degree to which large trading nations depended for critical balances on their exchanges with one another. The United States required both its European and Asian trade to balance its payments; in the same vein, Germany required its American and Middle Eastern trade; and Japan required its access to American and European markets to retain competitive advantage.

The institutions of credit and liquidity

The financing of trade, and the support for nineteenth-century trade growth, the period when modern trade developed, was provided essentially by Britain. That goods could be paid for internationally, that is across currency zones, turned on the stability of the pound sterling and its convertibility into gold. It was sterling which provided the liquidity of the system: the funds for borrowing, lending and credit. The stability of the pound was ensured by cautious lending in London, by trade bills (credits for goods actually en route), and by the persistent trade surpluses that Britain ran on its Indian trade, together with the gold and sterling earnings produced by the sale of Indian goods on the world market. The latter were carefully managed to keep gold from seeping back into the Indian economy and ensuring its continued circulation in the world economy. Not all trade at the end of the nineteenth century was conducted in sterling. By the end of the nineteenth century, a complex multilateral system had emerged in which trade balances (and trade growth) were happily achieved by the US and Canada selling wheat to Germany and Central Europe, who in turn sold machinery to Britain and Europe, who sold manufactures to India, who sold raw materials to America and Canada. But the British surpluses earned on the Indian trade were a vital link in fuelling the world trade chain and in providing a wash of gold-backed credit over the international trading system generally.[12]

The First World War interrupted this system, as governments controlled both expenditure and production to supply the war. The war also speeded up those changes which would eventually undermine it.

America's rising financial power and Britain's decline

The first of these great changes was the emergence of the United States as the major creditor country. In part, this had to do with the absolute growth of the American economy during the war, and a surplus of private savings induced by economic growth. It also derived from America's emergence as a large exporter of industrial goods which earned it a balance of payments surplus.

Parallel with the rise of the United States as a major creditor was a decline in Britain's financial position, due partly to the liquidation of foreign assets to finance the war and partly to confiscation of British assets in Russia. Britain's position as lender was also immensely complicated by its declining export position. During the 1920s, Britain had a stagnant economy which only slowly regeared to export performance. In consequence, imports grew faster than exports and ate away at the earnings margin provided by invisible earnings, that is, services. The result was that, during the 1920s, Britain's current account surpluses were seldom more than one-half or even one-third of their pre-war levels in real prices. This was not enough to meet what was in itself a new level of demand for international lending. During the 1920s, America's foreign investments grew from $7,000 million to $17,000 million, while Britain's new issues averaged little more than $390–440 million per annum. Paris also re-emerged as a financial centre and source of loans, primarily short term, after the stabilisation of the franc in 1928.

In consequence, by the late 1920s the source of international credit had become much more decentralised. New York was a major financial centre, followed by London and Paris; and each capital worked by different criteria and responded in different ways to the economic developments of the time. The close association between one government and one central bank, each following and correcting the other, which had been the characteristic pattern of the nineteenth-century informal system and which gave it a large measure of its stability, was no longer there.

A second change, prefiguring the pattern that would emerge after the Second World War, was the direction of America's investments and the changing balance between its imports and exports. Unlike pre-war Europe, much United States investment went into Europe; that is, it went to economies with which it was competitive, not complementary. Moreover, as a consequence of America's industrialisation, Europe sold fewer industrial goods to it relative to the pre-war position, while America was buying more raw materials to fuel its expanding economy, and from countries with whom European countries had surpluses. In consequence, the payments system of the 1920s came to depend not on Britain but on America, and on America's continuing to export capital and to import raw materials, particularly from countries with whom Britain held surpluses.[13]

As part of its response to the Great Depression, and indeed the efficient cause of it, the United States suspended both activities. In reaction to what had begun as a recession, American enterprises and public authorities reduced raw material imports, particularly from the sterling area, and repatriated capital abroad or saw it wiped out. In the ensuing financial chaos, sterling went off gold (this significant moment in international financial history occurred in 1931) and the dollar followed suit in 1933. The result was the development during the 1930s of monetary zones.

The currency zones

Whether the payments 'system' of the 1930s deserves the dignity of the characterisation is a moot point. It was highly ingenious and very disorganised; it was also brief-lived. First, there were the monetary zones – groups of countries with whom the major economic powers maintained limited convertibility. Within such zones trade moved relatively easily, and since they were, in the case of France and Britain, its imperial areas among others, this serves to explain the trade diversion witnessed in the later part of the inter-war period towards developing countries. With countries outside their zones, governments developed a bewildering array of swap and compensatory arrangements. They created bilateral accounts with traders in currencies that had to balance out. This development, more than any other, forced trade to take on an imperial pattern, since it was only within the monetary zones that exchangeable currencies were available to pay for goods and that expatriatable funds could be gained easily.[14]

The Bretton Woods system

The close relationship between the restrictions on convertibility, the reduction in trade and the growth of unemployment (as well as a perceived relationship between unemployment and the drive to war) determined both the United States and Britain to restore some of the elements of the pre-war financial system. Indeed, it became a central object of wartime planning. Begun in 1940 and finalised at a conference at Bretton Woods, New Hampshire, in 1944, the intention of their negotiations was to establish a system of exchangeable currencies backed by several internationalised forms of credit, so that trade growth might resume, and with it industry and employment.

Two forms of credit were created, the first by governments to stabilise their payments, in the form of the International Monetary Fund, a bank with foreign currency deposits and credits on which governments could draw. The IMF allowed governments to evade devaluations as part of their stability policies by making available secure loans without overtly political strings. (During the 1920s and 1930s, countries requiring loans often had to accept political conditionalities.) The other source of credit available to governments was the World Bank, a fund intended initially to aid post-war reconstruction, but which developed as a fund agency for underdeveloped countries.[15] Not all World Bank loans went into development projects; for some of the poorest it was used to pay the salaries of their officials and to support the provision of the most basic government services. Nonetheless, the post-war period was to see a major effort in international investment in developing countries. In the interim, a transitional arrangement was devised, in the form of the European Payments Union, which allowed European governments to balance out the debts they owed one another until they were ready to join the new arrangements. Countries who joined the EPU could aggregate the total foreign exchange surpluses and debits they held against other members of the union, leaving each government with only a single credit or debit, easing the problem of payments among the European states.

Bretton Woods was a rule-based system. It strove for a clear set of qualifying criteria for loans and for exchange rate shifts. It was also arguably norm-based, as that came to be understood in the 'regime' literature of the 1980s; in general, Bretton Woods supported the argument of regime theorists that implicit shared norms underpinned international agreements. Both major and minor powers agreed on the aims of economic development, relatively open competition and generally fair trade, without political strings.

The demise of gold exchange

The regulating mechanism of both the nineteenth-century 'informal' system and the original Bretton Woods system was the gold–specie link. In the informal system it was the gold–pound exchange, and in Bretton Woods the gold–dollar link. Bretton Woods thus represented a reinstitutionalisation of a gold-exchange standard: the dollar was pegged to gold and acted as the chief denominator of value and a universal currency of exchange. In effect, the United States took over the role of the financial hegemon which Britain had played before World War One. After 1945, dollar surpluses linked to gold provided the liquidity and the credit provision of the system. The system accordingly turned on the ability of the United States to produce trade surpluses and foreign exchange earnings, and to control government expenditure so as to keep the American balance of payments in surplus.[16]

By the late 1950s, several developments were threatening the gold–dollar link. In the first place, European countries had begun exporting manufactures to the United States in greater quantities, earning from it more dollars than they repatriated. Second, there was a continued heavy private American investment abroad, to be detailed in the next chapter. This had the effect of transferring production from the United States and reducing domestic exports and domestic foreign earnings. Finally, there was the high rate of government expenditure abroad, essentially to support America's allies, which turned into a flood through the financing of the Vietnam War in the late 1960s. Kenwood and Lougheed express the consequences of these developments with admirable terseness: '[they] made America's "deficit" policy in support of international liquidity clearly untenable.'[17]

When the dollar went off gold (this second major mark in twentieth-century international financial history occurred in August 1971), a period of exchange rate volatility ensued, within, however, noticeably narrow margins. The mark and yen, which had been deliberately undervalued in 1946 to aid post-war reconstruction, regained their more natural value. (The mark, set at 4 to the dollar, ended up at approximately 1.5 by the 1980s.) At the same time, the European currencies generally shifted by rates of between 2 per cent and 4 per cent vis-à-vis one another. What was most remarkable, however, was that the European currencies tended to move against one another *more* than they moved against the dollar. In other words, after the major readjustment of the mark and the yen, the dollar maintained relative stability against the other major trading currencies, despite going off gold.

The emergent pattern underpinned the managed-float system which succeeded the gold-exchange system. During the 1980s, the major industrial powers agreed to let their currencies float, but they also agreed to intervene to maintain relative degrees of exchange rate stability. The managed-float system was supported by the institutionalisation of frequent meetings of groups of seven (or ten or twenty) leading trading nations, where they agreed long-term growth rates and parallel interest-rate policies.[18] At the same time, and in keeping with its relative stability, the dollar continued to be the vital source of liquidity in the system. Unrepatriated dollars held in European banks, which kept their median value, became the source of a growing Euro-dollar market during the 1970s, and provided a vital source of funds for investment, international payments and liquidity.

Trade internationalism

Trade was international from before the First World War, and subsequent decades only demonstrated the continued durability of trade proportion. What was distinctive about the twentieth century was the increasing generalisation of the trading pattern that had been established among the major traders by the end of the nineteenth century. During the twentieth century, more countries made more of their wealth through trade. A second major change was in the nature of goods traded, from a long fifty years when trade in primary products was considered the heart of the trading system, to one where manufacturing came to equal it in value volume and to surpass it in competitive advantage.

The changing pattern of trade would highlight different ideal forms of political organisation at different times. During the 1930s, empires regained saliency as areas of relatively free trade, and this would seem natural for a short period of time, as many people understood trade in terms of an exchange between raw material producers (the colonies) and industrial centres (the metropolises). In the event, however, this would prove only temporary. The post-war pattern demonstrated the underlying rule of the emerging global trading pattern: that it turned on trade between industrial centres. This meant that it could not be contained within the established imperial zones. The major industrial powers exploited regional and other advantages but they sought competitive advantage on a global basis.

Central to this shift was the changing position of the United States, and its emergence as a significant importer of strategic raw materials and an exporter of manufactures. Within the context of an emerging global trade pattern which gave competitive advantage to manufacturing exports, and which demanded extensive provision of credits, the position of the United States would become increasingly vital. The United States' relative trading position, as well as its position as the world's major industrial producer, made it the lender of last resort for much of the century, within a system whose increasing scale it could not bank alone. Even more important, however, was the emergence of industrial competition as the crucial area of competitive advantage. This alone made the restoration of global trade and payments seem the obvious route of policy. The demand for open trade and payments, and their management by a rule-based system, was situated within and rationalised by a trading structure which necessitated a reliable and relatively stable credit system of, at least nominally, universal access and of considerable scope, and by the existence of major industrial traders who favoured access not only to a world product but to world markets.

Notes

1 In the years between 1933 and 1937, production in the thirteen most developed countries grew by 22 per cent, but trade by only 11 per cent. More revealing were the per capita figures: per capita production grew by 13 per cent, but per capita trade actually fell, by 3 per cent; C. Kindleberger, *The World in Depression* (London: Allen Lane, 1973).

2 P.L. Yates, *Forty Years of Foreign Trade* (London: Allen and Unwin, 1959).

3 A. Kenwood and K. Lougheed, *The Growth of the International Economy 1820–1980* (London: Unwin, 1983).

4 W. and E. Woytinsky, *World Commerce and Governments* (New York: Twentieth Century Fund, 1955).

5 Kenwood and Lougheed, *The Growth of the International Economy 1820–1980* (London: Unwin, 1983), pp. 223–5.

6 E. Heckscher, *Mercantilism*, 2 vols (New York: Allen and Unwin, 1955).

7 C. Kindleberger, *The Terms of Trade: A European Case Study* (Cambridge, Mass.: MIT Press, 1956).

8 M. Kaser, *Comecon: Integration Problems of the Planned Economies* (London: Oxford University Press, 1967).

9 See, generally, A. El-Agraa, *The Economics of the European Community* (Oxford: Philip Allen, 1985).

10 The general conclusion of A. Shonfield (ed.), *International Economic Relations of the Western World 1959–1971*, 2 vols (Oxford: Oxford University Press, 1976), sensitive to

the relations of politics and economics, especially T. Warley, 'Western Trade in Agricultural Products', vol. 1, Part III.

11 B. Pollins, 'Does Trade Still Follow the Flag?', *American Political Science Review*, 33(1989), pp. 465–6.

12 R. Triffin, *Our International Monetary System: Yesterday, Today and Tomorrow* (New York: Random House, 1968).

13 See especially Kenwood and Lougheed, *The Growth of the International Economy 1820–1980* (London: Unwin, 1983), pp. 237–40.

14 W. Arthur Lewis, *Economic Survey 1919–1939* (London: George Allen and Unwin, 1949–1970) pp. 156–64; League of Nations, *International Currency Experience: Lessons of the Inter-War Period* (Geneva: League of Nations, 1944).

15 J. Spero, *The Politics of International Economic Relations* (London: Allen and Unwin, 1985) is a useful guide.

16 L. Yeager, *International Monetary Relations* (New York: Harper and Row, 1966).

17 Ibid., p. 283.

18 R. Putnam and N. Bayne, *Hanging Together: The Seven Power Summits* (London: Heinemann, 1984).

4   Industry

As manufacturing came to prevail in the productive system, industrialisation spread, engulfing one country after another. New countries especially strove for industrialisation, pushing increasing numbers of countries into industrial competition. The growing number of industrialisers became linked, moreover, not only by market dependence but also by industrial organisation. As industry spread, the multinational enterprise took form, linking countries below the level of the state and forming the major channels for innovation, trade and common patterns of industrial management. Countries increasingly harmonised their domestic legislation, in part to attract, in part to control the new industrial agglomerations.

There was also the product cycle. The pattern by which industry spread demonstrated intimate linkages between more and less developed countries. The less developed took over the older industrial forms from the more developed, as competition forced the more developed into more advanced production.

These forms of interdependence supplemented trade dependence. By the end of the century, over a third of world trade would be accounted for by trade between subsidiaries of the same firm, and a similar proportion would consist of the exchange between the differing products of the product cycle. Countries thus came to be linked not only by trade, but internally by market organisation, parallel industrial policies and the process of product innovation.

The pace of industrial development

By the third quarter of the nineteenth century, industry had spread from Britain outwards to Germany and France, of sufficient scope to establish them as industrial countries. By its last quarter, a small industrialisation had begun in Russia (in 1900, Russia was providing 4.4 per cent of world output) and Japan was rapidly laying the foundations of an industrial economy. The features of the twentieth-century American industrial economy were also coming into place. In 1913, America was already responsible for 35.8 per cent of world industrial output and for 13 per cent of world manufacturing trade, at a time when Japan was responsible for 1.2 per cent and 2.5 per cent, respectively.

The First World War and the economic depression of the 1930s stimulated this outward movement. Cut off from European sources of supply during the war years, industry developed rapidly in a number of countries overseas. Industrialisation was particularly rapid in America, Canada and Australia during the 1920s, and high rates of industrial growth were also being achieved in Brazil, Finland, India, New Zealand, South Africa and Japan. Indeed, during the inter-war period, the older industrial nations experienced declining rates of industrial growth relative to the new generation of industrial states. Even in primary producing countries, industrialisation flourished, primarily because of the network of restrictions on trade in primary products which other countries enforced against them, though here developments occurred generally in secondary industry, to safeguard living standards and to keep down unemployment.

Treating 1913 as 100, the world index of manufacturing activity averaged 185 between 1936 and 1938, whereas the index for the United States stood at 167, Germany 138, Britain 122 and France 118, all well below the world average.[1] During the 1930s, many new industrialisers were industrialising at an enormous pace. Under Stalin's forced industrialisation, the Soviet Union's index may have been as high as 774, Japan's was 529, Finland's 289, India's 230 and Sweden's 223. In consequence, significant changes occurred in the distribution of the world's manufacturing production. It was moving out of the North Atlantic basin.

The pattern of industrial growth

Despite these enormous growth figures, there were significant differences in the nature of industrial growth between the newer and older industrialisers. In the newer industrial countries, growth took the form of the expansion of textile manufactures and other types of fabrication typical of a country in the early stages of industrialisation. On the other hand, in the United States and some of the 'older' industrial countries, inter-war industrialisation involved the rapid growth of new industries, such as motor-cars, household appliances and chemicals, as well as the rapid growth of new production techniques. The latter came to be known as 'leader' industries, so defined because they contributed towards maintaining a country in the advance of industrial growth. During the inter-war period, the leader economies were the United States and Germany: America's profile of industrial development concentrated on engineering products, while that of Germany was on chemicals and optical goods.

Kenwood and Lougheed, who produced the major economic survey of the period, note few startling new inventions during the inter-war period. What impressed them was the increased efficiency of already familiar techniques and the development of modern production methods. Fuel economies were achieved in iron and steel production and in the generation of electricity, with the best power stations halving fuel consumption between 1918 and 1989. New alloys became available for engineering, especially light alloys based on aluminium, and there was an increasing use of plastic. Refrigeration techniques improved greatly and, extended to ships, provided for, among other things, the enormous expansion during the 1920s of Argentinian beef exports. Efficiency and increased scale were also achieved in petrol and oil engines, including diesel and steam turbines.[2]

By far the most important of the new production techniques was the invention of the assembly line. Initially adopted by Henry Ford as the key to the efficient, large-scale and cheap production of motor-cars, the assembly line was widely used in the United States after the First World War to mass-produce such items as washing machines, radios and refrigerators. In addition, many other products including shoes, stockings, glassware and chinaware passed through factories in a continuous flow, enormously increasing the volume of output and thereby reducing costs. The rise in productivity attendant on assembly-line production led, in turn, to a rise in real income, which was partly used to buy the new industrial goods.

This industrial technique produced a distinctive and characteristic pattern of industrial production (and, indeed, of social organisation). On the one hand, there were the large, relatively stable workforces of industrial workers who worked the lines in repetitive fashion, generally organised into large trade unions. The trade unions became responsible for training and apprenticeships. On the other hand, workers were sharply distinguished from the smaller numbers of plant managers who also stayed in the same enterprises through their whole careers. The bigness of plant gave rise to specialised forms of management training, which stressed organisational competence, loyalty and organisational identification as much as the achievement of competitive advantage. This pattern of industrial production became known as 'Fordism'.

The assembly line points to an additional significant difference between the new industrial technology and that of the nineteenth century. Production for domestic use was as prevalent as the production of industrial machinery. This trend began around 1900 with the introduction of the telephone, the gramophone, the bicycle and the motor-car, and was continued after the First World War with the development of the vacuum cleaner, the washing machine, the refrigerator and the radio. In consequence, the demand for and consumption of electricity rose, creating a demand for electrical plant and equipment of all kinds.

The rise of protectionism

A good deal of the industrial development of the first half of the twentieth century occurred behind and under the protection of various tariff barriers. In Britain, the home of free trade, this was occasioned, at least initially, by the demands of prosecuting the war. The McKenna Act of 1915 imposed duties of 33.3 per cent on cars, motor-cycles and certain other manufactures in an effort to save wartime shipping space and foreign exchange; but the act also laid the foundation for a return to protection after the war, when it was extended to commercial vehicles and trucks. The war had, moreover, highlighted the role of industrial capacity in achieving ultimate victory and led to a concern to protect war industries. These came to be known as 'vital national industries', a new concept which identified industries vital to the prosecution of a successful war in modern conditions. In 1921, Britain passed the Safeguarding of Industries Act and the Dyestuffs Importation Act, which placed duties on the products of a number of such designated 'key' industries, including optical glass and instruments, and prohibited the importation of all synthetic dyestuffs and intermediate products.

Another war legacy was 12,000 miles of new tariff barriers. The war had led to the break-up of the Central European Empires of Russia and Austria-Hungary, and, in southern Europe, of the Ottoman Empire, creating nine new nations between Russia and the West. All adopted tariff barriers and quota systems to protect their nascent and incomplete economies.

Finally, the wartime developments encouraged new calculations of competitive advantage. In Japan, India, Australia and some Latin American countries, the disappearance of European competition in many lines of manufacturing for four years of war made local production attractive as well as necessary. Some of these 'war babies' died a natural death with the return of peacetime trading conditions, but many others, inspired by motives of self-interest as well as claims of national security, would clamour for and obtain tariff support. In Australia, iron and steel, machinery, railway materials and chemicals were given protection to maintain them when conditions returned to normal; in India, iron and steel, cotton textiles, paper and chemicals succeeded in making protection permanent; in Argentina, pharmaceutical manufactures were shielded from foreign competition.[3] In 1922, partly in retaliation, the United States introduced the Fordney–McCumber Tariff, raising American tariffs to the highest level in the country's history up to that time.

Tariffs were introduced not only for industrial protection or the encouragement of nascent industries. Currency disorders, occasioned by a lack of credit in the international economy, the appearance of new and often unstable Eastern European currencies, and the inflation which the war had imposed on the belligerents, also pushed towards tariff barriers to save scarce currency or prevent outpayments – in other words, for balance of payments purposes. Indeed, the use of commercial policy generally during the 1920s developed from the protection of particular industries to the protection of a country's balance of payments against declining export prices and the effects of the prevailing currency disorders. During the Great Depression, in addition, tariffs acquired yet another use, that of creating employment through the setting up of domestic manufacturing industries, in effect to replace demand satisfaction of the domestic market which had formerly been supplied by imports.

There was also the decline of economic liberalism, a marked feature of the inter-war period. A variety of political and economic doctrines which vaunted national protection and criticised notions of political and economic rights had been a growing feature of late nineteenth-century political thought. During the 1920s and 1930s, political parties and political leaders voicing such doctrines were swept to power, particularly in the countries of Central Europe, partly as a result of the economic depression. Among these, fascism and communism vaunted economic autarky as a positive good, and provided broad ideological justifications for closed economic systems behind which varieties of forced industrialisation were set in motion.[4]

The deep causes of protectionism

The deeper causes of the spread of protectionism formed the subject of a great debate between 'radicals', nationalists and liberals, but their differing conclusions were not incompatible. The radical theories had a broad Marxist origin. They saw the various types of protectionism as aspects of late or uneven development. They argued that the unevenness of the development process was causing a reaction formation, forcing the later developers to protect themselves from the enhanced power and capacity of the early developers. Nationalist, realpolitik and statist theories all stressed less the underdeveloped aspect than the rational and intentional aspect. They saw protectionism as the natural and inevitable effort to equalise capacity between emerging national entities: the various forms of protectionism were, consequently, rational acts of state power. The most prominent economic statist of the inter-war period was Eli Heckscher, who treated the various forms of protectionism as part of a 'new mercantilism', after the eighteenth-century policies undertaken by the European states to build up economic capacity in order to compete in power and prestige with their rivals.[5] (Heckscher's work highlighted the potential interaction between state power and economic power and encouraged a developing new political economy aimed at theorising the relations between the state and the economy, particularly in the context of inter-state competition.) Liberal economists, by contrast, tended to view them as an aggregation effect. They argued that, far from having a rational cause, protectionism was a resultant of a process of action and reaction, causing a breakdown in expectations with often unintended, and deleterious, consequences. They maintained that a rash of individual acts, reasonable in individual circumstances, were breaking down the system, and that the breakdown of the system was spurring on more protection – a vicious circle.

Whatever its causes, its effects were marked. Unique for the modern industrial age, output – and particularly manufacturing output – grew faster than trade during the 1930s.

Changes in industrial location after the Second World War

The Second World War gave a further rapid boost to the industrialisation of the United States, which had largely supplied the Allied war effort. Due to the destruction and dislocation of the war, the United States would also enjoy a comparative advantage over its European trading partners in its immediate aftermath. For at least four years following the Second World War, America was the main source of industrial products for rebuilding the war-torn industries of

Europe, the main source of engineering goods as well as the main source of coal and raw materials. It was also the main source of investment funds. Initially distributed in the form of Marshall Aid, purchasing credits were issued by the American government to enable European states to buy American goods to rebuild their war-damaged economies. These credits served the American economy as well, as they kept America producing through the immediate post-war years, avoiding a widely expected recession.

But industrial recovery in Europe was also surprisingly rapid following the Second World War. By 1949, both Britain and France had recovered their 1929 levels of production, though still behind tariff barriers. And by the mid-1950s, European industrial capacity had developed to the point where Europe was exporting manufactured goods back to America.[6]

The set of rules on international trade and payments agreed at Bretton Woods had led to a gradual resumption of, if not free, at least open trade. By 1958, all the major currencies were enjoying some convertibility. In consequence, the transfer of funds for investment became possible.

Partly in consequence, and also encouraged by deliberate policies of development, a third wave of industrialisation ensued. In Asia, what came to be known as the New Industrial Countries (or NICs), notably Korea, Hong Kong, Singapore, Malaysia and Taiwan, joined Japan as industrial states and became largely industrial economies, economies where economic life turned on the production of manufacturers. (In South Korea, by the mid-1980s, for every 10 people engaged in agriculture, 20 were engaged in industry; in Singapore, for every 10 people engaged in agriculture, 365 were engaged in industry.) In Europe, Ireland joined the already developed countries. In Latin America, Puerto Rico was developed into a manufacturing base, generally for affiliates of American firms, while Chile, Brazil and Mexico also joined the league of the industrial. In the Middle East, Algeria and Israel became industrial states, as did the oil exporters after 1973. By the mid-1980s, for every 10 people employed in agriculture in Kuwait, 40 were employed in industry; in the Emirates, 17 were so employed. Also, South Africa became sub-Saharan Africa's most advanced industrial state. Walt Rostow called the post-1945 world 'unique', in the growth of industry as well as in the growth of trade.[7]

These developments radically affected industrial location. By 1985, the USSR and Japan had become the world's largest producers of crude steel; Brazil was the sixth largest, Poland the ninth largest and India the fifteenth. China was the largest producer of cement, followed by the Soviet Union and Japan; India was sixth and Spain tenth. Hong Kong was the world's largest producer of radios with Singapore fourth, Korea fifth and Brazil eighth. Japan was the world's second largest producer of cars, West Germany the third largest, Spain the seventh largest, followed by Brazil. Japan was also the world's largest producer of ships, followed by South Korea and China. In textiles, China was the world's largest producer of cotton cloth, India the second largest, Japan the fifth largest; also in the top ten was Brazil.[8]

The pattern detected in the inter-war period was repeated in the post-war period. Industrial expansion tended to occur in the next generation of older industries, and even in the first generation. The newer industrialisers of South Asia produced smaller radios and televisions and ordinary makes of cars, largely for domestic consumption.

The relative concentration of industry

Despite the general spread of manufacturing industry, the implant of manufacture was not universal. If we include Japan and the Soviet Union among the new industrial powers of the twentieth century, alongside Canada and the European neutrals (Sweden and Finland), then the new industrial states outside of Europe and the United States – states where twice as many people were employed in industry as in agriculture – included no more than perhaps thirty. Taking countries classed as 'developing' by the World Bank in its post-war indices, which excluded the Soviet Union and its bloc, Japan and other developed countries, we may note that 75 per cent of the industrial exports of fifty developing countries was produced by just twelve states, and that Brazil, Korea, Hong Kong, Singapore and India produced 50 per cent of that.

The United States remained the largest overall producer with $1,000 billion in production in 1985, just under a third of total world production, followed by the Soviet Union and Japan with about $500 milliards each. The European countries came next, followed by Brazil and India.[9]

The causes of industrial spread

The spread of manufacturing activity was encouraged by, and in many cases the deliberate outcome of, direct and indirect investment from the more developed to the less developed countries. There were few entirely self-supporting industrialisers, the major exception being the Soviet Union after 1917. All others received funds from outside; and these were important spurs to indigenous development and in some cases formed the major portion of it.

The pattern of investment differed between the nineteenth and twentieth centuries. Up to 1875, foreign direct investment had consisted generally of direct purchases by corporations or individual entrepreneurs of controls in foreign companies. It was also the heyday of raw material and agricultural investments. In the period up to 1914, manufacturing activity accounted for only 15 per cent of total outward investment, while the primary product sector accounted for 55 per cent. After 1875, however, both patterns changed. Corporations began to set up foreign branches of the enterprises already operating in their home countries, primarily of manufacturing enterprises, a pattern which had become firmly established by 1914 and which would prevail again after the Second World War.[10]

The First World War had caused several European belligerents to sell some of their pre-war investments in Europe as well as overseas, while nationalist pressures and political and economic upheaval also reduced intra-continental European corporate activity. The 1917 revolution eliminated it altogether from Russia. But intra-European investment grew again towards the end of the inter-war period, and new mining investment from both Europe and the United States became especially important in the developing countries. There were significant new oil investments in the Mexican Gulf, the Dutch East Indies and the Middle East during the 1930s. By 1960, foreign-owned subsidiaries, numbering some 1,200 in 1938, had grown to 3,500, half of which were accounted for by mining and manufacturing, with trading and financial services making up a good deal of the rest. Already by the 1950s, the major European capital exporters were demonstrating a preference to invest in manufacturing, trade and service activities, and not in primary production. This would eventually direct investment towards other advanced countries. Thus, the US invested heavily in Europe during the 1960s, and Europe in the United States during the 1970s.

Originally, language, culture and political ties had played as great a role as geographical distance or economic conditions in determining the direction of investment. Before 1914, 72 per cent of American investment was in other parts of the American continent, and there was a strong colonial content to British, French and Belgian overseas involvement. France and Germany too primarily sited manufacturing activity elsewhere in Europe. These investments also tended to replicate the pattern of investment in the home country. Thus, British foreign branch plants were strongly oriented towards the production of consumer goods and heavy engineering equipment. United States foreign investment was already developing a comparative advantage in the newer technology-intensive industries and in those supplying standardised products and consumer goods, while the Germans led the world in chemical investments overseas.[11]

The product cycle

The generational movement of industry was first identified, and some of its causes analysed, by the American economist Raymond Vernon.[12] According to Vernon, production moved from old industrial centres to newer industrial centres in a regular cyclical form. Products were first produced in industrial centres where expertise, invention and funds for investment existed, and then moved out to the newer industrial countries to take advantage of cheaper labour and plant cost. The old producers turned to the production of new yet more innovative product lines, partly to compete with the new, cheaper industrialisers and partly to stay ahead of their main industrial rivals. Vernon predicted, moreover, that this would be an on-going process, characteristic of industrialisation generally.

The theory had important implications for thinking about processes of industrial growth and spread. It implied that there was one world-system, notwithstanding its unequal parts, and that industrialisation was, at least in part, a process with an autonomous dynamic, not a product of special talents. It also implied that industrial rivals were not only linked together but also dependent on one another, despite their rivalry. The less developed depended on the more developed to develop and simplify technology, allowing them to evade the costs of innovation, while the more developed were pushed by the less developed into new product innovation, allowing them to stay in the advance of industrial growth.

Why, however, the product cycle moved to some countries and not to others was not accounted for in Vernon's theory, and gave rise to a variety of contending explanations. Liberal economists tended to explain it largely in terms of the conditions of production. They maintained that new production tended to be located in those states which had relatively more educated populations, rational governments and stable political systems. Political economists, on the other hand, denied that such simple economic factors were sufficient in themselves. They pointed to, among other things, the external political relations of such states. According to some political economists, it was no accident that those states which were benefiting most from the product cycle were states which had military and security links with major Western powers.[13]

Industrial organisation

The rise in industrial productivity witnessed by the 1920s and 1930s, and its association with a rise in living standards, inevitably demanded large-scale operations. In secondary and tertiary industries, bigness became a necessity and oligopoly the predominant form of market structure. Industrial production became concentrated in a few large firms, each with heavy investment in plant and equipment. By 1967, some five hundred firms alone accounted for 25 per cent of all free world manufacturing production (and centralisation of production also became a feature of the socialist economies, partly for reasons of policy and political ideology, but also to achieve economies of scale). The same firms employed 17.3 million workers. There was also an unsteady but definite tendency towards greater concentration, that is, for increasingly more product to be produced by increasingly fewer firms.

Fewer firms not only absorbed production in a particular field (called 'horizontal development'). They also developed vertically: that is, they came to absorb the ancillary industries associated with their particular industry. This was most obvious, and most frequently noted, in the oil industry where companies not only explored for and pumped oil but also developed the exploration and pump technology, the 'upstream' processes, as well as refinement and transportation, the 'downstream' processes.

Industrial ownership by country was concentrated among the big three: America, Europe and Japan, with, however, significant variations over time. In 1962, of the 483 largest industrial enterprises, 292 were American-owned, 142 were European-owned (with Britain the largest single owner) and 29 were Japanese. By 1982, however, these proportions had shifted significantly. Among the 483 largest in the 1982 tabulation, America's share had decreased to 213 and Japan's had increased to 79. (Europe's increased slightly from 142 to 147.)

By 1989, of the top 200 companies, the alterations had become even more striking. Japan had 36 among the world's 200 top companies and 24 among the world's 100 top companies.[14]

The internationalisation of production

The post-war period was also marked by the increasing internationalisation of all types of production. First, there was a tendency, increasingly marked after 1970, for even relatively small domestic producers normally to sell abroad and to produce for international sales, competing across boundaries or offering products not available in domestic markets abroad. This was true especially in specialist clothing, such as that produced by the Italian firm Benetton, which became a household word across Europe, and in paper products. Second, there was the enormous post-war expansion in companies setting up or purchasing affiliates which produced parallel or complementary lines, producing the predominant form of multinational organisation with a firm in a home base and foreign subsidiaries. Finally, there was a limited though definite development of global production: that is, a real division of labour across boundaries, in which large firms produced not just parallel or complementary lines in different countries, but actual component parts for their products, which were then assembled in a number of different sites.

In the early 1980s, two British economists, John Dunning and Robert Pearce, carried out a major study, *The World's Largest Industrial Enterprises* which detailed the extent and sources of 'industrial internationalism'.[15] They calculated that, of the world's largest 800 firms in 1982, overseas production accounted for 28 per cent of their total production. Of this sum, estimated at $900 billion, American-owned firms were responsible for one-half of overseas production, i.e. $452 billion of production, and European industry for 44 per cent. Japan, on the other hand, was conservative, accounting for only 3 per cent of overseas production in 1982, though this figure would rise after 1989, due largely to the beginning of overseas car production. Viewed from the perspective of individual countries – that is, how much of each country's production was produced overseas – the figures were somewhat different, though perhaps more revealing. Thirty-nine per cent of Europe's production came from out-of-country affiliates, with Britain, Sweden, Switzerland and the Netherlands recording particularly high figures. But Japan again produced only 6 per cent of its total product abroad.

If the largest companies tended to produce more and more abroad, this did not mean that foreign production replaced domestic production for export or export sales. The same number of firms also sold on average 20 per cent of their 'home-produced' product abroad. Japan alone accounted for 21 per cent of all export sales of top companies, the US for 20 per cent (compared with 50 per cent of overseas production) and Europe for 44 per cent.

Overseas production and exports together represented the substance of industrial internationalism; and the proportion of total production these represented had become very high by the end of the century. In 1982, the two together represented 42 per cent of total production of the top 800 firms, who, it should be recalled, were also responsible for a great percentage of total world production (probably 30 per cent by the mid-1980s). Moreover, these trends showed steady signs of increasing. The top companies between 1977 and 1982 were more inclined to meet foreign markets with overseas production than they had been before.

The number of largest firms coincided with the number of multinationals, and the countries represented strongly among the lists of the world's largest firms were also those countries which recorded the largest numbers of multinational companies. Just under one-half were American; one-third were European, notably Britain, France and some of the smaller countries of Europe. The French economic index for 1987 calculated that one-half of world manufacturing plant owed its existence to 'American' capital investment (but this was a contentious figure, because the capital in question was often raised in Europe or by employing unrepatriated dollars, called the Euro-dollar market.) Germany and Japan were major exceptions, having rather large companies but rather fewer multinational companies; both followed a similar pattern of producing at home and selling abroad.

What these figures also revealed was that the majority of multinational investment went to other developed countries. The trend by which developed countries tended to invest in other developed countries, noticeable before the Second World War, became the prevailing pattern after it. Of the number of affiliates of American multinationals, 62 per cent were in Europe and other developed countries, while only 28 per cent were in developing countries, in America's case in Latin America. The largest proportion of American capital went to Europe in the 1950s and 1960s, and the largest share of Europe's investment capital was directed to the United States in the 1960s and 1970s.

If global international investment tended to be greater among industrial and developed countries, the saliency of the multinationals and the importance of their presence within less developed countries was not thereby less. While multinational production within developing countries was much less than the global figure, it remained vital because the multinational tended to represent a very large part of some less developed countries' domestic production. This was particularly the case since the developing world's share of multinationals tended to be concentrated in relatively few countries. For example, by the 1980s, 36 per cent of multinational companies, by investment value, were located in Brazil, Mexico, Venezuela, Indonesia and Nigeria, while India, Malaysia, Argentina, Singapore, Peru, Hong Kong and the Philippines accounted for another 22 per cent. In both Mexico and Brazil especially, foreign investment played a pivotal role in economic life, producing 23 per cent of their respective GNPs in 1970, and 28 per cent of all sales, and it was of course largely of American origin. In Brazil, in 1974, multinational companies controlled 29 per cent of all assets in the manufacturing sector and 44 per cent of all local sales; and foreign control was concentrated in the most technologically advanced and capital-intensive industries, including machinery, transportation and chemicals.

Why the multinational?

The most common explanation for the development of the multinational company was its more efficient use of the factors of production. In common parlance, it was cheaper for United States companies to invest in Europe in the 1960s than elsewhere, and for Europeans to invest in the United States in the 1970s than elsewhere. Cross-border agglomeration was also spurred on by the anticipation of tariff barriers. Once a subsidiary was established, the company became, in effect, a domestic producer and thereby evaded tariff restrictions.[16] Thus, the Japanese foreign production drive in the automobile industry in Europe during the late 1980s coincided with the announcement that the European Common Market would establish a truly single market, and a fear on the part of Japanese companies that the resultant dislocation within that single market might lead to prejudice against it.

Their pattern of organisation, as well as their decision-making styles, varied among multinationals, from loose federations to the highly centralised. The question appeared to be largely one of national style, and was in some cases the antithesis of what might have been expected, given the prevailing political culture within the home country. Thus, companies originating from within the complex federal United States seemed to prefer the more centralised structures, while companies whose home base was centralised France gave more leeway to local decision-making, especially among France's largest firms. Nonetheless, the large multinational of whatever type developed the capacity to take on decision-making for the whole.

The Défi Americain

As concentrations of foreign capital grew, so did concern for the potential social and political implications of such large-scale movements. Some commentators focused on the potential for undue political influence from the sender to the receiver state. In 1968, Jean-Jacques Servan-Schreiber published *The American Challenge*, pointing to the size of American investment in Europe and warning that within fifteen years the world's third largest industrial power might be American industry in Europe, placing Europe in a satellite position to the United States.[17] Others implied that the challenge was undue pressure from increasingly *autonomous* companies that were politically unaccountable and whose criteria of decision-making were determined by profit motives, irrespective of the social or political consequences of their decisions for the receiver country.[18]

The span of concern ranged from immediate threats to more long-ranging structural consequences. The former included the disturbance of development plans, the potential mobility of multinational enterprise and the consequences of mobility for domestic labour, conditionality terms, including the conditions of labour, the repatriation of capital, and direct political interference. The latter involved more diffuse concerns about cultural uniformity and the structures within which smaller, domestic industries were being forced to operate, including fears of peripheralisation within an emerging globally based capitalism.[19]

Some of these fears were undoubtedly exaggerated. Multinational companies proved to be not very 'footloose', as plant investment was very large and managers did not easily conceive of writing off such investments. Only in industries where initial investment was small, such as with semi-conductor or small electronic components, could companies contemplate rapid relocation.[20] Moreover, since they tended to produce for the local market, affiliates as well as their headquarters tended not to mind either tariff barriers or development planning. The various Proctor and Gamble enterprises in Latin America tended towards 'national' marketing strategies in which the various branches developed sectoral agreements among one another and sold at different prices in different – protected – markets.[21] Such strategies co-existed well with national economic planning and often, paradoxically, supported it, since a major economic enterprise might be well served by the shielding effects of such plans.

Of more immediate concern to governments was 'transfer price manipulation'. The great multinationals sold goods to their own subsidiaries, much of which counted as foreign trade. Moreover, such foreign trade made up a large part of foreign trade generally. By the 1990s, it was calculated that 30 per cent of all foreign trade was intra-firm trade, in which companies produced for their own affiliates in different countries. Transfer price manipulation included the adjustment of prices to affect profit and loss calculuses and, accordingly, rates of taxation; companies could also sell at lower prices to their own affiliates than to outsiders, a device which affected profit ratios, besides benefiting foreign-owned companies as against national producers in the same field. The more advanced industrial countries developed techniques for spotting and monitoring such practices, but it was more difficult for less developed countries.

Another was the political influence such companies might exert. It was feared that their financial resources might allow them to affect local election outcomes or to support local candidates. For this reason, political participation was, in general, forbidden to them. But this was not easy to monitor or to forbid in practice, since joint ownership between a foreign company and a locally owned affiliate was often the pattern. It was also the case that once such large companies were established they became ordinary political actors within the political system. They could not be forbidden from expressing views, at least in the liberal democracies; and their resources everywhere allowed them the possibility of exerting considerable influence, often by graft. Most learned to be cautious in public utterance, but they monitored political developments in their host countries closely. Large companies had political sections and developed their own styles of diplomacy; they developed insider political contacts, and they used them.[22]

Problems of culture and social structure were even more difficult to deal with, particularly from the perspective of traditional labour practices and regional economic inequalities. Liberal Western governments could do little to force foreigners to locate industries between richer and poorer parts of their states. In the circumstances, they had to offer incentives, which often took the form of competitive bidding, including terms of labour. The terms of such bidding were affected by market conditions, and in particular by how many multinationals were seeking location or acquisitions at any one time. Governments had more leeway in setting conditions when demand for foreign location was plentiful, as it was during the 1980s, than during periods when international investment was more scarce. The fact remained that, so long as the major sources of investment were international, a closer approximation of government policies among contenders for that investment would become irresistible.[23]

The potential consequences for labour practices and industrial location were highlighted by the changes in management doctrines. A 'post-Fordist' philosophy swept industry increasingly from the 1970s, recommending smaller and leaner industrial units with more flexibility, more mechanisation and less mass labour. The new doctrines stressed more flexible labour forces with more managerial as well as electronic skills. These affected host country educational policies as well as their policies towards trade unions. In general, de-unionising became a prevalent value among those states which wished to remain industrial leaders, and promoted the lifting of other devices of worker protection. It was also clear that monetary policies harmful to stable export earnings affected the consideration of industrial location, particularly in more competitive industries. The Japanese car company Toyota, which located in Britain during the 1980s to take advantage of the European single market, would warn the British government that it could not increase investment if Britain declined to enter an emerging European currency union.

The harmonisation of state policies

As early as the 1970s, international measures were undertaken to deal with some of these anxieties. The countries of OEEC established a country code of operations which forbade double book-keeping and which determined some rules of operation. At the national level, governments would increase their capabilities of bureaucratic management, by closer surveillance and enforcement. Some also became more astute negotiators, determining long-term conditions and demanding guarantees of establishment.

What governments found, however, was that companies could take advantage of differing national legislation, differing taxation regimes, differing banking rules, and differing rules on establishment to evade compliance. Complex accounting techniques and simple shifts in the balance of the operations could work to the advantage of the company operating simultaneously in different legal environments. From the 1980s, autonomous processes of common legislation began to appear, particularly among the more advanced industrialisers (who had also become major host countries). Banking legislation was among the first to be harmonised. The rules of establishment and company taxation increasingly paralleled one another.

Industrialisation, internationalisation and globalisation

The processes of industrialisation absorbed more countries more closely into the international trading web. It also linked them functionally into processes of industrial innovation. Less-developed countries imported industrial processes and copied them outright, taking advantage of their cheaper labour and plant costs; and the more innovative moved production to higher levels of technology and sophistication as the education and skills of their labour forces developed.

The spread of industrialisation was accompanied by its relative concentration in some thirty or forty countries, but few were left out entirely from the industrial network. Only the poorest states, with the most backward facilities or the most unstable governments – generally in Africa between the Sahara and the front-line states bordering South Africa – remained outside the emerging global network, and even in some of these the extractive mineral industries had some integrating consequences.

At the same time, bigness became the mark of industrial development, and this was reflected in an organisational pattern of purchase and oligopolistic organisation across territorial boundaries. Boundaries were crossed by an increasingly complex pattern of private investment, a horizontal spread of some thousand major companies with subsidiaries which organised spatially. Industrial organisation increasingly cut across state boundaries as more manufacture came to be produced by more multinational firms.

Technology transfer and management technique moved across this web, inducing common patterns of industrial practice and common policies both to attract investment and to combat its more baleful influences. They also induced a higher degree of common working patterns. But they did not induce equalities. Plants in the Third World tended to carry out the more mundane aspects of the industrial process, while investment decisions and innovation were carried out at the headquarter plants. Industrialisation processes and the form of the modern firm both induced more uniform social practices and also created greater inequalities between industrial leaders and those who were marginal to or had been excluded from the multinational web. Accordingly, industrialisation became identified, at one and the same time, as one of the central factors in the development of more uniform social practices around the globe, but also a central source of differentiation. Indeed, it was largely credited with creating a new form of differentiation, between 'cores' where people enjoyed more of what was available and 'peripheries' where access was being rendered increasingly difficult.[24]

These processes eventually gave rise to a new term to describe them. This was 'globalisation', a concept that was intended to supplement (though some argued that it should replace) internationalisation. Its inventors argued that the term 'international' confused governmental interaction with autonomous economic processes that crossed borders, and they wished to confine the older usage to inter-state relations. Globalisation, by contrast, drew attention to processes which occurred laterally, above and below the level of the state.

Scholars using the latter term also stressed the degree to which the processes associated with globalisation were autonomous social and economic processes, little affected by state policy.

The globalisation of industry was a bumpy process, however. The prevailing mode of political justification was not cosmopolitan; moreover, the source of regulation remained with sovereign governments, and nationalism was on the rise. Globalisation thus turned on demonstrating that such processes could serve national interests and national communities.

Notes

1 A. Kenwood and A. Lougheed, *The Growth of the International Economy 1820–1980* (London: Unwin, 1983) p. 182.

2 Ibid., pp. 183–4.

3 Ibid., pp. 185–6.

4 W.A. Lewis, *Economic Survey, 1919–1939* (London: George Allen and Unwin, 1949) Part II.

5 *Mercantilism*, 2 vols (New York: Allen and Unwin, 1955).

6 M. Postan, *An Economic History of Western Europe, 1945–1964* (London: Methuen, 1967).

7 W.W. Rostow, *The World Economy* (London: Macmillan, 1978) p. 66.

8 P. Ghosh, *Industrialization and Development* (London: Greenwood Press, 1984).

9 *Economist, The World in Figures* (London: *Economist*, 1987), pp. 53, 153.

10 J. Dunning, 'Changes in the level structure of international production' in M. Casson (ed.), *The Growth of International Business* (London: Allen and Unwin, 1983).

11 Kenwood and Lougheed, *The Growth of the International Economy 1820–1980* (London: Unwin, 1983), pp. 39–52.

12 'International Investment and International Trade in the Product Cycle', *Quarterly Journal of Economics*, 80 (1966), pp. 190–207.

13 J. Bhagwati and R. Eckaus, *Foreign Aid* (Harmondsworth: Penguin, 1970).

14 J. Dunning and R. Pearce, *The World's Largest Industrial Enterprises* (Aldershot: Gower, 1985).

15 Ibid.

16 M. Casson, *The Growth of International Business* (London: Allen and Unwin, 1983), anticipated in A. Cairncross, *Home and Foreign Investment, 1870–1913* (Cambridge: Cambridge University Press, 1953).

17 Published in Paris as *Le Défi Americain* (1966), *The American Challenge* (New York: Atheneum, 1968) pp. 3, 26.

18 R. Vernon, *Sovereignty at Bay* (New York: Basic Books, 1971).

19 R. Gilpin, *The Political Economy of International Relations* (Princeton: Princeton University Press, 1987) pp. 246–8.

20 See M. Hodges, *Multinational Corporations and National Governments: A Case Study of the United Kingdom's Experience* (Farnborough: Saxon House, 1974).

21 A story often told by the British political economist Susan Strange; see more generally G. Modelski (ed.), *Transnational Corporations and World Order* (San Francisco: W.H. Freeman , 1979).

22 E.g. A. Sampson, *The Sovereign State: The Secret History of ITT* (London: Hodder and Stoughton, 1973).

23 On the advisability of 'copying', see W. Hager, 'Protectionism and Autonomy: How to Preserve Free Trade in Europe', *International Affairs*, 58 (1982), pp. 413–28, and B. Hindley, 'A Comment on Hager', *International Affairs*, 59 (1982–83), pp. 77–86.

24 See e.g. R. Cox, *Production, Power and World Order* (New York: Columbia University, 1987).

5 National self-determination

While the material organisation of the age increasingly pointed to a shared economic future, its major principles of political organisation were becoming increasingly parochial. The demand for national self-determination spread steadily throughout the century, cutting across the nineteenth-century formal and informal imperial structures. It legitimated much smaller units of political rule, and established the well-being of discrete culture groups as the prime justification of that rule.

Culture groups were variously defined, with important implications for political spaces. Indian nationalists melded many linguistic groupings within a concept of 'Mother India', preserving a good deal of its seventeenth-century compass. China also avoided dismemberment. In other cases, accidental administrative units of the old empires became the carapaces for new nations, and a local nationalism was invented to base a claim to a specified territory. Whatever the case, however, each defined nationalism sought a separate state within which to pursue its political life; and, accordingly, the numbers of states and separate administrative jurisdictions grew. In 1919, 27 states joined the League of Nations. In 1998, there were 185 members of the United Nations, ranging from micro-states with a few hundred thousand in population to recast former empires of many millions. Despite the new diversity, however, in some respects the new nations would be uncannily similar. A cultural and political map of the world drawn as late as 1870 would have revealed a bewildering variety of social and political forms. A similar map drawn in 1970 would reveal common conceptions of citizenship, much more similar forms of political and social organisation and many shared social and political objectives.

The pacing and spread of nationalism

The claim for national self-determination was not a twentieth-century invention. It had made its first formal appearance at the Congress of Vienna in 1814, where the powers met to consider the reconstitution of Europe after the Napoleonic Wars. There, some Poles had demanded a reconstitution of a Polish state on ethnic principles, after its partition in 1772 between Russia, Prussia and Austria, and some German liberals had pressed for the unity of all German states into a single national Germany. In the event, each was ignored. The honour of being the first new nation fell to Greece: by 1830, the Great Powers had agreed to recognise it on the grounds of a cultural unity which distinguished it from that of its Ottoman overlord, making it the first country so recognised.

The development of nationalist sentiment, and the creation of movements to procure national liberation, took place only slowly through the remainder of the nineteenth century, and then primarily in Europe. The revolutions of 1830 and 1848 in Belgium, Spain and Germany were undertaken on the basis of the claimed right of cultural peoples to rule themselves. But they were not notably successful: the German and Italian unities only came in 1870–71 (though a long period of cultural definition had preceded each of their campaigns). Austria formed the Austro-Hungarian Empire in 1867 to take account of Hungarian national claims. But Serbians, Croats and other groups within the Austrian Empire only really began to press national claims at the end of the nineteenth century.[1] By the end of the nineteenth century, there was also some evidence that nationalism was spreading abroad. Japan under the Meiji restoration displayed nationalist symptoms: 'Rid Japan of the Barbarians' was one of the main rallying cries of the forces which had backed the restoration. In 1876, the Indian Association was formed to press for the entry of educated Indian elites into the Indian Civil Service. And Gold Coast transplanted ex-slaves had begun a form of nationalist movement from the mid-century, experimenting with ideas of negritude which imputed special qualities to the race, qualities which distinguished it from other races.

The contribution of the twentieth century to the development of nationalism lay in the formal establishment of the 'national right of self-determination' and its spread, together with some of these same animating ideas, to the rest of the world. It also saw the formation of often remarkably similar organisations with similar objectives in Asia, the Middle East and Africa. The twentieth century also added some new ideas to the older corpus.

Nationalism *outre mer*

It is hard to date the origins of the extra-European movements with any exactitude. Claims of cultural distinctiveness on behalf of specific groups of non-Europeans had made sporadic appearances throughout the nineteenth century. The British African historian P.E.H. Hair has pointed to the importance of the Freetown blacks in advocating both self-determination and a form of racial nationalism, known as Africanism, and their role in articulating and promoting liberation sentiment and defining a distinct cultural black experience throughout the nineteenth century.[2] In the 1860s, a linguistic movement was founded by some South African Boers to establish Afrikaans as a 'proper' language and to resist English cultural imperialism.

If the criteria for the appearance of a true nationalist movement were to include a political movement able to formulate and articulate political demands, we would find little evidence of any such activity outside of Europe before the turn of the century. The first Pan African Congress met in New York in 1900 with what was still a limited and vague agenda about the recognition of blacks. By 1919, however, the movement's leaders felt confident enough to demand from Clemenceau that blacks should have some kind of representation at the Paris Peace Conference to determine the peace settlement (one such demand was that the Congress become the mandatory power over the former German colonies in Africa). The first indigenous black African organisations were: the African National Congress, the ANC, established in 1912, two years after South Africa was given dominion status which, it was feared, might lead to a permanent white ascendancy; and the larger British West Africa Association, which held its first Congress in 1920. The Indian National Congress was formed as a self-help organisation in 1885 but only began to take on the appurtenances of a political movement in 1905, when the British authorities in India proposed to divide Bengal into separate administrative zones. (A separate Muslim organisation was founded in 1906.) In China, students had been going abroad in increasing numbers from the 1870s, carrying back reformist and nationalist ideas; but Sun Yat-sen only formed a political organisation after the Boxer Rebellion in 1900.[3]

The publication of Woodrow Wilson's Fourteen Points during the closing months of the First World War dynamised these extra-European national claims. The Points were the principles which would, Wilson declared, guide the United States in the drafting of the peace agreement; significant among them was an albeit ambiguous support for the principle of national self-determination.[4] It was also widely recognised that the Versailles settlement would be a victor's peace, and the developing nationalist organisations rushed to Paris to press their claims upon the victorious powers and to demand rewards for war participation. The India Congress insisted on a separate representation at the Peace Conference as a reward for war service, and gained some representation for the Indian elite at Paris; Blaise Daigne, the first black deputy to sit in the French National Assembly, demanded that he be allowed to represent a 'black voice' because of the role he had played in the military recruitment of black Africans. Many outside of Europe hoped that the principle of national self-determination applied to them as well as to their European counterparts, with the result that Versailles became a circus not only of Lithuanians, Latvians, Estonians, Poles, Serbs and Croats, but also of Indians and Japanese, all seeking representation and pressing for the right to be consulted on the final territorial settlement which Versailles would establish.

The exclusion of any black African representation at Versailles, when Indians and Japanese were given some consultative status, made many in the African Union fear that self-determination was primarily a European matter with some concessions to the yellow peoples. Indeed, a certain hostility began to develop in the black political movements towards Asian self-determination. Marcus Garvey, who founded the Universal Negro Improvement Association as a rival to the Pan African movement in 1914, became concerned that the achievement of political rights of other racial groups before Africans would lead to the permanent subjugation of the black races.

The structure of the new nationalisms

These early nationalist movements shared common characteristics. They all tended to be formed around a personality, a person generally from the educated classes and usually educated in Europe, or in the case of the Gold Coast blacks with a European experience via America. Just as Herder in Germany and Mazzini in Italy had been the focal point of their respective national movements, so too did the extra-European national movements have their own pivotal personalities. Sun Yat-sen, Sukarno, Kemal Ataturk, Kenyatta, Nkrumah, Ho Chi Minh, Gandhi, each defined the content of their respective nationalisms, articulated the particular spirit of the people, expressed its grievances and became either the organiser of the movement or the leader around whom a movement coalesced. These respective 'fathers of their people', lauded in national myth and history, came also to be seen as focal points by Western historians, who have stressed the role of elites as both receivers and transmitters of nationalist ideas and who, in consequence, have highlighted their historical roles almost as much as their nationalist chroniclers.

Despite the diversity of their circumstances, the majority of the national movements which appeared during the twentieth century followed a similar developmental course. They generally began as forms of self-improvement organisation, just as their European counterparts in the nineteenth century had done. Integral to self-improvement was a movement to recover or uncover a cultural past, expressed in poetry, fables or forms of dress. There was generally also a language movement directed to cleaning, reforming or modernising the tongue. Many Indian and African nationalists in the early days used English or French, either because there was no other predominant tongue among the populations they wished to reach or because the indigenous languages were considered too arcane for the purposes of self-improvement: an important aim of nationalist movements was to achieve dignity of consideration and equality of representation. The use of pre-modern and often pre-literate languages was felt to be prejudicial to this aim. Even where the language of the coloniser was used, however, it was deployed in a new context, to recover and record original oral traditions and express what was unique to the relevant culture group. Generally, then, a political movement became attached to or developed alongside the cultural organisation, pressing claims of representation in international and imperial fora. In 1906, Indonesians established the High Endeavour Society, which aimed to establish schools and to regenerate Javanese culture; in 1911, the Saschet Islam was founded, an Indonesian political movement, which in 1916 began to demand Indonesian self-government.

The ideology of these movements was also remarkably similar, despite their diversity of situations, histories and claims. In each case, the purpose of the movement was to recover a faded glory; the present declined state was generally conceived to have been the result of subjugation; and the removal of subjugation was generally seen to be the cure. All, moreover, stressed the rights of the so-identified peoples to some equality, either in political rights or considerations of dignity, with the European or Turkish overlord. In this respect, they all followed the first nationalist movement, the German national movement, which appeared, in consequence, to have established the model. Nineteenth-century German nationalists had claimed the special virtues of Germanness; Germany, it was claimed, had paid the price for European liberties; this could only be corrected, eventually, by a German state. German national ideas and the structures of nineteenth-century German national thought were prevalent everywhere in the early days of the twentieth-century national movements.

The role of the imagined past, when a national glory had been displayed, was meant to defend a case for rights; it did not generally imply arcadianism or political programmes directed towards the recovery of archaic social and political forms. None of the early movements in Africa wished to return to tribal structures, much less pre-modern agriculture. Regeneration was in this sense a misnomer, as such movements generally aimed to raise their peoples to European standards of literacy, self-respect and social capacity. The most successful of such movements welded together middle-class aspirations with peasant mobilisation. Gandhi's Young India movement combined the secular political ambitions of a rising Indian political class with the semi-religious, semi-traditional veneration of the peasants for Mother India.[5] There was some inevitable tension between going forwards and going backwards, witnessed for example in the conflict between the Pan Islam and the Pan Arab movements, the former of which wished to see a return to some of the tenets of traditional Islam, while the latter aimed at secularisation.[6] But generally all stressed the need for self-rule or dignity to achieve what would come to be called modernisation, and all aimed to transform the decayed people into modern citizens of modern polities, whose forms were, of course, to be infused with the genuine cultural sentiments of the people.

Increasingly, however, arcadian elements did creep in. The future imagined by African nationalists in the 1960s and 1970s was increasingly articulated in terms of a past golden age of co-operation and self-help which could provide a model for the contemporary society. Islamic nationalism, always complex, increasingly came to draw on divergent traditions, some of which stressed the more universalist elements in Islam while others emphasised the more traditional Bedu values of purdah and a strict reading of the Koran.[7]

The emergence of territoriality

Neither the Pan African nor the Arabic movements were originally territorial nationalisms. Pan Africanism had initially aimed at a general improvement in the condition and treatment of blacks everywhere, and it stressed the universal experience of slavery as experienced not only in Africa, but also in Europe and the Middle East, as well as in the New World.[8] Indeed, the Pan Africa movement originated, not in Africa, but in the West Indies and in New York, and its ideas were transmitted to West Africans; moreover, all three groups participated in the movement for West African liberation which began in 1905. This was reflected in the communications network which fuelled the movement: a circular route of newspapers and pamphlets between the West African coastal towns, across the Atlantic to the West Indies, and up to the northern American cities. The Pan Islamic movement, as it became known after the establishment of a Pan Islamic society in Paris in 1884, began with a poets' movement in Cairo. Many have stressed the Egyptian origins of the Pan Islamic movement, but the movement did not conceive of itself as Egyptian. Rather, it aimed at identifying what was unique to and shared between all Islamic peoples. Indeed, Egypt was not deemed by the early Egyptian Pan Islamicists to have a culture of its own.

The nationalist movements of the Arab world were particularly vague with regard to precise spatial locations. In Syria and Lebanon, nationalism was the special preserve of Christian Arabs, the Druse of Mount Lebanon and the Alawis of upper Syria, who all strove for the development of a non-Islamic movement, a Pan Arabic movement, which stressed secular nationalism but with no explicit reference to territoriality. Others among these same groups wished for a Pan Arab state based on Egypt. Copts and Armenians in the area joined neither, but became cosmopolitan or attached to forms of local nationalism.

Territoriality developed late in these pan movements, and largely in response to imperial policy. It was the establishment of varieties of legislative assembly by the imperial overlord in defined territories, where elections had to be fought, that, as much as anything else, defined territorial nationalisms. In the Arabian lands this occurred during the mandate period, when the French and British carved out Syria, Lebanon, Iraq and Transjordan from the former Ottoman Empire; as a consequence, Arab nationalist movements took on an increasingly territorial aspect. Parallel developments occurred during the post-war period in Africa. The establishment of colonial legislative assemblies provided a specific political arena for the political struggle between the coloniser and the colonised, and led to the enunciation of interests specific to the territory in question. Only then could one begin to speak of Ghanaian nationalism or Nigerian nationalism; and Ghanaian nationalism specifically retained substantial Pan-African elements. Nkrumah declared it an integral part of Ghana's liberation struggle that it should also aim at the liberation of the rest of Africa.

The early political aspirations of these movements varied, largely according to whether they were inside or outside a formal imperial relationship. To those outside a formal relationship, such as China, Japan and to a lesser extent Thailand, nationalism meant getting rid of or controlling the activities of foreigners and reducing excessive foreign influence, rewriting unequal treaties and being treated on a basis of equality with European states. To those inside empires, sovereign equality initially meant equal representation in the national assembly in the metropolis. Blaise Daigne enunciated this form, sometimes called 'assimilationist nationalism', when he said, in contrast to some separatist black Africans, 'We French natives wish to remain French, since France has given us every liberty.'[9] Influenced by American ex-slaves in Liberia, West African nationalists aimed originally for a United States of West Africa, a West African federation which would then be accorded dominion status within the British Empire. Many Christian Arabs, observing the slow modernisation of the Ottoman Empire under way by the end of the nineteenth century, began to speak of an Ottoman nationalism, and voiced a desire to remain within the great territorial range of the former Ottoman state and to partake in the construction of a new secular and liberal order within it, to protect their Christianity as much as anything else. In France's colonies, in particular, assimilationist nationalism largely defined local nationalist ambitions for a large part of the twentieth century: the achievement of equal rights with other Frenchmen, involving representation within the French National Assembly, remained the aspiration of most black African Frenchmen until the closing stages of the Second World War.

Some groups in the respective metropolises shared, endorsed and supported these aspirations. Some black Africans were introduced into the French National Assembly, albeit on a token basis, while a group of imperial federalists in Britain expended much effort on schemes to accommodate the entire British Empire within a single political order.[10] Intricate plans for a federated British imperial structure were still being proposed in the late 1920s and early 1930s, schemes in which local assemblies would legislate on much of the day-to-day business of government, while some sort of super-parliament in London would determine foreign and commercial policy, weights and measures and common currencies.

But such plans were frustrated, in the British case, not only by the desire for autonomy by the old white dominions, but also by the fear that the 'coloured races' might come to dominate a unitary parliament. Neither the prospect that the 'mother of parliaments' would be superseded by some kind of defence council or higher representative assembly nor, alternatively, that representatives from the diverse parts of the empire would take their place in it directly, with the prospect of British parliamentarians being out-voted, were acceptable. What frustrated these movements was primarily domestic sentiment in the metropolis; few Englishmen could imagine how to accommodate so many different peoples, each with their own nationalisms, within a single polity, nor could the government accept being one government among many. In the end, the British government – and, one cannot doubt, the people – preferred increasing autonomy of their colonies outside Parliament, maintaining a residual imperial role, rather than sharing a common polity with them. Largely in consequence, nationalism increasingly took the separatist – and in the end increasingly insistent separatist – road. In other words, territorialism was as much a result of the refusal to be allowed in than any autonomous growth of separatism from without.

The political socialisation of the nationalist movements

The direction of these movements and their individual political programmes were deeply influenced by the education and the political socialisation of their leaders, varying both over time and within it, according to where and when their formative Western education had occurred and the predominant ideas of social ordering then prevalent. Kemal, who led the Turkish army after 1920 and saved Turkey from further dismemberment after Versailles, had been strongly influenced by the German cultural, linguistic and strongly statist elements present in the movement for German unification. His programme took shape accordingly, to build Turkey on the single cultural rump of the Turks, abandoning any aspirations to a reformed Greater Turkey. He also had the language cleaned of its Arabisms, replacing words of Arabic root with those of Turkic root where possible, and rejected religion as the basis of the state, deeming that Islamicism in the case of Turkey, like Catholicism in the case of Germany, disturbed the drawing of boundaries. He also began a modernisation from above. Sukarno, by contrast, had been a student in Berlin after the First World War, where anti-imperialism was the dominant policy of the Anti-Imperialist League, a communist-front organisation. Largely in consequence, he carried socialist ideas into the national movement of the new Indonesia. Ho Chi Minh had come under French socialist influence during his student days in Paris during the 1920s, and spent the war in the communist-controlled part of China, imbibing many of the Chinese Communist Party's emerging ideas on the potential revolutionary role of the peasantry and on agricultural collectivisation as the road to modernisation. Many African leaders, by contrast, would imbibe their socialism at the London School of Economics a generation later, where they were introduced to the ideas of Fabianism in which an elite guided a socialistic but also pluralist development from above: a sort of Fabian socialism for Africa.

These varied historical experiences laid the basis for considerable differentiation between different generations of nationalist movements, as well as providing a source for conflict within them. The liberation movement in China became divided between the liberal modernist Sun Yat-sen's wing, led by Chiang Kai-shek during the 1930s and 1940s, and the younger, Moscow-educated Mao Tse-tung, laying the foundations for the bitter civil war which ensued. Gandhi's secular legacy has been variously challenged by those wishing to construct India as a Hindu state.

But aspirants to self-determination also learned from one another. Rheza Khan, the enterprising officer who seized power in Iran in 1921, followed Kemal's experience. He cleansed Iranian Arabic, giving it words of Persian origin, stressed the pre-Islamic cultural sources of the Persian state, controlled the mullahs and established a bureaucracy, also with the aim of modernising from above. Nkrumah read Gandhi and was inspired by the Indian examples of civil disobedience, while, a decade later, Tanzania, with a large number of peasant producers, followed Mao Tse-tung's China down the road of agricultural collectivisation.

Economic nationalism

Central to most national ideology was not only the achievement of equal dignity with Westerners and political rights. Nationalist movements also stressed the importance of catching up economically with European states and developing their territories. The model was again the 'new' Germany where the Prussian state had guided economic as well as social development from above, encouraging nascent industries and establishing special national schools. This implied enhancing the powers of emerging political leaders, as well as the acquisition of tasks which colonial authorities had seldom attempted: economic and planning ministries as well as social welfare programmes would be considered important requisites for new states. Nationalist ideas also tended to encourage tariff barriers, to protect nascent industries and to give them time to grow.

Claims to the invention of economic nationalism have been various. Some have given the credit to Mussolini, particularly as he was influenced by Giolloti, with his invention of the concept of *lo stato totalitaro*, which was to lay the basis for a revived and modernised Italian empire. Mussolini claimed the regulation of economic interests as a justified means to that end. The detail remained hazy, however, and the practice inconsistent. Italian fascist economic nationalism demanded little more than an optimum tariff, while *lo stato totalitaro* tended to become the focus for the protection of special interests.[11] A more convincing locus, argued in a work of that name by Harry Johnson, was Eastern Europe during the inter-war period.[12] Originally parts of large imperial spaces, they had to adapt what were often incomplete economies to the rigours of international economic competition in increasingly depressed economic conditions. (In the economic space of the former Austro-Hungarian Empire, Hungary had had the spinning capacity and Austria the looms; the area of Yugoslavia, formed by a union of South Slavs, had belonged to three different empires and had three different railway gauges, none focusing on Belgrade, the new capital.) Another causal factor was the demands of economic development in countries with large numbers of peasant producers. Eastern European economists who came to London before and during the war were prominent among the earlier formulators of 'nationalist' development policies.

This early development thinking was various. Peter Bauer, a pioneer of development economics, was noteworthy for recommending economic liberalism, arguing that this had been the development model of the most advanced industrial states.[13] Others emphasised planning: Indian nationalism was a particularly fruitful source of development thinking centred on the notion of planning. (But what was to be planned was the question; often, planning meant no more than greater knowledge of the wealth base of the territory.) Some tried to adapt Keynesian ideas to the requisites of national economic development, but with little success, since Keynes' had been a theory of underutilised capacity, whereas the problem in some new states was one of no capacity. Other schemes revolved around economic autarky; in Germany between 1935 and 1937, autarky was a serious policy (although it did not survive for long). The Soviet Union during the 1930s developed the idea of 'socialism in one country', which was, however, little more than the idea of national autarky directed and rationalised by state planners.

An allied phenomenon was nationalisation or expropriation, the seizure of foreign-owned private property by governments for social use. This was practically unheard of in the nineteenth century, not least since future credit would have been nil, but the Soviet Union engaged in a wholesale expropriation of all property after the 1917 revolution, an example which gave heart to Mexico, whose 1931 nationalisation programme extended to the seizure of foreign-owned oil plant and land holdings (most of the latter British). In 1951, Iran established the Aramco, nationalising its oil industry; in 1956, Nasser nationalised the foreign-owned and operated Suez Canal. When Libya nationalised its oil in 1964, Britain again was the chief victim. These nationalisers demanded, initially, to be freed from the requisites of compensation, and they tried to develop nationalisation-without-compensation into an internationally agreed practice, on the grounds of a new norm of thorough-going economic sovereignty. In the event, they failed. International law developed no such category; instead, sequestration with compensation became the norm. But new states did achieve the right of a government to abrogate agreements reached by previous governments, on oil exploration for example, provided compensation were made. As a consequence, nationalisation involving foreign expropriation disappeared as a *casus belli*.

By the post-war period, ideas of national economic development had come to centre less on national protection or even national welfare, much less the recovery of arcadian social forms. The main focus was growth, measured by universal criteria: 'nation-building' often became no more than a code word for economic growth. Nationalist and liberation movements, and the new administrations they formed, absorbed the economic ideas of the time, and came to power with ideas of rapid development, centred on social welfare, programmes of education and guided development. They tended to tax the original agricultural (and usually expatriate) producers heavily to earn revenues, and claimed equal shares of some international product.

The nation as a collective person

Other novel additions to the twentieth-century nationalist corpus derived from inter-war fascist doctrines of collective personality. Fascism avoided or denied rights-based notions of individuality, and constructed the individual as but one element in a collective, who owed both identity and duty to the state. It also introduced the idea that a war-right belonged to the nation, and that war was the ultimate test of the national virtues. Nazism developed the idea of special cadres, the Brown shirts and the Black shirts, whose members typified the nation's special qualities, and it vaunted ideal-typic individuals in propaganda as special instances of the national type. Both types of fascism also developed the idea that original and genuine peoples were those who had repelled various forms of Westernisation. The idealised German of Nazi propaganda was a pre-

Christian Teuton, the warrior of a tribal people linked by kin, blood sacrifice and ancient custom. The idealised Italian was a citizen of ancient Rome, a city which had civilised a vast empire through its Senate and its Legions.

The relation of fascism to nationalism perplexed and divided analysts of the inter-war period. To those who emphasised the cultural element, generally students of literature and discourse, fascism seemed to be a genuine, albeit 'distorted', form of earlier nationalist ideologies. Linguists generally argued a continuity between aspects of European nineteenth-century nationalism; for example, notions of recovery, self-autonomy and collective identity, and fascist notions of the value of discipline to the whole, the cleansing aspects of struggle and the subordination of the individual to the collective. Others argued, however, that fascism was an entirely novel social development which had merely grafted nationalism on, employing it in an instrumental manner. In the latter approach, what was emphasised was the political form, a form of direct plebiscitary democracy led by a charismatic leader who unified the state and its ancillary bodies in his own person, and which treated rights as a status bestowed by the state. In this latter argument, nationalism was generally presented as merely a conveniently available body of ideas to further justify the idea of the organic state.[14]

The new nationalism and liberalism

The new features of twentieth-century nationalisms confused Western liberals, and evoked conflicting responses. The 'new' liberals had generally supported independence movements based on national claims. The New Europe movement, formed in Britain during the First World War, saw the liberation of the subject peoples of Middle Europe and the Balkans from their various overlords as a positive move and the first step towards the construction of a more stable, and liberal, international order, against the more conservative views of the British Foreign Office.[15] When, however, the new nations turned to war glorification, suspensions of rights and harsh treatment or suppression of national minorities, liberals were stumped. Such claims could be made conformable to progressivist views only with difficulty. Some liberals tried to justify the 'aberrant' or non-liberal features of twentieth-century nationalism as the frustration effects of continuously disappointed national aspirations, which would be moderated when the grouping in question achieved a genuine democratic form. Others cautioned minorities to be less vociferous, less strident and less exclusivist in their claims.

The association between fascism, nationalism and economic closure was particularly disturbing. The liberal, as well as socialist, anti-fascist movements which formed during the 1930s came to distrust all nationalisms which justified the absolute subordination of the rights of individuals to the rights of collective peoples; and they refused to endorse war claims based on 'national' recovery. Liberal economists came to deplore nationalisms which supported doctrines of economic autarky as well as doctrines of national economic growth not supported by neo-classical economic rationality.[16]

There was also a more immediate practical problem. The ethnic nationalisms that clamoured for attention at the end of the First World War (and later) tended to co-occupy territories in middle Europe and elsewhere: liberal doctrine had no way of dealing with the often bewildering complexity of territorial claims, where distinct national groupings occupied the same territory. Whose claims took precedence became a vexing question, since national self-determination usually demanded a territory to express itself.

One early doctrine, to orient liberals towards the bewildering variety of nationalisms which developed during the 1930s, was the distinction between 'good' and 'bad' nationalisms. Good nationalisms were those that, raised to the level of independence and sovereign statehood, would be liberal and outward-looking, and promote equal citizenship and equal rights for all living within their territories. Bad nationalisms were those that, raised to state power, would use that power to invade their neighbours or repress the minorities that lived within them.[17] The determination of the validity of Germany's interference in the Czech Sudetenland during the late 1930s, based on shared culturality, was heavily influenced by this distinction. The behaviour of the Czech government to its German minorities became an important question in the corridors of the League of Nations and other liberal milieus, on the apparent grounds that if the Czechs were oppressing the German minority, this would establish Czech nationalism as a form of bad nationalism, not worthy of the protection of the international community.

This distinction did little to sort out claims during the inter-war period, but it survived into the post-war period, albeit in somewhat more sophisticated forms. The popular post-war distinction was between 'civic' and 'ethnic' nationalism. Civic nationalisms were so identified when they promised equal rights for all peoples and were integrationist in policy, while ethnic nationalisms were so classed when they displayed intolerance for the dignity of the ethnie within them. It continued, moreover, to influence liberal opinion. During the post-war period, and in particular during the century's last decade, when the end of the Cold War released a flood of ethnic claims and inter-ethnic conflicts, it was generally the weaker party which won the support of Western liberals, on the grounds that it was the one being oppressed.

International nationalism and human rights

At the international level, national self-determination did not develop into a doctrine of ethnic self-determination. It came to mean political and territorial self-determination: the right of a people living within an internationally defined territory to change its government without let or hindrance. The problem then became ethnic minorities. Seton-Watson describes the result in Europe after the First World War, where national reconstruction on a loose territorial basis of majorities led to numerous ethnic minorities, and to conflict between them and the 'hegemonic' national grouping.[18]

A brief-lived attempt to address this problem, which gave some status to ethnie, were the anti-discrimination provisions of the League Covenant. There was a Minorities Section in the League Secretariat, and the Council established the 'Committees of Three', to hear complaints on the treatment of minorities, which the Council was to resolve. Both received representation directly from minority groups, giving minorities a brief-lived international status.[19]

But even these minimal rights were done away with after the Second World War. The 1949 Universal Declaration of Human Rights, which in effect superseded the League provisions, gave no rights to ethnie: the Declaration stressed individual rights. Only towards the end of the twentieth century was an ethnie given international recognition, and then only very tentatively. The Palestine Liberation Organisation, which was not a political authority with any status in international law and which had no clearly defined territorial base (but which did claim to represent a genuine people), was given observer status at the United Nations.

Territorial claims in international law remained for this reason largely traditional in nature, even in the age of nationalism, and were based on sovereign rights, historic boundaries and legal facts.[20] There developed no right of cession in international law on ethnic or indeed on any other grounds. When cession occurred, it was because the ceding state or territory was strong enough to maintain itself and the defeated state forced to concede; and the international legal construct under which such cessions occurred was generally in the form of an international agreement to deed. The losing state was deemed to have 'consented' to the change of sovereignty.

Nonetheless, the political claim to be a legitimate putative sovereign authority was most frequently based, for much of the twentieth century, on some demonstrable cultural connection between a specific group and the party claiming the sovereign right. It was on the basis of a cultural claim that Germany annexed the Sudetenland and accomplished the Anschluss with Austria in the years immediately preceding the Second World War. Both were, in the event, restored to their original sovereign statuses after the close of hostilities, a restoration which underpinned the territorial (and denied the ethnic) basis of international claims. But the political effects of such cultural claims continued to be felt. After the Second World War, the re-established Czech government expelled three million ethnic Germans, to ensure that no such claim could ever be mounted again.

The continuing political relevance of some national claim to territory was perhaps most revealing in what it excluded. When, towards the end of the century, Britain was forced to cede Hong Kong back to China (its lease on the territory having run out), tentative attempts to establish a separate Hong Kong Chinese state, in the face of the agreed legal rights of China to the territory, failed to even get off the ground, largely because no separate cultural basis could be found to sufficiently distinguish the Hong Kong Chinese from their co-culturalists in China. By contrast, when Lithuania, Estonia and Latvia, each recognised territories who had enjoyed sovereign statehood between 1919 and 1939 and each with clearly identified culture groups, claimed sovereignty from the dissolving Soviet Union during the last decade of the century, they found no want of support, despite the existence of large Russian minorities within each of the territories.

States were conceded to have the right to make claims on behalf of their 'nationals' living in other countries who were threatened with harm. In the event, however, 'national' meant 'citizen' and, at the time the claim was being made, not shared ethnicity. Indeed, the process of new state-making both in Europe after the First World War and in Africa after the Second World War, which generally produced mixed ethnic states, dissuaded governments from making ethnicity the grounds for claims. The significant exception was perhaps the new state of Israel, whose authorities claimed a right in gaining reparations even for Jews living outside of Israel after the Second World War, and irrespective of Israeli citizenship.

The new nationalism and the new internationalism

The rise of ethnic nationalism presented many challenges to received internationalism. It challenged the emerging idea of an international law of consensus based on prevalent practice, insisting on strict consent. It challenged the sanctity of treaties which had been worked before the original ethnie had arisen to consciousness or political influence, and demanded that 'unfair' treaties be abrogated. It rejected the idea of external recognition and insisted on the 'internal theory', whereby a *de facto* government had a right to be recognised. It challenged the prevailing ascendancy of Lockean 'entitlement' theory, and demanded that property rights, especially of outsiders, give way to the rights of the nation. It also put rights of self-determination before concerns of international stability, and it let others bear the consequences of instability.

Liberals, for their part, had to determine on what terms the new nationalisms would be acceptable. On the less sympathetic side was Ada Bozeman, facing the release of many new nations in the context of decolonisation. She would argue that contemporary diplomatic practice was based on a common Western experience of rights and common Western values. She feared that the new cultural diversity displayed in the new nationalisms would disrupt the normative basis on which that order rested, and argued for limits to cultural pluralism.[21] In a similar vein, though on different grounds, Robert Jackson pointed to the phenomenon of 'quasi-states', artificial entities created on a fictional national basis which were maintained from outside, and regretted the granting of self-determination where the true requisites of internal statehood were lacking.[22] Other approaches were not so sweeping. The new liberal distinction between good nationalisms and bad nationalisms was intended to provide for a somewhat different way forward, in the idea of a set of discriminators which would endorse a limited cultural pluralism. Another set of terms was located in the idea of internationally guaranteed human rights. For some liberals, the new international rights agenda was of importance primarily because it set the limits of nationalism.[23] But liberals also had to concede some economic and social rights to new states and would grant, accordingly, some new collective rights, to language usage and to limited autonomy for minorities.[24]

Economic rights and entitlements were particularly perplexing. Concepts had to be found that would entitle new states to some *juste retour* without encouraging a new round of protectionism, granting economic and social rights within the context of the United Nations but leaving them unspecified, providing negotiating ground without conceding closure. Another was the development agenda, and a new international law of welfare which promised a rapid transformation so long as some economic rationality was conceded. Multilateralism was yet another new management technique. It implied a form of confederative decision-making, in which a negotiating agenda was agreed and rounds of negotiations pursued until a consensus was reached. The result was often the lowest common denominator, but some common norms were thereby articulated. These, in turn, provided negotiating ground for ensuing rounds.[25]

Nationalism was not all bad news from the viewpoint of unleashing an unmanageable cultural diversity. On the contrary, in the domestic arena, nationalism usually demanded that many archaic forms of social organisation be wiped away. This in fact had the effect of creating higher degrees of social uniformity.[26] If it levelled within, it also created a set of remarkably similar communities from without. New governments paralleled one another much more closely than had been the case for local administrations in the nineteenth century. They articulated similar demands and displayed common forms of organisation, and their citizens paralleled one another much more closely in aspirations and ideas of the good life. Moreover, nationalism carried many Western ideas of political organisation and political norms into non-Western areas, hence its association with modernisation and the idea of 'transition'.[27]

For their part, the new nationalists had to accommodate to an international order made up of other nation-states. They had to find some basis in reciprocity with other culture-based communities, and some common basis for claims on which to base new rights. Since, moreover, at least some of the new nationalisms were rather fictitious, and many more raised the prospect of cohabitation with ethnic minorities, they had to guard what were often incomplete nationalisms from minority claims from within and to stabilise their new, often weak states from without. It was notable that international law would give scant regard to ethnie; it remained territorially and sovereignty based. Nationalism also implied that small and poor states would have to find the requisites for security or economic well-being from within their own territories. In the days of empire, the empire had been valued because it seemed a way to contain a diversity of peoples at different levels within a single order. The new sovereignty implied that a new nation would have to manage on its own.

Most of the new nationalisers would prove remarkably agile in avoiding the less welcome implications of the new nationalism. They would discover new responsibilities for ex-colonisers, to redress past 'crimes'. They would articulate a new version of the 'haves and the have-nots' argument. They would, indeed, become the staunchest defenders of an international law which protected their rights to non-interference.

Notes

1 H. Kohn, *The Idea of Nationalism* (New York: Macmillan, 1944, 1967).
2 'Africanism: The Freetown Contribution', *Journal of Modern African Studies*, 5 (1967), pp. 521–39.
3 H. Seton-Watson, *Nations and States* (London: Methuen, 1977).
4 The Fourteen Points were more ambiguous on the national question than some representations allow. The most significant was Point V, which demanded that in determining 'questions of sovereignty, the interests of the populations concerned must have equal weight with the equitable claims of the government whose title is to be determined'. Point IX demanded that the frontiers of Italy should be drawn 'along clearly recognisable lines of nationality'; Point XI demanded that 'the relations of the several Balkan states to one another [be] determined by friendly counsel along historically established lines of allegiance and nationality'; Point XII demanded that 'nationalities which are now under Turkish rule should be assured an undoubted security of life and an absolutely unmolested opportunity of autonomous development', and Point XIII demanded an independent Polish state 'inhabited by indisputably Polish populations'. Autonomy, not sovereignty, was the significant usage, and the Points made no reference to the European overseas empires; *Foreign Relations of the United States: 1918*, Supplement 1 (Washington DC: United States Department of State, 1933), pp. 12–17.
5 Hugh Tinker, 'The Nation State in Asia' in L. Tivey (ed.), *The Nation-State* (Oxford: Martin Robertson, 1981) p. 111.
6 George Antonius' *The Arab Awakening*, first published in 1939, well expresses the early 'liberal' phase of Arab nationalism (New York: G.P. Putnam, 1969).
7 R. Dekmejian, *Islam in Revolution* (Syracuse: Syracuse University Press, 1995).
8 P. Worsley, *The Third World* (London: Weidenfeld and Nicolson, 1964) seems to have invented the concept of a 'pan-nationalism'.
9 A. Hughes, 'Nationalism in Colonial Africa' in L. Tivey (ed.), *The Nation-State* (Oxford: Martin Robertson, 1981).
10 An Imperial Federal League was founded in Britain in 1884; in 1984, the British historian (and federalist) Michael Burgess marked its 'forgotten centenary' in the *Round Table* annual of that year.
11 Renzo De Felice, *Mussolini il Duce, Part 2: Lo Stato Totalitaro 1936–1940* (Turin: Giulio Einaudi, 1974).
12 H.G. Johnson (ed.), *Economic Nationalism in Old and New States* (Chicago: Chicago University Press, 1967).
13 *Economic Analysis and Policy in Underdeveloped Countries* (Durham NC: Duke University Press, 1957).
14 E.g. A. Smith, *Theories of Nationalism* (London: Duckworth, 1971) pp. 58–60.
15 An influential argument in this vein was R.W. Seton-Watson's *The War and Democracy* (Cambridge: Cambridge University Press, 1915); Seton-Watson was a prominent member of the New Europe movement.
16 See especially J. Mayall, *Nationalism and International Society* (Cambridge: Cambridge University Press, 1990).
17 The genesis of such approaches may be found in Arnold Toynbee's *Nationality and the War* (London: Dent, 1916).
18 H. Seton-Watson, *Eastern Europe Between the Wars* (Cambridge: Cambridge University Press, 1945).

19 F.P. Walters, *A History of the League of Nations* (London: Oxford University Press, 1969), pp. 402–11.
20 See R.Y. Jennings, *The Acquisition of Territory in International Law* (Manchester: Manchester University Press, 1962).
21 A. Bozeman, *Politics and Culture in International History* (Princeton: Princeton University Press, 1960).
22 *Quasi-states: Sovereignty, International Relations and the Third World* (Cambridge: Cambridge University Press, 1990).
23 See especially D. Luban, 'Just War and Human Rights' and his quarrel with Michael Walzer in C. Beitz, M. Cohen, T. Scanlon and A.J. Simmons, *International Ethics* (Princeton: Princeton University Press, 1985).
24 See e.g. the International Covenant on Economic, Social and Cultural Rights, opened for signature in 1966.
25 J. Mayall, *Nationalism and International Society* (Cambridge: Cambridge University Press, 1990).
26 E. Gellner, *Thought and Change* (London: Weidenfeld and Nicolson, 1964) argued this was nationalism's main purpose.
27 See A. Smith, *Theories of Nationalism* (London: Duckworth, 1971) for a sympathetically critical account of such theories.

6 War

If nationalism was the predominant organising concept of the age, war was the forcing medium of the nation. Many of the twentieth century's new nations were born through war. War also speeded up industrialisation and was the crucible for many of the age's new industrial techniques. But the war experiences of the twentieth century also revealed the fissures within nations, the limits of national economies and the limits of national self-sufficiency. War was the twentieth century's most important teacher, and the century's two great wars called forth many political and social innovations. But they also demonstrated that social capacity was finite, that social cohesion was conditional, and that economic and political technique had in-built structural demands which could not be altered at will. Not the least of these would reflect on the use of war.

War and the academy

Traditionally, the study of war had been confined to general staffs and military academies where it centred on the analysis of past wars and the ways they had been fought. Nineteenth-century students of war concentrated above all on battlefield tactics. This was not exclusively so. In 1834, Karl von Clausewitz, a Prussian bureaucrat and staff officer, had drawn an analysis of war based on the Napoleonic Wars which related war to social resource, political will and popular morale, and which became a classic in the genre. There was also the Polish Jewish banker, I.S. Bloch, writing at the end of the nineteenth century, who drew attention to the ways industrial progress must alter war's shape.[1] But these were notable exceptions. In general, the study of war in the nineteenth century was the study of battles in isolation from their social origins or consequences, and it was what generals and staff officers did.

In the twentieth century this changed. War moved into universities and civilian institutes where it became a subject-matter for sociologists, social historians, political scientists and economists. These related war to changing social, political and economic forms, and drew the implications of battlefield technique for domestic political processes and for the peacetime economic and social life of nations. There also developed a core of civilian strategists who served on national defence councils and whose job was to devise new strategic concepts for use in the battlefield which were consistent with social, political and economic organisation.

The twentieth century's first great civilian study of war was Quincy Wright's, published in 1942.[2] Wright did not aim to develop a theory of war. He confined himself to drawing numerous social and economic indices, with the intention of identifying significant correlations. *A Study of War* was intended to prepare the groundwork for theory-building. But it identified one of the most oft-repeated correlations with regard to war in the twentieth century: the relationship between its incidence and its ferocity. According to Wright's calculations, warfare seemed to display a pattern by which, as society developed, the absolute numbers of wars fell and the phenomenon became less frequent; but it also became more intensive in scale.

The study also, although inadvertently, exposed one of the initial difficulties in the social science of war: the identification of the subject. Wright had employed an intuitive definition of war which contained certain presuppositions. His model of war was the First World War, through which the international system had just passed and the Second just entered upon. For Wright, war was an activity deriving from Great Power diplomacy, which tended to generalise. In 1975, a Hungarian scholar, Istevan Kende, chose different definitional criteria to identify and enumerate wars since 1945, identifying war by its internal nature.[3] His conclusions as to the number and nature of wars contradicted Wright's 'lessening phenomenon' thesis at several points. He noted the great number of wars since 1945; war did not appear to be lessening at all. He also demonstrated that wars involving the Great Powers were, on balance, less intensive and less destructive than wars involving less developed states.

But perhaps the most striking trend identification of the age was that claimed by Michael Doyle, a Harvard academic. In 1983, Doyle carried out a study which related war's incidence to the form or type of state engaging in it; and he counted the number of wars in which liberal-democratic states had been engaged, noting their antagonists. On this basis, he isolated a trend correlation of particular relevance to the twentieth century: that while liberal states had fought wars, they had not fought wars with one another. The claim that liberal states did not fight wars with one another implied a relationship between state form and proclivity to war, and initiated one of the great debates of late twentieth-century international scholarship.[4] It also began to influence policy: within a decade of its enunciation, statesmen from liberal states were claiming that democratisation was integral to the prevention of war and defending democratisation efforts on those grounds.

The pattern of warfare

Of the pattern of warfare in the twentieth century, war historians were much struck by rising costs and casualty rates. It is not certain, however, that modern war absorbed a greater proportion of what was a vastly expanded economic product (although it may have become more deadly).[5] What is more certain is that the twentieth century saw a more consistent and conscious mobilisation of society for war effort than previous ages. In both the century's great conflicts, government was turned over entirely to war, large sections of economic plant were directed to war production, labour forces were expanded and directed, and conscription became the norm. It was, indeed, precisely these features which made them great wars. In Italy during the Second World War, 64 per cent of the labour force directly served the war effort. Some small societies, such as Switzerland and, later, Israel, were able to achieve an almost total conversion of the citizenry into a fighting force.

There was also a tendency for war to spread geographically, and to call up social and political change over its widened terrain. During the twentieth century, the absolute numbers of states engaged in war tended to be high, and war tended to absorb more states the longer it lasted. At the same time, it enhanced and sharpened political and social fissures, bringing political orders into crisis. When the Paris Commune rose in 1870 to demand the resignation of the government in reaction to France's coming defeat in the Franco-Prussian War, a new stage in the political life of governments had begun. The experience of the Commune came to be considered paradigmatic of the fate which awaited other governments which lost wars.

The two together produced that flux, characteristic of the age, between international and civil wars. The two types of war often proceeded together or followed one another in rapid succession; and each opened the way for the other. Thus, the First World War occasioned revolution in Russia, in Germany and in the Austrian and Ottoman Empires, while the Second World War induced (or encouraged) bitter civil wars in Yugoslavia, Greece and China, wars which proceeded behind the main battlefronts. Each also left a legacy of colonial upheavals: following the Second World War, Malays, Vietnamese and Algerians turned their war potential, developed to fight against Japanese and Germans, against their colonial masters. Civil wars, in turn, induced international wars. Istevan Kende's study of wars since 1945 revealed a prevalence of civil, religious and internal wars in the Third World during the post-war period, but also the tendency of the Great Powers to become involved in them, converting them into international conflicts.

Total war

These different aspects came to be understood by the new concept of 'total war'. Coined by Mussolini in the 1930s, the expression was originally used as a threat and as an instrument of propaganda: it was intended to advise Italy's diplomatic partners, as well as to warn its potential antagonists, that the entire force of the Italian nation would be hurled into any coming military campaign, and that the fascist government would spare no resources in prosecuting its aims. In the course of time, however, it evolved into a descriptive and analytical concept, used to typify and analyse war's effects.

In its descriptive aspect, it came to denote a specific type of war: a total war was a war to which the entire social resource of a country was devoted, and whose close demanded unconditional surrender of the defeated side. In this form, a total war was contrasted with 'limited war', wars which were fought with forces in being and which were limited to specific material or political objectives. Thus, the First World War came to be described as the first total war, while Iraq's invasion of Iran in the 1980s was intended as a limited war, aimed at little more than settling the contested access to the Gulf of Aqaba and seizing some oil fields while Iran was in a temporary state of revolutionary upheaval.

Analytically, however, it identified a tendency which appeared to be a property of war itself, and a feature of all wars. This was a tendency to expand as hostilities proceeded, irrespective of the intentions of the belligerents. (A parallel tendency had been detected by Clausewitz in his 1834 treatise; the resultant phenomenon he had called 'Absolute War'.) In this form, the concept of total war was used to analyse the degree to which any war had absorbed the social, political and economic product of the belligerents.[6] Another term for this tendency became 'escalation', applied initially to nuclear warfare and to a reputed tendency for any initiations of hostilities among nuclear belligerents to rise to the level of massive nuclear exchanges. (The tendency to escalation was deemed to include geographical as well as social and material spread.)

From the analytical perspective, it identified a trend by which all the twentieth-century wars tended to expand, even the limited ones.

In its analytical form, it also gave rise to the idea of 'total strategy' or the 'unified war'. Increasingly during the twentieth century, the successful prosecution of any war was deemed to require an overall view of the total resources of the enemy, and twentieth-century strategic planning was generally directed towards the integrated campaign against all the enemy's resources. The theory of unified war imagined the interchangeability of political and military weapons, as well as rapidly shifting targets. The military historian J.F.C. Fuller identified Soviet revolutionary warfare as the first concrete expression of this idea.[7]

Finally, the term came to imply a relationship between war and social change. In a series of popular works, the British social and war historian Arthur Marwick set up a four-tiered system to register the effects of war on society, and it became a prevalent perspective of social and historical analysis.[8] From the social perspective, some of war's totalising effects were deemed to be positive. For example, the British social theorist R. Titmuss remarked on a tendency for total war societies to produce greater social equality.[9] In this sense, it became a contested concept, as some historians, while not underrating the effects of modern warfare on society, sought to test the concept more rigorously. Some of these studies demonstrated the ways in which society resisted war's effects or merely speeded up changes already in the course of occurring, and which may have occurred independently of it.[10]

War's internal features

Of war itself, the most significant feature of twentieth-century warfare was the application of industrial technique to the battlefield, with consequences for both speed and fire power, and ultimately for the ways in which wars were fought. During the First World War, the development of the railway allowed men to be delivered to battlefronts with greater rapidity, while the new machine gun provided them with more fire-power. To the offensive side, this produced the capability of the rapid massed deployment and greatly increased kill ratios. For the defensive side, it meant that gaps in defensive lines could be filled in with greater rapidity. The two together produced modern trench warfare, as troops dug in to preserve themselves and to establish secure defensive lines.

The application of motorisation to warfare produced the tank and the tank charge, while modern developments in communications allowed tanks to operate in dispersed formations, circling entrenched positions and taking advantage of mobility against a static enemy. The application of flight to motorisation made the aeroplane the support of infantry and tank. Aircraft spied out and destroyed fixed battlefield emplacements, and allowed for industrial plant, transport and communications behind enemy lines to be targeted and destroyed. And these were only the earliest examples.[11]

Industrial technique also meant the quantitatively greater production and replacement of weaponry of all kinds, as well as continuous qualitative improvements in weaponry, often during the very course of war itself. Prime examples are radio and telephonics, developed to operate alongside Morse code during the First World War, and radar, which replaced fixed ground sights to spy out and anticipate attack from the air during the early months of the Second World War. Michael Howard would identify continuous innovation as the central feature of weapons development, in peacetime as well as in war.[12]

The second significant feature of twentieth-century warfare was its lengthening time span, and the consequences of extended duration. Twentieth-century wars tended to last longer than their immediate historical counterparts, with multiple consequences. At the political level, the lengthening time span created the necessity to fix political will and purpose over an extended period. For the liberal democracies, this meant that the diverse groupings of pluralistic societies would have to be welded together for long periods, to fix them to the war effort, raising questions about their liberalism. On the other hand, preserving democracy would require limits in the type of force used and would force liberal governments to adjust their war aims. At the tactical level, extended duration meant that supply and resupply, of men and material, became crucial to all future wars, as well as logistics, the ability to deliver supply. Supply and logistics were essential to secure the advantages of the breakthrough, itself central to the accomplishment of victory in fixed position warfare, advantages which would be lost if sufficient men and material were not available behind the lines. But at the strategic level, extended duration also meant that even a significant battlefield defeat did not imply the loss of a war, providing the defensive side could regroup.

Extended duration also brought into play civilian morale, and gave greater play to the sharpened potential social and political fissures induced by the stresses of war. This would have consequences for both offensive and defending powers. The German victory on the Eastern Front during the First World War was not occasioned by a battlefield victory but by revolution in Russia. As the Vietnam War proceeded, the United States would face a growing civil revolt, which was exploited by the North Vietnamese government.

Time, moreover, created the potential for the mobilisation of alliances and for the incorporation of new belligerents into contests where they might affect outcomes. During the Second World War, the Battle of Britain was of the utmost strategic significance, not only or even primarily because it demonstrated the inadequacy of Germany's control of the skies, but because it extended the duration of the war, providing time for the mobilisation of the United States on the side of the near-defeated Britain, changing the balance of power which the German war machine would have to confront. Extended duration also meant that states could play for time, joining wars near their end to gain status and participate in the fruits of victory. States wished for short wars to avoid this as much as anything.

The third distinctive feature of twentieth-century warfare was the crucial role played by technological innovation in the achieving of advantage, particularly for the side operating from a position of weakness. During the First World War, the Germans brought in gas warfare and the U-boat campaigns at critical moments when they seemed to be losing advantage, while the Allies pressed forward tank developments and increased the fire-power of air gunnery. During the Second World War, weapons innovation continued throughout and hurried towards its end, as the Germans developed rocketry and the Allied powers the atomic bomb.

Technological breakthroughs were achieved by concentrating resources and throwing them at an innovative weapons project. It became a recognised peacetime technique, and was practised by the Soviet Union during the Cold War to equalise its disadvantages vis-à-vis the Western powers, as an integral part of the policy of 'peaceful co-existence'.

Above all, modern warfare demonstrated the strength of the defensive in battle, and the difficulty of bringing war to a determinate conclusion. Technical and organisational innovation always ended by strengthening the defensive side, whatever advantage to the offensive it first seemed to promise. Thus, the application of the railway and the bullet seemed initially to strengthen the offensive, but it also proved easier in practice to fill gaps in defensive lines, and to immobilise the attacker. The tank was developed to neutralise the bullet and to counter the power of spade and trench emplacements, while gas warfare and air power were developed to break the defensive line. Equally, however, dispersal, radar and inadequate fire-power threatened offensive air power, while the development of anti-tank weaponry threatened to blunt the tank offensive and forced tanks to disperse, shattering the psychological effects of the massed tank attack.

Initially, the invention of the atomic bomb seemed to change this 'historical law'. At first, the development in fire-power it promised, together with the advance in delivery systems, seemed to give an unassailable advantage to the side that struck first: that is, to the offensive. (It was this factor which explains the universal urge, other things being equal, for Great Powers to develop nuclear capabilities.) But, over time, even nuclear developments would demonstrate the classic rule of the natural strength of the defensive, as a successful nuclear offensive came to depend on the ability to wipe out the retaliatory capacity of the opponent, while the defensive side's ability to disperse and to conceal nuclear weaponry made it increasingly difficult to neutralise his ability to retaliate, particularly after the development of the nuclear submarine.[13]

The lessons of the First World War

Although past wars had displayed some of these features, it was the First World War which brought them together. The initial campaigns were marked by the failure of any side to achieve military supremacy. Within six weeks, the digging-in had begun. Politicians tried to escape immobilism by opening alternative fronts, into which, however, their forces immediately sank, widening fronts without achieving any military advantage. Commanders lost the advantage of hard-won breakthroughs when they could not bring up sufficient troops and material to carry the battle forward; and they constantly underestimated the amount of material they would require. Each of the belligerent powers had to turn during its course to the further rallying of public support, in part by claiming greater and greater objectives for the war, escalating their war aims and making defeat more difficult to accept.

It was because of these features that the First World War was called the 'Great War'. They gave that war its characteristic shape and its defining horrors. Moreover, they established its status as the model for the future requirements, and dangers, of all wars. Avoiding the impasse of the First World War became one of the guiding political as well as military principles of the age. For any war to be likened to the First World War became a term of abuse.

Avoiding deadlock became the central problem for the conduct of war in the twentieth century, and set its strategic agenda. Twentieth-century strategic thought revolved around the problem of how to regain mobility and how to break the enemy's defensive lines. Its numerous innovations were all devised to avoid entrenchment; each new strategic doctrine was framed in terms of its superiority in regaining mobility; and the great strategy debates which characterised the twentieth century concerned the adequacy of one solution or another to the problems of entrenchment (not least because different individual services were favoured, gaining in terms of status and budgetary allocation, in each of the various doctrines). The various doctrines also came to impinge on the ways wars were fought, and themselves began to define the features of the century's subsequent wars.

Blitzkreig

The first innovative doctrine was blitzkrieg (lightning war), conceived by Fuller when he was a staff officer in 1918 and theorised in its modern form following the Second World War.[14] The central principle was a concentration of forces in both time and space. The technique turned on the deployment of tanks in massed positions. The operational principle was to race to the rear of the enemy's lines. The central objective was the opponent's command posts, the brains of the armed enemy. Fuller proposed that without a brain, the enemy could not fight. Other theorists of blitzkrieg argued that the massed tank charge would also induce a psychological fright, causing the enemy's infantry to scatter.

Originally, the doctrine implied a concentrated strike against the enemy's strongest defensive point and, accordingly, the fixed battle 'breakthrough'. But, over time, it assumed other operational forms. During the 1920s and 1930s, it evolved into the war of manoeuvre, which implied forward movement and rapid strikes around and behind enemy lines. After the Second World War, it came to include pre-emption (which meant striking the enemy before his forces were off the ground). All three doctrines involved the same fundamental principle, however. This was an early concentration of offensive force. Its influence would be demonstrated in subsequent war practice, whereby huge amounts of men and material would be gathered for even limited campaigns.

The successful German campaigns against Poland and France during 1939 and 1940 initially seemed to support the soundness of blitzkrieg doctrine. Germany's early victories were easily gained, and on the basis of the massed tank attack.

After Germany's experiences on the Eastern Front, however, opinion wavered. In that campaign, the Soviet soldier did not scatter, not even in the face of Germany's tank offensives. He held his position in the face of tremendous punishment, operating a series of controlled retreats and forcing the German tanks down long corridors of fire-power. In the light of this experience, strategists began to reconsider the earlier successes, noting that, in the case of Poland, German tanks had faced a much inferior force, while in France there had been a collapse of political, as well as military, morale. After the Second World War, Fuller would continue to defend the doctrine, and would warn against generalising the Soviet soldier's fortitude, arguing that it involved a risky reliance on the will of the people. But strategic doctrine could never thereafter forget that the Soviet solder had stood his ground.

Attrition

Where forces were more even, and where sufficient of the enemy's forces could not be taken out in a single blow, the alternative favoured strategic doctrine became known as 'attrition', a practice which also became a common characteristic of modern warfare. Attrition involved weakening the enemy steadily over time while avoiding any large direct confrontation of troops until the enemy were so weakened. In the context of total strategy, it meant denying supplies, detaching allies, destroying plant and weakening morale. On the battlefield, it meant above all the use of artillery, which became the *sine qua non* of modern warfare. During the Second World War, 60 per cent of British casualties were caused by shell fire. The doctrine produced the expression, 'artillery conquers, infantry occupies'.

There were different techniques of attrition, most of which were developed from the various attempts to break the deadlock of the First World War. Initially, there was the massive bombardment, to destroy enemy positions and kill large numbers of enemy troops. The original promise was that advancing troops would only have to take empty trenches. One difficulty encountered in practice was insufficient fire-power. Fuller would point to another: that artillery broke the surface of the battleground and created obstacles to forward movement. This was important, since carrying the battle forward meant carrying forward vehicles, supplies and troops, and roads could only be constructed with difficulty across terrain so destroyed. A second technique was the creeping barrage. This was a curtain of shrapnel shells moving ahead of the advancing infantry. Barrages could be used either to break the enemy's positions or to neutralise him by breaking his morale, pinning him to his position and then overcoming him with an overwhelming assault. The First World War developed both methods, and refined them.[15]

Both techniques demanded enormous amounts of fire-power. The number of shells produced during the First World War alone were reckoned to have surpassed the fire-power of all previous wars.

Air power and modern warfare

By 1918, air power had already come to be considered essential to attrition technique, since aircraft became the eyes of gunnery. Hence, control of the air was deemed essential as early as the closing stages of the First World War. During the next decade, however, it would be proposed as an alternative to attrition, and a method of avoiding its burdens.

The strategic offensive based on air power was first theorised by the Italian strategist, Douhet, in a work entitled *The Command of the Air*, published in 1921. Predicting that all future wars would take on 'a static character very similar to that of the [First] World War', Douhet argued that continuous fronts would be the common pattern of future wars. Further, he maintained that air power, 'because of independence of surface limitations', as well as superior speed, was the offensive weapon *par excellence*. It could ignore fixed defensive lines, operate independently of armies and fleets, and come to grips with the enemy at once.

Douhet's doctrine involved several operating principles. First, there was gaining command of the air, which came to be seen as the absolute requirement of all modern warfare. Once this was gained, the air force would move on to the physical obliteration of the enemy. This involved targeting not only enemy forces but 'industrial and commercial establishment; important building ... transportation arteries and areas of civilian population'. Douhet envisaged not only carrying on the war from above, in which whole battles would be fought out in the air, but also carrying the war behind the lines, to cities and civilians as well as war-industrial plant, and subjecting them to direct attack. By such operating principles, he maintained, air power, and only air power, could achieve victory.

In practice, however, air power would suffer from technological limitations. During the great air campaigns of the Second World War, it was discovered that strategic targeting was not accurate enough to achieve what Douhet had promised. Allied bombers had to bomb by day to achieve any degree of accuracy, encountering losses which no belligerent could sustain, and not even this proved sufficient to strategically cripple the enemy. Civilian bombing, with its less stringent requirements, was in fact a last resort, entered upon when the technical capacity for controlled strikes failed. Moreover, both suffered from the inability to deliver sufficient fire-power.[16] Initially, the nuclear bomb was developed precisely to address this difficulty. The development of nuclear fire-power made sense within the context of a conventional war theorised in terms of air power. Its promise was the ability to deliver a sufficient 'payload' with, in some cases, just a single bomber.

The nuclear deadlock

But it was nuclear weapons, developed to fight the Cold War, which would eventually offer the greatest challenge to strategic doctrine. If only one side had nuclear weapons, it could convincingly threaten a massive strike against any opponent not so armed, with a reasonable expectation of political effect. But once both sides in a conflict could deploy nuclear weapons (and the Soviet Union demonstrated possession in 1949), it was not at all clear how they could be used without at once inviting massive destruction, and upon the initiator. Moreover, what a nuclear war would look like – how it would be commanded and organised in the context of massive destruction – required leaps of the imagination which took strategic doctrine to the very limits of rational force use. Nuclear weaponry, in short, threatened to vitiate at once both offensive will and defensive advantage. It threatened, in simple terms, to make war impossible.

Successive attempts to overcome the threat of nuclear stalemate only ended by confirming it. An initial doctrine, theorised in the early 1950s, was suggestively called 'broken-back' warfare. Its underlying assumption was that headquarters would be bombed early on in campaigns and that troops would have to operate in dispersed conditions without central command. Not the least of its problems was that, in such conditions, it would be difficult to determine who was winning. Nor could any strategist offer a convincing picture of how such a war could be brought to a feasible political conclusion. A succeeding doctrine involved limiting nuclear usage to force-to-force combat, whereby potential antagonists would direct their use of nuclear weapons to one another's forces and contain them to that use alone. In this doctrine, each side would declare its intention to avoid striking the other's cities and populations. Its proponents argued that 'counter-force', as the doctrine came to be known, could be maintained by targeting cities and threatening them with counter-attack, if the enemy broke 'the rule'.[17] But it was unclear that the rule would hold if one side were losing. A third solution was the pre-emptive attack to take out the enemy's nuclear capability and to disarm him immediately upon the onset of hostilities. But this threatened to create a very unstable environment, as the side which struck first would gain the advantage, and this would create a positive incentive to early use, whatever the cause at issue. The American civilian strategist Bernard Brodie conducted a sustained campaign against all three doctrines, in the context of an argument which insisted that nuclear weapons could only be conceived in the context of a 'non-use' or deterrent strategy.[18]

In the end, the doctrine of deterrence came to prevail. This meant that nuclear weapons should only be 'used', that is deployed, to dissuade the enemy from embarking on any nuclear usage at all. But it did not solve the problem of how to contain a war between nuclear belligerents, or how to keep such a war from rising to a nuclear level, once entered upon. Intricate 'combination strategies' were developed involving both ground troops and air power; and conventional as well as nuclear threats would be required to make a threat against a nuclear opponent convincing.[19]

The inner front

A concomitant feature of these innovations was the development of the concept of the 'inner front'. This was the area that lay behind the front, which supplied it with men, material and political stability. Total strategy came to involve these elements of the enemy's strengths, and they too became the subjects of estimation and the objects of war. Moreover, technique was developed with special reference to the new front.

Attacking the inner front

The most familiar was the blockade, scarcely new as it had been ancillary to the Napoleonic campaigns. But it would have more devastating effects on countries which had ceased being agriculturally self-sufficient. Propaganda was a new weapon; the British government set up the first propaganda office during the First World War, where Arnold Toynbee, among other impeccable liberals, set himself to writing pamphlets with such titles as 'The Murderous Tyranny of the Turks'. These efforts were directed as much to securing the home front as to weakening the enemy's inner front. A second novel technique was the encouragement of sedition and revolution. Lenin's arrival in Moscow through German territory via the courtesy of the German general staff is the best known of these, but Wilson also refused to deal with the Imperial Government, encouraging the revolution of 1919 in Germany. Encouraging sedition became a recognised technique, and one which most belligerents considered at one time or another.

A direct consequence of inner front tactics was that civilians came to be the direct objects of war, whether as political subjects who could be encouraged to revolt, propaganda subjects who would greet the invader with relief, or direct objects of attack, damaging among other things the enemy's war production capacity. Civilian targeting grew as the capabilities of weaponry grew and it became 'strategically respectable' to take the war behind the lines. During the First World War, there were about 1,500 British civilian casualties as a direct result of air attack. But between 1939 and 1945, more than 50,000 civilians perished in air attacks in Britain. Nor was this the least. The city of Hamburg lost 50,000 people each week during July and August of 1943, and that many again were killed on a single night during the Allied attack on Dresden. The loss of civilian immunity became a regular feature of the wars of the age.

The increase in state controls

State controls of the nation's physical plant jumped dramatically during the First World War and again during the Second. During the First, all belligerents nationalised their railways and turned them to war usage. Britain and France also established state control of mines and ship-building. Moreover, when Lloyd George took the premiership in 1916, he established the war cabinet, replacing the war council, a move which in effect turned the entire government, and all the resources it directly controlled, over to the war effort. (Lloyd George also founded a new ministry of labour and food, to co-ordinate food production.) In 1917, the United States federal authorities directed food production as well as munitions supply, and also established manpower policies, while Canada established the Imperial Munitions Board. During the Second World War, Britain additionally established a new ministry of supply as well as a section for economic warfare; and it controlled all food production, all shipping and all aircraft production. In the United States, federal government employment expanded from 1 million in 1940 to 3.8 million in 1946.

Governments not only controlled plant, they also controlled people. In 1914, Imperial Germany revived the 1851 Prussian Law of Siege, enabling the state to assume wide powers of public surveillance, among others. The British government prevented workers from moving and prevented strikes in both world wars, and it assigned labour during the Second World War. In 1943, the United States passed the War Labor Disputes Act which enabled the government to conscript strikers.

The mobilisation of society was not and could not be total. There were technical difficulties, what Clausewitz had termed 'friction', as well as frequent interruptions to mobilisation programmes when governments changed priorities. Moreover, governments had to try to preserve some features of ordinary life in order to maintain morale and to remind people of what they were fighting for. Both meant that valuable cargo space had to be reserved for the import of 'civilian' items, such as cigarettes and beer. In addition, many wartime measures were only finally perfected in the last months of the great wars: in Britain, co-ordination and distribution of mobilised resources was not effected until late 1917.[20]

War and society

Partly for this reason, the social effects of total war were uneven. The most frequently remarked upon, as well as the most immediately felt, was the recruitment of female labour with consequences for the self-images and aspirations of women. Some social historians insist that female emancipation would have come anyway. But there is no doubt that it came faster, and that it changed female expectations more quickly and more thoroughly than would otherwise have been the case. There were concomitant consequences for the work force: it doubled in some places and grew by a third in others.[21] The practice of incorporating businessmen into government was, by contrast, a relatively short-lived phenomenon, as they returned to their civilian posts once wartime controls were ended. Patterns of food consumption were also differently registered; in Britain, forbidden items and shortage products became demanded goods following the war, when fat and protein consumption soared, while in the United States, little affected by rationing, diets changed little.

There were important stimulation effects. Heavy industries such as coal, ship production and iron and steel were more heavily exploited as a consequence of war. There was also the rapid development of lighter industries such as chemicals and electrical goods. The Second World War in the United States saw a boom in synthetic rubber manufacture and in the production of artificial fibres.

Less welcome were the inflation effects; indeed, some would trace the tendencies of the twentieth-century economy to inflate to the world wars. In Britain, wages tended to stay steady through both wars, in part due to stringent government controls which directed savings, but many other governments were forced to print money in order to finance war effort. After the First World War, France would eventually be forced to devalue the franc by a factor of five, wiping out a generation of French pre-war savers.

Less easy to judge were the psychological effects, particularly as they came to affect political culture. In general, liberal opinion was strengthened in its negative attitudes to war, and mass movements based on war opposition became a familiar feature of the politics of liberal states during the twentieth century. But liberals also came to see in both the century's total wars a model for the mobilisation of society to a purpose. The Second World War may also have created a confidence in planning which would not have been there otherwise. There were also the effects on labour, both in the mainstream labour movements and on radical opinion: trade union membership not only grew as a result of increased employment, but having seen society so changed the working man would not go back to the old idea that there was a natural economic balance between labour and capital, nor that government action could not affect that balance. On the other hand, historians speak of a pacifistic effect, relating interwar appeasement not merely to the battlefield experience of the Great War but to the fears of the massive air bombardments and the enormous civilian casualties which were widely predicted at the onset of the Second.

Bringing war to a successful conclusion

The ending of wars became uncertain and fraught with risk. Historians still contest as to whether it was exhaustion which ended the First World War, the final tank charges in its last days and the evidence they provided of technological innovation, or the collapse of the German inner front. (The various analyses had important political as well as strategic implications: each rated Allied participation, and its role in the achievement of victory, differently; this applied, in particular, to the contribution of the United States.) The British historian A.J.P. Taylor, in a series of public lectures during the 1970s, pointed out that the Second World War kept starting and ending in its different campaigns, as France, officially defeated in 1941, had resumed hostilities in the colonies by 1943, and Italy, on Germany's side in 1940, had become a battle zone between Germany and the Allied forces by 1943.

The unendingness of war went far beyond the formal ending of war. Britain was still fighting in Malaysia in 1952 to contain communist insurgents, encouraged by the collapse of British power in the face of the Japanese. There were also stalemates, as governments hesitated to declare they had been beaten. Some conflicts dragged on for years in a state of 'no war, no peace' as belligerents refused to treat. It was less politically costly to continue low-grade hostilities than to accept humiliating peace terms. Bringing an antagonist to the negotiating table came to be considered the highest diplomatic feat.

Through the century, there was a noted tendency for peacemaking to begin earlier and earlier in the campaigns. This was partly due to the demands of the inner front. Publics demanded clear statements of peace aims from the onset of hostilities, forcing governments to declare their terms for treating the enemy increasingly early, not only to satisfy public opinion but also to counter the propaganda of the other side. This led them into declaring their war aims more readily, and sooner, than would otherwise have been the case. Such aims had also to be agreed with allies and were potential bones of contention among them, requiring periods for negotiation and agreement, and well before the end of war was in sight. When President Roosevelt declared the 'Four Freedoms', promising an end to 'foreign domination', Britain was determined to exempt the British Empire from its scope. Organisational preparations for the peace also began much sooner, particularly in the context of unconditional surrender policies; allies had to declare what and how they would occupy and what policies they would follow. Thus, a good deal of Allied diplomacy concerned not only tactics and grand strategy, but also the determination of peace terms.[22]

War effects were also being registered long after wars had ceased and peace treaties had been signed. The British blockade tactics of the First World War reduced the livestock of Central Europe by 90 per cent for some animals. Norman Angell, in a widely read work of the 1930s, argued that the Great Depression was, in part, a war effect, though this has been disputed.[23] The Second World War left a legacy of cross-cutting debts and credits, and an absolute reduction in liquidity, as governments expended their resources and off-loaded foreign assets, which jammed exchanges and impeded the ability of states to pay for goods in the required forms of exchange, disturbing reconstruction policies long after war's end.

In some cases, it required years for normalisation to ensue. It took successive French governments nine years to stabilise the franc after the signing of the peace treaty, while the damage to social and economic plant in the battlefield zones of eastern France was not made good until 1927, ten years after the war had closed. The conversion of the British war economy to peace conditions after the Second World War was reckoned to have taken five years, and rationing continued until 1954.

Partly in consequence, states came to anticipate their post-war needs and to make them the subject of Allied negotiations. At Versailles, the French demanded that the special prices for wheat and coal, a feature of Allied wartime co-operation, should continue for a period of time following the war to aid reconstruction, and the French government tried to avoid opening exchanges until normalisation had ensued. When France's allies refused both requests, France turned to Germany to extract the requisites of reconstruction. The harsh terms imposed on Germany at Versailles, which so many liberals came to criticise, were primarily the consequences of France's anticipated war effects. During the negotiations on the second German peace after 1945, the Soviet Union insisted on a high reparations bill against Germany, and made it a condition of its agreement to unify the occupation zones. Its seizure of the plant of Eastern Europe, when reparations were denied, was partly to make good for war destruction; and its refusal to allow its protectorates to participate in Marshall Aid was in part to prevent any accounting for those seizures. The closing of the blocs, and the beginnings of the Cold War, may have been little more than the unintended outcome of a failed set of discussions on the German war bill.

Thus, war also invaded peace and set central parameters within which diplomatic and political relations were conducted for years thereafter. The state of Israel, in essence a war creation, sat like a thorn in the Middle East for decades following its establishment, and limited the ability of Western powers to conduct normal relations with the other states in the area. North Korea, originally the Soviet-occupied area of Korea, in 1945, was still in existence in 1995, and still hostile to any suggestion of unification with South Korea. The occupation of Berlin by the anti-fascist coalition, undertaken in 1944, was only wound up when the country was finally reunited in 1990.

War and internationalism

In his classic treatise on war, Clausewitz had written that war was 'politics with an admixture of other means', implying a continuity between ordinary diplomacy and war. It seemed to Clausewitz that war was simply another political tool. And the same view was prevalent throughout the European chancelleries: the controlled use of force was a regular feature of even nineteenth-century liberal diplomacy, as well as statecraft. Moreover, the move to force, while it tested governmental skills, was not conceived as testing political or social institutions. Accordingly, the notion that war was an ordinary tool of diplomacy was widespread in the nineteenth century, and was reflected even in progressive opinion of the age. John Stuart Mill would recommend the use of force for subduing barbarian populations and as part of a progressive diplomacy.

During the twentieth century, this view became increasingly hard to sustain. War appeared as a disruptive phenomenon, breaking peace, undercutting diplomacy and threatening the very existence of a state. It also appeared to be a social phenomenon, not merely a political phenomenon, and one with unpredictable and deleterious social consequences.

The difficulty of fighting war was reflected in its justifications. During the twentieth century, war came increasingly to be seen as an instrument of last resort, as securing ultimate values and as a test of ultimate resolve. Moreover, states which went to war had to claim that the move to force was not merely on behalf of themselves, much less some narrow calculation of national advantage, but on behalf of larger collective purposes, like democratisation, or the spread of liberty, or the defeat of an aggressor. It did not suffice even for 'nations' to desire war; there had to be a unity of purpose among some significant section of the international community as a whole.

On the other hand, the large wars of the age spawned large collective efforts. Large coalitions had to be organised to fight the large wars of the century, coalitions which had to be kept going for durations of time, and into and through prolonged peacemaking efforts. These, paradoxically, provided experience in international co-ordination and became the models for peacetime diplomatic organisations. The functional method recommended by David Mitrany[24] in 1941 as a model for future international co-operation was derived from the experience of the joint war boards established by the Allies during both wars. The large organisational efforts which succeeded each war were shaped by the experiences of Allied diplomacy. Indeed, the very phrases 'United Nations' and 'League of Nations' were born of war efforts; each was conceived as the continued union of the victorious coalitions, together with those who shared their objectives.

The large wars of the century, because they were so large, also revealed the hitherto unnoticed connections between states and societies, their reliance on one another for diplomatic and political support, for food, for trade and for exchange. The First World War demonstrated Europe's dependency on the United States for balancing power among the European states. The Second World War would teach Germany that its wealth accrued from trade with the 'West', not 'living room' in the East. They would also reveal, most graphically, the consequences of disruption. It was no accident that, following each of the century's great wars, diplomacy would revolve around efforts to restore, and secure, the connections which war had revealed and broken.

Notes

1 The six-volume work was entitled *The War of the Future in its Technical, Economic and Political Relations*, published in 1897 in Russian, and in German and French in 1900. Its final volume was translated by the English journalist W. T. Stead as *Is War Impossible* (London: Grant Richards, 1899).

2 *A Study of War*, 2 vols (Chicago: University of Chicago, 1942).

3 'Local Wars 1945–76' in A. Eide and M. Thee, *Problems of Contemporary Militarism* (London: Croom Helm, 1980).

4 Doyle's findings were published as 'Kant, Liberal Legacies and Foreign Affairs', *Philosophy and Public Affairs*, 12 (1983), pp. 205–35; the subsequent points of controversy were collected together in M. Brown, S. Lynn-Jones and S. Miller (eds), *Debating the Democratic Peace* (Cambridge, Mass.: MIT Press, 1996).

5 The economic historian A. S. Milward was noteworthy for denying that it had become so, in relative terms; *War, Economy and Society, 1939–1945* (London: Allen Lane, 1977) p. 3.

6 The perspective of e.g. P. Calvocoressi and G. Wint, *Total War* (London: Allen Lane, 1972).

7 Fuller carried out a remarkable analysis of Lenin's military and political writings, showing his debt to Clausewitz, and his unity of military and political technique; it became the basis of Fuller's analysis of the century's two major wars; *The Conduct of War, 1789–1961* (London: Methuen, 1961) pp. 202–16.

8 The levels of war's effects were physical destruction, the social and political structures of states and societies, the participation of previously disadvantaged groups, and the psychological experiences left by war; *War and Social Change in the Twentieth Century* (London: Macmillan, 1974).

9 In *Problems of Social Policy* (London: HMSO, 1950), part of the British official history of the Second World War.

10 For these and other issues, see I. Beckett, 'Total War' in C. McInnes and G. Sheffield (eds), *Warfare in the Twentieth Century* (London: Unwin Hyman, 1988), useful throughout.

11 F. Barnaby, *The Automated Battlefield* (London: Tauris, 1986).

12 *War in European History* (Oxford: Oxford University Press, 1976).

13 B. Brodie's *Strategy in the Missile Age* (Princeton: Princeton University Press, 1959) accepted these as first principles.

14 Fuller's 1918 plan was not put into effect; he identified Hitler's General Heinz Guderian as the first practical exponent of the theory and drew on his strategic concepts in making its principles explicit; *The Second World War: A Strategic and Tactical History* (London: Eyre and Spottiswood, 1948). The doctrine of the 'indirect strategy', proposed by the British strategist Liddel Hart, was also a form of rapid and limited warfare.

15 See T. Travers, *The Killing Ground: The British Army, the Western Front and the Emergence of Modern Warfare* (London: Allen and Unwin, 1987).

16 See J. Pimlott, 'The Theory and Practice of Strategic Bombing' in C. McInnes and G. Sheffield (eds), *Warfare in the Twentieth Century* (London: Unwin Hyman, 1988).

17 Henry Kissinger's *Nuclear Weapons and Foreign Policy* (New York: Harper, 1957) recommended such a use doctrine and sought to demonstrate its feasibility.

18 See, particularly, Brodie's *Strategy in the Missile Age* (Princeton NJ: Princeton University Press, 1965).

19 See especially L. Freedman, *The Evolution of Nuclear Strategy* (London: Macmillan, 1982).

20 K. R. Grieves, *The Politics of Manpower, 1914–1918* (Manchester: Manchester University Press, 1988).

21 The judgement on the overall effects of total war on the position of women is, however, beset with difficulties. Ian Beckett, in an admirably succinct discussion of

the question, notes that trade unions in both Britain and America succeeded in protecting male jobs, that many women were employed for specific wartime functions which came to an end when war closed, and that there was a significant revival in domesticity in Britain in 1945; he also makes the important observation that 'wartime employment neither implied equality of pay nor an erosion of the sexual divisions of labour'. See I. Beckett, 'Total War' in C. McInnes and G. Sheffield (eds), *Warfare in the Twentieth Century* (London: Unwin Hyman, 1988).

22 Herbert Feis' *Churchill, Roosevelt, Stalin* (Princeton NJ: Princeton University Press, 1957, 1967) was an account of 'the war they waged and the peace they sought'; and its focus was determined as much by the high 'peace' content of the Allied negotiations as by the preferences of the author.

23 *The Great Illusion* (London: Heinemann, 1933); the point was disputed by two American political scientists in calculating the war recovery potential of major antagonists; A. Organski and J. Kugler, 'The Cost of Major Wars: the Phoenix Factor', *American Political Science Review*, lxxi (1977), pp. 1347–66.

24 'Territorial, ideological or functional international organisation', in D. Mitrany, *The Functional Theory of Politics* (London: Martin Robertson, 1975).

7 The changing balance of power

Relative power changed rapidly in the twentieth century, producing sudden and dramatic alterations in power status. Britain's ascendancy, still evident in the 1920s, had evaporated by 1939. The United States, an ordinary power in 1890, had become a rival to the European Great Powers by 1921. Russia turned from being the sick man of Europe during the 1920s to a super-power in 1945. As for the intra-European rivalries, France, considered at least Germany's equal in 1910, proved unable to exploit victory against a vanquished Germany after 1919, even with the help of the other major powers, while Germany's aspirations for global hegemony, a serious prospect in 1939, lasted a mere six years.

War registered these changes, and it certainly speeded them up, but it was not their primary cause. Rise and fall were rather the resultants of the large-scale social and economic changes which the century witnessed. Industrialisation favoured Germany over France, and Russia's imperial reach over Britain's imperial outposts. The idea of self-determination strengthened social cohesion in the United States, and expanded state reach, while it challenged imperial reach and eroded imperial controls. The demands of economic management advantaged large economies and threatened to exclude smaller economies from economic growth and prosperity, just as state power was coming to depend in large measure on economic growth.

Power did not involve merely long-term factors, however. It also meant being able to apply national capacity to a purpose. Power had, accordingly, to be measured in relation to a specific situation; and situation-specific power, while it could do little to change long-term prospects, allowed them to be circumvented for periods of time.

The calculus of power

The notion of 'national power' had emerged in the early modern period with the stabilisation of the absolutist state and the consolidation of its control over territory and social resources. By the late seventeenth century, a state's population, its armies and navies and its revenues were already central factors in policy choices, and they were increasingly recognised as important in the determination of outcomes. And if such factors could not be calculated with exactitude, nonetheless, absolutist monarchs and their advisors regularly estimated their value in considering policy goals and strategies.

Equally, however, such resources were relatively restricted. In the early modern period, fixed indirect taxes remained the rule; kings struggled, usually in vain, to extend them. Even absolutist monarchs had few autonomous powers over the economy. There were also no rights of conscription. During the early modern period, power resided essentially with the monarch's personal income, his treasury, the size of a standing army and his alliances. (A monarch's own resources might be supplemented through the claims he had upon others, sometimes in the form of gold, more often through the loan of a standing army.) The resultant power quotients were fairly static.

These restrictions were reflected in the pattern of seventeenth- and eighteenth-century European wars. There would be summer and autumn campaigns. Troops would then retire to winter quarters while diplomats would attempt to garner more resources, in the form either of special taxes or of a new ally who could be wooed to loan troops or resources. If neither were forthcoming, they would be forced to negotiate. It is no accident that most of the great treaties of the absolutist era were spring treaties, since it was then that governments knew whether they could proceed with a campaign or not.

In the twentieth century, by contrast, states found increasing ability to draw on the total social resource; moreover, that resource was growing. Equally, in the great twentieth-century conflicts, it was the total capacity of the state that was tested. Thus, it became the practice to reckon not merely population size and the health of the treasury, but a population's relative degree of education, its readiness to be conscripted, its overall industrial as well as its financial capacity, even the speed of converting between war industry and peace industry. Reckoning total capacity was an outcome of fighting total war.

But governmental reach was also a variable quotient. The power of the modern state may have been much greater than that of the absolutist state, but it was also more diffuse and in consequence more conditional. Seventeenth-century monarchs knew what they had at their disposal. In the twentieth century, by contrast, the greater the call on the social resource, the more citizens had to be convinced of the worthiness or necessity of an undertaking. Accordingly, twentieth-century governments had to expend energy and resources either winning support or shielding populations from their undertakings; and most governments found it wise to do both. This, in turn, made governing skill of great importance, while for the power analyst it meant calculating the consequences of governing patterns as well as the value of material resources.

The value of apparently fixed resources also changed, sometimes rapidly, as the value of currencies, for example, rose and fell.

There were also the implications of rapid and continuous technological change. Developments as diverse as the turbine engine and the railway affected the speed and the capacity of troop delivery and fire-power, and put a premium on a state's capacity to match or circumvent an opponent's innovations. Governments struggled, in the very midst of campaigns, to pull off technological advances. Since, moreover, sudden breakthroughs were always possible, each had to watch the other's scientific and technological developments, to anticipate them and to calculate their potential effects. Intelligence, particularly technological intelligence, became, in consequence, of the greatest importance.

Since economic strength was often dependent on production and resource capability far from home, states could also be crippled by adverse developments in areas outside of and even remote from their homelands: hence the importance of global reach and extent, whether provided by imperial possession, alliances or political guarantees on the part of other global powers. The conditions which secured global reach also had to be reckoned – the loyalty of colonies, for example, and the degree to which colonies absorbed or released capacity. As decolonisation proceeded, the stability and scope of alliances became a particularly important part of the calculus.

British power at the century's onset

If we take all of these factors together, we may understand why Britain appeared to be the paramount power at the beginning of the century. It was the single greatest industrial producer, providing some 35 per cent of world industrial product. Its banking and services, together with its industry, allowed it to command world trade. Its services accrued a steady balance of payments surplus which provided the capacity to loan. It was the ability of the Bank of England to secure a loan to the German banking authorities, which their French counterparts could not, that frustrated the efforts of the French government to secure an autonomous Rhineland zone in 1925. At the very beginning of the century, moreover, it was still rare for political fissures to invade foreign policy-making, while Britain's developing pattern of executive government allowed it to mobilise social resources within increasingly short periods of time.

Given the degree to which British wealth was externally sourced, global reach was a particularly important factor in the British power calculus; and, at the beginning of the twentieth century, that reach was extensive. Moreover, it commanded central strategic points of the globe. Colonial control of Gibraltar and Suez, together with the long-standing alliance with Portugal, gave it control of the entrances and exits to Europe. Its command of the Malay Straits, Singapore and Hong Kong, India and South Africa, Kenya, and the West African ports allowed it to command two other continents besides. There were also stations in the Caribbean from which it could mount a presence in Latin America. The world's largest navy gave it the ability to police these positions and to transport and garrison soldiers from great distances. Britain maintained a quarter of a million men in South Africa during the Boer War over a distance of 6,000 miles, the only power that could manage such a feat. She also had, in the Indian Army, a land force able to hold the Indian sub-continent against external threats from the north.

That reach was fragile, however. Empire could be supplied and serviced by sea but increasingly it had to be held by land, and the more it spread, the less sea power could do alone. (Being an island bastion had costs as well as benefits.) Moreover, other powers seemed better placed to achieve industrial innovation and scale, and the productive surplus released by innovation and scale. Finally, and most importantly, much British wealth, contributing a large proportion to its favourable balances, lay abroad in external investment, interest-earning bonds and invisibles, which would be affected by revolutionary and nationalist movements, further eroding its financial and earnings capacity.

The major factors in Britain's decline

Paul Kennedy has stressed the role of railways in changing the balance between sea power and land power.[1] In simple terms, railways allowed for the delivery of both goods and people faster and cheaper by land, and benefited land power at the expense of sea power. When Russia, with its vast population and potential resources, began constructing the Tashkent railway at the end of the nineteenth century, the power balance shifted to Britain's detriment, threatening its positions in both China and India. Railways also qualified the effectiveness of the blockade as a military and political tool, and not merely with regard to imperial outposts. Britain's ability to control the European continent was also immediately affected. Once Germany, for example, could receive supplies quickly and in quantity from the East European hinterlands, naval power alone could not contribute much to its defeat. In addition, British troop emplacements would have to be done by sea. In consequence, the continental powers gained a natural offensive as well as defensive advantage.

Germany had begun to outpace Britain in coal and iron production at the end of the nineteenth century. But it was the commitment to imperial competition and its form – a German naval building programme to match and surpass the British fleet – which was the main contemporary focus of concern, since together they threatened Britain's ability to maintain the open trading order upon which its wealth depended. These considerations had already begun affecting its policy before the First World War. Thus, we see Britain conceding the western hemisphere to the naval power of the United States increasingly between 1900 and 1914, in order to concentrate on matching Germany in Europe and Africa, while its 1902 alliance with Japan was undertaken to counter a Russian power build-up in the Far East. It also abandoned its traditional suspicion of France in the Mediterranean, allowing France to control and monitor Germany in Europe's inward sea.

Britain had, moreover, scarcely the population to emplace large garrisons on a permanent basis around the sensitive points of the globe, and the public would anyway not have permitted permanent peacetime deployments of large numbers of British troops to hold these far-flung places. Increasingly, therefore its ability to defend them required native recruitment. This depended, in turn, on internal pacification and on agreements with native elites; Great Britain won the Boer War, but had to accede to many Afrikaner claims in order to continue to exploit its base facilities there and to make the new-found gold and mineral wealth of the Transvaal available to exploitation by English South Africans. The raising of troops from all over the Empire to fight in the First World War affected the internal political balance within the Empire as a whole: increasingly, concessions would have to be made to self-rule to secure such defences, weakening the imperial bond.

Britain's external earnings also steadily eroded following 1917. A damaging proportion of its foreign assets was wiped out after the Bolshevik revolution – British investors had been prominent purchasers of Imperial Russian bonds which the Bolsheviks refused to honour; and overvaluation of the pound sterling after the First World War affected its favourable trade balances. These were reduced by one-third over its pre-First World War earnings, primarily through the loss of invisible earnings. External earnings were to be damaged again by the wholesale nationalisation of foreign-owned assets in Mexico in 1938: British investors held the majority of Mexico's foreign-owned assets. By 1933, Britain would begin to experience balance of payments problems, but already by the 1920s decision-makers were being forced to consider what might be foregone, in the event determining on a measure of 'self-government' in the newly acquired mandates of Jordan and Iraq. Such concessions did not weaken British power in the short term, since planners saved those elements essential to strategic mobility, notably the direction of both Iraqi and Jordanian foreign policies and the ability to sequester in time of crisis, but they were a portent of things to come.

The increasing industrialisation of war, and the degree to which it was coming to depend on technological innovation, also affected Britain badly. Britain was ill-placed, with small-scale and scattered industry, to remain a technological leader in an industrial environment which increasingly required scale and large investment, and it lacked capacity especially in the new leader industries, chemicals and electronics. Moreover, its more liberal traditions impeded the development of state-directed industrial policies. It was a defensive strategy against Germany which finally forced the government to encourage industrial take-overs in the chemical industry. The founding of the Chemical Industries in the 1930s corrected that situation, but engineering was still characterised by relatively small plants during the inter-war period. The British aircraft industry could barely supply the fighters and bombers required by the Blitz and the air campaigns over Germany. British engineering was a relatively small industry until after the Second World War, when a large open world market and the advantages gained in war production allowed it to concentrate and to grow. With this pattern of industrial development, it is not surprising that British industry was not geared up to war effort, nor that it took a long time to shift from peacetime to war production.

Had the Empire been industrially developed, this situation might not have been so serious. But it was not (Canada was in the course of becoming an exception, but only by the 1930s). The Empire could provide manpower, food and raw materials, but not the technical material required by modern warfare. Yet the Empire had to be held. In the circumstances, more and more fell on the homeland to produce and ship, which put enormous strain on the productive capacities of the metropolitan population, a population smaller than that of its rivals. Britain also had to recruit in increasing numbers from this self-same population to provide for the emerging continental and African campaigns, which it could not avoid. At the same time, the small industrial heartland was becoming increasingly vulnerable to air power. Moreover, an increasing share of naval capacity, which was shrinking in relative terms, had to be directed to getting munitions out to the colonies and bringing food to the home population. (Despite an enormous drive for agricultural self-sufficiency, Britain still had to import food during the 1939–45 war.)

The efficient secret of Britain's success in the Second World War was neither its industrial power nor its financial capacity nor even its naval strength, but its alliance strategy. An alliance with the United States secured it victuals, equipment and loans to pay for raw material production in the colonies. The trans-Atlantic alliance also ensured a combined force with substantial equipment when the invasion of Europe was finally undertaken. Its alliance with the Soviet Union provided it with a fighting force to combat Germany on the Eastern Front, a front which witnessed a series of brutal campaigns which steadily absorbed German power and weakened it, before the Western Front was opened.

By the end of the Second World War, its merchant fleet had been virtually wiped out, reducing its invisible earnings from shipping. Moreover, insurance, formerly the second great earner of invisibles, was not an earner but a pay-out. Destruction in the Far East had, in addition, reduced production which had been a vital link in Britain's trade chain: sales of raw materials and semi-finished goods had provided the colonies and countries of the Far East with the earnings to buy British industrial goods. Industrial production for peace was restored rapidly after the Second World War, but there was no liquidity in the international system to allow importers to pay for British goods. Britain became crucially dependent on a United States stabilisation loan and Marshall Aid to provide for restructuring and financial resources immediately after the Second World War, and it was only United States-supported rearmament policies after the onset of the Korean Front that flooded Europe with sufficient dollars to get trade moving.

Despite these severe limitations, Britain preserved much of its global reach into the post-war period. The political transformation of relations from colony to self-government was undertaken with an eye to maintaining global mobility, through a series of special defence relationships with key ex-colonies. It traded its physical location and its ability to provide the United States with base facilities close to Europe for an atomic relationship, important to the maintenance of Great Power status. The economy also grew.

But the economy of the home base was now the central factor in the calculus of British power, and it did not grow sufficiently to provide at the same time for social welfare benefit, industrial adaptation, weapons innovation and the maintenance of positions abroad. Attempts to retain a reserve role for the pound caused stop-and-go in the economy and slowed down industrial adaptation. By the end of the 1960s, slow growth and the financial demands of industrial and social adaptation at home led it to declare its intentions to withdraw from 'positions east of Suez'.

The sources of German power

Germany, unified after 1871, was centralised into a peacetime form of 'war government'. The first German chancellor, Bismarck, had built up a state machinery with limited accountability. In consequence, the chancellor was consistently able to bypass parliament. He outlawed the Marxist Socialist Party and outflanked a growing socialist movement through the first social welfare provision. The new German state was a federation, but in fact the power of the 'principalities' was weak in relation to the formal powers of the Kaiser, the chancellor and parliament.

But it was not so much its political form that determined German power; more relevant were its economy and geography. The three secrets to the rapid development of German power were, first, a close relationship between state, banking and industry, which became an in-built feature of German industrial development through the whole course of the twentieth century; second, organisational skills, gained in part from a long military tradition; and, finally, geographic position. These capacities became apparent during the Great War in the form of the Dreadnought, the U-boat and the machine gun, as well as in the speed of transmitting troops. They were also evident in the scale of German shell production.

Neither did Germany have an economy vulnerable to blockade, the stalwart of British naval power in the nineteenth century. Only 4 per cent of her 1914 income derived from extra-European exports, and only 10 per cent lay in overseas investments, compared to 27 per cent for Britain. She also had strategic raw material sources close at hand, especially Romanian oil, Silesian coal and the wheat of the Ukraine, all of which could be rapidly mobilised and delivered, through alliances, conquest or purchase. Germany did not have the largest army in Europe in 1914, but it had mobility, and it had a navy which surpassed Britain's in inshore waters. It was thus able to hold out at home, while attacking Britain and her allies at selected points around the globe.

The German empire was one million square miles in extent in 1914, but it housed only 21,000 Germans, took only 3.8 per cent of Germany's foreign investment, and contributed only 0.5 per cent to Germany's foreign trade. Losing its colonies after the First World War had, in consequence, little effect on German power since they contributed little to its raw materials, trading or industrial base. Indeed, losing them may have benefited it. The German government had actually subsidised them to the level of perhaps $100 million in the period up to 1914.

Fascist public works programmes and rearmament produced full employment during the 1930s and gave Germany market power. This was especially relevant in the context of the Great Depression and with regard to the Central European agricultural producers. Dependent on commodity exports, the countries of Central and Eastern Europe suffered severely from the sudden drop in commodity prices experienced by all raw material producers from the late 1920s. Germany could provide Central Europe with markets and earnings. It was essentially through market power that Germany gradually won the countries on its eastern hinterlands to its side during the 1930s. These areas were gradually enclosed into a centrally organised producing zone to fuel the German war machine during the Second World War.

The limitations on German power after the Second World War

Germany lost one-third of its territory and a similar proportion of its population after the Second World War, while the closure of Eastern Europe deprived it of investment opportunities and a resource base further on. But the latter may have not been essential in the changed circumstances of the open trading order of the post-war period: even during the Second World War, it was noteworthy that its trading surpluses with the western part of its 'empire' were used to finance deficits from its eastern producers. (During the Second World War, Germany actually gained surpluses from deliveries of industrial goods to France and used these to pay for its raw material imports from its allies and occupied territories in the East; it may accordingly have learned, earlier perhaps than others, that trade balances accrued from trade between advanced industrial producers.)

Its geographical position as the 'hinge' between East and West Europe continued to serve it in very altered circumstances. During the post-war period, in the context of the Cold War, Europe had to be defended to the east, and this allowed post-war German governments to gain political and military concessions from the Nato powers in return for base facilities and a military presence on German soil. Moreover, its own manpower became crucial to the United States in maintaining a strong military position in Europe. Increasingly during the 1960s, German troops replaced American troops along the central front of the conflict with the Soviet Union.

The rise of American power

The United States had had a form of standing army since the 1820s, but until the Spanish–American War it was essentially a frontier force directed to confronting native Indians. The South had conscripted during the Civil War, but the North had recruited essentially by advertising. Moreover, while some Northern citizens were called up, they could pay to get themselves released from war service. The American army which landed in France in 1916 was formed essentially from regiments of various states' national guard. A standing army only came into place during the 1930s, and it was difficult to justify because of America's official position of neutrality in any coming war: a standing army only made sense if the United States were planning to fight a war in Europe, a politically contested question.

Naval power caused less internal division. By the end of the First World War, it had a fleet equal in size to the combined strengths of France, Italy and Japan, and a fleet which dwarfed even the Grand Fleet in its prime. By 1919, the trident, symbol of sea mastery, was peacefully passing from Britain to America.

The American economy enjoyed a boom during the Great War, when mass-production techniques were first employed extensively; and after it, the increased productivity of the American economy began to be reflected in American investments in Europe and the Far East. Americans had money to loan, and the United States became a considerable diplomatic power on its ability to finance alone. The large internal market allowed it to further develop economies of scale which made production runs cheaper and also encouraged technological innovation. Moreover, during the Great Depression, it increased its relative economic strength through an open trading arrangement with Canada; both were industrialising powers, and they fed one another's industrial growth. During the Second World War, it supplied three-quarters of the entire Allied war effort, recovering and surpassing the industrial capacity lost during the depression.

The first American overseas bases were the legacy of its war with Spain, whose defeat gave it the Philippines and the Mariannas. The First World War also resulted in the possession of some of the ex-German colonies. It had, however, no bases in Europe, Africa or the Middle East. Its base operations during the European campaigns of the First World War were provided by France, and during the Second World War by Britain.

After the Second World War, it rectified this position. The United States began constructing a series of military alliances with states bordering the Soviet Union, which gave it global mobility. It covered the Far East from bases in South Korea, Japan and the Philippines; the Near East from Greece and Turkey; and Central Europe from bases in South Germany. It also had bases for nuclear submarines and aircraft in Britain, and it could port at Cape Town.

America's ability to mobilise its resources was affected, however, by its constitutional order. The federal system limited the economic powers of the federation: both state and county authorities had autonomous land-use and tax-raising rights. Moreover, the legal right of economic regulation belonged to the separate states, not to the federation. Washington had rights to take land for defence purposes from the states, but all other potential resources had to be negotiated between central, state and local government, as well as vital industrial bodies and trade unions. There was also the distribution of powers within the federation over the war right and treaty-making. After the Great War, a Congressional rebellion prevented the United States from being associated with the League of Nations or contracting permanent alliances. Immediately after the Second World War, and again during the late 1960s, Congress would again insist on close regulation of the war right. Thus, both the conduct of war and any large permanent alliances were dependent on building a consensus among groups and regions with very different interests.

Its political culture also affected the mobilisation of power. There was a long pacifist tradition, fuelled partly by religion and partly by the ethnic basis of the state: ethnic minorities opposed the use of American power against co-ethnicities and small states. Entry into both wars against Germany was impeded by its large German Catholic groupings, making it difficult to arm in advance or support allies before the event, except in secret and by indirect means. After the Second World War, the building of the anticommunist alliance and the association of anti-communism with nativism and adherence to the American way of life allowed America a wide-reaching world role, but this had not been part of America's political traditions. Woodrow Wilson, no less than Thomas Jefferson, would have been amazed at the extent of America's post-war commitments and incredulous at the post-war federal authority's capacity to direct American power to global policing.

Forty years of international involvement strengthened a growing liberal internationalist tradition which sanctioned American activism abroad, but the strength and durability of that tradition remained unclear. From the end of the 1970s, calls became more insistent for disengagement, particularly from Europe. Moreover, the dissolution of the communist bloc at the end of the century, and the emergence of Russia as a potentially weak and confinable power concerned with economic restructuring at home, removed the chief justification for continuous sacrifice of national advantage to the role of world policeman. This was bound to make the permanent securing of base facilities and the permanent stationing of troops abroad difficult.

The erosion of French power

France was considered the great European land power until its defeat in the Franco-Prussian War of 1870–71. By the end of the nineteenth century, there were additional causes for concern. First, there was its population, small in relation to the expanding German population, and declining, which increasingly obsessed French strategic planners as the importance of land power increased. France was also slow to industrialise, and its industry was characterised by many small specialist firms, particularly in the coal and steel industries, the basis of modern industrial power at the beginning of the twentieth century. The return of Alsace-Lorraine after 1919 had returned the minette of Lorraine, giving it a large potential iron and steel capacity; but France needed more coal with which to refine the Lorraine ores, making it increasingly dependent on external supplies. This deficiency was intended to be redressed by provisions of the Versailles Treaty which promised France large coal deliveries from the Ruhr; coal was finally secured by France's reoccupation of the Rhineland in 1921, as a result of which steel production expanded between 1928 and 1933. Deliveries stopped, however, when the Nazis came to power in Germany. During the immediate post-war period, it took care to secure permanent access to Ruhr coal, underwriting French modernisation. From the late 1960s, it secured indigenous supplies of energy from French-built and run nuclear power plants.

France had been a considerable financial power before the First World War: the thrifty French saver had produced a market for, particularly, Russian state securities. Moreover, providing access to that market had given French governments considerable diplomatic leverage. This power was virtually wiped out, however, by the war's inflationary effects. The French franc was only stabilised, and at one-fifth its pre-war value, in 1926. Reparations looked like restoring some measure of French financial power, particularly with the Dawes Plan, which allowed Germany to raise loans in the United States with which to pay its reparations bill. Moreover, the decision to speed evacuation in return for a final reparations settlement, agreed with Germany in 1930, put a large potential financial resource at France's disposal. But, with the onset of depression, Germany again suspended payments; and the development of closed economic orders across Europe militated against their resumption thereafter.

The other power the French could have used in the late 1920s and 1930s was market power, and in particular the power to open its markets to the Eastern European agricultural producers. The two things its potential Eastern European allies needed were loans to buy armaments and markets for their agricultural products. In fact, France could do neither. Its own large agricultural population demanded and secured protection during the inter-war period, leading to a price subsidy scheme and the closure of its markets to Eastern European agricultural goods. (The German government, with a much smaller proportion of its population involved in agriculture and with a more northern grain production, had no such difficulty.)

Colonial planners dreamt of joining French black Africa to the Sahara through an ambitious railway project, but France's economic weakness during the 1920s militated against the scheme. (It was also not clear what use a railway joining the Mahgreb to the Sahara would have been against German power, and it was clear by 1921 that Germany was once again France's major strategic rival.) The removal of German influence in the Mediterranean gave France a clear run there, however, and France's imperial status was not so disputed in its colonies as was Britain's. (Although here, too, there were portents of the future: France was in conflict in its Syrian mandate with the Druse in 1925 and 1927, and in Indochina from 1925 to 1930.) At the same time, its colonies were thinly held. Moreover, imperial producers were more successful in finding markets in France than vice versa. By 1938, France held a balance of payments deficit with the Empire of 4 billion francs.

The Grand Armée, often called the first modern army and created by the Revolution's *levées en masse*, was the source of French continental strength. But its tactics and fighting traditions were becoming increasingly outdated. It was a stationary army, trained to defend and hold positions, not in mobility or the war of movement. It was also deeply demoralised after the First World War and accepted change with difficulty. The future president of the Fifth Republic, de Gaulle, then a staff officer, tried in vain to bring the French high command to adopt the more flexible fast-moving tank strategy which modern land warfare in the twentieth century seemed increasingly to require. In the event, French strategic planners preferred a defensive strategy: to take advantage of the ratio in modern warfare which appeared to give the advantage to the defensive side. The Maginot Line was consistent with that preference.

Constitutionally, France was a strongly unified state, but the tradition of the revolution had left political power centred in the National Assembly without providing a set of strong or disciplined political parties. This meant frequent changes of government (but not always of personnel), and a good deal of political instability. This was particularly relevant in the area of foreign policy: the Fourth French Republic, established after the Vichy period, was prey to cross-cutting political interests, and proved unable to produce clear policies on the major issues of the day, including German rearmament and the growing series of crises and rebellions in its colonies, first in Indo-China and then in Algeria. Indeed, Algeria brought the country close to civil war at the end of the 1950s, when an army faction threatened to rise against any further concessions to the Algerian rebels.

This constitutional weakness was rectified, however, with the coming to power of General de Gaulle in 1958. President de Gaulle forced through a new constitution which shifted political power from the Assembly to a newly created presidential office. In the new constitution, the legislative powers of the Assembly were curtailed while the new president was directly elected, evading dependence on the National Assembly, and for a seven-year term of office. Powers over foreign policy were concentrated in the presidential office: the French president chaired all the high councils of state, including the defence councils, and could directly ratify all treaties which did not give rise to a financial commitment. Thereafter, French foreign policy became noted for clarity of both purpose and direction, establishing it as a model for other states.

Another important power-enhancing measure was the relatively successful economic modernisation programme, initiated through the first French plan, undertaken in 1946. French planners directed investment to the more advanced sectors of the economy while the government nationalised central areas of economic activity and gave them the protection of subsidies and protected markets. It took particular care to modernise the defence industries and heavily supported export sales, which allowed the industry to maintain economies of scale.

The failed promise of the Soviet revolution

The Soviet population equalled the rest of Western Europe combined, but the country's industrial backwardness negated the relative advantage of population size. The revolution and subsequent civil war destroyed what industrial plant there was, and the Soviet Union did not industrialise until the 1930s. When it did, moreover, the consequence was to weaken other central areas of the economy. The Soviet industrialisation was financed essentially by the collectivisation of agriculture, a process which was both destructive and economically costly. The Soviet Union fought the Second World War essentially with US material, and was dependent on the United States to supply it.

During the post-war period it rectified this situation, but at a cost. Driven by the demands of the Cold War, war industries came to be attached to the war ministry and were given the lion's share of the state budget. This allowed the Soviet Union to 'match' Western military technology, especially in the advanced sector of missile development. (The technique had been first systematically developed by Germany near the end of the Second World War, when it directed a large proportion of its declining resources to missile development to pull off a short-term technological superiority.) Practised for a long period, however, it distorted the civilian side of the economy, and it left the Soviet economy beached when the Cold War came to an end. Designed for Great Power competition, the gigantic and inefficient plants, tied to military production, could in no way compete in a civilian market situation.

A Soviet army was formed to fight the Civil War of 1920–23, building largely on the organisation and training (and a surprisingly large percentage of the soldiers) of the former Imperial Army. But it was not considered a serious offensive threat by the Western powers during the inter-war period, partly because it had little equipment. It was seriously weakened during Stalin's purge of 1937, when its officer corps was virtually wiped out. The rapid recruitment carried out to confront the German attack in 1941 was sourced largely through the release of 3 million prisoners from labour camps. Soldiers from such a source were a questionable asset, being both physically weak and untrained: few strategic experts expected the Soviet Union to be able to withstand the German onslaught in 1941. Nonetheless, the prisoner army eventually held the Germans at Stalingrad, a feat attributed not only to the long German supply lines but to the willingness of the Russian soldier to bear the most brutal conditions. It was in fact upon the 'Stalingrad army' that the Soviet Union rested its power pretensions in the immediate post-war period.

After the Second World War, the Soviet occupation of Eastern Europe from Stettin to Sofia turned the area into a buffer zone, providing a form of defensive space. But as defensive space, the zone was of questionable value. The development of air power rendered the buffer of little use in preventing surprise attack, the main fear of Soviet strategic planners in the post-war period. Moreover, its Eastern European allies were militarily and politically unreliable. Despite the Western tendency to include them in total numbers, partly to boost the 'Soviet threat', their actual use in war was questionable. The Balkan 'pseudo-armies' could not be relied on at all, and neither the Czech nor the Polish armies could be expected to fight to defend the Soviet motherland. Their actual military use to the Soviet Union lay in the provision of forward bases, allowing the Soviet Union to threaten the Western powers with rapid forward movement and a military occupation, in the event of a surprise attack. Militarily, they provided a springboard, not a buffer.

They had potential economic and some definite political value. In political terms, they buttressed the weak East German state and kept it out of West

German hands, thus limiting German power. They were also exploited economically. But Soviet central planning limited their economic growth without contributing significantly to Soviet economic development. The limitations of the zone would become apparent when, at the end of the century, the country turned from a war strategy to a peace strategy; one reason why the reformed Soviet state abandoned its European allies so readily in 1989 was their non-utility from the point of view of an economically reforming state who wished to join Western councils.

That the Soviet Union would enjoy such continuing influence over the West during the Cold War was due largely to its possession of atomic power. The atomic bomb, together with its forward emplacements in Europe, acted as an effective deterrent to any military force that might be ranged against it. Carefully graded nuclear threats also allowed it to secure its allies from Western interference, and to protect such global mobility as its allies provided. The nuclear shield also allowed it to maintain and to develop its revolution at home.

From the 1960s, the Soviet Union began to develop its naval power, first in the form of the 'blue water fleet', a surface fleet operating from its warm water ports. From the late 1960s, it also began a concerted programme of conventional submarine development, submarines which could operate below ice. (Nuclear submarine development continued throughout the post-war period; but these were expensive and relatively limited in number. Their purpose was to enhance deterrence, as well as to support the Soviet strategy of graded threats. The conventional force was intended as an 'ordinary' form of naval power.) By the mid-1980s, its submarine fleet had grown to two-thirds the size of the United States' submarine fleet.

However, Soviet naval doctrine remained conservative as to basing, with consequences for the fleet's offensive impact. Soviet planners preferred to concentrate basing at Vladivostock rather than to develop foreign basing. It had only one extensive naval base outside the country, in Vietnam, and some small stations variously between Ethiopia and Somalia. This limited the political and diplomatic use of the fleet, since the Soviet Union had only three exits from its territorial space into the high seas, each narrow: the Dardanelles, Greenland and the united waters north of Japan. Each could be and was heavily monitored by either a Nato or a US presence. No nuclear submarine got through these straits without being tracked.

Of greater relevance for Soviet global capabilities was air power. By 1977, it had developed an air capability sufficient for the long-distance support of its allies in local wars. This centred on troop and supply carriers. Until then, the Soviet Union would be conservative in offering direct military support to both allies and favoured client contenders in civil uprisings far from areas it could command from land. Thereafter, it would be more adventurous, supporting communist forces in the Horn of Africa and in Angola with troops and supply.

The 'civilian' power of Japan

Japan entered upon power politics with significant disadvantages. It had a small population relative to its chief rivals, and was raw-material dependent, especially on oil imports. Its coal reserves would prove insufficient even during the Second World War. The Meiji restoration had been accompanied by a rapid industrialisation, but during the 1920s and 1930s there was still only a shallow industrial base. Its industrial weakness, as well as its raw material dependency, would determine a war strategy which depended absolutely on a single devastating blow against American naval power. When it failed to achieve the freedom to seize control in East Asia, its only alternative was a co-operative development strategy, in alliance with one or another major liberal power.

Japan's economic development turned on the mimic technique. It learnt lessons from the advanced economies and reproduced them. This appeared to present no threat to the others during the 1950s and 1960s, when Japan's developing industrial economy was generally held in poor repute. But the technique had decided advantages; it was both cheaper and more reliable to copy others, since it was the others who bore the costs of innovation and who paid for mistakes. It was also the case that successive governments took care to lay the base of an increasingly trained work force, while copying occurred at the advanced edges of economic development. This encouraged a work force that learned to translate new ideas quickly into industrial goods, a technique which would lay the foundations for an eventually innovative economy to challenge the older economies, particularly in the production of consumer goods.

While apparently an export-driven economy, the Japanese took care also to develop a large internal market. This was protected to ensure the on-going domestic purchase of Japanese industrial goods.

The post-war alliance with the United States allowed it access to the large American market and, eventually, to take advantage of the opening global market of trade and exchange. (Japan joined the Organisation for Economic Co-operation and Development under United States sponsorship in 1963, its first non-European member.) A tight fiscal policy created funds not only for internal development but also external investment. Japan became a prime force in the development of the Asian 'tiger' economies during the 1980s.

The achievement of economic success, together with the eschewing of any active defence posture, created a new model of 'the civilian power'. This was a power which paid close attention to industrial development through state-sponsored initiatives and took advantage of an open global market to secure competitive advantage. Civilian power also seemed to imply measuring national progress in terms of performance in the global market.

The power calculus and internationalism

The rapid rise and fall of powers made the major powers very sensitive to developments that would affect relative advantage. It was equally clear that power balances depended on a complex mix of situation-specific power and objective power; that is, the factor bestowing relative advantage in the short term, and more long-term developments. Powers constantly sought to exploit short-term advantages, those which might disappear over time, to redress long-term disadvantages.

Partners were important to such endeavours, and accordingly competition depended, and depended increasingly, upon co-operation and on alliances. The powers constantly sought to get others to bear responsibilities, and they sought to hold others in relatively fixed positions for periods of time, in order to allow them to give duration to short-term advantages and to circumvent long-term disadvantages or permanent disabilities.

While the power calculus focused increasingly on relative economic weight in determining power balances, the central factors in this calculation were not easy to determine. In the short term, Britain's economic power seemed to depend as much on imperial reach as on domestic growth. The main indicators of economic weight also changed during the century. Just before and after the First World War, it was rates of coal and steel production that were considered to be the mark of a Great Power; and they served as the main indicators of relative power, engendering a competition between Britain and Germany before the Great War and France and Germany after it, both of which played their parts in destabilising Europe. Increasingly, however, innovation and the ability to stay ahead in leader industries became the mark of a Great Power. This made the conditions of innovation central to the power calculus. (But these were equally difficult to identify; increasingly, they would be seen to depend on financial capacity and research and development.)

That all powers were increasingly aware of the saliency of industrial power to the long-term well-being of states we may judge from the growing concern to restore the conditions of industrial growth after the Great Depression. That the Soviet Union rested its power on traditional considerations of military preparedness, as well as land-and-plant seizures, seemed old-fashioned and backward-looking, even during the peace negotiations which accompanied the closing of the Second World War, particularly when contrasted with the concerns of its allies. Britain and France, as well as the United States, were each as aware of the demands of industrial restoration and with restoring competition and the financial power on which innovation and competition depended, and as concerned to secure their requisites, as they were to contain the German threat, and they had been so steadily through the century.

Military preparedness did not, on that account, cease to matter, however. Germany may have been finally disarmed, but the Soviet military deployments and the forward military posture it adopted in 1945 seemed by 1949 to have become permanent. That, in turn, created the demand for some form of permanent security arrangement for Europe, and one involving some military element. And the lack of Europe's military preparedness, and the unwillingness of Europeans to provide it, would become a central concern, particularly on the part of the United States in the post-war period. If, moreover, that military element would eventually be secured by restoring German military power, it was clear that a carapace would have to be found within which to place and through which to control that power.

Note

1   P. Kennedy, *Strategy and Diplomacy 1870–1945* (London: Fontana, 1984), pp. 41–85.

Part 2

State policy

This second section concerns internationalism-as-policy. In this part is detailed the way in which state policies and governing intentions provoked the development of institutional internationalism and provided the organisational carapaces for the social anticipations previously discussed. Its focus is on the political motives for the building of the international institutions with which internationalism became associated. It will detail the ways in which political motives, and eventually policy choices, determined the construction of international instruments with particular ends. It is also about the way state policy limited institutional internationalism to certain forms, to specified compasses and to specified ends.

New political rhetorics accompanied institutional construction and defended their particular architectures. Concepts such as the 'free world', the 'united nations', and 'liberal development' provided justification for the new organisations and defended their provisions. They implied particular sorts of institutions and specified memberships. The 'one-worldness' displayed in such rhetorics was not meant to encourage universalism. It was meant to exclude rogue states and to limit the range of policy outcomes. They were counters in political struggles with opponents. The often-expressed claim of the 'union of domestic and foreign policy' was meant to give the institutional formulae of choice added weight.

Was there a single architect to institutional and rhetorical internationalism? Any account will reveal the prevalence of American thinking and American ideas in determining the shape of the new international organs, particularly after the Second World War, as well as the definition of the purposes they should serve. United States goals were not the only factor: they had to be negotiated with others who were necessary to their requisites; and the process of negotiation often changed their shapes and made their ends the subjects of compromises. The United States could seldom determine them alone. But it set the terms of the debates and generally succeeded in setting the limits of movement.

A common theme, which may aid in understanding the new institutions, was the reconciliation of irreconcilable demands. This was most obvious in France's early choice for internationalism. Its proposal for an international peacekeeping force in 1919, like the proposal for a European army in 1952, was driven by the need to secure German economic resources (and German compliance) for a

French economic revival, while limiting German political and economic power. Less obvious but not less telling was Britain's choice for 'collective security' involving the United States. The desire for a 'trans-Atlantic' collective security instrument rose out of the need to stabilise Europe without at the same time becoming entirely subject to the political, economic and strategic demands of the European theatre. With regard to the United States, there were the constraints of its federal system and political culture which offered the twin unpalliatives of isolationism or over-involvement. In the American case, institutional internationalism was intended to distribute the costs of global power, allowing the federal government to steer between the Scylla of staying at home and the Charybdis of becoming the world's policeman.

If there was a single rule or operative principle behind internationalism-as-policy, it was the pursuit of national interests understood as relative advantage within a confined political, economic and social space, and the relationship between internationalism and relative weakness in the game of seeking advantage. Internationalism was most persistently pursued by the weaker side, and it was the weaker side which generally argued for the deeper integration. Institutional internationalism was, accordingly, subject to re-evaluation, and the saliency and shape of the various organisations were altered according to calculations of relative advantage. It also threatened to be abandoned when one state or another felt strong enough to go it alone.

If that familiar concept appears much in this section, it is worth pointing out that the national interests of the respective powers were neither secular nor timeless. They, in general, reflected the interests of the new kind of state that states were becoming. Internationalism-as-policy was for most of the twentieth century an attribute of what became loosely known as the welfare state, and it reflected the interests, and the capabilities, of that kind of state. Accordingly, the shape and interests of that kind of state will be considered first.

What should be taken as understood is that internationalism-as-policy was not intended to produce internationalism as a fact. It was intended to produce economic growth or to secure alliances or to confine rivals. Above all, it was intended to supply various *points d'appuis* or platforms for national renewals. Policy internationalism was 'nationalistic' in the sense that it was intended to support revised and invigorated national development policies and to provide for more effective national foreign and security policies. It was the – often unintended – outcome of such efforts that was internationalist.

8　The changing state

The new state which came into place during the twentieth century was characterised by growing links between an executive-led bureaucracy and a widened, and more organised, social base. By contrast with the nineteenth century, cabinet government faded, to be replaced by 'executive government', a pattern of government in which chief executives increasingly held responsibility for domestic as well as foreign affairs. Executives, in turn, liaised increasingly with a growing body of organised social forces, which fed changing social demands directly into government. Executive government was consultative government; and consultation engaged organised social forces as well as parliaments and political representatives.

The legislative scope of the modern state also widened, bringing many new social concerns into the public arena, and accordingly, within the purview of government. These expanded the interests of the modern state, since modern government had to provide not merely for security or law and order, but also for a much wider definition of social need. Their widened legislative scope also gave them much more power to accomplish their widened responsibilities.

The old state and the new

The nineteenth-century state had progressively freed itself from the lingering constraints of Church and traditional authority. Increasingly after 1850, the limited constitutional state, in which a cabinet served a public regulated by private interests, had become the desired political form, and the object of revolutionary activity everywhere that it was not in place. The mid- to late nineteenth-century cabinet governments were sustained by concepts of customary and legal rights, including the right of private contract, which the state enforced, and increasingly by notions of nationalism and democracy. The limited state's prime political purposes were to maintain national unity, enforce law and order, regulate the public purse, and provide for the security of transactions, for defence, and for the stability of a national currency (the gold standard in the case of Britain). Much of the rest of social life it left to the self-determining activities of the populace.

The typical Western twentieth-century state displayed similar institutions of constitution, the ballot and citizen rights, but it directed them to quite different ends. Whereas the nineteenth-century state had used its growing prerogatives to lift restrictions on the citizen and to limit interference in his activities, the twentieth-century state used its powers to penetrate outwards into social life. State activity was increasingly looked to in social, economic and political matters, and the state came to be seen, and justified, as the main provider of an expanded range of public services. In the classic case, compulsory education would increase personal development and thereby effective freedom. Economic management would increase personal wealth and social stability. Cultural development would unify and equalise the citizenry, and release social potential. The twentieth-century state also claimed wide-ranging definitional rights, rights to decide how and in what areas of social life intervention should proceed.

These developments were spurred on by changing liberal concepts of rights. In the nineteenth century, an already expanding state prerogative had been used to consolidate civil and political rights, the right to due process of law and to private contract, as well as the right to vote and to petition government. The great political advance of the twentieth century was in the notion of 'positive' rights and 'welfare' rights: state power was justified in part by citizen rights to economic well-being and equality of consideration. Positive rights endorsed popular claims to increasingly higher levels of education, to social security, basic wages and health care. Moreover, such rights would be increasingly claimed by all of the citizenry.

The sum of the new positive rights, and their extension to the entire citizenry, encouraged the increase in the sovereign power, since by granting such rights the state was granting itself the legislative scope, and the political power, to provide the concomitant services. Welfare rights and state power grew in tandem.[1]

In the Western democracies, the line between the public and the private, a traditional inheritance of the nineteenth-century liberal order, was maintained, but it shifted continuously, as successive governments expanded, contracted or altered the balance among social policies. These shifts tended to erode the notion of a stable private realm, sacrosanct from government interference. Also, legislation where permitted (in France among others) increasingly took the form of enabling acts, giving the public authorities wide powers to define and implement general directives, widening the potential areas in which a policy could operate, as well as the discretionary powers of public authorities.

The routes to the new state

Instrumental to the unshackling of the nineteenth-century state had been the sustained liberal attack on the traditional powers of the Church and the old guild associations, whose erosion had steadily proceeded during the nineteenth century. It had also been encouraged by the great advances in positive law thinking. According to positive law doctrine, law was what a law-making body said it was, turning parliaments into the sole dispensers of law, and circumscribing the role of clerics, moralists and judges whose judgements had formerly enjoyed a quasi-legal status.

There was also the development of capitalist forms of enterprise which demanded the lifting of restrictions. Poggi notes how successful capital forces were in getting the nineteenth-century state to accede to capital's definitions of its requisites, altering long-standing social arrangements, such as Sunday observance and feast days, to suit the demands of regularised industrial production.[2] Indeed, the nineteenth-century state created a new form of corporation (the modern corporation was a company with limited liability) which was registered with the state, and which would in time develop into a substantial counter to state power. It was this development which made the large company and eventually the large multinational possible.

Its growth into a positive force was encouraged by many of the social developments already discussed. Modern forms of work gave rise to literate masses which pressed for political forms more suited to their circumstances. Trade unions demanded security of employment, minimum wages, decent schooling and health care – provisions which single-wage families of the poorer classes could not provide for themselves and which could scarcely be provided even by the emerging atomised middle-class family. Modern capital development required massive investment, investment which only the largest enterprises, or failing that the state, could provide, investment which in turn created firms of such scale that only the state could regulate them.

But there were also, and very importantly, the great political crises of the first fifty years of the century – the great wars of the age and the Great Depression. Governments not only had to take on powers to fight the world wars, they also had to reward the soldiers and the civilians who had sacrificed to support them, if only to circumvent the radicalism which threatened to follow them. The 'welfare state' became the prime method of incorporation.

Explaining the growth in state power

Some of these developments had been foreseen. As early as 1848, Marx had predicted that, as capitalism developed, economic and social power would shift from the owners of capital to the possessors of labour, upon which modern industrial development would increasingly come to depend. As economic and social power shifted, workers would also enjoy more political power, enabling them to direct public policy more to their advantage and interests. The new social power would also take on a more public aspect – in Lenin's terms, the 'administration of things' would enter into the public weal – and matters formerly regarded as private would come to be seen as *res publica*, or things of the public, enlarging the compass of public matters. But Marx, along with many liberals, had also predicted a narrowing compass to the formal institutions of the state, whereas the state grew in power and compass. Moreover, it seemed capable of rising above the mass of new public claims and directing them to its own purposes.

Twentieth-century political science developed a number of theories to explain why state power grew. One was 'pluralism', and the need for the state to intervene to balance the interests among new political entrants. In the Marxist version, this took the form of the idea of the 'fractionated class'. Instead of simplifying class divisions, as Marx had predicted, some new Marxists developed the idea that modern capitalism produced divisions within as well as between classes. Fractionalism, in turn, enhanced the saliency of the state and political power, since the various fractions needed the state to manage their conflicts with one another (such as between industry and finance, or between the advanced and more backward sections of industry). There was also the need to stem a potentially revolutionary situation. Modern, 'fractioned' capitalism required that some social benefit be directed to reducing the revolutionary zeal of the proletariat and to controlling it, requiring in turn a more extensive and empowered administrative apparatus.[3]

In yet another variant, the state institutions were conceived as independent of capital, but co-opted by it. In the theory of co-option, capital was portrayed as having adjusted itself to the parliamentary system, deploying electoral politics for the protection of value exchange.[4] Here, modern capitalism was deemed to work within the formal network of constitutional bodies, gaining natural advantages through its control of the media and its ability to finance election campaigns. In the theory of co-option, the widened state grew via the ordinary workings of liberal democracy, which transmitted the new social demands upwards.

A third form of theory explained these developments less in terms of conflict and the biased state than as a 'functional adaptation' on the part of a neutral state. One variant of the functional approach attempted to demonstrate a direct correlation between the achievement of the franchise by formerly dispossessed groups in society and the enactment of social policies. Peter Flora, in the major post-war study of the historical origins of the welfare state, noted a correlation between the achievement of 50 per cent of male suffrage in democracies and the beginnings of welfare provision.[5] Other liberal theorists argued that pressure from 'new entrants' was not the single most important factor, but rather the activities of middle-class reformers. They argued that middle-class elites, and their pressure for social reform, were the 'efficient' transmitters of social demands into state action and that it was their influence which widened state powers. (Britain and Sweden were frequently cited as political orders where 'progressive' elites had been prominent in formulating social programmes which enhanced governmental powers while benefiting formerly excluded sectors of society.)

The pace and locus of change

The growth of the state was not steady. It tended to increase during war, to fall back at its close and then to increase again, overtaking itself in subsequent cycles. The pre-1914 state had made tentative moves towards some social insurance provision, generally limited to industrial accidents. (It is noteworthy that industrial insurance could be made consistent with nineteenth-century liberal theory: it could be conceived as a 'market sanctioned' reward for taking on especially onerous occupations.) The First World War state, by contrast, took over extensive areas of social life, some of which prerogatives were retained after the war had ended, most notably the control of trade and the direction of industrial organisation.[6] The pattern would be repeated during the Second World War.

As between state types, provision was not even. It was noteworthy that the European constitutional monarchies came on stream first, then the European 'democracies', while America and Canada, along with some southern Mediterranean state orders, were dubbed 'social laggards'.

During the Great Depression, provision everywhere became more extensive, and it also tended to even out among the European states. In the 1930s, more European states moved towards more comprehensive insurance schemes which also covered more types of employment. They also established 'the dole'. At the same time, the targets of social policy also widened. Industrial workers and children had been the first beneficiaries of social policies, while agricultural interests became a prime focus in both the United States and continental Europe during the Depression.

It was during the Second World War that social control, management and direction became truly comprehensive, this time reaching close to total proportions. It was in the midst of this war, when Britain was facing Germany alone, that the term 'welfare state' was popularised. It was first used by Alfred Zimmern, one of the new liberals, during the 1930s to describe the compass of the 'new' liberal state; Churchill adapted it to war justification, contrasting the Nazi 'power and warfare state' with the superior British 'welfare' state. It was after this war that the complex of health, welfare, educational and housing allowances associated with the modern welfare state came into place as comprehensive programmes. Only then, moreover, did social provision become specified as the liberal state's *raison d'être* and a generator of its legitimacy.

The war powers and their effects

During the wars, governments acquired such powers as they conceived essential to war effort. Thus, the direction of the use of raw materials was claimed in respect of the production of war material. The power of stopping exports was seized in respect of items adaptable to war purpose and aid to the enemy. The right of cargo allocation was claimed to assure regular shipments of either food or strategic goods. The right of arbitrary arrest, confinement or expulsion was claimed in respect of suspected subversives, and control of information in respect of propaganda.

Since control of the economy came to be central in winning war, the economic controls were particularly far-reaching. During the Second World War, strike regulations were imposed, and imports and exports were controlled generally through licensing to ensure no seep-out of valuable credits or transport space. The state also regulated wages, rationed and directed the use of raw materials and guided industrial production.[7] In the United States, far more people were engaged in administering the wartime economy than had ever been involved in the New Deal, America's great experiment with social legislation during the 1930s.

These war experiences contributed in several ways to the welfare efforts that followed them. First, they provided a learning experience to governments in how to actually run an economy, direct a population and oversee its activities, as well as to social reformers in the way the social will could be directed towards a social purpose: the utopian dream of some nineteenth-century social reformers seemed to become a practical possibility after 1919 and 1945. Second, their scope and effect made post-war planning more ambitious than it might otherwise have been. Third, they provided a range of models by which social programmes could be initiated and carried out. (The most popular device, used by both sides during the Second World War, was corporatism, in which unions, businessmen and bureaucrats met to agree terms within a government's definition of a strategic purpose.) In Europe, post-war welfare schemes used such wartime administrative techniques, adapting them for different purposes: the habit of tripartite negotiations to determine wage levels which had been initiated during the war to forestall any tendency to work stoppage damaging to war effort, was widely adapted to the requisites of international competitiveness and economic growth following it. Hence, it is scarcely surprising that many historians of the period would detect a close association between the 'warfare' state and the welfare state.

The articulation of the new state

During the periods of its outward expansion, the direction and depth of the state's penetration into society was determined in large measure by the government's definitions of its needs. Early social reformers expressed dismay at the apparent ease with which governments subordinated early social welfare planning to war effort during the 1914–18 war. In Britain, the period from 1947 to 1964 saw steel nationalised and denationalised three times, as governments of different political complexions came into office. Economic growth, widely adopted after 1945 (and the political choice of governments), justified subsidies, the maintenance and management of whole industries and direct interference in interest and exchange rates.

Public safety became a prevalent concern, and measures against enemies of the state came into force in many democracies. In Britain, these originated in the 1904 counter-terrorist measures against Irish independence extremists, but they were extended to all enemies of the liberal state during the Cold War. On the continent, they had older pedigrees – the French revolutionary state began the fashion. But the political extremism witnessed on the continent during the 1930s and the terrorist campaigns of the 1970s led to their development. Public safety legislation tended to give wide discretionary powers to agents of the state in surveillance, arrest and expulsion, as well as in defining threats to the political order, all of which also tended to spread the legal net of the state.

The differing modalities of intervention

Differing political traditions tended to determine the methods and to some extent the depth and degree of social penetration. The British welfare state determined on a large public housing programme during the 1950s, to be carried out by centrally financed local authorities. In consequence, local authorities gained extensive rights to determine land usage as well as rents, which affected large areas of the economy. In the late 1970s, deeming these prerogatives too great, a Conservative government determined to curb them by allocating rights to purchase to citizen occupants, empowering local housing associations with the administrative duty to oversee such purchases (but setting purchase prices centrally). Health care, on the other hand, was initially more centralised, allowing government directly to regulate its price, besides controlling access to it.[8] In the United States, a more decentralised federal system required more indirect methods, employing special federal subsidies for nominated programmes and enticements to state governors to adopt them.

Most governments confronted the need for wage policies during the period of economic growth which followed the Second World War, if only to control inflation. Britain's long liberal tradition led it to generally abstain from direct involvement, and it discouraged centralised bargaining. Instead, it attempted to influence union demands by periodic warnings on the consequences of individual wage settlements. In other European countries, however, wages were determined in central sets of bargaining, with government representatives present in some cases, for much of the post-war period.[9]

There were various administrative beneficiaries to the enhanced power of the state. Initially, much of the execution of early social legislation lay with local government bodies who already held powers to improve local conditions and to help the poor. They used such powers to initiate policies of their own, to raise taxes and also to increase their own roles as administrators. As such, local authorities everywhere acquired enhanced political as well as administrative functions. But they were not the only beneficiaries. During both wars, liberal governments established boards of businessmen, unions and civil servants, which exercised power directly over enterprises under various sorts of emergency power acts. During the post-war period, many forms of quango appeared. These ranged from autonomous organisations like race relations bureaux and legal aid agencies to quasi-autonomous bodies. In Britain, the boards of nationalised industries, initially for gas, coal and electricity, were in theory responsible to government but had leeway in the practical management of their respective industries.

Parliaments, parties and interest groups

The putative political beneficiaries of the increase in the power of the state were the representative assemblies and parliaments, whose legal and supervisory rights grew. Thus, in a formal sense, the scope of parliamentary and representative powers increased enormously during the twentieth century. But this was an appearance only. Increasingly, organised social claimants, on behalf of various labour, capital and public interests, attached themselves to parliamentary representatives, checking their voting and demanding immediate accountability to the sectoral groups. At the same time, state administrators and bureaucrats, often working directly with sectoral organisations, eroded parliamentary prerogatives from above.

Enfranchisement had been completed among most liberal states by the 1920s, when women were generally granted the vote. What distinguished twentieth-century liberal political orders was the increasingly rapid development of popular political organisations, or 'interest groups', which sought to influence government directly. The first interest groups were the Grange in America, organised in the 1890s, and the European labour movements, who began to turn to interest articulation and the influence of legislation during the same decade.

In America, the decades of the 1920s and 1930s were particularly rich periods in the development of groups with permanent aims of influencing government, so much so that Charles Beard regarded the 'national interest' as a mere disguise of sectoral interests.[10] It was during this period that capital adopted more conscious political organisation, both by sector and through the establishment of 'political offices' within individual firms, sometimes at the behest of government. In the 1920s, Herbert Hoover, then US Secretary of Commerce, organised an impressive network of regional and international offices of the Commerce Bureau which liaised directly with regional industrialists, to monitor and report on the competitive pressures facing them from abroad. This, as much as anything, encouraged the establishment of political sections in large firms.[11] Increasingly, such groups would be aided by the development of lobby organisations which informed and lobbied on their behalf. During the post-war period, lobbying in the United States took on a highly organised form, with numerous registered 'political advice consultants' who offered their services to any group (and, indeed, government) who wished to hire them.

The main aggregators of these new interests were political parties, which became the major routes for feeding their claims into government, replacing cabinets in this function. (They also prioritised and excluded claims; this function became known as 'gatekeeping'.) Nineteenth-century parties had represented differences in political philosophy (as well as contingent coalitions of changing interests). Twentieth-century parties represented more permanent and more structured political and economic interests, and became identified with them, as Poggi has observed, 'more closely than liberal theory deemed decent'.[12] A large literature grew to classify parties, distinguishing, for example, between elite parties and mass parties, 'rational' parties and party democracies, ideological parties, catch-all parties and the party-in-office.[13]

Parties were, however, somewhat paradoxically, also 'private' associations whose internal organisation often eluded public control. They were run by party managers, and often without much say by the members; the latter were, on the contrary, disciplined to conform to party lines. These developments turned the open-ended parliamentary debates of the nineteenth-century liberal era into what often appeared routinised confrontations organised around ideological preference.

Parliaments everywhere retained rights – albeit varying – of legislative initiation, but as governments moved in and out of office with different policy agendas, the general pattern was for policies to be initiated from above: in 1990, the major source on European governing habits noted that, in Britain, 82 per cent of new legislation was initiated by government and 70 per cent in Germany.[14] Much of the new social legislation was, in addition, highly technical and specific, since it was intended to direct public officials to the accomplishment of specified tasks: this sort of legislation required specialist drafting. Parliaments increasingly found themselves in the role of mere sanctioners of legislation, and checkers of government abuse, rather than actual legislators. The constitution of France's Fifth Republic, established in 1958, went further, allowing French governments to declare organic laws, laws which had to be treated as whole packages, forcing the French Assembly to accept or reject the package in its entirety. Their distancing from legislation caused an immediate decline in parliamentary activity in France, where the power of the once all-powerful Assembly became limited to determining the political complexion of the prime minister and checking on government excess.

Where assemblies retained (or developed) rights of amendment, most notably in the United States and post-war Germany, specialist parliamentary committees developed which received legislation to consider, sometimes changing its intent. These became the main drafters of legislation, and indeed replaced full parliaments as the 'legislative power', as bills were scrutinised line by line; they also became the focus of bargaining and negotiations between government and parliaments. Here, parliamentarians acquired specialised knowledge with which to confront both interest groups and bureaucrats, and they became formidable opponents of executives, prime ministers and presidents. But such committees were also weighted according to party representation in the legislative body, and they were chaired according to party majorities. Both developments further empowered political parties and assured party interests in specific legislation, making the parties even more important donors of patronage and influence.

The growth of bureaucratic power

As government tasks grew and government became responsible for initiating, filling in and supervising legislation, so the administrative apparatus of the state also grew and became increasingly differentiated. The twentieth-century state became a vast segmented bureaucracy, personified by ministers perhaps, but which the citizen confronted as an often baffling array of offices.

Within these offices, bureaucrats often competed to expand their competences, and they became alert to the way different social programmes might expand or contract their roles. Bureaucracies also began to develop their own relationships with 'para-statals', the term for quasi-autonomous administrative bodies, and interest groups with close relations to government. The latter, in turn, deliberately encouraged close integration with the relevant bureaucracy, offering advice and even formative suggestions on the content of policy. Especially close relations developed in both Sweden and Britain between nationalised industries and the relevant ministry which oversaw their activities. The resultant power complexes came to be known as 'iron triangles'.

The growth of executive power

The task of co-ordinating these large bureaucratic apparatuses fell to the executive branch, which was increasingly pressed to undertake it. Co-ordination became important not least because the large state agencies often developed special interests of their own, sometimes to the point of impeding implementation of policies decided upon by presidents and cabinets. (The problems of implementation became a special branch of administrative theory.) Bureaucratic management took varying forms. Among Western governments, techniques ranged from special task forces, special cabinet committees on policy areas, and special co-ordinating offices.

The deliberative stage of legislation was also absorbed into the executive branch of government. Presidents and prime ministers not only proposed legislation: they also considered it, amended it, and sought public support for it.

In the process, they carried out extensive independent consultation with affected interests directly. These efforts targeted primarily the large organised professional sectors of society – lawyers, doctors, teachers and business groups – with the aim of ensuring a bill's eventual passage. They also sought to influence party managers, outside of their formal statuses in parliamentary assemblies. (The White House developed a special Congressional liaison office to anticipate Congressional reaction to policy proposals; it lobbied individual Congressmen for support, incorporating individual Congressmen's views into its policy packages, to ensure their votes.)

Increasingly, the executive branch of government was identified as holding the ring among political and social forces. Indeed, it became identified as 'the government'. The election of new representatives or of a new parliament was seen as important because it implied the election of a 'new' government, and the election of a new government implied a wide range of new policies. Within government, gaining the ear of the executive became essential to social, political and policy influence.

Executives not only co-ordinated, they represented. Increasingly presidents and prime ministers became identified as the only institutions capable of representing the nation as a whole.

Their representative functions, in turn, further enhanced their powers, since they could claim to be the only authorised representatives of the whole nation. But it also presented leaders with dilemmas between their roles as heads of parties, which represented sectoral interests, and their roles as leaders of states and nations, which implied operating above sectoral interests. Where party actually produced the leader, each new administration had to demonstrate that it was 'above party', while at the same time promising to implement a programme supported and endorsed by party.

The growing concern with civil rights

The growing compass of the state, not least in the realm of public safety, led to an increasing concern for traditional civil rights, which appeared to be endangered by the state's growing prerogatives. Civil rights movements appeared generally among the new political forces of liberal states to protect citizens' rights and to enhance them as against the powers of central authority, or, as in the United States, the state authorities with regard to the systematic exclusion of blacks.

In Europe, where liberal political and even social rights had been suspended by Nazi occupation during the Second World War, and where constitutional guarantees of rights were scarce, this impulse took on a constitutional and international form. In 1949, sixteen European countries agreed a European Statute of Human Rights and established a Court and an appeal system for citizens who could claim derogations of rights on the part of their own governments. The Statute included property rights, rights to presumption of innocence, and fair punishment. This produced in effect an incorporation of a bill of rights into the numerous European constitutional orders which had hitherto lacked one; and it made rights a concern of states vis-à-vis one another. (Although most European liberal orders had a constitutional court of sorts which acted as a watchdog on the constitution, and hence on government derogations of the constitution, few had bills of rights which applied to citizens directly.)

The practice of direct citizen appeal to the European Court pushed the legal orders of the signatory states closer together. A series of adjunct advisors to the European Court sifted a growing number of claims, as groups got used to the idea of a higher court of appeal for rights claims, and selected cases of general relevance for consideration by it. Particularly in social policy, such as women's and children's rights and employment law, the resultant judgements gradually led to policy change and legal adjustment in the separate political and legal systems of the European states, producing some harmonisation in these areas.

The new state and the new political theory

How the variety of group, industrial, party and bureaucratic influence was to be conceptualised, and how it affected the liberalism of the liberal state, occasioned the liveliest debate among political scientists in the pluralist orders after the Second World War. Some liberals believed that the centralised state as such was disappearing, to be replaced by a variety of plural forces operating at a variety of different administrative levels: local, national and international. This group tended to see in the modern developments an actual enhancement of liberalism. Others believed that the state was, on the contrary, growing, and that the state bureaucracy was absorbing society and subordinating it to state or sectoral interests. This group tended to be increasingly concerned that liberalism was failing.

On the optimistic side were ranged the majority of American political theorists. Americans in general tended to be fairly sanguine about the 'new state', picturing the vast array of political pressures as a form of political marketplace which, like American conceptions of the economic marketplace, would be eventually self-balancing, so long as it remained fairly open to entry. Indeed, in American political science of the post-war period, the 'state' conceived as a collective entity with a purpose of its own largely disappeared. It was treated as a mere outcome or 'resultant' of plural pressures, which served as the main focus of analysis, or as a varying administrative form, changing its shape as policy outcomes dictated.[15]

European political science initially adopted the interests-and-markets model and went looking for 'interests', but a stronger statist tradition eventually prevailed. The Europeans elaborated two rival models, both of which brought the state back in as an independent actor. The first was the corporatist model, reintroduced into the political debate by P.C. Schmutter.[16] Corporatism represented the state as a political regulator, potentially biased but capable of freeing itself and moderating the relations of classes and interests. In this view, the state was pictured as dealing with and between large sectoral organisations, essentially the large semi-professionalised trade unions and their employers, and setting the terms of their relationship (it was often called the 'triangular' model of the state). The model of incorporation, by contrast, pictured these interests as actually absorbed into the compass of the state, serving its interests.[17]

Which was the more appropriate picture depended to some extent on the state in question. In Austria, Sweden and Belgium, legal regulations demanded that major social and employment legislation be determined legally on a tripartite basis, setting some of the basic legislation within a corporatist form. But in both Britain and France the corporatist relationship was much more fluid. In Britain, it turned on shifting long-term relationships between different ministries and the groups they served, such as the education ministry and the teaching profession or the agriculture ministry and the farm lobby, and not on a balance between government, employers and labour. In France, it consisted of links between ministries and the large para-statal industrial organisations, which received government subsidies and took government direction, making France resemble the incorporation model rather than a true corporatist model. In Italy, however, the loose hold of the political parties on their appointees, as well as the state on public life, led to the characterisation of the political processes as a free-for-all, but one shielded from the true operations of a market by various forms of political exclusion, often exercised through corruption.

Administrative internationalism

The expansion of executive government internally was accompanied by a parallel development internationally. Each branch of government came to be shadowed in some of its functions by an international organisation of some sort which duplicated or supplemented its administrative tasks. Posts, health and the European railways timetable union were the earliest examples of this form of 'administrative internationalism'.[18]

These externalised bureaucracies developed along two different routes. In some cases, the more 'advanced' countries established a particular service, proceeded to international co-ordination where appropriate, and then urged the less advanced to follow suit (providing them with a model of organisation in the process). The International Postal Union was a characteristic example of this sort of development: the establishment of domestic postal services in Western Europe and the United States in the late eighteenth and early nineteenth century was followed by the creation of the International Postal Union during the 1850s, to which others then joined. In the same manner, regular central bank co-ordination began among the major powers during the 1930s, and central banks were urged upon the many states which did not have them after 1921. In both cases, the model was the 'advanced country' domestic service, international co-operation among the advanced, and then pressure from the international level for parallel development among others. In other instances, however, it was the perceived need for international co-ordination which spurred the development of the domestic service. Concern with the spread of plague began to appear in the 1850s, inspiring the need for international co-ordination to contain the problem. Domestic agencies were then established to carry out the co-ordination task. Here, it was the international requirement which came first, provoking the need for a domestic agency, to co-ordinate as well as to implement agreed international policies, which then acquired additional domestic functions.

The subjects of administration paralleled the progress of the liberal state. The first generation of international administrations, including posts and international health co-ordination, were a creation of nineteenth-century 'traditional' liberalism and conformed to its views of public purpose. They were seen as aids to the mobility of ideas and as solutions to some of the problems created by the enhanced mobility of labour. As the 'social question' began to concern governments, a second generation of 'new' liberal institutions began to be established, notably an international labour organisation, established in 1919, to equalise conditions of labour.[19]

The founding of the general international organisations, the League and later the United Nations, vastly encouraged the process of institutional development. By the mid-1920s, the League had expanded its concerns to include help for new states, encouraging a new international focus on development. This spurred the establishment of 'development' sections in foreign offices.[20] (But it should be noted that the League bureaucracy was itself modelled on the British civil service; i.e. from domestic to international.) The UN system incorporated these and added still more. Sixteen specialised agencies were established at the founding of the organisation in 1946, requiring the expansion of home services to liaise with them, including a new food and agriculture organisation, a maritime organisation, an intellectual property organisation and a telecommunications union. (During the subsequent decades, both permanent and temporary organisations developed very rapidly; in 1985, the United States was a member of over 200 intergovernmental agencies.)

Sometimes called 'functional' services, the early international unions were simple extensions of state bureaucracies. Their staffs were nominated by governments, and they were staffed by administrators from national administrations. They also were partial or single purpose orders, generally reflecting what their major participant governments saw as the predominant problems of the time in specific policy areas. The Food and Agriculture Organisation was established after the Second World War because of expected food and raw material shortages, and it was initially concerned with increasing food production as fast as possible. Its first task was to identify the obstacles to such an expansion and to propose solutions for overcoming them. As state demands changed, these were simply carried into the international bodies via executive action.

Since they were collectivised outreaches of domestic executive agencies, the autonomous powers of most of the unions were limited. They were primarily concerned with information-gathering and problem-spotting, and they administered agreed services in conjunction with the parallel home agencies. Their main purpose was to make suggestions to member governments on legislative and policy reform.

A few, however, were genuine regulatory agencies with substantial powers. The ITU, the telecommunications union, became the seat for negotiations on the allocation of airwaves after the Seond World War, and it also administered the agreed international broadcasting convention. IATA, the international air transport authority, was a private body of airlines, but it had effective powers over safety measures, determined airline routes and established operating procedures. The International Marine Consultative Organisation had considerable powers to set shipping schedules and to determine the rules of port entry and customs treatment.

The link between various home administrations and the growing plethora of international agencies came to be organised in different ways, depending on respective national administrative style. Some favoured the British approach of the 'lead ministry'. In this model, the respective allied home ministry was assigned representative responsibility to the parallel international agency, always with a watching brief and often with a negotiating brief. This suited the British style of executive government, where the cabinet served as the co-ordinating agency. In smaller counties, however, it was the foreign office which tended to carry the role of international policy co-ordination. After the Second World War, the smaller countries of Western Europe developed specialised sections within their foreign offices concerned with international organisation, which carried out representative and negotiating functions across a wide range of tasks, liaising with the relevant home ministry to establish the brief in a particular area.

Private non-governmental organisations, representing the general public, related to these outreaches of government in a variety of ways. In some, they had no presence at all. The FAO, for example, tended originally to think of itself as a purely technical body, dealing with a range of technical problems in food production, and it considered political representation from private bodies inappropriate to that task. Others allowed entry for consultation purposes, in the course of which government representatives could be lobbied (and where contacts with the relevant international secretariat could be developed). The UNCTAD conference on shipping became a semi-permanent fixture; and both public and private organisations concerned with shipping maintained close liaison with that section of the UNCTAD secretariat concerned with shipping. Others opened plenums to private organisations and even allowed them to address the various state representatives: Amnesty International was a regular appellate before the UN Committee on Human Rights.

Legal monism versus legal dualism

How these international creations were to be conceptualised in relation to the state's legal order divided political thinking quite sharply. Legal monists, associated with the German legal theorist Hans Kelsen, conceptualised them as emanations of a single legal order which was coming into place above the state. Kelsen maintained that, logically, the emerging international legal order must be seen as the higher order, while states were the subordinate parts. The precise legal process under which this was deemed to occur was one of transferred sovereignty: governments were considered to have handed powers up (or over) to such organisations, subordinating their own ministerial activity to them, gradually creating a legal order above the member-states. Legal dualists, by contrast, interpreted them quite differently. Georg Schwarzenberger, a leading international lawyer of German training but residing in Britain, tended to think in terms of two very different legal orders, the international and the national, with government providing the link between the two. In the dualist view, governments created two very different types of law, the one (domestic law) having a true legal nature, the other all the uncertainties of international or contract law, with no adjudicator above the states. In the dualist conception, the new bodies were simply parallel bodies to the state, with no necessary constitutional relation to all, unless the state created one. (Post-war France, Germany and Italy all made national law subordinate to international law. Dualists considered these autonomous decisions of the legal order in question, however, with no implication for the nature of international law generally.)

Administrative internationalism and state sovereignty

The implications of administrative internationalism for state sovereignty varied, depending on whether the focus was on legal sovereignty and formal decision-making or on 'political' sovereignty and the ability to control outcomes. The unions with no regulatory powers, which were the vast majority, had little effect on the ordinary workings of the expanded twentieth-century government; they were merely another expression of it. Being in effect extensions of respective national civil services, they involved no formal derogation of sovereignty. In political terms, however, their effects were significant. They promoted the internationalisation of issues; they also encouraged the more rapid development of joint policy-making. Moreover, they provided a setting for the development of shifting international coalitions on specific policy questions, which made governments more subject to concentrated political pressure than had formerly been the case. During the 1970s, the poorer countries forced the rich countries to consider closer control of their shipping companies, partly because of the existence of the United Nations Commission on Trade and Development, which allowed the poorer countries to co-ordinate their policies more closely. The foreign trade policies of the advanced states were also pushed towards more regard for the interests of less developed countries because of the sheer weight of their numbers in international trade fora. The regulatory bodies affected the exercise of governmental powers in more significant ways. The INMARSAT and IATA were each a form of legislative body which scheduled shipping and set airline prices respectively. Accordingly, their establishment had the effect of directly empowering the companies which participated in them. Where parliaments had direct powers of initiation, such powers could be 'got back', such as the United States Congress' great airline deregulation in the 1980s, but only with a good deal of effort. In effect, the internationalisation of both airlines and shipping shielded their activities from ordinary political control.

Internationalism and the enlarged state

What interests could be attributed to the new 'welfare' states? The most obvious was economic growth. So long as the state was determined to incorporate the mass of citizens into an active polity, it would need a steady increase in the gross domestic product, not only to provide it with resources but to provide its people with employment. Welfare budgets were never large enough to support mass unemployment. Nor could it be satisfied with national growth alone. The new state was the new industrial state; and it would seek to offset uneven rates of development at home with growth, and government expenditures in its markets abroad. States competed for growth when growth slowed, but they also looked to their major competitors to regear their economies as soon as possible, so that they could enjoy the benefits. The well-being of one was increasingly seen in terms of the well-being of (especially) industrial leaders, more generally. The new state would also value predictability; and it depended on majority consensus.

Its interests also lay with innovation while avoiding the costs of innovation. States watched one another and learned lessons from one another, while letting others make mistakes.

States gained more powers over more domestic matters of concern during the twentieth century. Hence, they also had more powers to agree international regulation of those matters. Nationalisation and internationalism were, in that sense, not contradictory. The concentration of power in the hands of executive agencies also allowed inter-state agreements to be reached more simply and with fewer impediments. Governments did not escape scrutiny, but it was often difficult for parliamentary representatives to know what executive agencies were doing, and much more so for ordinary citizens. The new state was, accordingly, freer to follow its interests.

The administrative unions facilitated policy transfer. They provided a web along which policy co-ordination could move easily. Since, moreover, international secretariats were linked to (and often derived from) home ministries, there was the possibility of bureaucratic co-ordination between the home ministry and its bureaucratic outreach. Thus, the development of the bureaucratic state encouraged the development of 'parallelism' in state policy choices.

Sovereignty was not much affected by the growth of the bureaucratic state, but power was moved around. The attachment of organised interests to the state's bureaucratic offices allowed for a direct feeding of 'interests' into the state apparatus. Equally, the habit of setting the terms of labour and production through regularised negotiations between the state and affected interests moved effective power out of parliaments and inter-party negotiation into 'side shows', shielded from constitutional checks and balances but with effective regulatory consequences for society. Power thus moved both up and down: upwards with regard to final decision-making, but downwards with regard to the range of interests decision-makers had to take into account. With regard to the traditional balance between executives and legislatures, this tended to enhance the power of political managers and executives. In respect to the traditional balance between the state and social interests, it tended to favour the large organised interests in society at large.

Notes

1 B. de Jouvenel, *Power, The Natural History of Its Growth* (New York and London: Hutchinson, 1948) especially Chapters xiii and xix.

2 Gianfranco Poggi, *The Development of the Modern State* (London: Hutchinson, 1978) pp. 114–16.

3 G. McLellan, D. Held and S. Hall review the efforts of Marxists to come to grips with the state in *The Idea of the Modern State* (Milton Keynes: Open University Press, 1984).

4 Ralph Miliband, *The State in Capitalist Society* (London: Weidenfeld and Nicolson, 1969) presented a variant of this approach.

5 P. Flora (ed.), *Growth to Limits: The West European Welfare State since World War II* 5 vols, (Berlin: W. de Grayter, 1986).

6 See e.g. K. Burk (ed.), *War and the State: The Transformation of British Government, 1914–1918* (London: Allen and Unwin, 1982).

7 A.S. Milward, *War, Economy and Society, 1939–45* (London: Allen Lane, 1977).

8 R. Brown, *The Management of Welfare* (Glasgow: Collins, 1975).

9 For the different modalities, see R. Scase (ed.), *The State in Western Europe* (London: Croom Helm, 1978).

10 The first study of the influence of groups on foreign policy; *The Idea of National Interest* (New York: Macmillan, 1934).

11 M. Fainsod and G. Lincoln, *Government and the American Economy* (New York: Macmillan, 1941).

12 Poggi, *The Development of the Modern State* (London: Hutchinson, 1978) p. 140.

13 Maurice Duverger, *Les Partis Politiques* (Paris: Colin, 1951), considered a classic, began the fashion for classification.

14 Y. Meny, *Government and Politics in Western Europe* (Oxford: Oxford University Press, 1990) p.165.

15 According to the American political scientist, A.F. Bentley, 'the balance of the group pressures *is* the existing state of society', *The Process of Government* (Evanston Ill.: Irwin, 1949) p. 258.

16 'Still the century of corporatism?', *Review of Politics*, 36 (1974), pp. 3–39.

17 A lively debate between advocates of the various corporatisms ensued, well represented in A. Cox and N. O'Sullivan (eds), *The Corporate State: Corporatism and the State Tradition in Western Europe* (Aldershot: Edward Elgar, 1988).

18 R. Jordan, *International Administration: Its Evolution and Contemporary Applications* (New York and London: Oxford University Press, 1971).

19 I. Claude, *Swords into Plowshares* (New York: Random House, 1964).

20 See e.g. D. Morgan, *The Official History of Colonial Development*, vol. 1 (London: HMSO, 1980).

9 The interests of the major powers

Analysing the political motives of governments fell largely to a new breed of international historian and to the new methods of 'technical' history. Technical history attempted to bring history closer to a true science. In the context of foreign policy, it demanded a close examination of the diplomatic record and discrimination in judging the status and veracity of other, more informal sources. Its major focus was cabinet or presidential records, as these were held to reveal the inner secrets of high policy decision-making and the actual, rather than claimed, intentions of governments. International history related intentions, in turn, to the broader movements of the time, to economic pressures, public opinion and ideological developments, to determine the degree of freedom decision-makers had actually enjoyed.

Policy motives, and the sources of constraint, mattered not only for outcomes but also in the context of the responsibilities which governments had to bear for the twentieth-century upheavals: the great wars of the age, the overthrowing of democracy, and the division of Europe. In each case, policy played a predominant part, and the reasons for those policies, whether driven or intended, and driven by what, became a matter of moral as well as political import. Whether Britain's appeasement policy reflected a loss of nerve, was an inevitable consequence of a lack of power or the result of some hidden sympathy with Germany, judgement mattered in the context of the growing belief that war, with all its consequences, might have been avoided had Britain taken a different stand. Whether Germany had intended total war or had, rather, miscalculated, reflected on considerations of war-guilt as well as on the inner nature of fascism. Whether the United States was ideologically inclined or economically determined mattered in the context of the belief that the Cold War, with all its consequences, might have been avoided had both sides communicated their intentions more clearly. The historian was expected to throw light on these questions, as charges of blame and responsibility were widely canvassed.

The diplomatic sources

How much could be known? The release of the German archives at the end of the Second World War made knowledge of that country's policy particularly detailed, accessible and immediate. Governments also wanted their own policies to be favourably judged by the growing public audience. Accordingly, both Britain and the United States issued large collections of documents at the end of the Second World War containing position papers, records of discussions and diplomatic correspondence between their ambassadors and the home government. For detail and nuance, however, the historian had to wait on the thirty-year rule and, in the case of France, the fifty-year rule. Assessments of French foreign policy for the inter-war period were rendered particularly difficult because of the destruction of the records of the inter-war cabinet meetings, undertaken as the Germans were marching upon Paris. As a consequence, historians of French inter-war policy tended to use the German records as they applied to France, giving the accounts of French motives a somewhat 'German-ist' flavour. As for the Soviet archives, these were closed in the 1930s with the advent of Stalin to power, after which there was virtually no history in the sense implied by the criteria of technical history. In the Soviet case, speculation and debate proceeded without clear issue. In the case of the West, speculation could be confirmed at thirty- (or fifty-) year intervals. As important papers were released, a growing army of diplomatic researchers settled a number of contentious questions. But of the Soviet Union, only the end of the Soviet regime promised more detailed knowledge, and some scholars doubted that there could be any proper history in the scientific sense of the term.

As to what such histories revealed, it was generally conceded that while the major powers had a multiplicity of interests, it was their relations with one another which tended to determine their major policy lines and to set the terms of their relations with other, smaller powers. So, too, must we understand the political complexions of the large number of international institutions that were created, particularly after 1945. The institutions that came to surround Europe, Africa and Asia took shape within a context of major power conflicts, and their operating principles were determined by calculations of advantage vis-à-vis one another. When France proposed an international authority for the Ruhr in 1947, it was to forestall a reascendant German power. When the United States rejected a regional organisation of a revised League of Nations in 1918, it was to forestall a further securing of the British Empire.

The diplomatic record also revealed the union of high politics and strategic advantage with considerations of commercial and economic advantage. Political and economic considerations were frequently blended, not only in respect to the way economic arrangements might enhance state power or outflank rivals, but also because of the growing understanding that economic systems demanded appropriate political frameworks.

The pattern of Great Power struggle

What did these struggles concern? If we concentrate on the large pattern and set aside much of the detail, we may discern six great movements during the century. The first was Britain's efforts to hold on to its global imperium in the context of relative decline. The second movement, part cause and part consequence of the first, was the rise of Germany to challenge Britain's global mastery. The third was the emergence of the United States to challenge the aspirant German hegemony, but equally to break Britain's imperial hold. The fourth movement was France's efforts to avoid falling under either ascendant hegemony. The fifth movement was the rise of the Soviet Union to fill the vacuum left by Germany in Europe after the second German war and to challenge America's global liberalism. The sixth was the absorption of first Asia, then Africa and the rest of the world into these struggles. Japan was the first non-European power to be recognised as a European equal: having defeated Russia in war in 1904, it was allowed a seat at the Paris Peace Conference. But it rode into Great Power councils on the back of the divisions among them. It was Britain's desire for a counter against Russia in the Far East which produced the first alliance of equals between Japan and a Western power. During the inter-war period, it was the German challenge to Britain which was crucial in firing Japanese ambitions for a larger role. Without it, Japan may not have tried, and would probably not have succeeded, in challenging Britain and France in Asia before and during the Second World War.

At the centre of these political struggles was the direction and extent of German power. The political movements in the relations of states in the twentieth century revolved around efforts to contain or direct German power, to blunt it or divide it; and the condition of Germany, whether rising, ascendant or fallen, whether unified or divided, came to determine some of the major arrangements within which the other powers conducted the main lines of their policies. What the twentieth century also showed was that no power could master Germany alone, no power could secure the peace autonomously, and all needed the others in reliable stances, in alliances or other secure understandings, in order to gain their own objectives.

The protection of the imperium

If the first great movement was the defence of that world-wide system of formal and informal influence that the British Empire had by 1900 become, it was being pressed at many points. Already at the end of the nineteenth century, Britain's imperial hold in Egypt and the Sudan was being challenged by France, by Russia in Persia, and by American power in the Caribbean. In 1904, moreover, Teddy Roosevelt declared the Roosevelt Corollary, a pledge that he would not only force Latin American states to honour their international obligations, but would keep British arms out of all Western waters. Germany was also developing a threatening stance. In 1900, the Reichstag had voted the second navy law in three years, pledging a fleet to match Britain's, challenging Britain's control of the European exits and promising Germany's acquisition of a global strategic mobility. Germany had also begun to challenge the existing Europe balance, not only by declaring an interest in the tottering Ottoman Empire but also by enticing Russia into an alliance to forestall a Franco-Russian bloc.

British decision-makers had been slow to comprehend the consequences of Germany's rise to a continental hegemony and the need for a new security architecture in Europe after 1870. Britain's continental policy remained largely determined by Metternichian considerations, even after Metternich's system had dissolved. Accordingly, Britain continued to view France as the most likely disturber of the status quo. (From London, the formation of the new German state had been regarded with relative equanimity, as merely providing a more secure European power than a bastioned Austria to counter French continental ambitions.) Even at the end of the century, Britain's European concerns were not so much with a new continental hegemon, but were focused on the Ottoman Empire, fast dissolving, and on Russian and French ambitions with regard to the Porte, particularly as they bore on influence and position in the Middle East.

With the Reichstag bill, however, the focus of concern shifted abruptly to the European status quo. The bill raised the prospect that the new Germany could use internal industrial and political might as a springboard to overturn, not to sustain, a European balance, threatening Britain in the Mediterranean and breaking its communications with India. Thus it was that, after nearly a century of relative uninvolvement, Britain returned to a concern with the question of how to reconstruct a European balance.[1]

In the light of that concern, the British calculus of advantage concerning its potential allies shifted. France now became the counter-weight against a potential German threat to the European balance. Accordingly, France's alliance with Russia, formerly deplored in Whitehall, began to be considered of value. As German action was also weakening and dividing that alliance, Britain began to bolster France directly after 1906, laying the foundations for their alliance during the First World War. (France reciprocated, fearing from 1904 that Russia was too weak a potential ally to forestall German ambitions.)

It was Britain's inability to secure with France alone the defeat of Germany on the field of battle which led Britain to back permanent arbitration and collective security, both of which were initiated in 1919 as part of the Versailles settlement. Of greater interest, however, were the ideas of a permanent council of Great Powers within the League, and the commitment of the United States to guarantee the Versailles agreement. Britain conceived the League's Council as a continuation of the wartime association of Britain, France and America in the regulation of the affairs of Europe, both to balance Germany and to reassure an increasingly uneasy France.[2] An American guarantee of the peace arrangements, first proposed at Versailles, was a second line of support. It was intended as a permanent snare, involving the United States in the affairs of Europe on a permanent basis. But the new organisation was still seen by Britain primarily in terms of securing the European balance, not as impinging on imperial or global matters. It only reluctantly conceded that those colonial questions arising from Germany's defeat should be made subject to the League, in the form of mandates; and it resisted any efforts by the League to make the mandates or any of her other colonies subject to League regulation or interference, a stance Britain also maintained through most of the period of the United Nations.

Thus, Britain aimed to free herself to manage her colonies autonomously outside of Europe while being assured of a permanent European condominium, in which she would also, of course, play a vital part.

The failure of the US Senate to ratify the Versailles Treaty put paid to these hopes and made Britain more dependent on the security concerns of France and more willing to conciliate them, at least during the early 1920s.[3] It also made Britain more hesitant about the League, at least as a political instrument to secure the peace of Europe, and more concerned to conciliate Germany.[4] Had Germany been seeking a *modus vivendi*, the two together might have determined some sort of loose spheres-of-influence policy over Europe. Britain would not have objected to a co-operative alliance with Germany within which the two would determine the political framework of Europe: this is what Chamberlain had hoped to gain from appeasement. But the idea of dividing the world between the sea power and the land power and organising it into two great imperia, an idea which attracted some on the far right of the Conservative Party after the Nazi accession to power, was quite another matter. Certainly such a policy never gained serious credence with the Conservative leadership, not even with Chamberlain. British appeasement was little more than a stand-off, at most an effort to see if Germany could be turned into a European partner. In the event, the tussle over Poland put paid to such hopes. When Germany invaded Poland, all interest in a *modus vivendi* dissolved.

German intentions during the inter-war period

Initially after the First World War, Germany was concerned to 'revise the treaties'. This meant breaking the Versailles territorial settlement, regaining lost territories and re-establishing itself as a Great Power. In 1925, it agreed to the Locarno Treaty, largely in return for France's agreement to limit the military occupation of the Rhineland. (The Locarno Treaty guaranteed Germany's borders to the west and promised an economic normalisation, which France earnestly required.[5]) But it refused to abandon any claims to the lost territories in the east. It also delayed making reparations and refused to deliver the promised coal or monies to France, turning instead to develop the Silesian coalfields to re-establish its commercial and economic strength.[6] By the late 1920s, it had begun a 'secret' rearmament, raising small local militias. By the time of its military reoccupation of the Rhineland in 1936, and with the national rearmament programme openly declared in 1935, that programme of re-establishing national strength was virtually completed.

The Anschluss with Austria and the seizure of the Sudetenland from Czechoslovakia signalled the onset of a new phase, in which Germany aimed to establish itself as the hegemonial power on the continent and to force the capitulation of France and Britain to its rights to a hegemonial position. Its alliance with the Soviet Union via the Ribbentrop–Molotov pact was designed to pacify the Soviet Union and remove it from the European equation.

In economic policy, it moved from the internationalisation implicit in receiving the Dawes and other loans to autarky; and then, from 1937, to building a form of total war economy. The countries of Central Europe were increasingly integrated into the German economy on terms which indicated that German policy aimed at a form of widened 'bastion' economy.[7]

Whether total war was ever intended, however, is debatable. On the side of total war, Richard Overy, one of the new 'technical' historians, maintained that Goering's economic policies, instituted in 1937, were intended to enclose Europe within a rational economic structure which would provide Germany with means to carry out a total war, and which, in his view, gave it the distinct promise of winning such a war.[8] Others, however, followed the 'Milward thesis', after the British economic historian Alan Milward, who argued that Germany's economy was not so organised, nor the sacrifices undertaken so consistent, as to make the 'total war' thesis credible.[9] That Germany attacked Poland before any 'European system' sufficient to the fighting of a total war was achieved gives support to the Milward thesis. By 1938, Hitler seems to have chosen to break British power, and British power in Europe, essentially through humiliation and capitulation, an integral part of which would be a short military campaign to subdue France. It did not appear that Germany wished for a long European war.

If Germany did not intend total war, what of Hitler's long-term ambitions? Did he aim eventually at a global imperium (total war also implied global war), or would Germany have been satisfied with the role of a continental hegemon? In the event, Hitler declined to declare himself, and his actions remain subject to various judgements. On the side of 'continentalism', there is the evidence of the Russian campaign: after the failure to bring Britain to the negotiating table following the 1940 summer air battles, Hitler turned the German armies against the Soviet Union in a surprise attack which betrayed their alliance. This seemed a bid to secure a continental imperium since, had he sought a global role, such an attack would have been inadvisable. The problem is that he seems to have initiated the Russian campaign rather *faut de mieux* than from any serious long-term strategic plan. The subsequent German feelers that were put out for a compromise with Britain, and which entailed a promise of peace against the Empire, also implied a limitation of Germany's ambitions. But they, too, were ambiguous. They were clearly intended to entice Britain to sue for peace, but it is not clear that they were anything other than opportunistic efforts on the part of the Nazi Reich to extract itself from the invidious military position of the two-front war, and so they were interpreted by the British government.[10]

To apply the standard questions of diplomatics to the Nazi Reich, may, however, be inappropriate, given the internal nature of the Nazi regime. The true nature of German interests under Nazism lay in continually revitalising the Reich through the commitment to strike, and there was no way of predicting which direction such strikes might take.

The sources of French internationalism

France had sought, through Versailles, to achieve two central objectives: to secure a permanent weakening of Germany, and to build up its own economic power. For France by 1919, German power meant economic power and had to be met in those terms. This meant, among other things, eventually harsh reparations, in part to weaken Germany but even more to provide funds for the modernisation of the French economy. Even more than Britain, however, it had also counted on the guarantee status which was to be attached to the Versailles Treaty, and eventually to the League framework, to provide for France's military security. Despite later appearances to the contrary, France of all the Allied powers placed the most hopes in a guaranteed League as a security system and as the political framework for its economic development.[11] Indeed, France had compromised some of its initial demands against Germany to secure such a guarantee; and one of the sources of its bitterness against the United States during the 1920s was its failure to honour an understanding for which France had made sacrifices.

By 1921, when France had had to move alone to forcibly extract reparations from Germany, it had abandoned hope in the League as then constructed. It did not, however, abandon hope in internationalism as such. Through the remainder of the 1920s, it tried to reintroduce a guarantee to the shaky Versailles system under a variety of guises, including pulling America into the continent under a disguised guarantee system. (This was the origin of the famous Kellogg–Briand pact, in which signatories abandoned war as an instrument of policy.[12]) When these efforts failed, it began toying with the idea of a Pan European Union for Europe, to secure Germany within a tighter legal framework than that offered by the League. (The proposed Pan European Union also had a second use: to protect Europe from America's emerging economic power, which was then also beginning to be felt.[13]) It also proposed a permanent international army, to be attached to the League, to provide for a permanent military force able to be called up in defence of the Versailles provisions should Germany attempt an autonomous revision.

The failure of all of these efforts left it reliant on its own devices and on more traditional balance-of-power strategies. Accordingly, by the late 1920s it had begun to woo Italy in earnest with the promise of favours, to tempt it away from Germany, and to build the Maginot Line to defend its territory. (The Maginot Line was intended as a deterrent; in the event, it failed.) The only other hope, and it was a desperate one, was to tighten its economic and political alliances with the countries of Eastern Europe. In consequence of the latter, the 1930s saw an intense race for the favours of Eastern Europe between Germany and France, one of which, however – France – had increasingly little to offer. (Partly in consequence, the centre-right government which took power in France in early 1930 tried to entice Germany into a number of joint economic efforts in Eastern Europe to evade a competition which it would surely lose.[14]) In the end, its only real provision for security was the Maginot Line.

The growth of neutralism in small power Europe

So far, little has been said of the small powers of Europe. Of those in Europe's north-west triangle, both Belgium and Holland were increasingly caught in the pincer movement which they feared would take Germany across their lands into the battlefields of France once again, and they sought desperately to ameliorate Franco-German antagonisms, to strengthen neutrality and to solidify Britain's guarantees. In Scandinavia, the movement accelerated to non-involvement and to 'Scandinavianism', the development of a neutralist, social democratic, anti-colonialist bloc in Northern Europe.[15] Neutralism did not, however, equate with small-poweredness. In Central Europe, Poland played dangerous games, trying to provoke first the Soviet Union against Germany and then Germany against the Soviet Union.

The United States and global economism

In refusing to ratify the Versailles agreement, the United States Congress had rejected any permanent involvement in the political tangles of Europe. It was also evading any legal obligation to act in respect of the League's Covenant (although the Covenant of the League, in fact, provided few such obligations). Both revealed a lack of concern with the European balance of power on the part of American policy-makers, a desire to avoid European political and military entanglements and a wish to preserve autonomy of action.

More central to United States foreign strategic policy was the gradual rejection of an imperialist role, determined by Congress in a series of debates during the 1920s and early 1930s. As a result, the United States formally committed itself to eventually giving up the Philippines and to acquiring the novel status of a non-colonial Great Power. Roosevelt abandoned the 'Big Stick' with regard to Latin America, declaring in his inaugural address on 4 March 1933 the policy of the 'good neighbor'. By 1935, America had turned definitively from the imperial road, as that was understood in the context of the European empires. Already suspicious in 1919 that the mandatory system of the League allowed for a joint Anglo-French condominium to protect imperial gains, the United States government became increasingly insistent through the 1930s that the empires of others had also to be dissolved.

The abandonment of a direct imperial role implied, however, a more vigorous foreign economic policy. In Latin America, the American Export-Import Bank became an important device for securing Latin American economic openness and 'indirect hegemony'.[16] Growing as an economic power, the United States had already demonstrated hostility to the private economic arrangements that European countries were proposing in order to evade the economic restrictions bequeathed by the First World War, including the cartel movements of the 1920s. But the abandonment of political imperialism made it more determined to establish global economic liberalism, particularly as against the economic protectorates set up in the 1930s around imperial zones to protect against depression.[17] It also opposed the tendency towards state economic management in the European and other economies which accompanied such developments.

The eventual choice of Britain as an ally, and its entry into war on Britain's side, was not the natural alliance of two liberal powers. The US government was antithetical to British aims of retaining its colonies and to the construction of an imperial economic retreat. There was also a haunting fear in the United States, which grew during the late 1930s, that British appeasement was aiming at achieving a spheres-of-influence pact with Germany, and that Britain and Germany would divide up the world between two great empires, while conceding Japan a sphere in the Pacific.[18] The fact is that the US could scarcely have wrested concessions from Nazi Germany, and Roosevelt did think he could do so from Britain, as part of the price for preserving the British Empire from falling under Nazi domination prior to its conversion into a liberal political and economic order.

The device for wresting concessions from Britain was the 'Four Freedoms' enshrined in the Atlantic Charter of 12 August 1941, the implicit conditions for America's entry into the second German war. Often presented as a vague manifesto of Anglo-Saxon idealism, the Atlantic Charter was no such thing. On the contrary, the Freedoms were intended as an anti-imperial device and were aimed directly at British imperial ambitions, to push Britain to commit to the principles that all peoples must be able to freely choose their own governments and that all states should be committed to economic co-operation on equal terms. It was the first volley in the United States' efforts to secure an open political, financial and trading order following the war. The Atlantic Charter encapsulated American, not British, war aims, and these were directed as much against Britain imperialism and closed trading orders as against Nazi aggrandisement.

It was the attack by Japan on Pearl Harbor at the end of 1941 which finally brought the United States into the war, although the German declaration of unrestricted submarine warfare would probably have done so in any event.

United States' war aims

During its course, the United States was caught between the contrary pulls of the Pacific front and the European front. There was strong pressure, particularly from the navy, to regard Japan as America's first enemy and to concentrate its resources on the Pacific front. Roosevelt, however, strenuously resisted these demands, arguing (quite correctly, in the event) that Germany was the centre of gravity of the Axis war effort. He also devoted much time, energy and resources to maintaining joint Allied co-operation, which Roosevelt viewed as the *sine qua non* for Germany's defeat, going so far as to endorse the opening of an Italian front, to pacify Stalin, and providing military material for the British efforts against Rommel in the Western Desert, despite continuous criticism from within the country and official doubts that either would directly contribute to a German defeat.[19]

Following the early formulation of its war aims, a good deal of America's wartime diplomacy was directed to accomplishing them. Nearly as much time was given during the meetings of the inter-Allied war councils to the United States' political and economic agenda for the post-war period as to strategic planning, and considerably less time to concrete plans on how the immediate enemies would be treated after their defeat. The United States directed the meetings of the Big Three to two aims, differentially appropriate to its two allies. With regard to Britain, it aimed to bargain a set of rules to regulate foreign economic policies following the war, to which states would have to commit themselves if they wished to gain American diplomatic and military support; and with regard to the Soviet Union to the maintenance of the alliance of the Big Three into the post-war period.

US plans centred first on the Bretton Woods agreements, the set of economic arrangements which would commit states to free trade and open monetary exchanges, for which negotiations with Britain began in December of 1941. These were not merely economic agreements, but integral to its political strategy of preventing the recreation of the closed economic zones, which had been the pattern in the mid- to late 1930s and which America saw as the source of much of the tensions and hostilities which had led to the war. In the course of those negotiations, United States representatives resisted anything which smacked of imperial preservation or guided economism.[20]

The second American aim, though it grew more slowly, was a replacement organisation to the League. Roosevelt had initially been hostile to any revival of the League, seeing it as a body with no power and no teeth. His first ideas recalled the British and French proposals of 1919 (which the United States had then rejected) of the permanent alliance. Here, three or four major power 'policemen' would mobilise power against any future miscreants. By 1942, however, his advisors had convinced him that the smaller powers of Europe and Latin America would never agree to a Great Power condominium without a form of League body attached to it. Thus, the double structure of the United Nations gradually took shape in American planning, a Security Council semi-detached from a General Assembly. Of the two, it was the Security Council on which America's first committed internationalist government placed its main hopes. Through the Security Council, the Allies would be harnessed together to provide a permanent overseeing of the international situation, preside over decolonisation and sort out the quarrels of the world.

Reconstruction of their political and social orders along Western liberal lines was to be the eventual policy imposed upon the immediately hostile powers, to produce an internal as well as external bastion against fascism. For the United States more than any other state, internal reconstruction became the key to international peace. Liberal, pluralist democratic orders in Germany, Italy and Japan (it was less concerned with democratic governments in the smaller states of Eastern Europe), together with the construction of a global liberal economic order and an agreed global security system within which to place the recon-structed states, would secure their pacificity. In Germany's case, this would involve creating a decentralised federal system. In Japan's case, it would involve a new constitutional system in which the Emperor would serve as a form of constitutional monarch, as well as demilitarisation.

But this policy took a while to emerge. America's first ideas for Germany involved its dismemberment into a number of small states and a permanent economic weakening.

Three-power diplomacy over Germany

The origins of the Morgenthau Plan, named after the American Secretary of the Treasury who formulated it, need not concern us here, except to point out the degree to which it represented the view that Prussianism and Nazism were co-extensive phenomena, and that the one would have to be totally eradicated in order to deal with the other. The plan involved not only the dismemberment of modern Germany into its pre-1870 statelets, but a determined de-industrialisation. (Morgenthau proposed that Germany should become a largely pastoral area of small states.)[21]

Having initially agreed to the idea, both Britain and the Soviet Union began to object as soon as Germany's defeat became imminent. At Yalta, in June of 1944, Churchill pointed to the implications for the European economies of an 'economic corpse' in the middle of Europe. It was also clear to British planners that the defeat of Germany would lead to an increase in the power of the Soviet Union in Europe, with the result that Britain became increasingly concerned during 1944 to limit its extent. (Hence, Churchill's attempts to save Poland as the war came to a close; it was also that intent which lay behind the 'spheres of influence' agreement with Stalin which eventually secured Greece.) There was also the problem that any division of Germany into small states, besides creating a power vacuum in Europe, would create a set of competitor statelets capable of playing off the Great Powers against one another. The Soviet Union appeared to concur on the question of creating new sources of division among the Allies. When they met at Potsdam in 1945 to make the final arrangements for Germany, all agreed to abandon division. Accordingly, an entirely new set of institutional arrangements had to be negotiated.

At Potsdam, the three powers established separate zones of occupation to avoid tangling with one another during the period of occupation, and agreed on the eventual establishment of a common German administration which they would jointly oversee. They also agreed on a joint programme of denazification and political education: Nazi party members would be extirpated from high office and removed from all positions in the civil service, including the educational service. Denazification would be supported by war crimes tribunals: the Allies declared that they would prosecute for crimes against humanity; and they named the initiating of aggressive war also as a crime, criminalising those who had been directly responsible for carrying out war planning and the murder of civilians.[22] The first international criminal tribunals met during 1946.

Britain's aims in Germany were shaped in the context of its increasingly dire financial position – it was 'diplomacy on a shoe-string'.[23] It had to retool its industry for export and to underpin the exchequer. At the same time, it was facing severe liquidity shortages. British debts were large and cross-cutting, and there was no way they could be cleared unless exports resumed. (Immediate post-war British diplomacy centred largely on efforts to gain a large American loan for financing reconstruction and supporting the pound.) It was also facing a variety of difficulties in the re-establishment of its imperial possessions: there was an emerging civil war in Malaya and insurgency in Palestine. It had fought hard to gain the industrial zone in Germany, because of the role that the Ruhr had played in Franco-German hostilities at the end of the First World War, but in the event it discovered that it had little use for it in the context of uncondi-tional surrender. On the contrary, the zone came to be a drain on British resources, since it did not produce sufficient food to feed its inhabitants, and the Germans there had to be fed largely at the expense of the British tax-payer. Increasingly from early 1946, Britain began to press the United States for a fusion of their two zones, to enable cross-trade to begin and to relieve it of the large drain on its resources in supporting the zone.

Soviet policy was initially directed to creating an all-German administration receptive to Soviet influence. Like the United States, it adopted an 'internal' view of security; and 'democratisation' was a genuine war aim, although in its case democratisation meant the emplacement of political parties friendly to the Soviet Union. In the event, it began its occupation of Germany by calling for the formation of German political parties, and then pressed for a fusion of the smaller German Communist and larger German Socialist Party into a common-front organisation. (Its strategic interests also dictated a buffer zone to its west, and it was laying the foundation for such a zone, essentially by building reliable political parties and putting them in power in united front governments in Central Europe behind the line of its troops. But it does not seem to have aimed at total control: up to the end of 1947, there was travel to and fro, and dissident parties were allowed voice.) Moreover, it also had a severe economic deficit and had suffered massive destruction. The Allies had agreed that Germany would pay reparations, and in respect of this the Soviet Union had begun dismantling plant in its zone of occupation; but no reparations bill was set, and the Soviet Union pressed its allies to set a high reparations bill.

Soviet aims were reflected, initially, in a generally co-operative diplomacy. With regard to Germany, the Soviet Union anticipated its allies in declaring that it had no enmity towards the German people. It raised no serious objections to the Bretton Woods scheme, nor initially even to Marshall Aid, and it welcomed ideas concerning a post-war security structure which would institutionalise wartime collaboration.

The problem lay in its efforts to achieve a socialist Germany, via a fusion of the German Socialist and German Communist Parties. The German socialists resolutely refused to condone a fusion between themselves and the German Communist Party, at least not without a popular mandate via a referendum, and the Soviet Union had no power other than in its own zone to oversee such a referendum which, in the event, it refused to allow. When such a referendum was held across the other zones, moreover, the proposal was defeated.[24]

In the changed circumstances, the Soviet Union refused to consider any immediate zonal unification, refused any immediate dropping of the zonal boundaries and began to insist that elections should not determine any future German administration; rather, it should be appointed by agreement among the occupying powers. It also proposed a relatively strong German administration without too much interference by the other Great Powers. Equally, however, it still wanted a strong lien against the defeated state in the form of a high reparations bill.

Neither Britain nor the United States were prepared to accept this package, presented to them at the Moscow conference in March of 1947, where they met to sort out their differences. They argued that the new German administration should be either appointed and weak, or elected and stronger. They also insisted that reparations had to be postponed until the German economy was built up (so that a realistic assessment could be set). But they also tried to comprise Soviet demands.

Marshall Aid and its consequences

It was the German dilemma which lay behind Marshall Aid. The United States proposed Marshall Aid, which was credit to aid reconstruction, in the context of circumventing immediate Soviet demands for reparations.[25] Marshall Aid was intended, first, to raise the level of European economic activity, in which the Soviet Union could participate, then to restore German economic life which would, finally, allow for the determination of reparations. The proposal was also linked to America's aims at economic opening, in Europe at least. It was intended to force the pace of economic re-opening among the Western European states, still disastrously slow after the end of the war. (By 1947, virtually no progress had been achieved in establishing regular trade and payments; countries were still controlling trade and directing the use of resources.) The conditions of Marshall Aid will probably long provoke dispute, as they became the break-point in the relations among the Allies, but what was intended by them was not mysterious. They were intended to force the Europeans to concede to economic liberalism, by making receipt of aid conditional upon establishing monetary exchange and freeing trade. This was proposed to the Soviet Union, in turn, as a reason for suspending its reparations demands, until a level of economic activity had been restored

The Soviet Union was tempted by the offer, but ended by rejecting it. It feared the diplomatic advantages the United States would gain in making credits available to countries in its erstwhile zone of influence. There was also the requirement for joint accounting and planning. Britain and France had seized the offer to set up a planning agency in Paris in June of 1947; and the OEEC, the planning agency which would disperse Marshall Aid to the agreed recipients, receive countries' requests and vet them, was in the course of being established. (The US demanded also that country plans should be co-ordinated, which in the event, however, never occurred, since its two allies wanted to avoid being forced into opening their exchanges just yet.) But even the rendering of country plans required that the Soviet Union should account for what was happening in Eastern Europe, and would have put the countries of Eastern Europe in the position of having other sources of political support available to them. The Soviet Union did not want either. (The problem the Soviet Union faced was that, in much of Central and Southern Europe, communist and even socialist parties were weak, and it could not count on automatic alliances with them, whereas paradoxically in Western Europe they were more firmly established and the war had made them stronger still.)

When the Soviet Union expressed its antipathy to the plan, Britain and the United States moved ahead with the reconstruction of a transitional German state, planned to include the three western zones in Germany. By 1948, Britain and the United States had determined on a federal constitution, with limited and divided powers, proportional representation and trade unions disciplined to market conditions, together with the freedom of religious observance and a free media. For much of 1948, they pressured France to come into the scheme with them.[26]

France, the odd man out

France's aims for Germany remained centred on dismemberment, long after it had been abandoned by the other powers. Accordingly, it refused to accept the results of the Potsdam meeting, where the united Germany policy had been agreed. It continued, in the event unsuccessfully, to woo the Soviet Union back to support for such a policy; and it semi-integrated its German zone into the French economic space, reconstructing it as a form of organic statelet. It also detached the Saarland from Germany, directly incorporating it into French territorial space. Accordingly, its conditions for reversing its policy and agreeing zonal incorporation were extensive. It demanded a permanent guarantee of limited German sovereignty, no army and a control over German war production. France supplemented these demands with an insistence on an international authority for the Ruhr, to oversee the shipping and production of coal and to remove it from the control of the new German authorities.[27] A Ruhr authority was established, largely to win French compliance with a common German authority and the recreation of a united German economy.

The United States did not like the scheme, however, and the new Federal Republic chafed under it bitterly. Within months of its initial establishment, the United States agreed with the German authorities that the scheme would be temporary and that Germany would eventually regain the control of its own coal resources.

Faced with an emerging US–German entente, French policy abruptly changed tack. In one of the more imaginative moves of French policy, in 1950, when the Ruhr authority had been in operation barely a year, the French government proposed the 'domestication' of the Ruhr's international controls. It proposed that an autonomous administration of a non-state technocratic sort, a functional body, be established to oversee the coal and steel production of all the European states joining the scheme. The coal–steel pool, or European Coal and Steel Community, would establish and maintain an open market in production and sales, operating within rules previously agreed by the state members, and it would be overseen by a Council of member-states.

The coal–steel pool looked both backwards and forwards. As a solution to one aspect of 'the German problem', it was modelled on the Allied control councils, developed during both the wars to co-ordinate the Allied war effort. Thus, it grew out of great nationalist wars of the twentieth century. At the same time, it created the second true international regulative authority in peacetime (the Security Council was the first). Finally, it began the process of putting in place a second, European, tier of international organisation.

Great Power antagonisms and institutional growth

The first generation of international political institutions emerged as integral parts of the peace-making that followed the great wars, and they reflected the lessons of those wars. These included the difficulties of defeating Germany, the strategic necessity of maintaining allied cohesion, and the necessity of security guarantees. The League was understood by the Great Powers primarily in terms of a guarantee system which would secure the borders arrived at during the Versailles peace arrangements and contain Germany; the United Nations was understood as the continuation of the Great Coalition necessary to defeat Germany, and it was intended primarily as a diplomatic mechanism for keeping it subdued.

The diplomacy for the ending of the Second World War witnessed a particularly intense period of institutional innovation. Not only were new institutions created, but they demonstrated a greater imaginativeness in range and architecture than anything previously witnessed. The League had been a relatively simple structure, based on the idea of an *assemblée générale*. The new United Nations displayed a complex division of power as well as a new and wide-ranging division of function. The idea of internationalising a contested area of Great Power control, in the form of an international authority for the Ruhr, was startling in its contrasts with the conflicts that had marked the 1920s; and the Marshall Aid programme was positively visionary in linking national wealth restoration to international co-ordination.

It is tempting to see in such innovations political far-sightedness: in fact, they were the results of diplomatic failures. Marshall's aid programme was a response to the failure of the powers to maintain Allied cohesion, as well as a response to the failure of the Bretton Woods system to restore global exchange. The internationalised Ruhr, with the promise of future slackened controls, represented the failure of France to gain support for its view that Germany remained a potential threat, while the division of Germany, and the attachment of its larger part to the Western Allies, represented a double failure. It resulted from the failure of the Allies to convince the Soviet Union that reparation was a false goddess, and the failure of the Soviet Union to convince friendly Germans that there were advantages to an entente with the Soviet Union.

As the construction of Germany ensued, the Soviet Union placed a tighter hold on the countries of Eastern Europe. In response, the Western powers moved ahead more quickly with the construction of the transitional German state. Soon, the old Reich would be divided, Eastern Europe would fall completely under Soviet hegemony, and much of the rest of the world would be cast into opposing camps. By 1949, the Cold War had begun to take on a concrete institutional shape, in the form of antagonistic blocs.

Notes

1 See M. Howard, *The Continental Commitment* (Harmondsworth: Penguin, 1974).
2 The different ideas, and the eventual ascendance of the Kerr–Hankey conception, are detailed in G. Egerton, *Great Britain and the Creation of the League of Nations* (Chapel Hill: University of North Carolina Press, 1978).
3 A. Wolfers, *Britain and France Between the Wars: Conflicting Strategies for Peace* (New York: Harcourt Brace, 1940).
4 W. Jordan, *Great Britain, France, and the German Problem* (London: Frank Cass, 1971).
5 E. Keeton, *Briand's Locarno Diplomacy* (New York: Garland, 1987).
6 J. Bariety, *Les Relations franco-allemandes après la première guerre mondiale* (Paris: Editions Pedone, 1977).
7 R. Overy, *War and Economy in the Third Reich* (Oxford: Clarendon, 1994).
8 Ibid.
9 *War, Economy and Society 1939–1945* (London: Allen Lane, 1977).
10 The various positions are discussed in N. Rich, *Hitler's War Aims*, 2 vols (London: Deutsch, 1973–74).
11 R. Boyce (ed.), *French Foreign and Defence Policy 1918–1945* (London: Routledge, 1988).
12 R. Ferrell, *Peace in Their Time: The Origins of the Kellogg–Briand Pact* (New York: Harper and Row, 1952).
13 C. Navari, 'The Origins of the Briand Plan', *Diplomacy and Statecraft*, 3, 1 (March 1992), pp. 74–104.
14 D. Kaiser, *Economic Diplomacy and the Origins of the Second World War* (Princeton: Princeton University Press, 1980).
15 N. Orvik, *The Decline of Neutrality, 1914–41* (London: Cass, 1971).
16 See W. Keylor, 'The Confirmation of United States Supremacy in Latin America' in *The Twentieth-Century World* (Oxford: Oxford University Press, 1984); Keylor is also useful throughout.
17 H. Feis, *The Diplomacy of the Dollar: First Phase 1919–1932* (New York: Norton, 1950) and L. Gardner, *Economic Aspects of New Deal Diplomacy* (Madison: University of Wisconsin Press, 1964).
18 A. Offner, *The Origins of the Second World War: American Foreign Policy and World Politics, 1917–1941* (New York: Praeger, 1975).
19 See H. Feis, *Churchill, Roosevelt, Stalin* (Princeton: Princeton University Press, 1957).
20 See R. Gardner, *Sterling–Dollar Diplomacy: Anglo-American Collaboration in the Reconstruction of Multilateral Trade* (Oxford: Oxford University Press, 1956).
21 For this curious episode, see W. Kimball, *Swords into Plowshares? The Morgenthau Plan* (Princeton: Princeton University Press, 1976).

22 Herbert Feis, *Between War and Peace: The Potsdam Conference* (Princeton: Princeton University Press, 1960) is the standard account.

23 As characterised by F. Northedge, *British Foreign Policy: The Process of Readjustment 1945–1961* (London: Allen and Unwin, 1962).

24 P. Windsor, *Berlin, City on Leave 1945–1962* (London: Chatto and Windus, 1963).

25 J. Gimbel, *The Origins of Marshall Aid* (Stanford: Stanford University, 1976) stresses the 'German' origins.

26 B. Kuklick, *American Policy and the Division of Germany* (Ithaca and London: Cornell University, 1972).

27 F.R. Willis, *France, Germany and the New Europe 1945–1967* (Stanford and London: Stanford University, 1968).

10 The Cold War

'Cold War' was the term used to characterise the global struggles which ensued among the major powers during the second half of the twentieth century. During it, none directly exchanged fire with one another (hence the term 'cold'), but they came to be involved in bitter hostilities with a wide variety of local forces around the globe, forces which were, or were believed to be, in alliance with their antagonists. Sides were also drawn up, and fixed political allegiances became characteristic. Almost every state became tightly enmeshed in a Cold War 'system' of blocs whose relations were regulated by implicit rules and common understandings. No region or state avoided incorporation, on some terms or other, in the conflict.

The hostilities varied in intensity. The two major antagonists enjoyed a limited detente during the 1960s (antagonising some of their allies), while both the super-power and intra-European rivalry ameliorated during the 1970s. Between the two super-powers, intense hostilities revived again during the 1980s; and the unwillingness of their respective allies to share in its revival caused a new generation of intra-bloc quarrels. But central aspects of their conflict continued to structure their relations until near the end of the century.

Its consequences for internationalism were significant and far-reaching. First, it politicised 'external' liberalism and forced the major liberal powers to both defend and extend it. After 1947, liberalism became tied to a dynamic policy of containment. Second, it absorbed the new international institutions created at the end of the war and gave them immediate political saliency. The United Nations, Marshall Aid and the emerging Western alliance all came to be seen as instruments in a defining global struggle. Its duration, moreover, meant a continuing commitment to institutional adaptation, as their hostilities varied and as the demands of prosecuting the war changed. The inter-war period had demonstrated the limitations of the League, and the new institutional order created between 1941 and 1947 was altered in the light of it. But the Cold War forced institutional learning on to a much higher plane. Finally, it engaged government directly and minutely with the internal arrangements of other states, with popular movements and with economic policy-making, and made these everyday matters of diplomatic concern.

The parameters of total Cold War

The Cold War ensued at a variety of levels. At the level of the mundane, the powers struggled to establish and maintain global mobility and alliance loyalty along traditional nineteenth-century diplomatic lines. But they also struggled to establish and maintain particular forms of political society in the areas they were contesting; and, what was even more novel, they battled to gain ideological ground with the general populations in those areas. The Cold War was also an economic struggle, not merely to outpace opponents in economic growth, but to incorporate regional zones into global trading systems. The major powers supported their allies' economic efforts at home (and set conditions for them), as well as protecting and enhancing their trading efforts abroad.

The struggle did not engulf the entire globe at once. Initially, it seemed capable of being confined to Germany alone, as each of the Allies sought to outmanoeuvre one another in achieving its favoured scheme for German reconstruction. By late 1947, however, when the Soviet Union forced the governments of Poland and Czechoslovakia to withdraw from the United States' Marshall Aid programme, it had clearly begun to absorb Europe; and by 1949 it was moving outwards from Europe to Asia. Asia came on stream first, followed by the Middle East and then Africa.

The outbreak of the Korean War in 1950 signalled the onset of the Asian stage, while conflict within the Middle East began to appear as an aspect of the Cold War from the mid-1950s, as certain Arab countries adopted indigenous socialisms and threatened to nationalise economic plant. Africa, by contrast, was not seen as a potential site of Cold War struggles until the beginning of the 1960s, when a secessionist movement in the Congo found the United States and the Soviet Union on opposite sides. Nor was communism a prevalent issue in Latin America until after a socialist revolution in Cuba in 1958, and the increasing identification of the Cuban leader, Fidel Castro, with the Soviet Union. Thereafter, however, the United States' Latin American policy centred on efforts to prevent Cuba's revolution from spreading, which turned mainly on isolating Cuba from involvement in the diplomatic affairs of the rest of the Americas.

As to what these quarrels concerned, they had begun as a struggle among the Allies to determine the political and geographical shape of the defeated Nazi Germany. When the quarrelling began in earnest, it was about what kind of government to impose on their former enemy within what kind of state. But the German struggle soon became a struggle to determine the allegiances of Europe, as each side pulled in allies and dependants across the growing European divide. It also became a struggle to contain the Soviet Union outside of Europe, which made it a global struggle to restrict that power's strategic and political mobility. Finally, it became a struggle along the fissures of the old empires, which also made it a colonial struggle.

How the major powers regarded their quarrels changed during their course. Initially, it appeared to be a matter of sometimes discrete, sometimes connected, efforts to gain and repel political influence, primarily within their respective zones of military occupation, and primarily with local contenders for power. In 1947, in an internal State Department paper, George Kennan, the American architect of containment, called it a 'traditional conflict fought with new methods'.[1] Within two years of Kennan's analysis, however, the United States was casting the conflict in ideological and global – rather than in political and local – terms as a struggle between a 'free world' and a new totalitarianism, while Britain continued to regard it as a simple power struggle which was spreading. (Initially, the Soviet Union regarded it as a dupe to deprive it of the just rewards for war participation.)

In its initial phases, local communisms and well-meaning fellow-travellers were the main focus of attention – initially, it was felt that circumventing local antagonists would contain global antagonists. At the global level, however, definitions of the strategic enemy differed. Britain consistently regarded the Soviet Union as the critical opponent, while the United States initially looked upon France, and at times even Britain, as presenting obstacles as difficult to overcome as any offered by the Soviet Union. By the early 1950s, as well, the United States was coming to regard China as its chief opponent in the Asian arena, while Britain continued to regard the Soviet Union as the major threat and had, in fact, recognised Communist China. France, on the other hand, tended to view the Cold War in terms of its troubled relations with Germany, and it responded to all policy initiatives with a view to the continued suppression of its neighbour.

During its course, patterns of struggle in one arena were held to prefigure intentions in other arenas, whether the analogy fitted or not. The struggle of German communists in the zones of occupation to suborn German socialism – the first evidence of 'cold war' – seemed to prefigure the intense party conflict which began to occur in the rest of Western Europe during 1946 and 1947, despite the very different socialisms, communisms and liberalisms involved. A coup in Prague in 1948, however, signalled an entirely different sort of danger – the military-backed putsch. (The Prague Communist Party, a partner in a socialist coalition, had seized control of the Czech government in February backed by Soviet military force.) As the Western powers began to see Western Europe in terms of threats from minority political forces with external military backing, so their views of Korea and, later, Vietnam also changed. They also came to fear that the loss of resolve to hold on to gains and positions in one area would reflect upon their resolve in other areas.

The same phenomenon was observable with regard to the modalities of the conflict. At the beginning, it was primarily a matter of political and economic supports: the weapons of its early stages were aid and statements of commitment. Moreover, during 1946–49, the European tactics of political support and economic aid were employed in all regions, irrespective of the relative rationalities of doing so. But when the Korean conflict rose to the level of armed hostilities, and the powers found themselves engaged in a large and bitter conventional war in Asia, the European conflict acquired a parallel military definition, though no external military threat was much in evidence. The formation of military alliances in Europe promoted, in turn, Western-sponsored military pacts with clients and recently liberated colonies at strategic points over the globe, in part (but not only) to hedge in the Soviet Union and prevent it gaining allies at significant points around the globe. And global militarisation would have serious consequences when nuclear weapons became involved in their struggles.

In some conflicts, local powers played off global powers to gain local and regional advantage, in arms or political and economic support. The major powers, in turn, sought aid from their Cold War allies in their local and colonial conflicts on the sometimes dubious grounds that the struggle in the locale or colony was part of the more general global struggle. In other cases, the modalities of the Cold War forced local as well as major powers into confrontations not of their choosing and into definitions of their quarrels which they would prefer to have avoided. The Cuban socialist revolution became 'sovietised', not least because it came to be seen in the light of a global struggle and not because the Soviet Union was a natural ally, while France sought to evade Cold War definitions of the European situation (since these definitions benefited the rapid reconstruction of Germany) until it was no longer possible to do otherwise. Major as well as local powers were often forced to choose sides along a whole range of issues upon which they might otherwise have had more diverse and differentiated positions.

Soviet policy and the onset of the Cold War

Responsibility for beginning the Cold War has been variously contested, as that question, too, became part of the ideological battle. But it would not strain the historical record to observe that the end of the Second World War had placed the Soviet Union in a favourable position, both geographically and politically, to establish a wide influence at relatively little cost, reversing its pre-war diplomatic isolation. Troop movements and war exigency had left it the sole occupying power of the former belligerent states of Hungary, Romania and Bulgaria. It was also one of the four occupying powers of both Germany and Austria. Moreover, at Potsdam, it had been given a zone of occupation in Korea, down to the 38th parallel, as a reward for joining the war against Japan.

Outside of these immediate zones, left-wing and progressive forces were contesting power whose local victories promised to aid the Soviet Union further afield. The Chinese communists, for their part, did not seem certain in 1945 to win the civil war, raging since the Japanese invasion in the 1930s, nor were Chinese allegiances yet determined. But left-wing forces in Vietnam and in Korea, as well as in Europe, had largely carried out the resistance to fascism, and it seemed reasonable to suppose that their participation in or mastery of post-war administrations would benefit the Soviet Union and extend its influence beyond its formal areas of occupation. This was particularly likely since, as one of the 'Big Three' victorious belligerent powers, the Soviet Union would have a vital say in the many political settlements to be determined following the war.

Soviet policy was initially concerned with the political balance in the countries immediately on its western littoral, with Eastern and Central Europe and the South Balkans. Its policy was to nudge reformist forces in those areas in the direction of participation in or domination of post-war administrations, creating friendly governments not merely in the occupation zones but across Central Europe more generally. It dispossessed the legitimate government of Poland, in exile in Britain during the war, and replaced it with a communist government, the so-called Lublin government, which agreed a loss of eastern territory in return for compensation in the west. In its occupation zone in Germany, it immediately entered upon a campaign for the unification of the German communist and larger socialist parties. It also moved its own borders west, re-incorporating the briefly independent Baltic states of Lithuania, Latvia and Estonia, and seizing territory from Romania as well as Poland. (Post-war Poland was moved in its entirety about 100 kilometres to the west, as the Soviet Union compensated the new Polish authorities with Soviet-controlled territory in eastern Germany.)

The main instruments of Soviet influence in these areas were the Soviet-loyal party organisation participating in a broad-based socialistic People's Democracy. The latter was a form of centralised state with a government drawn from a broad front of socialist parties endorsed via managed elections, with at most a small opposition. In Hungary, the strategy required bolstering what had been a small pre-war communist party; in Bulgaria and Romania, where socialist parties were weak or non-existent, the Soviet Union employed peasant parties, ensuring their acceptance into common front organisations. Begun immediately upon Soviet occupation, these processes were speeded up in the autumn of 1947, after the United States, supported by France and Britain, refused to agree Soviet terms for the dispersal of Marshall Aid. Initially, the Soviet Union differentiated its economic treatment of countries which had collaborated with Nazi Germany from defeated 'victim' countries such as Poland and Czechoslovakia. The economic plant of the collaborators was immediately integrated into the Soviet economy via joint ventures, and their currencies, reformed under the occupation, fell under regulation by the Soviet central bank. Poland and Czechoslovakia, by contrast, were allowed to re-establish autonomous economic systems. After each had expressed interest in receiving Marshall Aid, however, external direction of their economies was also established, in their case via ideological control. Soviet economic planning was eventually declared the model for all the People's Democracies, and the countries of Eastern and Central Europe were expected to follow Soviet policy. To ensure ideological and policy conformity, Soviet advisors were placed in relevant ministries from Warsaw to Sofia and Bucharest.[2]

These political and economic measures were combined with the rapid elaboration of local secret services staffed by new party trustees which controlled social and political dissidence. Approximately 10,000 people disappeared into labour camps in East Germany between 1946 and 1950, as the new Soviet-friendly parties and their apparatuses were put in place in the emerging East German state.

The evolution of Western policy

The Western powers, as the coalition eventually led by the United States came to be known, had initially regarded revolutionary Russia with a mixture of suspicion and outright hostility. This included the United States which had been considered, and behaved like, a revolutionary state through most of the nineteenth century. Until the Mexican revolution of 1911, revolutions against autocracy could generally count on unofficial American aid, particularly in Latin America, and official silence. It was when the Mexican revolution declared itself not merely a political but also a social revolution that American policy changed. Thereafter, revolutions of an economic character, involving expropriation of property as a principle of policy, particularly when this impinged upon American interests, were opposed, though with varying fervour. The Soviet revolution was no exception.[3] The failure of the White forces during the civil war, which raged from 1919 to 1923, and which the Western powers had supported, had, however, marked the beginnings of an uneasy status quo. The British and Poles ceased active hostilities against the Red Army in 1921. In any event, few feared a military or even a diplomatic threat from the Soviet Union during the inter-war period. It was the idea of the Soviet revolution as a model for other potential revolutions which disturbed.

During the 1930s, quarantine had turned to engagement as the other powers turned increasingly to win Soviet support in their diplomatic struggles to balance the rising German power. The French broke ranks first, out of fear of the proposed German–Austrian customs union, and signed a non-aggression pact with the Soviet Union in 1931. The United States recognised the Soviet Union in 1933 and eventually welcomed it into the anti-German coalition, supplying it with arms and war material. It was also President Roosevelt who played the mediator between the Allies during the course of the 'second German war', a role which expanded towards its end, as Britain became increasingly alarmed about Soviet troop movements and the Soviet Union's occupation of forward positions in Central Europe during the final months of the campaign.

The onset of containment

Britain was the first power to express alarm at the Soviet Union's European policies and the first to insist that joint policies be undertaken to combat them. It was also Britain which first publicly dramatised them. In a speech at Fulton, Missouri, in April of 1946, Britain's eminent wartime prime minister, Winston Churchill, then in opposition, declared that an 'iron curtain' was descending through Central Europe, the first acknowledgement to the general public that all was not well among the victors. (The popular history books of the time generally date the onset of the Cold War with Churchill's speech; and though there was plenty of evidence of deep divisions among the Great Powers before it, the decision to 'go public' indicated that, for Churchill, at least, the quarrel could no longer be contained within Allied councils.) Its purpose was to bring the United States to adopt a more active stance of opposition to Soviet behaviour.

The first sign that the United States was viewing relations with the Soviet Union in terms of an extended struggle was provided by a series of statements and speeches beginning in late autumn of the same year, warning the American public that Soviet behaviour in Europe was becoming increasingly unco-operative. In September, the United States had agreed with Britain that reparations deliveries to the Soviet Union should be stopped until the Soviet Union accounted for its behaviour, and it wished this departure from Allied co-operation to be understood and publicly endorsed.[4] Gradually, over the winter of 1946–7, it began to provide the American people with more aggressive anti-Soviet propaganda.

France, however, remained much more concerned with limiting German political reconstruction than with any putative Soviet threat. It was initially slow to respond to any rallying cries from either Britain or the United States and evaded joint policy co-ordination against the Soviet Union.[5]

The 'Europe-first' strategy

The first priority for Britain and the United States, after securing the German Socialist Party in the inner-German party struggle, was the rump of Western Europe. There had been a delegitimation of traditional parties in all the occupied countries of Europe, accompanied by the emergence of strong socialist and communist parties, the legacy of the resistance, who were aspiring to political power. In France and Italy, indigenous left-wing parties had won large minorities in the elections of 1946; French communists had entered the French cabinet as a result; and, in late 1947, the Italian Socialist Party declared it would fight the next elections on a united socialist–communist ticket. The first task of the newly created United States Central Intelligence Agency was to organise a campaign among Italian-Americans to warn their relations in Italy against voting for any united front containing communists. In France, the centrist premier, Ramadier, was urged to eject the communists who had been serving in the coalition cabinet, which he did in July.

The institutional carapace of these endeavours was the 'tri-zone'. Britain and the United States agreed to hold joint elections in their occupation zones in Germany with the aim of creating a joint German-staffed administration to oversee both zones in tandem. It would be a liberal administration (but still under their joint control). When France initially showed reluctance to reform its zone accordingly, Britain offered to undertake a permanent commitment to its defence. In 1948, the Brussels Treaty was signed, an assurance from Britain to France that it would not stand alone against any renewed German threat. But its immediate aim was to speed the restructuring of Germany and to provide for the rump of a liberal, non-communist West German state to secure Germany, and the rest of Western Europe, from internal communisms backed by Soviet support. The early objectives of Western policy were, accordingly, the bastion liberal state under semi-permanent external administration, with a British security guarantee.[6]

Attention was next directed to Europe's southern littoral. The restored Greek monarchy was under increasing pressure from former partisans, and Britain was struggling to maintain the monarchy against the KKE. (Greece was important to the mastery of the eastern Mediterranean and to the maintenance of Britain's access to the Middle East and India.) In early 1947, it warned the United States that it could no longer maintain aid to the restored monarchy. The United States administration, now headed by President Truman, agreed to take on the task, America's first ever peacetime permanent guarantee to another sovereign state. It would involve continuing to maintain the restored monarchy and a substantial bilateral military and economic aid programme to Greece; Greece would also become a significant recipient of Marshall Aid.

The 'Truman Doctrine' justified this innovation in liberal, democratic terms. Truman did not name the Soviet Union as the source of the problem. Rather, he argued (to Congress) that aid to Greece was necessary to support Greek democracy. At the same time, he declared, however, that forces anywhere seeking to seize power through internal processes of disruption were enemies of democracy and should be combated. The definition of the Cold War had begun to widen.[7]

Agreed Western policy until the end of 1947 centred on the re-establishment of collaboration: the European chancelleries in particular wished to avoid a final break with the Soviet Union. Accordingly, in June of 1947, when US Secretary of State Marshall announced his programme of economic aid to Europe, it was offered to all European states, irrespective of their client status. (The 'Cold War' aspect of Marshall's scheme was to reunite Europe through joint participation in a guided aid programme.)[8] During the summer and autumn of 1947, however, left-wing parties in Western Europe called a series of strikes to protest at the imposition of Marshall Aid on conditions antithetical to Soviet wishes, which became more widespread and more vocal after Czechoslovakia and Poland withdrew from the aid programme. By late 1947, Marshall's programme had perceptibly changed its objective. Rather than uniting Europe, the United States increasingly saw its credit programme in terms of securing weak Western European governments from left-wing pressure.

Britain and France, facing the choice between credits and keeping lines open to the Soviet Union, chose the former. Planning the distribution of credits proceeded without the Soviet Union, (though still not to America's entire satisfaction since its economic objective was global liberalisation, and neither Britain nor France wanted any immediate economic opening). Germany's economy was unshackled from the occupation rigours during 1948, in part to receive Marshall Aid, while the ensuing popular protest was directly cast as communist-inspired and, if not directed by, then in aid of Soviet geopolitical scheming.

Asia enters the equation

Asia was absorbed into the European conflict along three tangents. One was Soviet policy and the failure of the Soviet Union to achieve an ascendant position in Korea, itself a result of the growing European divide. The second was the success of the communist forces in China: in 1949, Chiang Kai-shek's nationalists had abandoned the Chinese mainland, seeking refuge on the island of Taiwan, some hundred miles off the South China coast, but vowing to return. Shortly thereafter, Mao Tse-tung had declared a decided tilt towards the Soviet Union with a series of aid and friendship pacts; and the United States was determining how the events in China should be viewed. The third determining factor was the decision of the United States, occasioned finally by North Korea's aggression, to view both sets of events as evidence of a single emergent Asian communism, supported by the Soviet Union.

In Korea, internal resistance to the Japanese had been primarily left-wing, and the Russians had recognised a left-wing alliance as the caretaker regime in its zone. In June 1947, a Joint Commission had been established between the two major occupiers to prepare for elections. In the Soviet zone, all pro-Marxist elements were fused into a National Democratic front, confirming the ascendancy of the Muscovite group over its opposition Yenan group within the North. But this was the smaller part of the country and the Soviet-backed political grouping faced certain electoral defeat in any united elections, leading the Soviet Union to evade all-Korean elections. Gradually, administrations were built up in each side along the lines of the emerging German model. A Korean Republic was declared in the Soviet zone early in February 1948, following which a parallel republic in the South was hurried into existence, taking power on 15 August 1948. How much the subsequent events owed to Soviet initiatives or to local pressure is debatable, but what cannot be doubted was the North's reliance on Soviet material.[9] In June, 1950, Pyongyang sent a large force over the Yalu river to seize the South and reunite the country.

In the United States, a great debate had developed, centred on the State Department, as to how the Chinese developments should be regarded: the old 'China hands', those traditionally in charge of America's China policy, argued that the hand of friendship should be shown to the new Chinese government. Britain, for its part, had recognised Communist China almost at once; and, as late as January 1950, the United States had indicated that it, too, would be willing to accept Communist China as a member of the Security Council, implying also a willingness to recognise the new regime. When North Korea invaded the South, however, American policy abruptly changed. The United States announced that the North Korean attack had been encouraged by the Chinese communist victory, as well as by direct Soviet backing. A large General Assembly majority declared, in February 1951, that China was the aggressor in Korea.

The United States responded to the Korean attack by mobilising a Security Council resolution declaring North Korea a threat to the peace, the first state so named. (The Soviet Union had declined to attend the crucial meeting.) The ensuing counter-force was American-organised, as there was no Security Council force in existence and no prospect of organising one. At the same time, the effect of the General Assembly resolution was to sanction the United States to directly attack China. The Cold War at once became not merely a local but a global military struggle, a definition confirmed when China, increasingly fearful of the troop movements to its south, joined North Korea in a brief military operation to ensure that United Nations troops did not cross into Chinese territory.[10]

The onset of military hostilities had two immediate consequences. First, it turned the whole of the United Nations into a fighting force: to fight the Korean War, the United States mobilised the United Nations via the General Assembly, not the Security Council, involving all members in the struggle. (It was the General Assembly which eventually endorsed the undertaking of the peace-keeping force.) Second, it heightened the ideological struggle and widened its institutional deployment. In the United States, Senator McCarthy, already warning of 'communists in our midst' as well as fellow-traveller associations, succeeded in establishing the House Un-American Activities Committee, bringing the Cold War into the domestic environment. It was also thereafter that the Chinese began a much more vigorous form of communist rule, through a systematised programme of ideological education throughout the country (it was also after the Korean counter-attack that it determined upon agricultural collectivisation).

A third set of consequences would be registered along the growing European divide. The Korean War set the Europeans along the road of constructing a form of total alliance which would not only institutionalise the European division, but which would produce a global system of blocs.

The institutional militarisation of the Cold War

Up to 1949, the use of force had been very limited in the European theatre. There was the Albanian adventure, when Britain landed a small force of indigenous Albanians on the coast across from Corfu, a last effort to use exiles to change the balance. The Soviet Union, for its part, blockaded the routes to Berlin, jointly occupied and located deep in the Soviet zone of occupation, to which the Western powers had responded with minimum force in the form of an air lift, forcing the Soviet Union to weigh up the costs of armed interdiction, which, in the event, it declined to undertake. The Western powers had also signed the North Atlantic Treaty in June 1949, in which they maintained that an attack on one was to be considered an attack on all, but few considered the treaty as other than a form of political guarantee linking the United States with the Brussels treaty powers. Certainly, there were no arms.

The decision to rearm Europe, and to arm it heavily, was initiated by the United States. The calculation was primarily a military one, based on the experience of the Second World War, whose lessons appeared to have been confirmed by the Korean campaign. This was that occupying forces could move quickly and with devastating consequences for the weaker side: Korean troops had advanced rapidly south during the summer of 1950 and the UN troops had suffered a devastating loss of men and material. The proposed source of troops, to be raised by rearming Germany, was a political calculation, arrived at in late 1950 when it became clear that neither Britain nor France was prepared to make large forces available for a 'European army'. In the autumn of 1950, the US began to insist that West Germany should be rearmed, to provide a barrier against any rapid overrun of the country.[11]

The conditions which the European powers would demand for German rearmament reflected their major security concerns at the time. For Britain, the defining issue, and the concern which had occupied it since the rise of the Nazi threat, was how to commit the United States permanently to the defence of Europe: in the event, it made its agreement to rearming Germany conditional on the creation of a joint general staff, a common command, to be led by an American commander-in-chief. On Germany's part, the strategic interest was the recreation of a German sovereign state and an autonomous German power: Chancellor Adenauer, leading the first post-war German administration, made West German rearmament conditional on the lifting of the occupation regime. The French terms would, eventually, be a genuine joint army with a permanent American military presence on the ground. For France, rearmament meant facing the new German power alone, or agreeing to the creation of a genuine military and political alliance of duration for the foreseeable future, if not on an 'Atlantic' then on a West European basis. It also tried, however, to forestall both eventualities. France's initial 'European' scheme proposed the creation of a sort of German mercenary force, small German units with no autonomous command, which would be integrated into a small West European army to be controlled by Britain and France under the general framework of the Brussels Treaty.[12]

The eventual carapace for the new European army, which displayed an ingenious complexity, was determined primarily by the United States' definitions of the threat and Britain's refusal to join any political control system with France alone. Britain was not enthusiastic about a 'European army', since it wanted the United States directly involved in any military organisation of the European continent. The United States, for its part, deemed the proposed 'mercenary' force much too small for the task. Not only did it insist on a high level of German rearmament, but it was willing to give Germany more and more independence to secure it.

As Germany promised to liberate itself from Allied control, and with a large army in tow, France began to fear subordination to a rising German power. After the negotiations were completed, it reneged on its own scheme and refused to join Germany in any joint military structure without either Britain or the United States as joint partners.[13] After four years of acrimony between France on the one hand and the United States and the German authorities on the other, the United States and Britain agreed, in late 1954, to place troops in Germany on a permanent basis and to participate in a permanent common command structure. A virtually sovereign Federal Republic joined Nato in 1955, committed to rearmament but also to full integration in the new Nato. The new German army, together with the British and American forces, would be located within a widened and more tightly organised alliance and would be commanded by an American general. A second tier of controls was fashioned, based on the Brussels Treaty, which gave France and Britain the right to oversee German rearmament and to ensure that the new Germany developed no autonomous control of nuclear weapons.[14]

National troops with their own commanders would eventually be sited on bases in the eastern part of the new Federal Republic and provided with specified roles in a series of jointly determined strategic plans, which would change with differing definitions of the threat and evolving war-fighting concepts. These forces never saw battle during the whole period of the Cold War; their function was to convince the Soviet Union, by displays of continuous preparedness, that the Western powers were willing to confront it on a European battlefield were it to attempt a seizure of any part of the Nato area by main force or threaten a Nato ally in adjacent areas. They were also there to provide the institutional framework and command structure for what would rise to over half a million armed Germans.

The result of this construction was to render Nato into a permanent peace-time organisation with a large bureaucracy in being. It also made it the organisational basis for a permanent diplomatic entente. Germany's insistence that its new allies accord sovereignty to the Federal Republic meant recognising it as the only German government. This implied that no Nato government could recognise East Germany without the Federal Republic's concurrence.

Consolidation in the West and consolidation in the East

The isolation of communist parties in France and Italy continued though the 1950s by means of counter-propaganda and, primarily, military aid on the part of the United States. This was paralleled by the Soviet suppression of the residual opposition parties in Eastern Europe. Gradually during the early 1950s, the Balkan peasant parties were converted into parties fully obedient to the Soviet Communist Party, and full Stalinist-style peoples' democracies were solidified. Increasingly after 1948, the Soviet Union displayed relative indifference to the fate of the communist parties of Western Europe, although it continued to aid some of the smaller parties indirectly, such as the Greek communists, through cheap delivery of the Soviet encyclopaedia and the financing of Communist Party newspapers.

The Soviet Union responded to West Germany's incorporation into Nato by the creation of the Warsaw Pact in 1955, a weak cover for a series of bilateral military pacts with its client states in Central and Southern Europe. It also formally abandoned efforts to achieve the reunification of Germany. It recognised West Germany in 1956; and it pressed the West to accord simultaneous recognition to East Germany. By the late 1950s, it was openly arguing for a European settlement along a 'two Germanies, two blocs' basis.

Following Germany's incorporation into Nato, the smaller West European governments proposed a customs union among the Western European states whose economies demonstrated particularly close interdependencies. The United States did not like the closed trading aspect of the scheme, and would press for global trade negotiations directed to keeping the new Common Market's external tariff low. But France and Germany proved enthusiastic, particularly after the French had ensured continued protection to their agricultural producers.

The project was initiated by the Benelux countries, whose entrepot position between Germany and France militated towards low tariffs between them. It also gained immediate support from Italy which depended on the triangular trade between it, Germany and France. The proposal had been mooted from as early as the late 1920s to create larger economies of scale in Europe and to counter the protectionist tendencies evident since the First World War. In the immediate post-war period, it had gained additional saliency in the context of reconstruction. But the instability of the European situation had militated against it. With a divided Germany now locked into a Western alliance with a permanent American guarantee, it could proceed.

The Cold War *outre mer*

In their colonial domains, the imperial powers had had to continue or resume fighting after the defeat of the Axis powers. Neither Indo-China nor Malaya nor Singapore wanted a return of colonial rule, having in each instance had to face the Japanese alone after British and French power had collapsed. In Malaya, confronting 10,000 armed guerrilla fighters, Britain shifted a large part of the population to safe havens and thereafter fought back. In Vietnam, where Ho Chi Minh had established a government in Hanoi in the north, France declared that it would not recognise its sovereignty over Cochin China in the south. (The Malayans as well as Hanoi had sought and gained Soviet aid, taking advantage of the break-up of the wartime alliance.)

The United States, antithetical to imperial reconstruction, had initially viewed these struggles in a light rather favourable to the local partisans: in 1945, the forces of Ho Chi Minh were regarded by the American military missions there as a legitimate nationalist uprising against French imperialism.[15] Increasingly, however, as the Korean struggle took shape, the Vietnamese conflict was redefined. By 1950, it, like the Chinese revolution, had become yet another arena in the struggle between communism and the Free World. The United States did not thereby reconcile itself to the French position, recognising full well the colonial nature of France's aspirations. It began, instead, to insist on the construction of an independent and democratic Cochin, or South Vietnam as it came to be known, to be built around a 'third force', neither a communist–socialist government nor a colonially dominated pro-French government.

With the growing identification of colonial struggles as also struggles between global antagonists, there began a rush for uncommitted allies, sometimes with conflict among the Western allies to secure preponderant positions. Britain and the United States quietly contested influence in Saudi Arabia and Iraq. Turkey and Greece were incorporated into the Nato alliance in 1952, despite protests by other Nato members at having to take on responsibility for their defence. (In fact, the United States took on the main responsibility for Greece and Turkey, who were semi-detached Nato members through the 1950s and 1960s.) The Philippines, South Korea, Israel and South Africa were all offered, and accepted, military aid and other forms of alliance with the United States. In Iran under the Shah, the Communist Party was outlawed.

By the late 1950s, the Western powers had become involved in a complex web of bilateral and multilateral military pacts at the centre of which were five regional arrangements which policed what they considered strategically crucial areas. Besides the North Atlantic Treaty Organisation, these were the Baghdad Pact, covering Pakistan and Turkey, the Central Treaty Organisation (CENTO), covering the Middle East, the South East Asia Treaty Organisation (SEATO) for South East Asia, and the ANZUS, linking the Western powers with Australia and New Zealand. Containment was largely a matter of securing reliable governments in strategic areas of Western interest, and flanking them militarily.

Indigenous political processes in these areas were increasingly identified in Cold War terms, not only by the outside belligerents but also by the predominant local power, usually to secure its ascendancy over some contesting local force. In South Africa, the Nationalist Party which came to power in 1948 was soon claiming that the anti-apartheid forces confronting it were communist-dominated, that supporting them could lead to a communist-dominated South Africa, and that aid was required to keep it from falling under communist influence. (South Africa offered the Western powers access to a large South Atlantic base facility which became strategically vital after the closing of the Suez Canal in 1967.) Syngman Rhee in South Korea resisted calls for reform on the part of students and intellectuals, in part through labelling them communists, and excluded reformists from any participation in government, as did the conservative Centre Party in Greece and the Marcos government in the Philippines. (In the latter, a prolonged civil war in the interior was cast in terms of communists-versus-democrats, though there was little that was democratic about the Marcos regime.)

In Africa, free of Cold War conflict until 1960, a post-colonial struggle in the former Belgian Congo brought the Soviet Union in to support Congolese breakaway rebels with military aid. Thereafter, Britain speeded up the preparation of its African colonies for independence, maintaining, however, residual control of foreign policy in the emerging new states. In 1963, the United States Congress agreed a large aid programme directed at securing Africa. Among the local African states, Zaire began to experiment with socialist rhetoric, but only Tanzania really declared a decided tilt. With a large number of peasant producers, the new Tanzanian government began to experiment with agricultural collectives, guided partly by the Chinese model. Eventually, it sought and secured aid from China to construct the Tanzam railway, long thereafter a source of pride to the occasional Chinese traveller.[16]

The United Nations Security Council fell an early victim to the Cold War. After the United States had North Korea declared a 'threat to the peace', the Soviet Union steadily used its veto right, paralysing the institution in the crucial area of its peacekeeping function. The General Assembly was affected in another way. Its early majorities favoured the Western powers, who used it to mount a series of resolutions against the Soviet Union and its allies. This tactic, which incorporated the general body of states into the Cold War conflict, gave the Assembly enhanced political weight. But it proved a risky tactic in the long run, as more newly independent states with different policy agendas entered the organisation.

The developing economic instrumentalities

Military and political institutionalisation was accompanied by economic conditionalities, not surprising since a crucial aspect of the quarrel between the United States and the Soviet Union had been the nature and extent of the latter's control over its own and its client's domestic economies. But the economic devices were shaped more by the immediate needs of the Cold War than by any liberal economic orthodoxy. There was, for example, little objection on the part of the United States to state planning in the emerging post-colonial states of Africa and Asia. (The Western colonial powers had established frameworks for 'economic intervention' during the late 1930s, a form of 'New Deal imperialism', and these structures were elaborated by newly independent governments to put in place what were often high degrees of planning.) The development economics practised in many new states (much of which turned on state intervention) was, besides, a Western invention. The Cold War foreign economic policies of the major Western powers demanded no more than that Western holders of plant and resources be allowed to continue to operate undisturbed, and that aid should not be received from the Soviet Union or its allies.

The major instruments of Western economic diplomacy towards new states became the GATT and the World Bank, which became in effect Western institutions and to which access was gained through sponsorship by a Western power. (Initially intended to aid the reconstruction of Europe, the new World Bank rapidly acquired the role of major lending agency to the new states being created by decolonisation.) Securing World Bank aid involved demonstrating at the very least neutrality; and World Bank funds were enlarged, and its programmes elaborated, to allow it to perform the role of managing economic growth without communism. Few new states were economically strong enough to join the GATT, but achieving GATT reciprocity was initially considered the proper and eventual aim of a new state: early aid programmes were directed with that aim in mind. Each Western power also established its own aid and development funds with which to aid those new states with whom it had special relationships.

Not all economic aid was informed by Cold War considerations. The large domestic and international aid agencies which came into being after the Second World War operated by a variety of changing criteria (initially 'development' but, increasingly, relief of poverty). But World Bank loans could be strategically directed by the voting power of the United States, while the existence of aid allocations within national budgets made aid funds available for political purposes. It was no accident that countries in strategic locations whose fate was of particular concern to one or other of the major powers always enjoyed more aid. When Nasser's Egypt failed to gain Western support for the immense Aswan Dam project in 1956, Egypt turned to the Soviet Union, which responded immediately, creating fears that Egypt was lost to the Western bloc (but also assuring to Egypt the acquisition of a valuable electricity asset). Accordingly, to be strategically sensitive in Cold War terms became an asset that new governments in such areas exploited, notwithstanding the considerable diplomatic skill and hard nerve required to do so. The Cold War struggle also influenced the size of aid donations.

The critical economic instrument of the global conflict was, however, not World Bank funds, nor even the loan resources of the IMF, but military aid routed through the growing number of military alliances. Both bilateral and multilateral alliances became the routes for large financial donations from the major powers, usually in the form of military equipment and training but also credits and outright monetary grants. The terms 'security donors' and 'security receivers' were coined to characterise the system. The major donor was, undoubtedly, the United States. Special ties developed between local military forces and the United States Pentagon, which approved the level and direction of American military aid.

Military aid, and the military ties which grew in the wake of aid, became another important political resource for receivers: they helped to secure new or reformed regimes as much against internal dissidence as any external threat. (The system had other, unintended, consequences. It tended to put, particularly new, receiver states in the hands of generals and military-backed autocrats, and it encouraged military coups.)

Non-alignment

Countries seeking to avoid incorporation into one camp or the other developed various avoidance tactics. The most important of these was the non-aligned movement, initiated by the Indian prime minister, Nehru, in 1955. Since independence, India had followed an anti-colonial policy accompanied by tight control of Western capitalist firms operating in the domestic economy; it also practised a form of mild state-directed socialism which included agricultural and other subsidies aimed at supporting the poor. It was, however, not anxious to exchange British for Soviet tutelage. At the Bandung Conference of 1955, Nehru proposed a declaration of non-alignment and the establishment of a non-aligned movement which would create a neutral space between the emerging blocs.[17]

By the middle 1960s, the non-aligned bloc had grown to include Cuba, Yugoslavia, Ghana, Indonesia and Egypt, and its orientation would influence the political balance in the General Assembly. Negotiating in the interstices between the Soviet bloc and the West, the non-aligned states would succeed in bringing issues of decolonisation to the floor of the Assembly, as well as structural issues of economic inequality.[18] A United Nations Conference on Trade and Development was formed in 1964 with the radical Latin American economist Raul Prebisch at its head, and became a permanent organisation which continued to press revisionist claims.

As decolonisation speeded up, the new entrants into the organisation helped codify these efforts. The General Assembly became the *locus classicus* for revisionist smaller powers during the late 1960s and 1970s. They learned to exploit a developing committee system within the Assembly, and the growing numbers encouraged its development. The rules of the emerging 'parliamentary diplomacy' favoured, in turn, the maintenance of coalitions: groups of states working together could control resolution outcomes. By the late 1960s, there were some thirty new members; and political scientists began regularly calculating the weight and durability of the expanded 'Afro-Asian bloc' in the General Assembly, to assess its consequences for the balance of power within the organisation.

The delicate central balance

European stability rested upon a Western Germany which increasingly identified itself with the West, in economic and cultural as well as political terms. West Germany's growing alignment with the West was due partly to a strong economic recovery (by the middle 1950s, Germany was already on the way to again becoming the economic powerhouse of Europe). Also, joining the West was rewarded with increasing influence in Western councils: none of the Allied powers was inclined to recognise East Germany or to deal with the Soviet Union's client states. Towards the West German electorate, Adenauer argued, in the event successfully, that the building of a strong West German state was necessary to achieve reunification on Germany's terms and that unification would eventually be achieved. The Christian Democratic Party, which had overseen the creation of West Germany and had forged Germany's links with the West, was confirmed in power with growing majorities throughout the 1950s, creating a strong bulwark to the west against Soviet influence.

The three pillars of West German foreign policy during the height of the Cold War were the 'Hallstein Doctrine', close adherence to the Nato alliance and, finally, integration into Western Europe's developing economic and political organisations. The Hallstein Doctrine, declared in 1958, aimed to steadily weaken the East German proto-state and to turn it into a liability for the Soviet Union. Germany made its adherence to the Nato alliance conditional on supporting this effort; and its membership of the Common Market as well as Nato secured it political legitimacy and diplomatic support.[19]

By 1961, East Germany had lost almost 3 million people in flights to West Germany, the majority of whom were young to middle-aged, urban and educated, depriving the new quasi-state of its most valuable population asset.

Unfortunately, European stability also depended on a Soviet Union that could look forward to bloc stability. Soviet Union's European allies were not strong states, and some had accepted Soviet domination only on terms that they be left relatively alone: the Warsaw Pact was a source of weakness to the Soviet Union, not a source of strength. Governments in Eastern Europe were, moreover, only maintained by the force of the Soviet army; a Hungarian uprising in 1956 had demonstrated that the Hungarian government could only maintain domestic control by calling on Soviet military support. The Soviet Union depended on East Germany to provide the bulwark for Eastern Europe. Had the West recognised the Soviet zone as a legitimate sphere of Soviet influence, these weaknesses might have been corrected. The Soviet Union might even have welcomed Western help in developing them. But the commitments gained by the Adenauer government forestalled this possibility, even had the other Western powers been tempted to accept it. West Germany's success, in short, left the Soviet Union with a weakening East Germany confronting a strengthening West Germany, which was backed by the predominant power of the Western alliance and increasingly free to disturb what was an unstable Eastern European situation.

The relationship between the balance of power and the balance of forces was also changing. During the 1950s, Nato had developed the doctrine of conventional force use behind a nuclear shield. The 'shield' dissuaded others from excess adventurism, besides allowing for massive force delivery should central Western interests be threatened. This depended, however, on an effective Western monopoly. By the late 1950s, the Soviet Union had not only broken that monopoly but had demonstrated the capacity for accurate targeting and long-range delivery. For the disadvantaged side, there was accordingly a rational temptation to use nuclear capabilities, in the form of veiled threats, either to change the status quo or to preserve it, as interest dictated. By 1961, the Soviet Union was regularly using veiled threats to destabilise the central balance unless the Western allies recognised its sphere of influence.

As the prime target of these endeavours, the United States became increasingly concerned to contain Soviet threats, if only to regulate an increasingly dangerous nuclear competition. How this was to be done, however, was not easy to determine. The McNamara Doctrine, which had established Mutual Assured Destruction (MAD) as the US's basic strategic posture, had also proposed matching the Soviet Union blow for blow from within a tightly organised alliance. Both 'matching' and MAD implied force increases, besides 'use' doctrines; and the United States had hurried its own missile developments and increased the range of its nuclear targeting. But it also depended on the possibility of giving ground, and it required Nato concurrence for this. The efforts of the United States to bring the Federal Republic to concede some changes in the status of Berlin in 1961 and 1962 were greeted by near-hysteria on the part of the Federal authorities, as they implied that the alliance was no longer committed to a change of the status quo in its favour, and was indeed retreating.

The McNamara Doctrine was also inherently destabilising. It invited nuclear competition. When McNamara announced, in mid-1962, that US missile development had surpassed that of the Soviet Union, and that it was now in a position to 'match' its opponent's developments, the Soviet Union moved some of its short-range missiles on to the island of Cuba, its only client state in the western hemisphere and located some 90 miles off the coast of the United States, primarily to demonstrate its own albeit more limited capabilities of matching. In October, the United States retaliated by declaring a zone of exclusion around the island, manned by a naval blockade. For a tense thirteen days, an actual nuclear confrontation appeared possible, a confrontation which few at the time doubted would engulf Europe as well. In its aftermath, European governments would express increasing concern with the control of the American nuclear arsenal and displayed an increasing determination to maintain independent control of their own nuclear weapons, in the hope that they could escape the consequences of American or Soviet nuclear adventurism.

The missile crisis was widely vaunted as demonstrating the soundness of American strategic doctrine, as well as its ability to manage political and military confrontations. In fact, it did neither. At the European level, it called into question the wisdom of the 'total' alliance, and led to a greater differentiation of interests among the Western allies. At the global level, it inspired the first detente, and much more caution in the use of graded threats.

The missile crisis and the two-centre alliance

France emerged as the leading dissident power. In 1961, President de Gaulle had proposed the Fouchet Plan, a proposal for intra-European political and diplomatic co-ordination to be built on the European Economic Community: in the aftermath of the missile crisis, he offered the new European 'political community' as a 'second pillar' to Nato.[20] He also promised to lead a cartel of European states towards greater strategic independence via a 'European deterrent' based on French and British nuclear forces (exploratory talks were held at Rambouillet in 1961 and 1962), an idea which gained increasing attraction among important European elites after the missile crisis. Finally, he initiated discussions aimed at creating a special Franco-German relationship which would supplement the proposed Anglo-French deterrent with a political entente between France and Germany. In early 1963, a Franco-German treaty was initialled by Adenauer.

The motives for these initiatives were entirely political. They concerned, first, the legitimacy of France's new constitution: de Gaulle wished to demonstrate that the reduction in the powers of the National Assembly and the enhancement of the new presidential office, the central elements of the Fifth Republic's new constitution, brought immediate benefits in terms of Great Power status. Second, France had been denied direct entry into the Anglo-American entente: de Gaulle's first proposal upon assuming the new presidential office had been tripartite management of the alliance, which the United States had refused.[21] Restructuring the alliance along 'two centres', with a European deterrent and a special Franco-German relationship, would have had the effect of making France the central pivot of a new Europeanised alliance.

The United States moved immediately to forestall France's initiatives. It proposed a multilateral nuclear force (MLF), to be located in Nato, offering to the Europeans direct political control of some Nato nuclear forces, denying the need for another European organisation. Alliance members were also called upon to demonstrate their loyalty to the alliance by signing up to the MLF. A strong anti-Gaullist rhetoric accompanied the MLF proposal: 'Gaullism' was declared a dangerous doctrine which would destroy the alliance and open Europe to direct Soviet influence. The CIA undertook the support of several magazines and encouraged research institutes which were loyal to Nato: a new Italian Institute for International Affairs was founded with (secret) CIA funding which strongly supported an 'Atlantic' construction of Europe.

The immediate result of this quarrel was a free-for-all among the Western powers. Germany moved uncertainly between the French and American demands, agreeing to a special Franco-German relationship but also agreeing to join the multilateral nuclear force. The United States, about to undertake a detente with the Soviet Union, insisted that its partners not do the same. The Kennedy administration urged British entry into the European Community in the hope of controlling allied dissidence, in return for which, however, it had to aid and abet British nuclear development, producing a second-generation independent British deterrent, a development antithetical to a centralised alliance. The French government rejected British entry of the European Community, splitting it thoroughly, which eventually frustrated its effort to build a European political community: Belgium hesitantly and Holland absolutely refused to proceed with any European construction 'outside' of Nato. In mid-1964, the alliance appeared momentarily on the point of disintegration.[22]

In the end, France abandoned the effort to restructure Nato and satisfied itself with weakening it. It recognised Communist China at the beginning of 1964, breaking the Western diplomatic front on the question. Two years later, it withdrew from the military structures of the alliance, forcing it to relocate to Belgium, and began a series of daring initiatives aimed at inviting the Soviet Union directly to partner France in a new European settlement.

Germany, fearing France's efforts would undercut its reunification strategy, was forced, in the event, also to break Nato ranks. It too began to move unilaterally, undertaking cautious initiatives towards the countries of Eastern Europe, while continuing to isolate East Germany. Between 1966 and 1968, it offered an ambiguous normalisation of relations with Czechoslovakia, Poland and Romania, hoping to lure them into a special relationship with the Federal Republic.[23]

These developments had contradictory consequences for the Western alliance. At the institutional level, France's departure and its relocation produced, paradoxically, a tighter and more coherent alliance structure. With no alternative in view, the remaining allies settled to reform Nato, producing some significant alternations. The multilateral force was dropped in return for something much more substantial, the establishment of a nuclear planning group which determined the targeting of Nato nuclear warheads and became the locus of co-ordination between the United States and its European partners on nuclear strategy. At the same time, however, there was no co-ordinated control of the detente process – each power was moving independently and with different policies towards the Soviet Union. An important question at the end of the 1960s was whether the future would produce a Europe with blocs or without them.

The Common Market entered a period of stasis, with its existent policies intact but with no immediate prospect of development.[24] Enthusiasts for European union began to fear for its future.

The cautious global detente

France's abandonment of Vietnam after a military defeat at Dien Bien Phu in 1954, and the creation of two Vietnams in 1955, as well as the incorporation of Germany into Nato, might have been understood as laying the foundations for an increased global stability. In fact, they did not. To demonstrate their resolve to maintain their positions over the European divide, both super-powers had continued to engage in quite confrontational policies outside of Europe. Also, China had entered upon the road of revisionism: in 1958, the Chinese had seized the Quemoy and Matsu Islands, inducing nuclear threats from the United States. At about the same time, the Soviet Union had begun an active Middle East policy, directed at weakening the Western links with the major oil producers.[25] It was during this period that the United States declared that a threat at one point was a threat across the whole front, and had begun strenuous efforts to woo uncommitted Third World states. The missile crisis had been but the latest effort to use peripheral politics to change the central balance.

After the Cuban missile crisis, this changed. Whereas before it, their political interests seemed to be served by deploying and developing their nuclear arsenals, after it their strategic nuclear relationship began to set the terms of their European and global struggles, not vice versa; and their strategic relationship was deemed to demand greater control, not only of the nuclear relationship and alliance dissidence, but of also of their more wide-ranging global confrontations, particularly confrontations involving third or 'local' parties which could trigger nuclear war or miscalculation. During the subsequent decade, beginning from the spring of 1963, and the establishment of a 'hot line' between Washington and Moscow, the two super-powers began a limited detente, the 'first detente' as it came to be known, aimed at controlling the nuclear confrontation. More significantly, they initiated a set of self-limiting policies *vis-à-vis* their allies across the globe.

Initially, the super-power detente centred on limiting arms levels, and was aimed essentially at leaving each side in possession of a mutual assured destruction capability without destabilising their confrontation. By 1967, they had managed to achieve one arms agreement, the SALT I, limiting the number of warheads on each side but with a sufficiency to leave each vulnerable to a second strike. This detente produced no major amelioration of the general conflict, but it implied that their quarrels would not be driven by nuclear confrontation.

During the parallel period of peripheral restraint, control in the peripheries was determined essentially by who got there first. Cuba continued to build socialism, now free of the threat of direct American intervention, but at the cost of a distorted economy dependent on Soviet purchases of the sugar crop. (Equally, however, the Soviet Union resisted all efforts by Cuba to join the Warsaw Pact.) During this same period, the Vietnamese civil war escalated, with the United States, as an already engaged power, becoming increasingly involved. Through the middle 1960s it sent first advisors and then greater and greater levels of troops. The Soviet Union became the major supplier to the North Vietnamese as well as to the partisans in the South, but it did not seek to support either by any direct engagement with the United States, either diplomatically or militarily. Even a vigorous bombing campaign undertaken against Hanoi in 1968 and eventually spreading to Cambodia did not inspire countervailing measures by the Soviet Union against the United States.

The China 'normalisation' graphically demonstrated the new priorities. In 1970, the Nixon administration had determined that an approach to China might restrain the Vietnamese, and a visit by Nixon to Peking was scheduled for the beginning of 1971. It promised to regularise relations between the two countries. One week before the visit, however, the US carried out an extensive bombing of Haiphong harbour, the port through which the Vietnamese received arms, raising doubts as to whether the Chinese government would receive the American president. In the event, the visit was not called off, and an historic agreement was made in which the United States finally recognised Communist China and recognised it, moreover, as the government of all of China, delegitimating the status of Taiwan.[26] (The Vietnam War continued, however, as before.)

The practice of restraint in the peripheries left little hope for governments and political forces who found themselves in the wrong zone of influence. A seizure in Dominica by a military junta was declared by the United States as potentially opening the way for Castroite forces, and the United States intervened. A putative socialist revolution in Chile led eventually to the unseating and murder of its leader, Allende.

Germany breaks the European impasse

If the delicate European balance shaped the field within which major power priorities were determined, it was Germany which held the key to that balance.

Undeterred by US pressure for a unified detente, the West German government had commenced a series of political initiatives in 1966 following France's departure from Nato, aimed essentially at Eastern Europe. In substance, it began to offer to normalise relations with selected Warsaw Pact states, threatening to split the Soviet bloc. (With hindsight, we may say that France and Germany were in a race during 1966–8 to influence the political shape of Central Europe.) The Federal Republic's initiatives went so far as to encourage a democratisation in Czechoslovakia, the Prague Spring of 1968.

In response, the Soviet Union began accusing the West German government of 'adventurism' and, by implication, aggressive intent. It moved first to control its dissident Czech ally by political threats. Then, somewhat nervously, it moved tanks into Prague during the summer of 1968, in which exercise three of its client states participated. (This unexpected coalition was explained by Western analysts as the attempt by clients to protect the fragile autonomy which they had gained during the earlier years of the decade.) Germany's initial efforts appeared, in consequence, to have strengthened Warsaw Pact cohesion.

Faced with the impossibility of splitting the Soviet bloc by even the most cautious of political initiatives, and by the failure of all other initiatives, the West German government took a fateful decision. In the spring of 1969, the new socialist chancellor, Willy Brandt, cautiously proposed recognising the 'other' Germany, implying also a recognition of the legitimacy of the Warsaw Pact system and an end to a policy of actively seeking to undermine either. A treaty between the two Germanys was signed in 1972, containing a pledge that neither would attempt to affect their relations by force of arms.[27] The agreement also accorded the East German state a form of limited recognition. The Federal German government also abandoned the Hallstein Doctrine and regularised its relations with Poland and Czechoslovakia, implying also the abandonment of territorial claims against them (although this was not clearly stated).

This development had significance at several levels of the encounter between the major powers. With regard to the 'German question', the body of agreements worked by the Federal Government settled the majority of the territorial questions left over from the Second World War in Europe. (West Germany recognised the post-war territorial settlement in Czechoslovakia, and agreed to no border changes by force of arms with Poland, agreements which were sanctioned by the former Allied powers.) Accordingly, they served to accomplish that 'German peace' which had eluded the Allies at the end of the war. Moreover, if they did not sanction, they nonetheless accorded a certain legitimacy to Soviet-controlled governments in Central Europe. After these agreements were finalised, there were no more stable borders than the European borders, and no greater expectation anywhere that governments in power would remain in power. In consequence, the Soviet Union became less concerned with contacts between its client states and the West, so long as communist parties stayed firmly in control in Eastern Europe. (Indeed, the Soviet Union took advantage of such contacts: during the 1970s, the Western powers began to make funds available to support economic modernisation in Poland, relieving the Soviet Union of the financial burden of doing so.)

The Western alliance was affected accordingly. With the territorial situation in Europe stabilised, it became reduced to an approving mechanism of the allies' various future detente policies.

After 1972, the United States was left to continue the last major military struggle of the Cold War, in Vietnam, alone.

The new European stability and a changing global balance

The new European stability also allowed for more economic differentiation. Increasingly during the 1970s, Third World countries discovered that they could experiment with different aid partners and with different development goals without being accused of 'going over to Moscow'. They also started to rebel at the restrictions of the development route offered to them, in particular the idea of competing on a level playing field with advanced industrial countries under the rules of GATT and in conditions of strict reciprocity. A group of 77 developing countries, formed in the late 1960s, began to press more steadily for revision of the post-war trading rules. The United Nations Commission on Trade and Development (UNCTAD) encouraged a 1974 Declaration on the Establishment of a New International Economic Order, and the UNCTAD secretariat largely managed its programme of action, which became the locus for a wide variety of revisionist efforts throughout the 1970s.

Economic dissidence was not limited to the Third World. During the late 1960s, a serious economic recession had struck the advanced industrial states, and each had responded with short-term measures intended to protect growth, including subsidies and trade restraints. The terms of economic competitiveness among Western trading states became, in consequence, a major issue, as economic recession led first one major trading state and then another to engage in forms of economic protectionism. The United States found, moreover, that it could not call on imminent danger to moderate the growing protectionism, nor could it claim special benefits in respect of its own economic difficulties, at least not to any effect. Its allies were enjoying too much peace to justify the subordination of national economic interests to the economic requirements of the alliance leader.

At the same time, however, the new European status quo changed the balance of risks in the peripheries, and changed it differentially for the two super-powers. For its part, the Soviet Union began to practice a much more active interventionist policy outside of Europe, and it demonstrated a new capability to act far from its own borders. In both the Horn of Africa and in Angola, where an intense civil conflict had been triggered by Portugal's abandonment of its African colonies, the Soviet Union became an active participant, delivering large quantities of arms and advisors to the Horn, as well as a Cuban fighting force to the 'progressive' side in the Angolan dispute.[28] The United States, however, facing a growing internal protest at its engagement in Vietnam, had found it increasingly difficult to justify the Vietnam War in Cold War terms. In 1973, it had abandoned the use of force, suing for peace with the North Vietnamese to allow itself a graceful retreat. It allowed the southern part of the country to eventually fall to control by the North. By contrast with the Soviet Union, America seemed to have become more constrained in acting abroad, as it became increasingly evident that domestic constituencies would not allow it any easy military interventions after the retreat from Vietnam.

The 'unilateral' Cold War

Alarmed by this disparity in their respective freedoms of action, the US undertook a series of unilateral actions. First, it began a massive domestic rearmament. Initiated by the Reagan administration, which took office in 1980, rearmament was designed, some argued, to push the Soviet Union to a crippling level of defence expenditure. The programmes were wide-ranging, including 'smarter' guidance and new bombers, but the centrepiece was the 'Star Wars' project, as it came to be known. Star Wars was a spaced-based defence system designed to make the United States invulnerable to any Soviet missile attack. Second, rearmament was accompanied by demands that America's allies limit their economic engagements with the Soviet Union, and that they adhere more closely to strategic embargoes. In particular, the new administration began a vigorous campaign against the construction of a pipeline from the gas fields of the Soviet Union to an energy-hungry Western Europe; and it threatened European companies with subsidiaries in the United States (and vice versa) with sanctions if they broke embargoes.[29] Finally, the Reagan administration undertook a steady attack on those United Nations specialised agencies which promoted the interests of revisionist Third World states, by refusing to pay its 'debts' to the organisation, reducing agency funds in some cases by as much as half; and it pushed the IMF and the World Bank to more rigorous neo-liberal economic criteria in the granting of development loans and the provision of monetary stabilisation funds.

In the event, its allies began to demand rewards for sanctioning the Star Wars project (a popular reward was to share in Star Wars contracting). Moreover, they refused to significantly restrict their economic competitiveness to aid America's new Cold War.

By the mid-1980s, Western solidarity, not to mention the major Western institutions, was demonstrating signs of noticeable decay. Nato had become little more than a negotiating forum for the terms of Star Wars and other weapons contracting. It was, moreover, a notably ineffective forum for restraining United States behaviour towards the Soviet Union.[30] At the global level, the GATT regime was weakening in the face of intra-Western economic competition, particularly as Japan was rapidly emerging as a powerful economic actor with protectionist instincts, which further threatened the global economic order.

The only Western institution which really showed vital signs was the European Community, which gained increased salience in the face of both American pressure and the Japanese ascendancy. It not only enlarged to include Spain,

Portugal and Greece, it was emerging as the major locus of co-ordination for the West European powers in their policies vis-à-vis both Japan and the United States. The Community allowed the Europeans to confront Japanese competition in tandem, as well as to resist American demands for special economic treatment in its renewed conflict with the Soviet Union. (It was partly in consequence of both that, in 1985, the Community agreed to the achievement of a fully single market.)[31]

The end of the Cold War

The abandonment of the Cold War struggle was finally undertaken by a new Russian premier with a background in the KGB, the agency perhaps most alert to the long-term balance of forces. Gorbachev came to power in 1985 after a decade of stagnant Brezhnev rule with a radical political agenda for the internal restructuring of the Soviet system. He initiated a series of internal domestic reforms during 1988, the first in economic policy. (The significant new economic measure was citizens' property rights.) The new economic policy implied a turning from the high-cost military sector, which the Cold War struggle had caused to be the preferred sector, to the production of ordinary consumer goods in an ordinary economy.[32] A political reform, or *glasnost*, took place the following year. The political reforms included citizen rights to criticise the state machinery, rights to form other political parties and the promise of genuine elections between competing political groupings.[33] The aim of both sets of reforms was political accountability, a revitalised and efficient bureaucracy, and an end to the administrative and economic stagnation into which the Soviet Union had fallen.

The chief question raised by the reform process, to insiders as well as to outsiders, was the role of the CCCP within the reformed state machinery. Initially, Gorbachev had sought to create a new locus of political authority based on a freely elected parliament. But he also wished the Soviet Communist Party to be accorded a special role in the new political marketplace, essentially through the continued enjoyment of special state privileges. A special status would assure the party electoral advantages and, accordingly, a probable parliamentary majority, providing Gorbachev and any future leader with a double power base, based on both party and parliament. The proposal became a major bone of contention within the country, both on the 'right', which objected to any power-sharing, and on the 'left', which wished no special privileges for the party at all (and some of whom wished it dissolved). An attempted coup by the 'right' would be forestalled by the direct action of the Soviet vice-president, Yeltsin, himself committed to ending the special role of the party.

These changes were accompanied by a new foreign policy stance, an 'external glasnost'. Instead of confronting the West, it became Gorbachev's policy to seek Western support during the Soviet Union's transition. Such support would be required to maintain the territorial integrity of the country (vital since the old Soviet Union was not a homogeneous national entity) and to provide restructuring loans and backing for a convertible rouble. The new policy would have immediate consequences for its relations with the United States, reflected in a new willingness to collaborate with Western-sponsored initiatives: a move by the United States within the Security Council to condemn an Iraqi invasion of Kuwait at the end of 1990 (and to raise a coalition force to restore the *status quo ante*) was not opposed by the Soviet Union.

Both aims limited the degree to which the Soviet ruler was willing to support the puppet regimes of Eastern Europe, at least by any show of force. Gorbachev urged the various parties of the Soviet bloc also to enter upon glasnost. What was more significant, he refused to secure them in the face of a series of rapidly emerging popular protests and reform movements.[34] One by one, the regimes of socialist Central and Eastern Europe were swept away during 1989, to be replaced by a variety of experimental governmental forms. The East Germans voted to join the Federal Republic, under that country's constitutional order, without alteration. On 3 October 1990, five new Länder joined the Federal Republic, enhancing its population by one-quarter and its land space by one-third.

The future of the Cold War structures

War was, once again, the occasion for the articulation of a 'new world order'. In the months following the Soviet collapse, Iraq had invaded Kuwait, and the United States moved to build a coalition to repel the invasion. In September 1990, President Bush, Reagan's Republican successor, made a major speech to Congress defining the coalition's goals, which he set within a framework of the new possibilities created by the end of the Cold War.

There were four pillars to the Bush structure. The United Nations was to be reformed to make it more efficient and more cost-effective; Europe must henceforward take more responsibility for its own defence; and the super-powers would collaborate. Finally, Bush signalled America's commitment to global liberalism. This implied a continuation of 'Reaganism' in the distribution of financial aid, as well as the encouragement of liberal state forms globally; in addition, reform of the global trading order would be undertaken to counteract economic regionalism. His Democratic successor, Bill Clinton, would unambiguously throw United States support behind a new global trading organisation, the World Trade Organisation, enshrining a new set of universal rules for the management of economic protectionism.

At the global level, 'liberal political systems' was soon defined to mean party competition for electoral advantage. The United States began to press governments of remaining one-party states, generally now in the Third World, to allow the formation of opposition parties. Particularly in Africa, indigenous political cultures and local conditions had favoured the development of the coalition government in which diverse, particularly tribal, forces were united into a single party under a single strong leadership. These were now pressed into abandoning this political form.

In Europe, there was an initial fear that the European Community would not be able to contain an enlarged Germany, with its increased economic and political might, and that unification would engender a process of splitting and weakening, particularly given the commitment to a single market.

France took the lead in setting the terms for Europe's post-Cold War construction. The French government announced it would only agree to the unification of the two Germanys if Germany abandoned any remaining territorial claims in Central Europe and agreed to continue 'Europe building'. This meant Germany's commitment to an eventual monetary union, regulated by a new European Central Bank, and enlargement of the union to take in at least some of the newly liberated countries of Central Europe. For France, an enlarged European Community with enhanced central powers would contain the new Germany and ensure its impulses served Europe as a whole.

With regard to the formal alliances, there was initially a strong tendency to try to maintain the traditional structures on the part of both sets of alliance leaders (although on the part of Britain and the United States at reduced cost – this was called the 'peace dividend'). The maintenance of the alliances now depended, however, solely on the willingness of the respective alliance participants in each bloc, a variable quality. Within the former Soviet bloc, Russia's former allies proved distinctly unamenable. First Hungary, then Poland and Czechoslovakia quietly announced that they would be leaving the Warsaw Pact. After initial protests, the emerging Confederation of Independent States, formed under Gorbachev's successor, Yeltsin, did not demur.

The Western situation proved more complex. Both Germany and France wished to see the alliance maintained in some form, but with radically different structures. Germany urged the United States to remain an integral member of a reformed alliance. France initially proposed a more European-based alliance system, perhaps built on the Western European Union, partly out of an inclination to see the United States out of Europe and partly out of a fear that it would leave anyway. The determining issue for France, however, was the nuclear question, and whether a new European grouping would endorse a European-based nuclear defence. In the event, none of its putative partners in the proposed new venture proved willing even to discuss nuclear weapons. By the end of 1995, France had signalled its willingness to return to the military structure of Nato, foreclosing the European defence option for the immediate future.

The choices of the major Western powers, and the eventual shape of the Western alliance, were to be affected by the emerging situation in Eastern and Central Europe. As the newly independent states of Central Europe watched a reformed Russian-based Confederation of Independent States rise to their east in the context of a possibly dissolving Nato to their west, they began to enter into the Nato equation. They began to demand entry into some sort of reformed Western security system, pointing to their isolation if Nato did not take them in.

Faced by the choice between maintaining the old Western-based system in the context of a set of unstable states to its east, abandoning it for an entirely new and yet undetermined arrangement to include those states, or building a new system from within its structures, the major Western powers, with varying degrees of enthusiasm, determined on widening the existing alliance. In 1994, led by Clinton, they agreed on a major expansion of its remit. Nato would take in some of the states of East and Central Europe and explore the undertaking of peacekeeping roles with regard to the rest, as a supplement (and some argued as a replacement) to United Nations peacekeeping. At the same time, they drew the line at the Baltic states, choosing either not to antagonise the CIS beyond recall or to avoid confronting Russia on its immediate borders.

The question of what kind of security system the Western powers were building by such measures dominated discussions among security analysts during the last years of the century. Some deplored the decision as creating renewed conflict with the former Soviet Union. Others maintained that widening Nato's remit would result in an ineffective security structure: it became a matter of debate whether Clause 5, which regarded 'an attack on one as an attack on all', could or should be maintained under enlargement. It was clear that none of the original Nato members wished to be involved in securing undetermined borders in Central Europe nor in resolving disputes among contending national minorities, both features of several potential new members, including Hungary. An important qualification for entry would be the settlement of border disputes and the clarification of the position of minorities in Eastern and Central Europe.

The IMF and the World Bank had already been reformed through the late 1980s in a neo-liberal direction, but the ending of the Cold War, somewhat paradoxically, gave them enlarged scope and new tasks, at least for the transitional period. The IMF was given the task of co-ordinating and overseeing the terms of Western aid to the former Soviet Union. (The EU became the primary overseer for the transition of the newly liberated countries of Central and Eastern Europe.) The World Bank was to oversee the liberalisation experiments in the Third World. During the last decade of the century, a more rigorous set of conditionalities was set for restructuring those Third World economies which were in debt or which sought restructuring loans, and which turned on the establishment of genuine market economies and limiting government expenditure. The 'free world' institutions took on the task of seeing that such conditions were met, approving projects and channelling funds to them in the degree to which they ceased uneconomic subsidies and liberalised their political orders. (In this effort, the former Soviet Union was not a player, offering neither political support to those who objected to the conditionalities, nor alternative sources of needed aid. Without such alternative sources of support, there was little choice for debtor states but to obey.)

The Cold War and internationalism

By 1995, it was generally conceded that the Cold War had ended and that the West had prevailed. Which among the Western powers had precisely gained the relative advantage was, however, not easy to determine. For those who had been colonial powers at its onset, those colonies had gone. Moreover, a revised economic clientelism was scarcely a viable future option: the question for the immediate future was one of national and regional economic competitiveness among economic leaders. So far as the United States was concerned, this represented a considerable victory. But, equally, the modalities of the Cold War had raised two formidable economic competitors against it: Germany and Japan. Moreover, the one power which had been enhanced by the dissolution of the Soviet bloc, politically as well as in geographical extent, was Germany. Finally, China had been left in place as a major revisionist state.

What was less disputed was that the Cold War, even more than the war against fascism, had firmly entrenched forms of political and economic liberalism as the declared aims of liberal foreign policies, while its end had generated those aims throughout the international system. The 'New World Order' implied economic and political liberalism for all states.

Moreover, the institutional carapace built to fight the Cold War had, in fact, been converted into the major modality for securing those aims. The World Bank, the altered Nato and the expanded European Community would set conditionalities for achieving eventual membership (and for receiving Western aid and private investment) which would include guarantees of human rights, open economic exchange and secure borders. The new World Trading Organisation would set the rules of economic exchange among them. A major question for the immediate future was the role of an increasingly sidelined United Nations among these other, more vibrant, institutions.

While the end of the Cold War had immediately strengthened institutionalisation, however, its course had demonstrated that the precise institutional formulae of choice (not to mention the definition of 'liberalism') had all varied with major power interests, and that institutions had been deployed in quite different ways in the context of quite different diplomatic initiatives. It had also shown that the commitment to institutional multilateralism rose and fell, particularly on the part of the United States, now the only remaining superpower.

Notes

1 'The sources of Soviet conduct', *Foreign Affairs*, 25 (July 1947), pp. 566–82.
2 Zbigniew Brzezinski, its most skilled observer during the late 1940s and early 1950s, pointed out the Soviet leaders' lack of skill in managing an international empire; *The Soviet Bloc* (New York: Praeger, 1961).
3 D.F. Fleming, *The Cold War and its Origins, 1917–1960* (London: Allen and Unwin, 1961).
4 J. Gaddis, *The United States and the Origins of the Cold War, 1941–1947* (New York: Columbia University, 1972).
5 A. Werth's *France 1940–1955* (London: Robert Hale, 1956) is particularly good on the debates at the time, including the neutralist 'heresy'.
6 W. Le Feber, *America, Russia and the Cold War 1945–1980*, fifth edition (New York: Wiley, 1985).
7 See H. Jones, 'A New Kind of War' in *America's Global Strategy and the Truman Doctrine in Greece* (Oxford: Oxford University Press, 1989).

8 J. Jones, *The Fifteen Weeks* (New York: Harcourt, Brace and World, 1955).

9 R. Simmons, *The Strained Alliance: Peking, Pyonyang and the Politics of the Korean War* (New York: Free Press, 1975).

10 See A. Whiting, *China Crosses the Yalu* (Stanford: Stanford University, 1968).

11 R. McGeehan, *The German Rearmament Question: American Diplomacy and European Defense* (Urbana: University of Illinois, 1971).

12 A. Grosser, *The Western Alliance* (Paris, London and Vienna: Macmillan, 1978) is especially illuminating on French attitudes.

13 D. Lerner and R. Aron tell a story of demoralisation and confusion in *France Defeats E.D.C.* (London: Atlantic Press, 1957).

14 The idea for two tiers was Anthony Eden's, conceived in his bath and recalled in his memoirs, *Full Circle* (London: Cassell, 1960) p. 151.

15 R. Scigiliano, *South Vietnam: Nation Under Stress* (Boston: Houghton Mifflin, 1964) p. 191.

16 J. Mayall, *Africa: The Cold War and After* (London: Elek, 1971).

17 G. Kahin, *The Asian–African Conference, Bandung* (Ithaca: Cornell University Press, 1956).

18 See P. Willetts, *The Non-Aligned Movement* (London: Pinter, 1978).

19 One of the best analyses remains W. Hanrieder, *The Stable Crisis: Two Decades of German Foreign Policy* (New York: Harper and Row, 1970).

20 R. Bloes tells much of the inside story: *Le 'Plan Fouchet' et le problème de l'Europe politique* (Bruges: Collèe de l'Europe, 1970).

21 A. Kolodzie, *French International Policy under de Gaulle and Pompidou: The Politics of Grandeur* (Ithaca: Cornell University, 1974).

22 R. Aron, *The Great Debate* (Garden City: Doubleday, 1965) and H. Kissinger, *The Troubled Partnership* (New York: Mcgraw Hill, 1965) managed to stay calm.

23 Or fostering polycentrism; Philip Windsor, *Germany and the Management of Detente* (London: Chatto and Windus, 1971) pp. 60–4.

24 M. Camps, *What Kind of Europe?* (London: Oxford University Press, 1965).

25 Deriving partly from Soviet underwriting of the Aswan Dam; W. Laquer, *The Struggle for the Middle East* (London and New York: Penguin, 1969).

26 L. Gardner (ed.), *The Great Nixon Turnaround* (New York: New Viewpoints, 1973).

27 J. Mayall and C. Navari (eds), *The End of the Post-War Era: Documents on Great-Power Relation 1968–75* (Cambridge: Cambridge University Press, 1980); the volume contains all the 'German' agreements.

28 T. Farar, *War Clouds on the Horn of Africa* (New York: Carnegie, 1979).

29 See F. Halliday, *The Making of the Second Cold War*, second edition (London: Verso, 1986).

30 K. Myers (ed.), *Nato, The Next Thirty Years* (Boulder and London: Croom Helm, 1980) is a catalogue of woes from the Atlantic establishment, one contributor inquiring, 'Does Nato Exist?'; see also S. Serfaty, *Fading Partnership: America and Europe after Thirty Years* (New York: Praeger, 1979).

31 J. Lodge (ed.), *The European Community and the Challenge of the Future* (London: Pinter, 1989) expresses the optimism surrounding the development.

32 A. Anders, *Gorbachev's Struggle for Economic Reform* (London: Pinter, 1991).

33 M. McCauley (ed.), *Gorbachev and Perestroika* (London: Macmillan, 1990).

34 K. Dawisha, *Eastern Europe, Gorbachev and Reform*, second edition (Cambridge: Cambridge University Press, 1990).

11 Decolonisation

As the Cold War proceeded, decolonisation was speeded up. Colonisers could not give the same time and energy to maintaining colonies when the Cold War required resources, of domestic modernisation and nuclear development. In the colonies, the Cold War conflict expanded the ideological resources available to indigenous liberation movements: 'actually existing' communism, as opposed to 'actually existing' liberalism, demanded liberation at once. The rivalries among the major powers also gave rebellious colonials potentially potent sources of aid in their struggles. The British, in particular, hurried decolonisation in Africa to forestall the transformation of colonial theatres into arenas of Cold War conflict and to prevent the radicalisation of local political movements. It was vital that colonial possessions be transferred to local personnel who could be trusted to protect the remaining British interests in the ex-colony.

Decolonisation, in turn, widened institutional deployment. It was not merely that many new members of the developing international community were created. It was also that the old imperial bonds had to be transformed into new self-standing post-imperial mechanisms which at the same time would continue to link former colonies with former imperialisers. Few colonies could simply be abandoned. Economic and military plant vital to the former mother country had to remain accessible for exploitation, particularly given the political environment of the Cold War. Nor did ex-colonial governments wish to be abandoned without recourse to aid or political and strategic support. The process of decolonisation, accordingly, saw the creation of new forms of relationship between former colony and colonial master, and novel administrative devices which continued to link what had become putative sovereigns.

The rise and fall of the colonial game

The nineteenth century had witnessed the acme of colonial expansion. More and deeper colonisation occurred during its course than at any time since the 'gold and silver' empires of the sixteenth century. It also witnessed the establishment of direct imperial rule. Eighteenth-century imperialism had consisted primarily in the establishment of factories and trading sites in Asia and Africa which co-existed with local rule. The nineteenth century saw the incorporation of entire territories and pre-existing political orders into formal areas of direct colonial administration.

The period following 1870 was a particularly hectic time for colonial expansion. Having settled Algeria between 1830 and 1870, France annexed South East Asia – Cambodia, Laos and Vietnam – between 1870 and 1890.[1] The British Crown had taken over administration of the great commercial empire of the East India Company in 1856, formally establishing the British Empire (with the declaration of Victoria as Empress of India in 1887), while Egypt, British Malaya and Singapore were incorporated into that Empire as forms of protectorate during the 1880s.[2] Britain's African adventure had begun much earlier, with the seizure of the Dutch Cape Colony during the Napoleonic Wars (to keep it out of French hands after Napoleon's invasion of the Lowlands), but African colonisation speeded in its last quarter, driven by Cecil Rhodes' dream to establish a railway from the Cape to Cairo.[3] At the end of the nineteenth century, the great Berlin West African Congresses of 1884–5 divided the remainder of Africa between France, Britain, Germany and Belgium, and recognised the Portuguese old coastal colonies of Angola and Mozambique.

The causes of this eruption were puzzling, particularly in the light of the 'liberalising' tendencies spreading through the metropolitan centres. After the loss of its American colonies in 1776, Britain had begun handing increasing autonomy to its old white colonies, whose conversion to dominion status was well under way by the time the new imperialism was undertaken. The emergence of the new 'administrative colonialism' became, accordingly, an historical knot to be untied.[4] There was also the increasing ascendance of liberal political forces within the colonial countries, registered in Britain by the reform of the Corn Laws and in France by the Anglo-French commercial treaty, which were antithetical to imperial renewal. Accordingly, any theory accounting for the onset of 'new' empire had to do so in the context of an apparent dissolution of 'old' empire; it also had to explain why liberalism was being suborned to the imperial drive.

Three different explanations emerged, each of which sourced the new imperialism in different contexts. The first pointed to the gradual dissolution of political, economic and social structures in the colonial theatre, often as a result of informal colonial activity. It became known as the 'theory of the peripheries'. The 'peripheral' theory highlighted the erosive effects on traditional societies of informal colonialism, and the cumulative consequences of the separate activities of missionaries, traders and guarantor powers. It also insisted on the gradual nature of the assumption of local administrative functions by colonial governments, which was in fact a feature of the 'new colonialism'.[5] Its major theoretical rival pointed, not to changes in the peripheries, but to changes in the metropolitan centres, which were witnessing the onset of industrialisation, and a growing conflict between older and rising economic forces. The 'metropolitan' theory stressed economic forces and economic demands in the mother country.[6] Both tended to ignore the third, 'systemic theory', but it pointed out yet another, important, parallel development. It stressed the rise of global power, an important aspect of which was the emergence of aggressive 'have not' powers, and colonial competition as an aspect of a changing global balance. It also pointed to the fact that, due to the developing nature of power in the later nineteenth century, colonies had to be more firmly held and more widely exploited.[7]

Whatever its efficient causes, however, its effects were dramatic. By 1914, all of Asia and Africa had fallen under the direct administration of five European powers, with the exception of Japan, China and Thailand in Asia, and Ethiopia and Liberia in Africa.

The twentieth century, by contrast, saw the steady disbursement of this vast tract, slowly during the inter-war period, and then with increasing rapidity following the Second World War. France and Britain gradually relinquished formal controls in the Middle East during the 1920s and 1930s, while they were pushed into hurrying independence for India and South East Asia during the 1940s and 1950s. The great period of Africa liberation occurred during the 1960s, resembling at times a scramble for decolonisation as countries dumped even possessions scarcely ready for independence.

The decolonisation process was also marked by the adoption of implicit policies of parallel development. Not merely were the empires dispersed, but former colonial possessions were constituted into states resembling the emergent states of Western Europe and incorporated into a single system with them. Indeed, the new European states and the new, post-colonial states emerged together. It was the disbursements of their empires which converted the great nineteenth-century European imperial powers into the medium-sized national states of post-1945 Europe, interacting as 'ordinary' sovereigns with other legally equal sovereigns. If England became Britain and Overseas Dominions at the end of the eighteenth century, and the British Empire in the nineteenth century, she finally became Britain after 1968.

The onset of imperial retreat?

The onset of retreat may be differently assigned, depending on the differing meanings of 'retreat'. One was the emergence of responsible government in territories formerly ruled directly, a definition implying the transfer of administrative competences. Another was power and evidence of inability to hold. Finally, there are the ideological criteria, involving the abandonment of the colonial vision altogether. Responsible government (but scarcely full powers) was conceded by Britain to some of its territories as early as 1917, in the midst of the war, and was reaffirmed and clarified by the Declaration of Westminster in 1926. But nobody then was thinking of a complete severance of political or administrative ties. Indeed, the wartime behaviour of the Allies would lead even the most casual observer to conclude that the colonial game was in full swing. Not only were Turkey's Arabian possessions partitioned between Britain and France during the First World War, but even the Turkish 'homeland' – that is, Turkey itself – was up for grabs. Moreover, an integral part of the war strategy of each of the colonial powers was to get into as many 'liberated' areas as possible to forestall the others. In few of these new possessions was real liberation entertained, despite a series of ambiguous promises to Arab chieftains and urban elites (and these were made primarily for strategic reasons). It was also taken for granted that Germany's Asian and African colonies would be shared out among the victors. The dispersal of the German and Ottoman possessions went through several phases as the First World War came to an end, with much unseemly scrambling, but it is the result that commands attention. Both the British and French colonial empires reached their greatest respective extents in 1920, after the formal partition of Arabia.

If the defining criterion is failure to hold – that is, inability to impose a will otherwise desired – the significant dates for Britain would be the mid-1920s. In 1925, Britain was forced to relinquish direct administration of Jordan, the first (albeit briefly held) colonial possession to escape the imperial net since Britain had lost the American colonies (although Britain continued to direct its foreign policy).[8] More significantly, the British government announced to the House of Commons in 1926 that old dominion status, concerning Canada, Australia and New Zealand, no longer required obedience in foreign policy, the final attribute of sovereignty as far as the old dominions were concerned; and it, too, was not a freely willed donation but rather an obedience to necessity.

The ending of the colonial vision is much harder to judge, since this was a question of attitudes, and these changed only slowly and over a long period. At the level of state policy, the United States was the first colonial power to abandon the colonial dream. It had entered upon the colonial game in a small way with the seizing of the Philippines from Spain after the Spanish–American War. During the First World War, it sometimes attempted to forestall the imperial ambitions of others and sometimes behaved as rising colonial competitor itself. Increasingly, however, the image of America as a potential colonial power in competition with other colonial powers faded, even in the midst of frequent interventions in Central America. During the 1930s, the Roosevelt administration rejected empire as an objective of policy or a method of determining relations, even in Latin America. In a series of landmark Senate debates, the issue was finally settled: in 1934, the United States government announced its intention to cede the Philippines to independence, at the latest by 1946. With this announcement, moreover, United States policy shifted towards encouraging the development of modern institutions and economic growth in less developed parts of the world. (Indeed, the increasing mondialism of American economic thought after the Second World War derived, in part, from American ideas on how to live with countries that it was not going to colonise.) This objective determined others in its wake: one of the major objectives of American foreign policy both immediately before and after the Second World War was to rid the world of colonialism generally and to detach Britain in particular from imperial habits. Indeed, it became, with varying emphasis, one of America's war aims.[9]

For Britain, some have dated the relinquishment of the imperial vision with the abandonment of India in 1947; and in terms of unintended consequences perhaps it was. Much of the colonial drive during the early 1920s in Arabia, as well as the effort to maintain the informal controls established during the last quarter of the nineteenth century in Egypt, had been undertaken in the context of a perceived necessity to secure the routes to India. Abandoning India would inevitably make the protection of intermediate imperial strongholds seem less important. But, at the time, few Englishmen thought that leaving India implied the end of empire more generally or even the ending of a special relationship with India. Indeed, its incorporation into the Commonwealth was widely viewed as the continuation of an imperial relationship in a different form. It is also noteworthy that the idea of 'trusteeship' invaded both major British political parties during the 1950s, and that maintenance of the Commonwealth as the carapace of trusteeship was supported by both parties precisely because its meaning was ambiguous.[10]

Attitudes also differed as between elites and the general public. Many ordinary working people in Britain were distinctly unenamoured of the imperial vision and could scarcely grasp the importance of India to imperial enthusiasts, particularly after the fall of Singapore. Among the ruling elites, attitudes also differed. It was from within the Treasury, taking a hard look at the actual benefits of colonial possession to Britain in the late 1950s, that the idea first clearly emerged that Britain's future well-being lay in developing its economic and trading relations with other advanced industrial countries, and not within the Empire.[11] It took time to distinguish the colonial role from the global role.

A single process or multiple processes?

Decolonisation was scarcely a single process. There was little that tied the Senate debates of the 1930s to the long parliamentary stasis which confounded French colonial policy during the 1950s. Also, it was affected by different criteria at different times. For example, the loss of control over the Suez Canal in 1956 made Britain all the more determined to hold on to Cyprus, with the consequence that while responsible government was being conceded in other British territories, it was actually being denied to Cypriots, spinning off the bitter civil and anti-colonial struggle of the late 1950s. Likewise, the French military became more determined to hold on to Algeria after the defeat at Dien Bien Phu in Vietnam in 1954.[12] Moreover, the question of Algerian independence largely drove the efforts of officers of the French Algerian army to unseat President de Gaulle and to destabilise the new Fifth Republic. (Hence, liberating Algeria, as well as France's other overseas territories, became linked to the securing of the new French Republic.[13]) The rise of local fighting forces and the appearance of forms of guerrilla warfare to push the coloniser out also affected the process. Where local forces adopted modern forms of guerrilla warfare, this had effects on the terms of the donation, and tended to produce greater degrees of independence, greater degrees of coherent leadership among the anti-colonialists and sometimes greater degrees of popular solidarity.[14]

At the same time, the colonial powers faced similar requirements in extracting themselves from colonial territories. Also, the methods they employed, if they varied with time and place, displayed a limited variety of solutions. Moreover, it is the legacies that are the subject of our concern. The question is less what drove the powers in each instance than what was donated or handed over during the process, and how this process structured the many new states that would be created.

The internal legacies of decolonisation

The first requirement was an intact territory with more or less delimited borders. Administrative competence for the new dominions had to be defined territorially in order to define the domain of competence for each responsible new governing or administrative authority. These were the result of various criteria at various times. Sometimes protectorates in the British case were simply tagged on to a Crown Colony: for example, Western Province in Zambia, which had had a separate political identity and a separate administrative structure. Others, like Botswana, survived.[15] In other cases, the new borders simply reflected imperial administration at the time of liberation, as with the tripartite division of West Africa in the 1930s, or derived from international obligations. (The mandate system and mandatory responsibility for Turkey's Arabian provinces demanded their early partition between Britain and France and, accordingly, a clear definition of their respective borders, particularly since some were in group A, singled out for early self-government.) In the case of India, however, it was a political decision which determined the borders of the new state, a decision which emerged in the course of a long process of contrary political evolution between Hindus and Moslems and which eventually resulted in partition between a new India and a new Pakistan.

In some cases, federations were tried. The India Act of 1935 had promised to resolve Muslim–Hindu differences within a federal structure. In Malaya, there was a short-lived scheme in the 1950s to satisfy the Chinese minority; there were also proposals for a federated Arab state that might include an autonomous Jewish state. Usually, however, they ended in either partitions, or as in the case of Malaysia, a unitary state.[16]

Where a clear division of some sort had existed historically, as in the case of French Indo-China, the old kingdoms were re-established. But they were also given 'hard' boundaries, which most had previously lacked.

The experience of Asia also demonstrated that it was not always the colonial power that defined a new state's area. France tried to limit independent Vietnam's extent to two northern provinces and to constitute the South into a separate entity with a continuing colonial status, which became the basis of a war. The ultimate borders of Vietnam were finally determined by the military action undertaken by the North, first against France and then against the United

States. In the Dutch East Indies, the Dutch tried to limit self-government only to Java; Sukarno determined in 1954 to break the limitation and declared all the islands the subjects of decolonisation.

A second process involved removing traditional local and regional rulers or incorporating them into new rationalised state machineries. Empire, particularly in the British case but also elsewhere, had often involved operating through traditional rulers who were subordinated via treaties to the status of representatives of the British Crown (with British advisors close at hand). Political and constitutional evolution, as well as the ideology of national self-determination, demanded bypassing traditional rulers and avoiding the restoration of traditional rights. Chiefs, local kings and maharajas had to be removed legally from centre-stage, to be replaced by new leaders with a populist base in new nationalist groupings. This involved an often undignified process of buying off the maharajas in India, while in Africa traditional chiefs and kings were jollied along by local British administrations and challenged by newly formed political parties fighting in representative assemblies. In British Africa, traditional chiefs lost many of their formal powers but retained local patronage and effective control in the countryside, leaving each new state machine to deal with the novel problem of unauthorised but still legitimate power in different ways.[17] In Uganda, where the issue of the relative rights of traditional kingship intensified with independence, it was 'solved' by direct violence on the part of Idi Amin. (In the short term, the more serious problem was the settler problem.)

A third donation was a constitution and a machinery of state. The constitutional form was generally liberal democratic. The state machinery included a judiciary in principle free from political interference, a governor-general in the case of British colonies to perform the roles of the monarch, and a prime minister to determine the business of the day. It also included a parliament, a cabinet and a leader of the opposition, a central bank and an appropriate currency.

If constitutionalism was paramount throughout, the shape of specific institutions was determined by the institutional pattern of the former metropolitan power. Each new state machinery was essentially a replication of the host country institutions injected into the new territory. The French outline law of 1956 established governmental councils (equivalent to the French cabinet), to be eventually raised from territorial assemblies which would direct centralised administrations. The model in the case of the British Empire was the transformation from Crown Colony to Dominion status that had taken place in the white colonies, and which had involved a gradual handing over of powers, and their elaboration, to a local administration until a more or less complete state had been created, once again resembling the mother country, which then joined Britain in the Commonwealth with, of course, the British monarch as the titular head.

These processes of constitutional development were supported by elections. Elections identified a legitimate group to whom the constitution and the new state machinery could be entrusted. These periods of electoral contestation in preparation for the full granting of autonomy were periods of something like genuine party politics, particularly in Africa, as different groups contested elections to win the mantle of the new powers that were being created.

Later commentators would characterise as naive the belief that a newly created state machinery could simply be passed intact to new and untried political entrants, or that such processes could create political stability in their wake. In fact, few serious observers expected these formulae to guarantee stability or to remain unchanged. This is not to say that one-party rule, which became the prevalent form in Africa and elsewhere, was either foreseen or welcomed. It is that both colonisers and new aspirants to political rule wanted a regularised exit, on both sides, which these processes enabled. Nor in hindsight were they unwise. In Angola and Mozambique, where the Portuguese simply abandoned the territories during the 1970s without any preparation for decolonisation, administration simply dissolved, and politics degenerated into unregulated violence.

In many cases, powers were reserved, some for a transition period but some in perpetuity. The British government everywhere typically retained control of security, domestic and cross-border, and all aspects of foreign relations. Many ex-African colonies began independence without the control of their foreign policies and without autonomous police forces or security services; and they had to push hard to gain these as of right. The French government reserved not merely security, but also communications, higher education, finance and foreign exchange. It fixed the new African currencies in its former territories to control by the French central bank and regulated the exchange rate between the local currency and the franc. The currency link became, moreover, a permanent feature of francophone Africa.

Ex-colonial powers also tried to ensure some degree of economic viability to new states. This was taken to exist whenever local taxation could support the administrative machinery required to sustain an independent government. (Borders were drawn partly with a view to viability, to assure a sufficient tax base or a share of valuable raw materials.) Where this was not seen to exist, initially at least, a territory was not considered ready for independence, and decolonisation proceeded more slowly. But viability also became subject to varying criteria as the slow became anxious to catch up. Moreover, the more countries became independent, the more pressure fell on the colonial powers to speed up the process, and the less lack of viability impeded the decision to render full sovereignty. By the 1970s, powers were agreeing to the independence of even micro-states with no prospect of economic viability.

The external legacies of decolonisation

Internationally, new countries all joined the United Nations under sponsorship, and all enjoyed the protection of international law. They became equal legal entities, theoretically free to diversify their foreign policies. But they did not enter into the international community free of more specified obligations; they were expected to honour treaties and commitments already entered into on their behalf.

But decolonisation also involved the creation of a special set of international institutions which were intended to be of particular service to new states and to support them. Partly because they were creating 'weak' states, partly because they had left behind imperial plant, partly because of the existence of important 'private' ties, especially economic links into the old metropolis, and partly because of defence requirements further on, a great variety of new arrangements were created (and some old methods returned to) within which new states' foreign policy would be conducted. Not a small part of the institutional density of mid-twentieth-century international relations was a resultant of this parallel effort to 'place' the newly independent countries.

Some of these new structures were directed to maintaining some political or strategic relationship between the former imperial overlord and the new state. Others were designed to aid their passage as fully independent states, albeit within a specified type of international order.

The political union

The most obvious were the new political unions. In the case of the French Community and the British Commonwealth, these were originally intended to be containers of responsible government and the location of the reserved powers, rather than with France or the United Kingdom.[18] The French Community, created by the new Fifth Republic in 1958 as part of the new constitution, was a transition device intended to provide a framework for rapid 'self-administration' for twelve overseas territories, and indeed their independence if they so desired it. (It was widely understood as a form of semi-federation in the interim.) But it was revised to allow for continued membership by completely independent states, of which six agreed initially to remain within it, and it became the locus of co-operation in the fields of foreign policy, economic and financial policy and higher education. In the case of the British Commonwealth, biannual meetings between Commonwealth Heads of State were regularised during the 1950s, and a foreign ministerial meeting was held annually.[19]

They also had important economic functions. Those states who remained in the French Community (as well, eventually, as those who left) received generous economic, financial and technical assistance from France. The British Commonwealth served importantly during the 1950s and 1960s to regulate the economic relations between the sterling area and territories moving towards independence. The Commonwealth also remained an important residual link, not least of all because it came to serve as a route of development aid. A newly created Ministry of Overseas Development served as the immediate donor agency. This proved important to the maintenance of the Commonwealth, since to be a member gave access to a special aid relationship, just as French Community membership did.

In the Americas, a Pan American Union had begun to take shape in the late 1920s which provided for recognition among equals, arbitration, and non-intervention. (It was at the conference in Montevideo in 1933 that the United States fully accepted the principle of non-intervention in Latin America.) In the American case, the Union served as a negotiating forum for determining the rules of the game within which inter-American relations would take place, emphasising international law and including agreements to consult if the continent's peace were endangered, as well as commitments to adjudication in the case of disputes between them.[20]

In 1948, at Bogota, the loose Union was transformed into the more formal Organisation of American States. One of the central provisions of the founding document was a generalisation of the Monroe Doctrine, which forbade interference by any external state against the territorial integrity, sovereignty or political independence of an American state. It represented a quid pro quo between the United States and the states of Latin America, assuring that if America was not going to colonise Latin America, then neither should anyone else.

Defence co-operation and regional pacts

A variety of defence arrangements were created which were directed either towards maintaining the security of the government in place, to strengthen its defence wing, and/or to continue to allow the former imperial power the use of the territory for defence purposes. Some were forms of the 'imperial alliance' prominent in the latter part of the nineteenth century, and represented a reversion to older types of imperial relationship, while others were more novel forms of defence community.

The imperial alliance had been a prevalent device of late nineteenth- and early twentieth-century informal empire. The regulation of Egyptian finances, which gave Britain such a prominent place in Egyptian affairs, was via an alliance which gave to Britain the power over the Egyptian state finances. The same formula was repeated with regard to Bahrain and the Trucial kingdoms in the Gulf during the early twentieth century. Britain's treaties with Iraq in 1922 and Jordan in 1925 tied the countries in foreign policy and provided sometime military training; in the case of Iraq, the treaty also gave Britain control of Iraqi finances. The transformation of British relationships with the Trucial kingdoms and small Gulf states (formerly small Gulf provinces) was also through a policy of alliances. French imperial alliances tied former colonies into military exchanges, guarantees to help France protect the rest of the former or still existent colonial area, military training and permission to site French troops.

These arrangement were adjusted over time. France, which had 27,000 troops spread through its colonies in 1964, reduced that number to 6,000 in 1980, located at four support points in Dakar, Abidjan and Fort Lomy and three locations in Madagascar.

The more novel arrangement was the regional pact. A form of multilateral defence arrangement, they were created by joining several countries together with their former imperial masters. Set in key strategic areas, regional pacts became an important adjunct of the policy of 'containment'. The pattern was for two or three former imperialisers to join together with key regional partners. The pact provided security to the local partner, global mobility to the major powers involved and a barrier against military incursion by the Cold War antagonist or his local allies.

There were four major regional defence communities which linked former imperial powers with former colonies. The CENTO, the Central Treaty Organisation (sometimes called the Baghdad Pact), signed in Baghdad in 1956, linked Iraq, Iran, Pakistan and Turkey with Britain and the United States. The SEATO, or the South East Asia Treaty Organisation, agreed in Manila in 1954, linked Britain, France, the United States, Australia and New Zealand with the Philippines and Thailand. The ANZUK, formed in 1957 was an agreement between Australia, Britain and New Zealand to defend Malaysia and Singapore, and it accompanied and provided the larger carapace for an Anglo-Malaysian Defence Treaty of the same year. Both were supplemented by the ANZUS, based on a treaty of 1951 between Australia, New Zealand and the United States, which brought the US into the defence of southern Pacific Asia and provided the basis for defence collaboration between the ANZUK and ANZUS partners.

A key feature of these regional pacts was the emergence of the United States as a partner to a revised colonial relationship. Sometimes, United States entry was requested by one or other Great Power to enhance its military capability. In other cases, it represented a quid pro quo between them in the context of their global manoeuvrings. At other times, it was at the behest of the new state, and was intended to deprive the revised defence relationship of any untoward colonial aspect. Its most important role in the middle 1950s was as the material donor. The regional defence communities were built on an emerging political relationship between the old metropolis and the new self-governing elite legitimated by it through the decolonisation process, which provided the political stuffing to the alliance. This was supplemented by a material relationship between both parties and the United States, which provided the economic stuffing and an enhanced assurance of strategic security.

The forerunner of all such regional defence communities was the Rio Pact of 1947, which brought together and made explicit mutual security commitments agreed upon at Buenos Aires in 1936, at Havana in 1940 and at Chapultapec in 1945. Members of the original inter-American community had agreed that an armed attack upon one would be considered an attack on all. They had defined various forms of threat, including aggression short of armed attack, intra as well as extra continental conflict and 'any other fact or situation endangering the peace'. A notable feature of the Rio Pact was the inclusion of Canada as a signatory, and Greenland and Antarctica as areas of applicability.[21]

Economic linkages

Special trading ties were maintained through a variety of devices. Initially, there were the preferential trading agreements, generally inherited from the 1930s when the imperial powers had retreated to their colonial domains as a defence against economic depression. These could not be got rid of in the immediate aftermath of the war, as countries had to conserve scarce exchange, with the result that the new GATT rules had had to be designed around them. In the case of Belgium and France, where the process of decolonisation accompanied the negotiations for the European Economic Community, both argued, in the event successfully, that their preferential trade relationships with their colonies and former colonies should be converted into general obligations for the EEC as a whole. The Yaoundé Convention brought Belgian and French former colonies (and some of continued colonial status) into a preferential relationship with the emerging European Community as a whole.[22] (The convention provided for a governing Council made up of all member-states.) In Britain's case, the preferential trading arrangements became an attribute of the Commonwealth, to be enjoyed by all entrants upon achieving independence. But the Yaoundé pattern was replicated when Britain came into the EEC in 1973. As part of the entry package, its Commonwealth partners were offered the choice of joining a widened preferential trading arrangement with the European Community, or floating loose on to the world trading market. Eventually, 46 states signed the Lomé Convention, giving them preferential access to the European Community for raw materials and some industrial goods. The new Convention also provided a commodity price stabilisation scheme, which the European states agreed to fund.

There were also diverse monetary arrangements. Within the Commonwealth, a dollar pool had been established in the immediate aftermath of the Second World War to conserve scarce exchange, and it continued to operate through the 1950s. Accordingly, a number of Commonwealth countries pooled their dollar earnings and gained, as a reward, limited convertibility with the pound, which allowed their currencies to operate as exchangeable currencies on the world market.[23] The Franc Zone arrangements went much further. Ten West African countries and former French colonies, including Senegal, Ivory Coast, Burkina Faso and Chad, established the CFA, the African Community franc, which exchanged with the French franc at a fixed rate of 50 to 1. The rate was maintained by an African Community Central Bank which was directly linked to the French Central Bank. The effect was to establish immediate convertibility for all CFA countries. In turn, these arrangements allowed the French government to continue to influence economic policy in its ex-colonies.[24]

The elaboration of the new international organisations

Beside these special relationships, the recently created general international organisations were elaborated in various ways to support new states, generally by an enhancement of their tasks or through the addition of new sub-institutions.

The International Bank for Reconstruction and Development (the 'World Bank') had originally been intended to support the reconstruction of war-torn European economies following the Second World War, to avoid both the economic disruption which had followed Germany's defeat in the First World War and the withholding of loans as a form of political blackmail which had been a feature of inter-war diplomacy. The original task of the IBRD was to issue more or less commercial loans for reconstruction. In the early 1950s, however, its remit was widened to encompass development loans for new states. By the late 1950s, as more and poorer countries were made independent, the commercial loan basis of the IBRD was proving inadequate to the new demands being made upon it, and a new International Development Agency was established as a special agency of the IBRD which made softer loans available at lower rates of interest from a fund to which major powers subscribed, the International Development Bank.[25]

International loan facilities were supplemented by special joint development programmes. Often tied into the alliance systems, these provided an additional institutional framework for joint initiatives among a number of old and new states and were aimed at addressing the particular resource problems of new states. The Colombo Plan of the 1950s and 1960s joined Korea, Laos, the Philippines and Thailand with Australia, Canada, Japan, New Zealand, Britain and the United States. It was in the context of the Colombo Plan that the experiments leading to the 'green revolution' and enhanced rice yields were initiated and largely conducted. Yet another was President Kennedy's Alliance for Progress, proposed in 1960, a form of multilateral Marshall Aid programme for Latin America; it was attached to the OAS and became the largest continuing US foreign aid programme over the next decade. The Latin American participants pledged themselves to self-help and domestic reforms while the United States promised substantial financial assistance aimed at economic development.

Intervention as a post-colonial phenomenon

Another aspect of the decolonisation process was an increasingly frequent habit of intervention. During the 1950s and 1960s, Great Powers intervened regularly, sometimes by direct military action, in the political processes of their ex-colonies to affect outcomes or to discourage the undertaking of policies inimical to their regional or global interests.

The general pattern of Great Power interventions during the 1950s and 1960s almost precisely replicated the pattern of former colonial activity. In 1952, Mussadiq had assumed dictatorial powers in Iran and seized British oil assets; in 1953, by direct encouragement of both Britain and the United States, the Shah was returned to power. (Britain and the United States acted together again in the brief military incursions into Lebanon and Jordan in 1958.) France undertook military operations in Guinea Bissau and Chad in 1962 and 1968 respectively, quite apart from the prolonged struggles to restrict or affect the terms of decolonisation which were proceeding in Algeria, Morocco and Tunisia. In Central America and the Caribbean, Guatemala (repeatedly), Dominica and Grenada all witnessed armed intervention by United States forces in areas the United States had determined not to colonise; and the United States both organised and encouraged 'Contra' forces during the 1980s, to unseat the Sandinista government, a left-leaning political regime in Nicaragua.

The fear of untoward military intervention eventually influenced the shaping of new regional organisations. An Organisation of African Unity had been agreed at Addis Ababa in 1963, in response to the schisms created by the war in the Congo, to provide a framework for the pan-African dreams of the early African liberators. Its most important initial feature was a guarantee that new states in Africa would not attempt to change borders established during the decolonisation process. Increasingly, however, African governments began to see the OAU as a resolution device for intra-African rivalries and as a method by which civil wars and intra-African quarrels could be shielded from Great Power attention. The general secretary of the organisation was given the task of conflict resolution and provisions were made for the raising of OAU peace-keeping forces, to obviate the need for UN Security Council forces. In 1967, an Association of South East Asian Nations, the ASEAN, was formed among Indonesia, Malaysia, Thailand, the Philippines and Singapore to provide for a common diplomatic front, but also for the mediation of quarrels among their respective societies.

Decolonisation and internationalisation

The major powers could not control all the outcomes in ex-colonial countries. South Asia witnessed the autonomous emergence of the 'development state', where autocratic rule directed indigenous economic forces through a developing bureaucracy. In Africa, the one-party state which developed was a unique and indigenous political form – a coalition among diverse tribal forces which was maintained by deliberate policies of inclusion and exclusion and which provided handsome bureaucratic rewards for the included. Their lack of other intermediate social organisations and their low levels of political development also made military coups difficult to resist, especially in Africa, where the military was often the only strongly organised social grouping.

Nonetheless, their efforts to do so, and the various devices they employed to that end, had their effects. African socialisms had perforce to operate within the restrictions of English Fabianism or French dirigist planning respectively. Countries like Zaire or Tanzania, which tried to operate further afield, found themselves isolated and deprived of much-needed aid and political support. In Thailand, Malaysia and Indonesia, by contrast, a long mercantilist tradition and larger urban middle classes, not to mention the existence of armed, and contending, communist and guerrilla forces in Indo-China, made their governments independently anxious to control indigenous radicalisms, and provided a supportive foundation for Western regional security systems, open economic orders and non-communist governments. (The existence of large Chinese minorities in the context of efforts to create new national identities also aided the Western coalition's efforts to preserve South Asia from Chinese communist influence.) These policies, and the ancillary social features of many ex-colonial states, could not direct but they did limit the range of political and economic experimentation open to new states.

These limitations provided the substantive international framework within which new states had to operate. The new institutions reflected Great Power interests and definitions of their requirements rather more than the needs of new states. Where the two coincided, moreover, this was the result of contingent social accidents rather than intentions.

At the same time, new states would elaborate that framework in some directions of which the old liberal internationalists would have approved. They developed self-help coalitions. They endeavoured to introduce ethical considerations into the agendas of international organisations, and they stressed the responsibilities that old states had for new states. The new states also encouraged analyses of the international order, which would highlight the structural links between old and new states, usually for purposes of revealing the structural inequalities between them, but which also encouraged the habit of seeing the system as a whole.

Notes

1 J. Cooke, *The New French Imperialism, 1880–1910* (Newton Abbot: David and Charles, 1973).

2 J. Pluvier, *South-East Asia from Colonialism to Independence* (London: Oxford University Press, 1974).

3 T.H.R. Davenport, *South Africa: A Modern History* (London: Macmillan, 1977).

4 See e.g. H. Wright (ed.), *The 'New Imperialism'* (Lexington: Heath, 1976).

5 See especially R. Robinson and J. Gallagher, *Africa and the Victorians* (London: Macmillan, 1961).

6 A. Hopkins and P. Cain, *British Imperialism*, 2 vols (London: Longman, 1993).

7 E.g. C.J. Bartlett, *The Global Conflict 1880–1970* (London and New York: Longman, 1984).

8 E. Monroe, *Britain's Moment in the Middle East: 1914–1956* (London: Chatto and Windus, 1963).

9 W. Louis, *Imperialism at Bay: The United States and the Decolonisation of the British Empire, 1941–45* (Oxford: Clarendon, 1977).

10 D. Goldsworthy, *Colonial Issues in British Politics: From 'Colonial Development' to 'Wind of Change'* (Oxford: Clarendon, 1971).

11 Macmillan set up the cost-benefit review; D. Morgan, *Official History of Colonial Development*, vol. 5 (London: Macmillan, 1980) pp. 96–7.

12 R.F. Holland, *European Decolonisation 1918–1981* (London: Macmillan, 1985) pp. 166 and 252; but invaluable throughout.

13 C. Kelly, *Lost Soldiers: The French Army and Empire in Crisis* (Cambridge, Mass.: MIT Press, 1965).

14 See e.g. H. Jackson, *The FLN in Algeria: Development of a Revolutionary Society* (London: Greenwood Press, 1977) and L. Pye, *Guerilla Communism in Malaya* (Princeton: Princeton University Press, 1956).

15 W. Henderson, 'Reality and Illusion in the Acquisition of Statehood' in C. Navari (ed.), *The Condition of States* (Milton Keynes: Open University Press, 1991) provides many other examples.

16 M. Kolinsky, 'Federation and partition in the transformation of empire' in C. Navari (ed.), *British Politics and the Spirit of the Age* (Keele: Keele University Press, 1996).

17 P. Gifford and W.R. Louis (eds), *The Transfer of Power in Africa* (New Haven: Yale University Press, 1982).

18 N. Mansergh, *The Commonwealth Experience. Volume 2: From British to Multicultural Commonwealth* (London: Macmillan, 1982).

19 P. Lyon and J. Manor (eds), *Transfer and Transformation: The Political Institutions of the New Commonwealth* (Leicester: Leicester University, 1983).

20 S. Inman, *Inter-American Conferences 1826–54* (Washington: Washington Universtiy Press, 1965).

21 J. Mecham, *The United States and Inter-American Security 1889–1960* (Austin: University of Texas, 1961).

22 W. Zartman, *The Politics of Trade Negotiations between Africa and the EEC* (Princeton: Princeton University Press, 1971).

23 B. Tomlinson, *The Political Economy of the Raj: The Economics of Decolonization* (London: Macmillan, 1979).

24 W.H. Morris-Jones and G. Fischer, *Decolonization and After: The British and French Experiences* (London: Frank Cass, 1980).

25 E. Luard, *A History of the United Nations. Volume 2: The Age of Decolonization, 1955–1965* (London: Macmillan, 1989).

12 Political economy

As governments everywhere became important economic actors, they looked to economic science for guides to promoting growth and competitive advantage. Partly in consequence, economic theory grew rapidly, sometimes to support, more often to correct, government policy. Economics increased its claims to be a 'science', largely on the basis of providing more precise policy guidelines for the new 'welfare' state. In turn, it became a major influence on government policy.

Its general tendency would be to support the idea of international economic openness. Protectionist theory was not lacking, but theories which recommended international competitiveness in a relatively open international economic order generally predominated. The new economic theory also promised to solve the apparent conflict between the claims of national economic protectionism and the claims for more open trade and monetary exchange.

The new economic science

The new epoch in economic science has been characterised as 'marginalism'.[1] Its foundations were laid at the end of the nineteenth century with the development of cost-benefit analysis. In the decade between 1890 and 1900, Menger, the Austrian economist, had laid out the concept of marginal utility, which pointed to the different value of the same resources under different conditions and which highlighted the comparable value of resource allocations. An Italian social theorist, Pareto, had developed the concept of optimality which defined the point at which the economic system, as well as its parts, was operating to achieve its maximum product. In Britain, Alfred Marshall was in the process of inventing 'statics', a technique of identifying misallocations in particular sectors of the economy, and within particular industries, which were creating a drag on productive processes.

These theoretical developments enabled a clearer identification of costs and promised a more rational utilisation of resources. The theory of marginal utility allowed economists to identify the point at which investment for new processes should desist. It also combined utility, cost and value, ideas that had been opposed as late as Sidgewick: it not only allowed for a sophisticated determination of costs, it provided a way of judging whether a new enterprise was worth bearing the cost. Statics identified the specific points within the productive process which were slowing the economic machine and, accordingly, the particular problems which should be addressed in improving the economy as a whole. Optimality determined the distance between an efficient operation and its present productive level.

Not only did it appear that the agenda of classical economic theory was about to be completed, but during the 1930s a whole new economics emerged which built on the classical corpus. This was Keynesian economics, which appeared to free economic policy from the rigid dictates of constraints during economic downturns and expansions during upturns, promising thereby to reduce the scourge of unemployment and to liberate economies from the terrors of the business cycle. It appeared that economics was becoming not only a science, but a science which could produce an amelioration of the human condition. During the twentieth century, economics freed itself from the charge of being the 'dismal science'.

The new economics as public policy

These theoretical innovations were driven by social and political purpose. 'Statics' was intended to increase the national dividend to achieve a welfare effect. (Marshall believed that, if economic activity could be regulated so as to produce more efficiently, it could also produce an increasing surplus which could then be allocated to alleviating social want.) Pareto's optimality was intended to demonstrate that socialist economies could not escape from 'bourgeois' economic laws, and that the problem of the distribution of the social product faced socialist as well as market economies. J.M. Keynes developed the *General Theory* to give liberal governments guidelines about how to cope with economic downturns and how to create employment.

Its social goals influenced its presentation. Keynes, no less than Marshall, wished to communicate his findings, and both put the mathematics in the footnotes.[2] During the early part of the century, economics was still a readable subject.

Initially, expanding social provision was a classical liberal as well as a 'welfare' goal. Indeed, Marshall's successor and the major neo-classical economist of his time, Charles Pigou, devoted his major theoretical effort to proving that there was no inherent conflict between the individualist orientation of classical economics and the holistic orientation of the new 'welfare' economics. (Pigou proposed that, if the overall product grew and if the poor were better off, then there need be no contradiction between individual economic choice and social betterment.) He used this proposition to underpin an argument for marginal redistribution consistent with the neo-classical corpus, but also quite radical in its implications. It was only after Keynes, and partly as a result of his polemical tone, that a distinction between neo-classical and 'welfare' or Keynesian economics developed.[3]

Many of the mid-century's theoretical developments derived from the policies that governments undertook to deal with the Great Depression. During the 1930s, governments experimented with a variety of forms of economic regulation, including trade blocs, currency controls, currency swaps and monetary regulation; and the new science turned to evaluating not merely the consequences but also the assumptions behind such policies. Inspiring a good deal of the new trade theory, for example, was the claim that economic autarchy and self-sufficiency were better than reliance on the vagaries of a changeable world market. (A popular idea in the 1930s, self-reliance would recur in a milder form among the developing countries of the post-war period. Economics moved to evaluate both sets of practices.) Other theoretical innovations derived from the variety of government experiments with tariff and exchange controls. During the 1930s, economic theory followed policy as much as it led it.

Keynesianism

Keynes' *General Theory* began as an effort to demonstrate that public works programmes were more than an immediate, short-term palliative for unemployment, the claim of many neo-classical economists, and that government-created employment could achieve long-term benefits. In the course of proving this case, Keynes elaborated an entirely new approach to economic management. Indeed, Keynes became so prominent precisely because he introduced the then revolutionary idea that an economy could be managed.

The argument rested on the proposition that falls in wages did not necessarily create incentives to expand production, the classical position, if there were disincentives to either investment or consumption. A key factor identified by Keynes was lending resources. He analysed the causes of the Great Depression in terms of the disappearance of liquidity, as well as the policies of deflation which were the universal initial responses to the depression, and which, he argued, further worsened conditions. In simple terms, Keynes maintained that, instead of trying to balance the economy, governments had responded to what may have been no more than a relatively mild depression by a disastrous deflation, throwing both national and international economic activity into such disarray that there was no way it could recover 'automatically'. As a correlate to this proposition, Keynes proposed his counter-cyclical theory of economic management: governments must not go with economic cycles, they must move against them. Public works was one such counter-cyclical policy.[4]

Central to the new theory was a new view of interest rates. The classical position had been that interest rates were an automatic reflection of the general economic condition, and that they would adjust in keeping with that condition. Keynes maintained that, on the contrary, they reflected the supply of liquidity and would only reduce if money supply were enhanced, providing a defence of the proposition that government should supply needed liquidity if the market threatened to deny it. (This would lead Keynes in time to an advisement of the necessary availability of international liquidity – funds available on which governments could draw.)

These innovations, much as they drew from the new marginalism, differed in two crucial respects. First, Keynes' was a macro and not a micro approach; second, it was systemic, not evolutionist. Marshall was an evolutionary socialist: he viewed the economy as a developing and evolving system which had its own nature. It did not occur to him that an entire economy could be directed. Accordingly, improving the efficiency of the economy turned on examining particular elements of it; and hence Marshall's concern with the development of micro-economics and with advising businessmen. Keynes, on the other hand, looked to government regulation of the economy as a whole; and those in the Keynesian tradition addressed their works to state economic planners. Keynes criticised Marshall for having taken economics away from its true direction of macro-economics – that is, away from looking at the economy as a whole – and for ignoring feedback, central elements in Keynesian economics.

One important effect of 'Keynesianism' was to enhance the importance of business cycle theory and to make it a special tool of government. Business cycles were the patterns of rise and fall in economic activity, which economists had been attempting to predict since the end of the nineteenth century. If they were natural, as many economists in the classical school had supposed, downturns could be anticipated, by discovering either their causes or their patterns. But Keynesian theory added the idea that policies could be prepared to correct them, providing an added incentive to their prediction. (During the 1950s, the ascendance of Keynesian ideas of counter-cyclical fine tuning, together with the experience of continuous growth, led some economists to believe that the business cycle had finally been conquered. But concern with business cycles would return in the 1970s, by which time older industries were developing in the Third World while declining in the advanced industrial countries. The new theories would emphasise continuous innovation as the central feature of modern economic life.)

Another allied contribution of Keynesianism was to encourage planning, often seen as the 'big idea' of twentieth-century economic thought.

Economic planning

The idea of planning had been anticipated in the corpus of nineteenth-century German nationalist writing, where the economy was presented as 'belonging' to the nation and of use in promoting its development. Two early German nationalist ideologists, Jahn and List, had both developed schemes for government intervention – Jahn with regard to common national education systems and List with regard to the protection of infant industries. These ideas had been given a powerful impetus by the German nationalist historian, Schmoller, who virtually invented the idea of national economic development: after the 1917 revolution in Germany and the imposition of economic controls, Walter Rathenau provided a detailed account of a form of planned economy.[5]

But it was also implicit in socialist ideas. The contributor to the 1934 *International Encyclopedia of the Social Sciences* on 'Planning' observed that:

> Every variety of socialism desires to eliminate economic exploitation of one individual by another, to make society master of the economic process and to provide for an equitable distribution of the most abundant production possible. This goal, however, implies the regulation of the flow of goods in accord with the needs of the masses, and the imposition of control over the anarchy and inequity of capitalist production.

The depression, which strengthened criticisms of anarchic capitalism, dynamised the notion. German economic science was again in the forefront of planning theory, now based on the limitations of pure capitalism.[6]

The Keynesian contribution to planning centred on the hope that, once the techniques of economic management had been refined, they might be directed to broader purposes than the mere escape from depression. A variety of Keynesian-inspired proposals appeared during the late 1930s which recommended using Keynesian demand management to improve social welfare, to encourage growth, or to develop particular sectors of an economy which were deemed to be in the national interest.

Initially, the new liberals greeted planning with enthusiasm. Indeed, they saw it as a naturally emerging aspect of social development. Hobson and Woolf, the 'gas and water socialists' of the First World War, had predicted that 'co-operation' would automatically arise following the identification of common problems among advanced countries; and following the First World War, they proposed a number of national and international institutions to regulate problem areas. David Mitrany, a leading new Fabian and the emerging theorist of functionalism, would propose the establishment of many common problem-solving international authorities on an international as well as sub-regional basis.[7] Most new liberal theorists saw the new idea of planning as simply the rational aspect of social co-operation.

Nor did they anticipate its potential consequences for the concentration of state power. This was not a new question: Menger had developed the concept of marginal utility primarily to demonstrate the limitations and flaws in Schmoller's ideas of national economic growth, and Max Weber had intervened in the debate to argue the necessary liberal limitations to planning. In the same manner, the leading English enthusiasts for planning were also pluralists, and most were, in fact, against the growth of the centralising state. But their enthusiasm for autonomous social co-ordination led them to generally ignore the implications of planning for the growth of governmental prerogatives.

Gradually, however, the implicit tension between planning and pluralism began to be recognised. At a Fabian summer school held on the subject in 1931, Mitrany would point out that planning must increase the reach of the state, as well as its centralising tendencies. He also pointed out that private groups would become more dependent on the regulative authority of the state.[8] H.N.

Brailsford, one of the new liberal planning enthusiasts, recorded at least one sleepless night over the problem of how to make planning consistent with liberty.

This tension was at the root of the debates which began to ensue in the late 1920s and early 1930s among liberal economists as to which elements of the economy should be planned: a central feature of the debate was the concept of planning itself. One important argument centred on the concept of price. According to the Austrian 'liberal' economist, von Mises, echoing Max Weber's argument in the Menger/Schmoller debate, planning in the sense of social engineering was impossible in the closed economy because authorities and businesses would lose the capacity to know the real cost of things. Another 1930s critic of planning, the American economic historian Howard Ellis, studying the German system of exchange controls, would note not so much the inefficiency of a planned system as the degree to which it made the state the arbiter of economic choices and opened economic policy-making to 'uneconomic' political considerations.[9] (Many of planning's opponents evaluated planning in terms of the experience of the closed economies, which were *ipso facto* planned to a degree.) But the 1934 *Encyclopedia of the Social Sciences* continued to express confidence that these shortcomings could be overcome, provided that production was not so centralised as to preclude comparison within the country itself.

At Geneva, the idea of national planning was seized upon by League enthusiasts to support the idea of international planning centred on the League. The American Political Science Association *Annals* of 1932 was given over entirely to 'National and World Planning', and the 1934 World Economic Conference provided the occasion for a flood of proposals to deal with the economic depression through co-ordinated action. These took various forms, from suggestions for agreed indicative planning among governments to the theory of rationalised economic zones. The enthusiasm for planning was such that everyone wanted to call their idea 'a plan', including schemes that were little more than suggestions for diplomatic co-ordination.

The 'national economy' in the world economy

One question enthusiasts and critics alike had to consider was how the planned economy would operate within the world economy. One scheme, of German origin, proposed the development of large economic spaces which could be used to either dominate, or provide a shield from, the world economy. The idea of planning as a shield against adverse international conditions became a popular notion during the world depression, partly because the Soviet planned economy appeared to have evaded the effects of depression. Even Keynes, generally considered an internationalist, seemed to give some partial recommendation to national closure in 1933, on the grounds that 'a greater measure of national self-sufficiency and economic isolation among countries than existed in 1914 may tend to serve the cause of peace'.[10] Public works also gained support: there was a good deal of praise for Germany's public works programme in maintaining economic growth.

The shield idea would be used to justify the maintenance of colonial involvements, just when the old liberal idea that colonies were economically unnecessary had begun to prevail.[11] Quite a different idea emerged from the English new liberal school, concerned with the planning of international public services. Here, the idea was for a simple extension of public service provision into the international arena, primarily through the establishment of specialised agencies attached to the League of Nations.[12] To early British enthusiasts for the idea, national planning would lay the foundations for and give direction to enhanced international co-operation.

Of course, any sort of planning assumed a national economy capable of being protected from the winds of international economy. But whether protection provided the ideal solution was another question. In fact, Germany attempted autarky between 1934 and 1935, only to abandon it thereafter. There was also increasing scrutiny and criticism of bilateralism.[13] In America, the association between economic closure and totalitarian systems gradually influenced opinion against closure doctrines. Eugene Staley, in an influential work which was published by the Council of Foreign Relations in America in 1939 and which represented something of an establishment view, noted that the closed economic system was an integral feature of totalitarianism, a sure sign of condemnation, and that trade was necessary to increase wealth and to direct the rational allocation of resources.[14] The social costs of autarky were also reckoned and became the subject of formal theories.

Equally, however, there was increasing belief during the 1930s that capitalist, as well as mixed, liberal welfare economies would require international co-ordination of some sort. Charles Beard's *America Faces the Future*, published in 1932, set out an agenda for increasing economic co-ordination between what he foresaw as increasingly mixed economies, whose precepts were summarised at some length in the American Political Science Association's annals of the same year.[15] In 1937, one of Britain's leading liberal planners, Lionel Robbins, produced the most widely read tract on the subject, *Economic Planning and International Order* (London: Macmillan). In the tract, derived from a series of lectures in Geneva, Robbins devised the term 'liberal planning' and identified its major precepts. In general, the liberal consensus moved towards Robbins' idea of open 'liberal' or indicative planning, in which governments would set economic targets and use budgetary allocations and interest rates to achieve them, while operating within an open market economy.

Keynes' internationalism

The idea that there was a relationship between national economic well-being and international economic conditions had been popularised, and some of its mechanisms demonstrated, by Keynes in his widely read 1919 tract on the *Economic Consequences of the Peace* (London: Macmillan). In it, Keynes had demonstrated that Germany was the economic powerhouse of Europe, and that to destroy it would entail damage to all the European economies. Partly in consequence, his refusal to back the 1936 World Economic Conference, which called for an expansion in international trade, was viewed with some perplexity.

Keynes had not, however, abandoned internationalism. His refusal to back trade expansion during the latter years of the depression was due, rather, to a growing belief that expanding trade was a mistaken approach to recovery. Increasingly after 1933, he argued that world liquidity had to recover before trade could recover; and by the time of the 1936 Conference, he was proposing the creation of 'gold credits' to accomplish such an aim. The concern with international liquidity would increase with the onset of war: in 1940, then a civil servant, he would begin to consider how Britain, a country for whom trade was vital, was to pay for the war. In the event, Keynes' recovery programme would eventually revolve around the idea of a regularised source of international liquidity. When he was called upon in 1943 to draft the British proposals for a post-war international economic regime, the central pillar of his plan would be the idea of an international monetary fund.

The new trade theory

Trade theory became one of the liveliest areas of inter-war economic theorising, partly to evaluate the totalitarian experience of Nazi Germany, and partly to gauge the probable effectiveness of the neo-mercantilist policies of the new developing countries which gained independence after the war. (In the latter, planned economic development was to be based on protected industrialisation and deliberate import-substitution.) The new trade theory would become particularly important in rebuilding a consensus for open trading orders in the post-war period.

The major trade theorist during the inter-war period was Bertil Ohlin. A Swedish economist, Ohlin sought to correct aspects of classical trade theory, where trade benefit had been related primarily to comparative advantages. Comparative advantage had, in turn, drawn primarily on a theory of comparative costs: Ohlin, while not overthrowing the idea of comparative costs, added the idea of the consumption effect of trade. He calculated the gains from substituting lower-cost for higher-cost goods, and the gains from diverting resources from direct higher-cost to indirect lower-cost production (this came to be known as the production effect of trade). Ohlin concluded that gains from trade were dependent on the commodity terms of trade – the prices of exports in terms of imports. If a country were in a favourable position vis-à-vis the terms of trade (if its exports cost more than its imports), then it would make economic sense for it to trade.

Another important new concept in the trade calculus was labour productivity. Productivity had been a familiar feature of classical theory, but its importance in the analysis of the differences in comparative costs and its relation to trade benefit were merely assumed in much classical theory. Ohlin did much of the original theoretical work, but his findings were confirmed and expanded upon by other economists.[16] They concluded that the benefits of trade turned on the ratios by which nations were endowed with factors of production: where a country had a relatively high endowment of a particular factor of production, such as relatively cheap labour in an industry which demanded such labour, then it would have the advantage in an open trading situation. This was so because increases in the demand for that good would exploit the relative advantage accruing to the country which possessed the factor in question. (Paul Samuelson developed the analytical techniques which demonstrated and refined the case; and the relationship between factor price, commodity price and trading position eventually came to be known as the 'Stolper–Samuelson' relationship.)[17] What it meant was that relative factor abundance would give rise to comparative advantage in an open trading system.

The Stolper–Samuelson relationship also threw light on the consequences of tariffs, and clarified the tariff position, by demonstrating that tariffs would shift production towards import substitutes and would raise the real income of the factors used intensively in producing them. Equally, however, it demonstrated that a country would lose if the tariff were sufficiently high to restrict trade volume. The point at which tariffs increased incomes without reducing the volume of trade became known as 'the optimum tariff'.

(But there were important exceptions to the new tariff 'rule'. First, a country's trade position would worsen if those who spent the tariff proceeds had a higher preference for imports over their own country's products. Second, it would worsen if domestic consumers had a stronger preference for their own country's products than did foreigners, such that the internal price of imports fell.)

Other refinements in the new trade theory pointed to a variety of other limitations to the 'trade benefit'. First, there was the relationship between technical change and trade. According to Harry Johnson, emerging as the *enfant terrible* of American liberal economists during the 1960s, technical change would make the country more dependent or less dependent on trade, and worsen or improve its terms of trade, according to whether the change occurred in the export- or the import-competing industry.[18] Second, there were the effects of transfers, either through reparations, foreign investment or balance of payments surpluses. Generally, economists concluded that transfers were likely to impose secondary burdens on the country making the transfer, because they shifted purchasing power from one country to another. It depended, of course, on whether transfers were accompanied by an increase or decrease in world demand for the exports of the country making the transfer, but there was a general presumption that the effect would be to worsen the terms of trade. Third, there was the important proposition that 'while trade is always superior to self-sufficiency, restricted trade may be superior to free trade'. Harry Johnson pointed out that if a country had any monopoly or monopsony power in world markets, exploiting such power made rational economic sense. He went further to maintain that the exploitation of a monopoly position was a 'necessary condition for maximising the country's welfare' (so long, of course, as it stayed within the strictures the optimum tariff rule).[19] Finally, there was an increasing recognition that an inauguration of trade or any change in its conditions, as for example, through the erection or removal of trade barriers, would have different effects on different individuals and groups within the country. In other words, trade did not automatically achieve a welfare effect. (Johnson would insist that trade only maximised welfare in the 'potential sense'.)[20] Accordingly, the new trade theory emphasised the ability of the state to carry out some economic redistribution.

Despite their qualifications, the conclusion of these arguments was that trade was an important factor in allowing countries to realise their natural advantages, and that trade was the dynamic element in wealth creation. They also, however, demonstrated that free trade was a qualified good. Benefiting from trade depended on the efficient representation of alternative social opportunity costs by money costs and prices in domestic currency, on the social consequences of the resulting distribution of increased income and on possible need for internal income transfers. It also depended, significantly, on the maintenance of international monetary stability.

On the other hand, the new body of theory also justified tariffs of a certain level, and not merely with regard to underdeveloped countries. Both the 'terms of trade' or optimum tariff argument and the 'infant industry' argument were also applied to advanced economies, in the latter case when they were innovating. There was also the Manoilesco argument. The Manoilesco argument justified industrial protection if wages in the industrial sector exceeded alternative opportunity costs; that is, if industrial wages could not otherwise be earned.

Another important justification for tariffs was around customs unions. Customs unions had been seen as an attractive alternative trading arrangement for close trading partners since the late 1920s, when Europe had begun to suffer intense economic competition from the United States. But their economic effects had been little understood, and free trade doctrine seemed to contradict them. In the late 1940s, the Carnegie Fund asked Jacob Viner to study the question; and Viner gave them a qualified approval. Viner argued that any customs union could increase general welfare to the extent that it created trade by diverting demand from higher-cost domestic to lower-cost partner products. Alternatively, it would decrease welfare to the extent that it diverted trade from lower-cost foreign to higher-cost partner products.[21] The theory allowed for a calculation of the benefits of any potential union. (They were, however, widely regarded as 'second-best' options.)[22]

Monetary theory

On monetary affairs, the era saw the overthrow of the gold standard. The theoretical work was done by Cassel using the idea of 'purchasing power parity'. Cassel demonstrated that it was not the abstract value of one currency in terms of another which mattered, neither could their value be determined in terms of gold. What mattered was the value of the goods that each currency could purchase: it was when this changed that currency values would tend to shift.

This theory implied that competitive devaluations, a prominent feature of inter-war protectionism, would have merely short-term effects.

Another policy implication was derived from Keynesian monetary theory. While classical economics had tended to treat money as a fixed quantum and a reflector of other forces, Keynes demonstrated that money was a commodity in its own right, a commodity that people might prefer to hoard rather than to do what economic logic said they should do. This theory implied that confidence-building was an important part of monetary management.

Popular ideas on international trade and monetary management

These theoretical insights were accompanied, and strengthened in their general effects, by pervasive popular ideas drawn from the experience of depression and war. One such idea was that the world economy could destabilise the domestic economy (an idea which implied that, if closure were not the best option, international economic management was important for national economic well-being). Another, particularly widespread, was that economic closures had caused a general lowering of trade, and that lower trade had resulted in a loss of national income.

The belief that protectionism lowered incomes became widespread, notwith-standing experience to the contrary. Countries had suffered in different degrees during the Great Depression. Moreover, such differences did seem to be associated with the ability to shield the domestic economy from foreign disturbances. It was widely recognised, for example, that the United States, which had maintained freedom of trade for longer, and which had fewer domestic economic controls available to it, had been most seriously affected by the prolonged economic downturn. Much analysis of the Great Depression was given to demonstrating a hierarchy of sufferers, attributed to a variety of factors. Despite these differences, however, it was reckoned that all were worse off for the collapse of the international economy and the decrease in trade and exchange. Sir Stafford Cripps, Chancellor of the Exchequer in the first post-war Labour government in Britain, expressed a general view when, in 1946, he declared to the House of Commons that, 'If, on a basis of self-defence and timidity, trade and financial restrictions of every kind are to spring up again, we shall all be the sufferers, however much we try by economic and financial devices to protect our own people.'

Yet another general body of thinking implicated widespread economic want directly in the causes of war. This became a particularly prevalent view in the United States, and would emerged as a rhetorical staple of the Democratic Party's commitment to internationally agreed rules for economic trading. Roosevelt's close adviser, Colonel House, preparing the way for the Havana Conference, would declare to Congress on 3 October 1946 that the 'cumulative despair of restrictionism has proved itself the worst friend of the masses … and has been a powerful factor in bringing about the crisis of war'. By the end of the

Second World War, economic reconstruction, and the type of reconstruction that would produce full employment, had acquired political as well as social value.

The idea of development

A third important body of ideas with implications for international ordering was the emerging body of development economics. Development theory emphasised the importance of industrial investment, the necessity of administrative and planning skills and the need to integrate the new developing economies quickly into the international economy.[23] Most of the resources for these tasks had to be found outside the countries in question.

It was also the case that most of the early development theorists worked within the context of international organisations. The idea of 'welfare development' had first emerged in colonial offices in the 1930s, but it had been given a powerful impetus by the specialised agencies of the League of Nations. During the 1930s, the League's specialised agencies had sponsored schemes to alleviate poverty and hunger in the poorer parts of the world, and provided an institutional basis for their development. In return, the early development economics tended to link their schemes for poverty alleviation to enhancing the capacity of international organisations for monitoring, the distribution of information and international administration.[24]

The increasing mondialism among American economists regarding the poorer parts of the world was especially significant. One of America's rising young economists, Kenneth Boulding, produced a popular essay in the war's immediate aftermath entitled *Technically Advanced and Technically Backward*. Boulding identified the advanced parts of the world with an equilateral triangle in Europe whose points were Rome, Belfast and Riga, and a band in North America bounded by the Missouri and Ohio rivers to the west, the Mason–Dixon line to the south, and a line from Maine to Minneapolis to the north, with some enclaves on the Pacific coast. There were then a number of smaller sectors, including parts of Australia and New Zealand, a few enclaves in South America, notably Buenos Aires and Montevideo, and a few coastal cities such as Cape Town. 'Once we pass beyond them,' he wrote, 'the whole level of economic productivity falls rapidly.' Boulding identified the most fundamental world economic problem as that of 'improving the level of technical productivity of the backward three-quarters of the world', a task which would require large-scale investment on the part of the technically advanced regions.[25]

The tasks envisaged by development economics were not only or even primarily 'economic' in nature. Boulding's work stressed the necessity of increasing educational levels and training in the poorer parts of the world. Basic health care provision was also a prevalent recommendation in early development writing. There was also the need for statistical surveys and the collection of basic economic indicators. Many poor countries did not have even basic population statistics, much less information about earning levels in different sectors of their economies. Development implied a multiplicity of social as well as economic undertakings by new governments.[26]

Economic policy

During the 1930s, the foreign economic policies of the trading nations were thrown into disarray as monetary values shifted rapidly and countries began to engage in various forms of protection. In the years between 1929 and 1933, countries closed their exchanges, supported commodity prices and raced one another in currency devaluations, to try to achieve competitive advantage for their export goods. They closed colonies into preferential trading areas and set up protected currency zones to protect domestic production and to conserve scarce external exchange.

By 1938, the results of these policies had proved unimpressive. Unemployment in Europe was still above 12 per cent, and production had fallen below 1929 levels by 5–7 per cent. Even those countries which had been able to fall back on large closed economic zones, such as Britain and France with their imperial preference systems, could not be said to have prospered.[27]

In the years immediately following the Second World War, the general pattern was quite different. Governments generally aimed at full employment, which they accompanied with policies of deliberate international economic competitiveness. Despite the enormous dislocations caused by the Second World War, they gradually opened their borders, lifted trade restrictions and set par values for their currencies which they agreed to maintain.

They accompanied these policies of international openness by a deliberate economic restructuring of their economies. Traditional sectors such as textiles were deliberately cut down, and coal and steel were at first fostered and then rationalised. At the same time, through subsidies or grants or temporary protection, they fostered entire new growth industries which were directed deliberately to international competitiveness. The major exceptions were the communist countries, the Soviet Union and China, with their newly acquired satellites, and the newly independent and developing countries, the latter of which were allowed to discriminate and to engage in protectionism in order to create viable economies.

Explaining the shift

The absence of economic restraint on the part of Western countries after the war was so sudden, so spontaneous and so general, particularly when viewed against the caution and fear of the inter-war period, that it became a subject of theory-building in itself. Different factors were emphasised, not all of which were strictly economic. Some economists saw it as the result of pent-up economic energies demanding to be released after the depression; some saw it, by contrast, in social and political terms, as the social price which had to be paid after the century's second great war. The massive Labour victory in Britain in 1945 appeared to those on both the right and left of the political spectrum to be the result of social forces demanding a recompense for war service and war suffering, and not just for the recent war but also for the previous war and the depression. (One piece of evidence supporting the 'social approach' was that the declared aim of virtually all post-war economic policies was full employment.) Others emphasised the reticular nature of policy origination: the desire for economic reconstruction called forth promises of social welfare while the fulfilling of new social welfare plans necessitated increased production and growth. Still others emphasised the international environment, the expected competition into which states would necessarily be projected, and the need to push forward reconstruction as quickly as possible in order to meet such competition.

From full employment to growth

By the mid-1950s, policies aimed at full employment had progressed to deliberate strategies of economic growth. London University's Professor of Social Policy during the 1960s, David Donnison, castigating those who would place emphasis on equality irrespective of its contribution to growth, would point out that a 'high rate of economic growth can be achieved without alleviating social injustices, but injustices cannot be remedied without a high rate of growth'.[28] Michael Postan's economic history of Western Europe in the post-war period plotted the varieties of what he called 'growthmanship'.[29]

Doubts about growth as the guiding objective of economic and social policy would only appear in the late 1960s, by which time the post-war reconstruction had produced the most continuous sustained growth in history. They would also prove remarkably short-lived. By the 1990s, critics of growth had been consigned to the fringe of a developing environmentalist movement.

The achievement of economic openness

Internationalisation was initially quite difficult to achieve, in part because of the very drive for economic expansion. By 1947, expansion was producing severe liquidity shortages which were being reproduced as raw material and plant shortages, as a consequence of which governments refused either to open up their borders or to settle their accounts. A renewed 'vicious circle' threatened as Britain, still the major world trader and whose policies would inevitably set the limits to world economic reconstruction, reacted by instigating a dollar pool within the Empire, in order to distribute scarce dollar resources. This allowed movement of goods within the Empire, the world's largest trading zone, but it shored up imperial closure and scarcely contributed to international openness. By 1949, both European and global exchanges were as controlled and trade as frozen as they had been in 1945, despite continuous diplomatic pressure, particularly on the part of the United States, for economic liberalisation.[30]

Liquidity appeared to be the major problem, and particularly the problem of 'dollar scarcity'. In the years immediately following the war, the United States had emerged as the major source of both coal and wheat, vital to reconstruction, as well as the new machinery for retooling. Accordingly, the absence of dollar earnings either in Europe or in the colonies was identified as a major factor keeping European trade and exchanges closed. The immediate economic aim of the Marshall Aid scheme was to provide dollar liquidity. The central economic feature of Marshall Aid was that it was a dollar credit programme; participants in the scheme could purchase American goods on credit, easing the dollar shortage and allowing for the reduction in tariff barriers and the opening of financial exchanges.[31]

Generous as the United States was in offering credits, the scheme was not without its political conditions. The United States authorities demanded that Marshall credit should serve the aims of economic liberalisation. Specifically, they demanded that reconstruction plans be co-ordinated among aid recipients. Moreover, as countries received the credits and refuelled their economies, they must also open their financial exchanges, establish par values for their currencies and re-establish open trade. The aim was to create an open economic order at least among the European states.

These demands gained a different reception in different countries, depending largely on their short-term monetary balances, on whether they were mainly creditor or debtor nations and the direction of their debts. Thus, Belgium, Luxembourg and Holland, potentially creditor countries whose debts could be balanced by an opening of the European exchanges, were very anxious to secure large-scale economies through the lifting of economic barriers. They were, accordingly, more willing to consider the establishment of a free trade and payments regime in Europe. Indeed, by 1948, they had begun to press for supranational institutions which would have regulatory powers in those areas. Britain and France, still colonial powers, held large debts which could not be settled on an intra-European basis alone, and both were determined to resist, so far as possible, any immediate opening of the European exchanges. A short-lived alignment between Britain and France emerged during 1947 and 1950 which rested on a shared interest in frustrating the immediate objectives of American policy, while gaining access to Marshall Aid. The two also maintained a common front in resisting any supranational development of the OEEC, the agency created in Europe to receive and distribute Marshall funds.[32]

Congressional threats to suspend Marshall Aid entirely inspired a moderated scheme with regard to financial exchanges. In 1949, the European countries participant in Marshall Aid compromised on a payments union, an ingenious arrangement modelled on the international bank set up in 1931 to manage the final German reparations settlement. The new payments union would balance the payment requirements of its members against one other and set up a simple balancing device by which all debts and all credits were multilaterally cleared, leaving only one set of deficits and one set of credits for each country. The European Payments Union allowed governments to continue with controls and to allocate scarce resources, while freeing them from the hampering effects of international cross-deficits.[33] Not the least of its benefits was that it allowed for more or less rational growth policies, and for competitive growth, by allowing states to take advantage of trade. But it was not free monetary exchange.

The reconstruction of trade was more planned still, although it too fell short of American hopes. The United States had aimed for the establishment of open borders at once, and plans were drawn for the creation of an international trading organisation which would set the rules of fair trade and adjudicate trade disputes. At Havana in 1947, however, it had proved impossible to get countries to agree to an open trading system, in part because no workable international payments system had yet been achieved. In Havana, they had signed instead a more limited instrument, the General Agreement on Tariffs and Trade. The GATT signatories agreed the achievement of open trade as their ultimate objective, but they adopted the 'most favoured nation' principle as their immediate operating rule.[34] As countries gradually liberalised trade, they would make available to all other GATT signatories the benefits of their bilateral trading arrangements. Over the long term, it was hoped that trade would become more open (and such it did: during the 1950s, the number of GATT signatories expanded rapidly, as countries saw the benefits of getting in on others' trade deals). But in the short term, the scheme did little to ameliorate the closed trading situation.

In the interim, countries began to turn to their immediate neighbours to explore the possibilities for a more rapid opening of closed trading zones. In 1948 and 1949, France, Belgium and Italy began to negotiate a series of closer trade pacts with one another, designed to take advantage of their close trading relations and the natural compatibilities of their economies.[35]

Crucial to all of these reconstruction, full employment and growth schemes was the German economy, increasingly recognised as central to both European and indeed world economic recovery. As noted previously, early plans for 'pastoralisation' were dropped. By late 1947, Marshall Aid was extended to include the emerging West Germany, and the occupiers agreed plans for its gradual economic reconstruction, including the lifting of some of their economic controls.[36] Italy, Belgium and Holland especially waited to see the results of these efforts, and held up their separate arrangements with France until a secure political regime for the emerging German state had been agreed. Each was particularly anxious to seize the German trade, provided the political conditions of security could be achieved. This was accomplished when Germany joined Nato in 1955, laying the political foundation for the customs union between the six original signatories of the Rome Treaty.

The relative contribution of these institutional devices to the unprecedented high growth rates of the post-war period, indeed of reconstruction itself, was differently assessed in the years following their elaboration. Most economists eventually agreed that Marshall Aid alone was not sufficient to have induced open exchanges (although most conceded it was useful to domestic planning). Several pointed to the economic consequences of the Korean War, and the function of 'war aid' as a significant adjunct to Marshall Aid. In fact, much of the international liquidity important to financial and trade recovery was provided by the military re-equipment which the United States fostered in Europe and the Far East in the wake of the early military defeats suffered by the United Nations forces in Korea.[37] A second equally unintended source of dollar liquidity was United States investment in Europe during the 1950s. As American traders earned dollars through the European purchases of their goods, they recirculated them back to Europe in the form of investments. One piece of evidence which supports the saliency of the post-Marshall Aid developments was that convertibility did not become general among the industrialised states until the latter end of the 1950s.

Planning and growth

The contribution of planning to the rapid economic growth enjoyed during the post-war period was more difficult to assess, not least because governments adopted a variety of planning strategies, and these would differ considerably both in extent and instrumentality.

Planning was not unknown before the Second World War, but it was sporadic and its results, where capable of being assessed, were either unimpressive or strictly conditional. The first real national economic planning experience of any sort had been the first German war effort, organised by Rathenau after 1915, and from which Lenin had consciously approached the problem of Soviet planning; the Soviet machinery was established by 1925.[38] Soviet planning may have been admired in the West, but in fact little was known about it, since the second and third five-year plans were shrouded in secrecy.

Elsewhere during the inter-war years, planning had scarcely occurred. There was the fascist practice, evident in both Italy and Germany, of national economic councils which, it was claimed, would guide production to a social good and within which all sectors would engage in co-operation. But this was more rhetoric than reality. In fact, Nazi enterprises tended to make special deals with the various ministries to carry out what were in effect government, not social, objectives, and these were seldom co-ordinated. As for 'liberal planning', it was true that the liberal governments had intervened during the depression in various ways. Also, a few initiatives had given rise to large co-ordinated enterprises: the Tennessee Valley project in America was frequently instanced as an early example of planning, in that it tied the development of water resources to a planned programme of replanting. But most planners refused to bestow the name of planning on the organisation of a single sector in what was, moreover, a discrete geographical area.

Experiments with international planning during the inter-war period were similarly unimpressive. The planning enthusiasm which had taken the World Economic Conference of 1934 by storm was directed essentially to the planning of commodity production so as to eliminate surpluses and to push up prices. Wheat became an early target of concrete proposals. But Australia refused to be involved in any indicative planning of wheat production out of a fear that its own wheat industry would be planned out of existence, which killed the scheme.

Commodity schemes also suffered from the more fundamental problem that people were in want, and that to further restrict production would only increase want. In general, advocates of increasing demand held the theoretical high ground. The central dilemma of the Great Depression, which no government seemed able to solve, was how to recreate the capacity to fulfil demand. Restricting supply would not provide a solution to that problem.

The first Western planned economy in any real sense of the term was the British wartime economy, which displayed some of the mechanisms other liberal planners would later employ. During the Second World War, the British government had established a rigid allocation of the entire national product, including import allowances, to fuel the war effort. Even so-called 'non-war' imports, such as beer and tobacco, were controlled so as to conserve exchange. After the war, the British planning strategy fixed export targets at a 75 per cent increase over 1938 levels, a figure arrived at in a rather slap-dash manner according to what would be needed to maintain the pre-war British standard of living. It then encouraged investment by precept and example. The cotton, coal-mining and iron and steel industries were identified as central sectors and pressed to install new equipment. It also set an exchange rate, in the event unsustainable, and continued the wartime system of bulk purchases of imports.[39] Norway and France were other early planners.

The conditions which the United States had set for Marshall Aid demanded some indicative planning on the part of all participant governments, since each participant was required to justify its credit demands and to demonstrate how expenditure and investment would aid the reconstruction of an open economy. Also, the availability of Marshall Aid credits fuelled hesitant and under-financed national efforts. France used Marshall Aid credits as a source of investment for modernisation, making it available to some enterprises and not to others, thus achieving an economic rationalisation. Greece first established a form of planning agency to monitor the use of Marshall Aid and to determine fund allocation.

At the end of the 1950s, by which time financial exchanges had been opened, planning spread to the European laggards. Belgium, which had eschewed it (and where slow growth was increasingly related to its absence), began to set up the instrumentalities. Germany established the mechanisms for some indicative planning in the early 1960s.

Among the liberal economies, Keynes' ideas were very influential for determining the theoretical direction of planning as well as in the selection of its policy instruments. Liberal planning was generally directed to demand control; and the major instruments of demand control were tax incentives, credit provisions and wage regulation. But supply-side measures also crept in, as various governments made new investment available and established different terms for inward investment.

The declared objectives of planning varied. For France, the aim of the plan was accelerated growth. Others aimed to manage wages and incomes so as to achieve 'stability': that is, to manage growth so as not to overbalance the economy by producing wage inflation. (Inflation was a perennial problem which all the trading economies faced during the 'rush for growth'.) Some eschewed the use of the term 'planning' altogether because of its anti-liberal overtones, notably Germany and the United States. But the new West German authorities engaged in activities which in other countries would have been considered planning, in its case aimed initially at the rationalisation of its heavy industries, especially coal and steel, still considered the heart of the advanced economy.

If the objectives of planning varied, so did its scope and direction. The French planners may have spoken in macroeconomic terms, but what primarily occupied them was 'output, employment and, above all, investment, considered sector by sector and industry by industry'.[40] Its historians have agreed that its greatest achievement was the ability to assign available investment capital to uses which would produce the highest returns. (French planners directed about 50 per cent of available investment through a variety of institutional devices.) In the Netherlands, the planners operated through wages, a field that the French plan hardly touched. An economic and social council was set up soon after the war representing various economic interests which negotiated wages across all the major sectors of the Dutch economy: wage contracts for individual industries were agreed nationally and subject to approval by a government board. In Scandinavia, planning operated neither through wage agreements nor through controlled investment but through forecasting. By 1962, the Swedish planning commission had prepared three successive five-year economic forecasts which set the parameters for monetary controls, an anti-cyclical company investment policy and wage levels.

After 1962, planning everywhere would become more intense and less permissive, and government economic intervention more intrusive. In Britain, the new Labour government attempted to fashion stricter rules for investment and pricing in the nationalised industries, and it took the steel industry back into public ownership. In the United States, under the Kennedy and Johnson administrations, large domestic economic reform programmes were undertaken which aimed to expand the proportion of the economically active by using federal programmes to benefit deprived sectors of the population and to equalise employment across the states. These operated by enhancing educational and housing provision.

Planning and internationalism

By the mid-1950s, the devices of post-war economic growth were in place. Governments had generally abandoned tariffs for quota schemes which had as their end the controlled lifting of quotas. (Tariffs were still in place, but with a commitment to their gradual lowering.) They had abandoned monetary protection as a long-term device and established regularised exchanges, albeit protected by rules and the availability of long-term international borrowing. Britain, the United States and Japan had settled for interdependence: the acceptance of a degree of upheaval which they would manage by diplomacy.

The countries of Western Europe, perhaps because their trade was already so close, had gone further towards integration: the management of their economic relations by common policy-making within a legal framework. Both approaches were backed by commitments to domestic reconstruction, often aided by subsidy policies, which had as their aim international competitiveness. Everywhere growth policies were generally financed by loose money, a policy which would lead to the inflationary tendencies which Milton Friedman would identify as the necessary price, as well as the chief curse, of Keynesian economic practices.

A major exception was Japan, on whom a strict fiscal policy was imposed by the occupation forces. Under the occupation statute, government operating expenses had to be kept within current revenue, a policy which the Japanese government at first opposed because of unemployment and need for industrial restructuring, but which proved beneficial in the long term. As employment grew, the government gained more in receipts than in expenditure, and every year tax schedules were adjusted downwards to enable successive administrations to reduce receipts and to balance the budget. It only broke with the practice with the Dodge Plan in 1966, a plan to undertake public works and large infrastructure projects, at which point it began to issue governmental bonds.

Protectionism was not absent from the economic policies of the major traders during the post-war period. Agricultural sectors in particular were protected, in Western Europe through controlled prices established by the European Community's Common Agricultural Policy. Fixed internal prices were combined with subsidies which made European agricultural products competitive at world prices. Subsidies for industry also developed, distributed in part through the planning mechanisms, and contributed to a policy of 'national champions', which began to develop consciously through the 1970s. 'National champions' were restructured major industries that were deliberately fostered to seek advantage in international competition. (France especially encouraged the development of 'national champions' which could compete on an international scale.)[41] Full employment and stability were also protected by market management: Austria and Sweden, the former with rising deficits, placed increasing restrictions on market forces during the 1960s to protect full employment. There were also various forms of social contract with labour, vital in directing the national dividend to savings and investment and in keeping export competitiveness. Sweden deliberately maintained low wage differentials, combined with a very high tax policy.

The respective contributions of deliberated planning and autonomous growth to the internationalised international economy of the second half of the twentieth century were difficult to determine. But that there was a relationship was clear. Growth allowed for tariff cuts, while the growth of trade was closely associated with prosperity. Prosperity made it easier for populations to bear the costs of adjustments, not least because it moderated political objections to those costs. Planning created confidence that economic competition could be met; it also provided the mechanisms and opportunity for internal economic restructuring, to achieve economic and competitive advantage in the new, more open economic environment.

Development and internationalism

During the 1950s and 1960s, the developing nations, particularly the larger ones, opted for a policy of import substitution, not only to raise incomes but to stimulate industrialisation. They protected their infant industries, or stimulated their birth, with effective tariff rates that rose sharply with the degree of processing. The initial goal was to encourage the relatively simple step of assembling foreign parts. But there was the hope that more of those parts, as well as the intermediate products associated with them, would eventually be produced domestically (called 'backward-linkage' in the development jargon). The heavy protection of domestic industries stimulated the establishment of factory tariffs. Rates were very high: 100 and 200 per cent were common during the 1950s and 1960s in India, Pakistan, Argentina and Brazil.

In much Third World planning, the political aim of developing administrative and social capacity was generally more important than the economic logic. In the degree to which there were factors of production which could be developed, the requirements of the import substitution argument were satisfied. But this was often not the case. There was also the need to identify local elites with new governments and new political spaces, creating political incentives to economic allocations which often made little sense in strictly economic terms.

Industrialisation through import substitution generally met with only limited success. The economies of many developing countries suffered from inefficiency, as well as high prices. Some of their products cost more to produce than to sell, often because the imports required to produce them cost more than the export price of the finished goods. The highest priority was given to the construction of new factories and the purchase of new machinery. But the practice often left little money for sufficient raw materials or fuel imports, with the result that much new plant existed in theory only. A large new dam project in Ghana absorbed so much governmental resource that there was little left to encourage the factory development which had been intended to use the great electricity resource it created.

The governments of developing countries also undertook extensive social welfare programmes in areas which appeared consistent with the development task. Early social welfare programmes concentrated on education and health care. These programmes were intended not only to fulfil the economic promises of independence, but to build a new sense of community among often diverse populations by identifying their well-being with the existence of the new state administrations.

Both economic and social policies demanded high rates of investment, in the event lacking within most developing countries. Accordingly, they made developing countries very dependent on external provision and secure sources of trade earnings, with the result that the political unions developed during decolonisation became important economic carapaces, providing secure markets and special aid relationships. (The saliency of private economic ties between former metropolis and former colony also increased, often because it represented the most developed sector of the developing country's economy.) By extension, they also required a high rate of economic growth in the more developed countries which would release funds for aid and industrial and technological investment.

During the 1950s and 1960s, considerable sums were transferred from developed to developing countries from both public and private sources. International public provision varied, as the governments of the more developed countries responded with various degrees of individual generosity, which also varied over time. Development budgets sometimes amounted to as much as 3 per cent of government expenditure and sometimes to less than 1 per cent. (France was a particularly generous contributor to development.)[42] International funds for development were also available through the World Bank. Growth, the enthusiasm for development on the part of Western development economists, and the existence of international organisations with instruments which could mobilise funds from the open market, led to considerable private investment during the 1950s and 1960s (and the earlier period was, in any event, a prosperous period for raw material producers). The international economic organisations quickly developed their capacities for planning, evaluation and the securing of loans for development projects.

Recession and the moderation of economic internationalism

During the 1970s, a baffling form of economic recession began to affect the industrialised countries. It was characterised by a gradual onset of economic stagnation which was, however, also combined with continued inflation: the combination was called 'stagflation'. It was gradually understood to be the effects of competition for smaller margins of growth domestically as well as internationally; that is, within sectors of organised labour and between industrial enterprises, as well as internationally among states. 'Competitive growth' was apparently exacerbating an inevitable economic slow-down as economies absorbed their growth margins. The Commission of the European Community began to call for a regulation of growth policies among its members, and to recommend both more moderated and more co-ordinated growth policies.[43]

Gradually, tight money policies were established across all industrial economies, as differential inflation rates caused a series of speculative currency movements, against first one currency and then another. Particularly vulnerable to upward pressure were the yen and the mark, belonging to relatively low-inflation countries whose currencies became in consequence desirable, causing them to rise in value. The franc, the lira and the pound all tended to fall, as inflation in France, Italy and Britain proved more difficult to control. The movements of the European currencies against one another threatened the common pricing policy established within the European Community to regulate agricultural production, and had the effect of reinstituting border controls in agricultural products, as a complex system of intra-European subsidies and payments was put into place to redress the effects of the differential currency movements.

Credit squeezes and limitations on government spending were accompanied by a rapid growth in piecemeal protection. During the 1970s, governments everywhere 'took measures not sufficiently thought through to be called industrial policies'[44] but which were intended to protect existing economic structures against foreign competition and the decline in demand, as well as to stimulate new production and employment. These included 'orderly marketing arrangements' by which governments agreed to restrict their exports to economies under pressure and new quotas against textile producers, as well as the imposition of temporary tariffs in sensitive areas such as steel.

In initiating such policies, governments exploited the GATT provisions which allowed countries 'temporary protection' against immediate economic harm. Accordingly, the new protectionism was often presented in terms of short-term measures; and the formal principles of the GATT rules were adhered to. But the accumulation of temporary measures and orderly marketing arrangements created growing fears for the future of the GATT order and for open trading more generally. The Uruguay Round of trade negotiations, which formally opened in 1979 and which became the longest round initiated within the General Agreement on Tariffs and Trade, would pay particular attention to short-term protectionism and 'orderly marketing arrangements'.

The international monetary order also suffered. In 1971, after a prolonged debate about the creation of additional international reserves to enhance government borrowing and exchange rate stability, the United States unilaterally ceased the fixed relation between the dollar and gold, which had been the central mechanism of the Bretton Woods system. (The US unilateral move was in response to an increasingly acrimonious quarrel between the United States and its European partners concerning the causes of the growing American payments deficit and the amount of new credit to be created in relation to domestic economic restrictions. The Europeans had insisted that America's balance of payments problems were being caused by domestic inflation and the unjustified higher cost of American goods and labour. The United States had refused to accept the analysis, and chose to protect its internal economy rather than discipline it for the sake of international exchange rate stability.) Gradually, other governments abandoned the effort to maintain fixed parities, spelling the end of the Bretton Woods system of fixed exchange rates.

The Bretton Woods system of relatively fixed exchange rates was replaced by a looser system of co-ordination among the major industrial powers, combined with the 'dirty float'. In the post-Bretton Woods system, never really dignified by a more positive designation, governments allowed their currencies to float. But they also intervened periodically to support their own and other major trading currencies to secure a measure of international monetary stability. (They also intervened to protect the stability of their banks.) They enhanced the International Monetary Fund credit provision, generally avoided competitive devaluations and sometimes aided one another, often in a 'private' capacity, with bilateral credits.

The European exception

Within the European Economic Community, the tendency towards competitive growth in an environment of economic stagnation and shifting and unregulated exchange rates created fears that the Community's development would be halted or even reversed. In the event, the Commission proposed a series of measures which would protect intra-European competitiveness and secure some measure of protection as well as some measure of continued growth. Long- and short-term indicative goals were established to guide national economic ministries in their domestic policy-making, indicating a continued commitment to international competitiveness but with more cushions.[45]

Most importantly, there was the elaboration of the ERM, an exchange rate mechanism among the member-states of the EEC. The ERM, set up in 1977 after six years of volatility in the European exchanges, multilateralised the exchange rates among the Community members. The system distributed the costs of adjustment between those who had to reflate and those who had to devalue, and created a rough par value system among the currencies of Western Europe. In the case of Western Europe, the economic difficulties of the 1970s enhanced institutionalisation, and led to the creation of new co-ordinating mechanisms, and mechanisms of a tighter nature than had existed before.[46]

Notes

1 A. Dasgupta, *Epochs of Economic Theory* (Oxford: Blackwell, 1985).
2 See especially J.M. Keynes, *Essays in Persuasion* (London: Macmillan, 1931).
3 T. Hutchinson, *On Revolutions and Progress in Economic Knowledge* (Cambridge: Cambridge University Press, 1978).
4 See T. Hutchison, *Keynes versus the 'Keynesians'?* (London: Institute of Economic Affairs, 1977).
5 *Die neue Wirtschaft* (Berlin, 1918).
6 E.g. R. von Ungern-Sternbery, *Planning as the Ordering Principle of the German Industrial Economy* (Stuttgart, 1932); P. Schroder, *Die Uberwindung der Wirtschaftkrise durch den Plankapitalismus* (Jena, 1932); O. Frieder, *The Method of Socialist Economic Planning* (Berlin, 1932); C. Landauer, *Planwirtschaft und Verkeswirtschaft* (Munich, 1931).
7 Reviewed in D. Mitrany, *The Functional Theory of Politics* (London: Martin Robertson, 1975).
8 The debate is reflected in F. Mackenzie (ed.), *Planned Society: Yesterday, Today, Tomorrow* (New York: Prentice-Hall, 1937).
9 *Exchange Controls in Central Europe* (Cambridge, Mass.: Harvard University Press, 1941).
10 'National Self-Sufficiency', *Yale Review*, 22 (1933), p. 758.
11 See J. Gallagher, *The Decline, Revival and Fall of the British Empire* (Cambridge: Cambridge University Press, 1982).
12 E.g. L. Woolf, *International Government* (London, 1916).

13 H. Ellis, *Bilateralism and the Future of International Trade*, (Princeton: Princeton University Press, 1945), was influential.

14 *World Economy in Transition* (New York: Council on Foreign Relations, 1939).

15 In the special volume on National and World Planning, edited by E. Paterson, *AAPSS Annals*, clxii (1932), pp. 1–180.

16 The American Economic Association, *Readings in the Theory of International Trade* (Philadelphia: Blakiston, 1949) produced the findings.

17 P. Samuelson, 'International Trade and the Equalisation of Factor Prices', *Economic Journal* 58 (1948), pp. 163–84.

18 In *Money, Trade and Economic Growth* (Cambridge, Mass.: Harvard University Press, 1962).

19 'International Trade Theory', *International Encyclopedia of the Social Sciences*, vol. 8 (New York: Macmillan, 1966), pp. 83–95.

20 *International Trade and Economic Growth* (Cambridge, Mass.: Macmillan, 1958).

21 J.Viner, *The Customs Union Issue*, Carnegie series on International Organisation and Law (New York: Carnegie, 1950).

22 E.g. R. Lipsey and K. Lancaster, 'The General Theory of Second Best', *Review of Economic Studies* 24 (1956), pp. 11–32.

23 See H. Arndt, *Economic Development: The History of an Idea* (Chicago: University of Chicago, 1987).

24 See G. Meier and D. Seers (eds), *Pioneers in Development* (Oxford: Oxford University Press, 1984).

25 *Collected Papers Volume 1: Economics (1932–1955)* (Boulder, Col.: Associated University Press, 1971). Quotes are taken from pp. 326–37.

26 Compare A.I. Qureshi, *The State and Economic Life* (Madras: Oxford University Press, 1938); C. Clark, *The Conditions of Economic Progress* (London: Macmillan, 1940) and W. Rostow, *The Stages of Economic Growth* (Cambridge: Cambridge University Press, 1960).

27 W.A. Lewis, *Economic Survey 1919–1939* (London: George Allen and Unwin, 1949–1970).

28 'Social Work and Social Change', *British Journal of Psychiatric Social Work*, 8 (1966), 4, pp. 3–9.

29 *An Economic History of Western Europe 1945–1964* (London: Methuen, 1967) pp. 22–51.

30 See A. Milward, *The Reconstruction of Western Europe 1945–57* (London: Methuen, 1984).

31 H. Price, *The Marshall Plan and its Meaning* (Ithaca: Cornell University Press, 1955).

32 N. Waites (ed.), *Troubled Neighbours: Franco-British relations in the Twentieth Century* (London: Weidenfeld and Nicolson, 1971).

33 W. Diebold, *Trade and Payments in Western Europe* (New York: Harper, 1952).

34 See K. Dam, *The GATT: Law and International Organization* (Chicago: University of Chicago, 1970).

35 Often called 'refrigerator' plans, because they had names like Fritalux; see Diebold, *Trade and Payments in Western Europe* (New York: Harper, 1952).

36 J. Gimbel, *The Origins of the Marshall Plan* (Stanford: Stanford University Press, 1976) takes the somewhat unorthodox view that German reconstruction was the whole point of the plan.

37 W. Brown and R. Opie, *American Foreign Assistance* (Washington: Brookings, 1953).

38 E.H. Carr, *The Bolshevik Revolution*, vol. 12 (New York: Macmillan, 1951–3).

39 A. Shonfield, *Modern Capitalism* (London: Oxford University Press, 1965).

40 Postan, *An Economic History of Western Europe 1945–1964* (London: Methuen, 1967), p. 33.

41 A. Jacquemin, *European Industry: Public Policy and Corporate Strategy* (Oxford: Clarendon, 1986).

42 W. Friedmann, G. Kalmanoff and R. Meagher, *International Financial Aid* (New York: Columbia University Press, 1966).

43 I. Tsoukalis, *The Politics and Economics of European Monetary Integration* (London: Allen and Unwin, 1977).

44 W. Diebold, *Industrial Policy as an International Issue* (New York: McGraw-Hill, 1980) p.2.

45 Commission of the European Community, *Industrial Policy in the Community* (Brussels: Commission of the European Community, 1970); also, at this time, H. Wallace, W. Wallace and C. Webb (eds), *Policy-Making in the European Communities* (London: Wiley, 1977).

46 P. Ludlow, *The Making of the European Monetary System* (London: Butterworths, 1982).

Part 3

The new international management

This section will focus on internationalism in its aspect as new forms of international management and the criteria that were used to judge them. The new management includes, most obviously, the development of the 'new diplomacy', including the widening of the diplomatic agenda; the innovations in international law, in particular those associated with the 'new' international law; and the new forms of international organisation. In addition, the new security instruments, particularly the permanent alliance, and the 'new Europe' were also understood as relevant types of new internationalist experiment which would further the internationalist agenda. Permanent alliances were among the most novel of the twentieth century's political innovations and many saw in the permanent alliance the most substantial of the diplomatic revolutions of the time. As for the 'new Europe', the European institutions which took shape after the Second World War represented the furthest development of internationalism and its most complete expression, and to many they seemed the model towards which other internationalist experiments should be aiming.

The criteria of judgement reflect the century's movements in thought, not external or 'abstract' criteria. They were how the people of the time judged the institutions, the values they believed organisations should pursue and their ideas of effective international management. They measure, accordingly, the things twentieth-century people valued, judged in terms of the criteria most prevalently used.

These tended to mix normative, juridical and social solidarist standpoints. The normative criteria ranged from common law and peace to more programmatic goals, such as democratisation or rational planning. Here, the criterion was the degree to which any organisation or legal innovation encouraged the pursuit of the favoured value. At other times, it was the degree to which common law-making and common decision-making were emerging in fact, evidenced by substantive co-operation and the degree to which international organisations began to resemble genuine constitutional orders. 'Solidarism', by contrast, implied a more broadly based form of social judgement along two related tangents: first, the coverage of the social programme: that is, the degree to which an international institution incorporated the range of social interests usually associated with the liberal or socially progressive state; second, the union between governing and social interests and the degree to which decision-making at the top reflected social concerns at the bottom.

These were not always mutually coherent. Noteworthy, for example, was the division between the ideals of *Gemeinschaft*, the 'warm' community based on common values and common ends, and those of the *Gesellschaft*, the community based on legal regulation, contract and obedience to law, each of which implied different starting points for international constructions and different emphases as to the direction of innovation or reform. There was also a strong utilitarian tendency in judging the new creations which cut across both, as well as a continuing value for the national community which might live in freedom from insecurity and unjust domination.

In either case, what should be observed was a strong tendency to domestic analogy; that is, an inclination to use the internal order as the ideal model for judging and reforming the external order. When people thought of the new international developments, they tended to judge them by reference to domestic institutions and domestic values, and by the same criteria they would apply to the domestic social order.

The most obvious of these was the degree to which institutional innovation would chain or restrict the autonomous state and control unregulated state power. This tendency derived from the claims, frequent in the twentieth century and its major contribution to state theory, that the autonomous state was dysfunctional to political order, domestic as well as international, and that traditional concepts of sovereignty were outmoded. The most frequent justifications for setting up new organisations or for institutional innovation were claims to the now-limited saliency of the traditional state. Accordingly, many judgements about the new innovations were based on, and argued in terms of, the degree to which they limited state constitutional prerogatives and/or political autonomy. Moreover, the escape of states from internationalised control was often regarded as the failure of an organisation to do its job.

Both emerged out of the liberal movement and its new thinking about the requisites of the liberal state. The new liberal thought established institutional pluralism as the mark of the good state and carried the idea of the limited state into the arena of international management. It expanded the scope of institutional pluralism to include the idea of social and economic as well as political regulation at the international level; and it produced the institutional specificity which put much of the meat on the bones of international co-operation. It also articulated many of the guiding values and laid out many of the specific criteria by which the new management techniques would be judged. During the twentieth century, liberal internationalism occupied the high ground for theorising the international more generally; and the new institutional forms deemed necessary for a union of new liberal states provided the basic templates for unions of states in general.

13 The new liberalism

The 'new liberalism' was the term given to the development of liberal ideas, well under way by the end of the nineteenth century. Isaiah Berlin would characterise it as a movement from 'negative' liberty to 'positive' liberty, as a shift from 'freedom from', to the concept of 'freedom to'.[1] The new liberals placed less stress on freedom from government interference and much more on the freedom to enjoy work, the achievement of social equality and the provision of social benefit. They shifted from an emphasis on the sanctity of contract to the idea that the worker could strike to change his contractual relations. They shifted from the idea of the family as a private association to the idea that children should be protected by social and government intervention and, eventually, more equal rights for women. They also demanded more positive action by governments. Whereas the old liberals had insisted on the limitation of government, the new liberals demanded that government should take the lead in achieving social betterment.

But the new liberalism involved more than the expanded state at home. Whereas the 'old' liberals had imagined a growing world of private international exchange, of goods and ideas, supported perhaps by an expanded public law of Europe, the new liberals, increasingly suspicious of private exchanges at home, would increasingly doubt their efficacy in the management of international relations. Already, by the end of the nineteenth century, they were supporting the expansion of international law; regularised international adjudication and the creation of international courts; and they demanded permanent engagements by governments in such efforts.

Some even came to support empire. In Britain, during the latter part of the nineteenth century, a liberal imperialism had developed which aimed to transform the accidental, ramshackle structure of the British Empire into a progressive vehicle for liberal aspirations. Liberal imperialists argued that empire was a positive element, if responsibly run. They argued that, reformed, the old empires could secure liberal values in backward countries and implant liberal institutions, that they could educate and transform colonial subjects into modern citizens, creating a new, progressive commonwealth of nations. It seemed at the time an extension of their ideas: L.T. Hobhouse would claim that the 'socialist development of Liberalism paved the way for Imperialism'.[2]

The more radical of the new liberals continued to harbour a suspicion of empire, even of 'liberal' empire. But during the 1930s, under the press of depression and the collapse of the League of Nations, even their numbers dwindled. In that context, Britain's empire seemed to be one of the few remaining bastions for the protection of a dwindling number of liberal orders in the face of a spreading and increasingly aggressive fascism. In 1937, Norman Angell, the voice of new liberal foreign policy in Britain, who had resisted the new liberal enthusiasm for empire, would argue that the British Empire was the potential siting of a new security system, to supplant the failing collective security system of the League.[3]

There was also a new interventionism. Cobden and Bright, the most prominent and influential of the old nineteenth-century 'free trade' liberals, had both deplored intervention as an instrument for the maintenance of the balance of power and for the support of oppressive and unreformed autocracies. They had condemned each as an outmoded instrument of the *ancien régime*. But by the latter part of the twentieth century, an old liberal, Michael Walzer, would be isolated in defending non-intervention against numerous new liberal enthusiasts for the practice.[4]

Above all, there was a changed attitude to war. The old liberals had condemned recourse to arms, but as the First World War approached, the new liberals made a pact with war, and they supported the war effort. They urged their governments to war, and saw in the war positive outcomes for their vision of society. That pact would lead them into theorising the need for new collective security arrangements, for a new diplomacy and for wider links between states. Indeed, the new internationalism was the new liberalism as its doctrines were hammered on the anvil of war.

The progenitors of the new liberalism

In Britain, the foundations of the new liberalism were laid between 1879 and 1882 by T.H. Green, the Oxford political philosopher, in a famous series of lectures on political obligation.[5] Green drew on an Hegelian organicism and an evolving social Christianity to revise notions of the relations between the individual and society. He argued that the solitary and autonomous individual of Manchester philosophy was an unreal entity, characterising man instead as a political and social animal. Instead of seeing society as a simple aggregation of individuals, and government as an unfortunate necessity whose role should be limited to regulating relations among individuals, he argued that society was an organic whole, of which both citizenry and government were integral parts. In his view, the self could only be realised within the life of a community. Government, accordingly, had a moral duty to provide for the good life of the citizenry as a whole.

Green's organic liberalism had provided the philosophical foundations to the Factory Acts and the regulation of children's and women's work, which formed the main parts of Britain's new social programmes during the last quarter of the nineteenth century. His ideas influenced both right and left of the political spectrum; and they had begun to inform ideas of international organisation by the first decade of the twentieth. Arnold Toynbee, Leonard Hobhouse, H.N. Brailsford and Leonard Woolf, Britain's 'new internationalists', would all be influenced by Green's view of integral social linkages.

In America, the new liberalism's main philosopher was John Dewey, the American pragmatist; and its attendant political movement was known as 'progressivism'. Dewey argued that the American spirit had brought forth a new philosophy based on empiricism and experimentation; and that society as well as science should be guided by pragmatic criteria, not by *a priori* philosophical argument.[6] His substantive point of departure for political organisation was that the American limited state, established by the founding fathers, was an inadequate response to the new social brew produced by America's recent industrialisation and its increasing ethnic mix. Dewey believed that both society and state should be more closely integrated, failing which their continued separation would produce both social and political stagnation. His ideas would influence Walter Lippmann, Woodrow Wilson and others associated with the 'New Republic' movement.

In Germany, central tenets of the new liberalism would be articulated by the sociologist Max Weber, in the context of a more troubled German liberal tradition. Max Weber would draw on an historical understanding of the development of capitalism to pinpoint the dangers of social anomie and individual isolation present in traditional economic and political liberalism, and he would criticise socialism for an inadequate understanding of the ideological element present in social structure and an inadequate understanding of the state.[7] He would emphasise bureaucratisation and an accompanying tendency to social extremism unless the citizen were more closely integrated into the political order.

The new liberals and the new democracy

The crucible of the new liberalism was the advent of mass democracy. Some liberals feared that the widened suffrage would bring a mass of particularised interests into the political arena, to sway policy without concern for the social order as a whole. Others emphasised the irrational aspects of crowd behaviour. A spate of publications of a decidedly anti-liberal tone had appeared at the end of the nineteenth and during the early part of twentieth century on the new subject of mass psychology, which stressed the involuntary tendencies which emerged when crowds gathered and acted together.[8] Woodrow Wilson, then Professor of Politics at Princeton University, wrote in one of the crucial documents of the new liberalism, his *Constitutional Government*, of the nation 'unconscious of its unity and purpose' and he characterised America's system, famously, as 'leaderless government'.[9] Another American new liberal, Walter Lippmann, coined the phrase 'herd politics', describing America's political class as 'blown hither and thither like litter before the wind'.[10]

There were several distinct dangers in 'herd politics', each variously stressed by the different liberal complexions. One was the rise of an uncritical tyranny, in the classical sense of the demagogue. Demagoguery identified an irresponsible or self-interested leadership which would mobilise an uncritical mass movement, a movement which could be turned against established rule.[11] (That this concern was not misplaced would be more than amply supported by the march of Mussolini on Rome in 1921. Mussolini directed hundreds of thousands of his followers in a disciplined surge on the Italian capital from all parts of the country, leading to the fall of the established government and to the installation of the first fascist regime. It sent shock waves throughout Europe.) Others feared that the age of the masses would lead to the routinisation of politics. In 1918, commenting upon the coming German democracy, Max Weber would point to the dangers of bureaucratisation which mass society seemed to imply, and to a consequent immobilism.[12] Yet others feared new political forms emerging from within liberalism itself, which an unshackled individualism was creating. Those on the right of the liberal movements feared a socialistic upsurge and the unseating of liberalism from below; those on the left feared the monopolistic and oligopolistic tendencies in large industrial organisations, and their increasing domination of political power, which they argued could not be contained by the traditional device of anti-trust legislation.

The question at the turn of the century was how to seize these movements and direct them to a continuation of liberal progress. It was how, in Lippmann's words, to 'harness political power to the nation's need'.[13] The forge of the new liberalism lay in the efforts of liberal thought to adapt liberal institutions to the age of mass democracy.

New institutions for the new democracy

The new liberal programme moved in three directions. One was to reconsider the role of the leader in liberal democracy. Traditional liberalism had stressed representation and the control of leaders; the new liberalism would advocate freeing them and giving them a more dynamic role, opposing both parties and parliaments. Paralleling the new leadership were various forms of revived public education. Everywhere the new liberals pledged faith with directed educational programmes built around new concepts of citizenship, after which the nation's young could be entrusted to rule. Finally, there would be new forms of political participation which would supplement or even replace political parties and parliaments.

Leadership

The idea of a new form of democratic leadership was especially strong in the United States. In America, Walter Lippmann had identified America's political challenge as the choice between 'a blind push and a deliberate leadership, between thwarting movements until they master us, and domesticating them until they are answered'.[14] Woodrow Wilson, in a discourse redolent of the German and Hegelian philosophy still prevalent in America at the time, characterised the leader as the interpreter of the mass will and the pivotal point in America's political reform.

To Wilson, indeed, the whole art of the new politics had become 'the seizing and formulating of mass opinion'.[15] He devoted chapters in *Constitutional Government* to the qualities that would be required of the new leader, including initiative, strong will and independence from the legislature. He also stressed the importance of a new direct relationship between the new leader and the new citizenry.

In Germany, Max Weber, scarcely less concerned with the importance of leadership in mass politics, was more sceptical of its availability within a Germany corrupted by the illiberal practices of the Wilhelmine monarchy. He bewailed the lack of political talent in the new Germany as much as he feared the initiative and the referendum. For him, one solution was political parties along the British model which he believed produced a trained and disciplined political cadre.[16] Alternatively, he drew a new model of the isolated leader who was self-responsible. In his famous 'The Profession and Vocation of Politics' (which was also, though not often recognised, a testament of a possible German liberal politics), he portrayed a new form of charismatic leader who would bear a special burden of responsibility for the twists and turns which mass politics would require. Such charismatic leaders would require a special sense of duty.

In Britain, yet another idea of leadership emerged from within Fabian socialism. Here, a wise and scientifically educated elite would guide the people by means of a scientifically based social policy.

Public education

Ideas of political education and 'new citizenship' drew on different traditions. In America, their source was a revised Renaissance humanism. Dewey preached the importance of political education from a young age and the inculcation of the values of republicanism, including active engagement, patriotism and a continuous dialogue between leaders and led.[17] Such doctrines had a wide influence. (Dewey is remembered in America as much for his educational programmes as his philosophy.) This essentially republican and secular image was replaced in Britain by an organicist and Christian developmental image of individual transformation into a growing awareness of social responsibility. In Britain, the predominant liberal solution would be paradoxically a Christian education, carried out in progressive institutions of a Christian stamp, which would turn the individual will into a truly progressive social will.[18]

Political and social incorporation

The method of their incorporation into the political process was no simple matter. The new liberals had confidence in neither representation nor political parties, the central institutions of nineteenth-century liberalism and its solutions to political participation. Lippmann criticised representatives as being directed as much by the leaders as informed by the led, while political parties were condemned as little more than 'the stale toing and froing of interests'. Graham Wallas, a British pioneer in the study of mass political psychology, introduced his students at London University to the notion that parliament was weakening as a central focus for discussion and policy-making.[19] The challenge was to achieve new forms of participation that would cut across discredited parties and immobilised parliaments; there was also the problem of how to achieve a single will out of a mass of emergent and contradictory interests.

Their solutions ranged from direct plebiscites to new forms of intermediary political associations. In Woodrow Wilson's writings, he proposed the initiative and the referendum, forms of direct appeal from leader to the citizenry which would allow the new leadership to directly respond to popular views, bypassing entrenched interests and a blocked Congress.[20] Confronting this option in Germany in 1919, Weber was not so convinced, fearing the direct mass plebiscite as a temptation to social extremism. Instead of the direct plebiscite, Weber began to theorise a new form of more organised political party to replace the loose coalition of interests which nineteenth-century parties generally were. The new type of party would discipline the masses and control political extremism, and would serve as the gatekeeper for informed social opinion.[21]

Other alternatives revolved around notions of social incorporation. In America, the progressives looked to labour, especially to organised labour, to articulate citizen demands (as well as to balance large emerging industrial interests). In Britain, an analogous solution took shape as 'functional representation'. Its main proponent, G.D.H. Cole, outlined a widened role for worker organisations involving not merely representation but direct worker control in the workplace. In Cole's scheme, new forms of political organisation would be located in factories and offices, providing for local workers' democracies.[22] Advocates of 'guild socialism' pictured these new expanded trade organisations as revived forms of the medieval guilds, which had provided for identity and lifestyles as well as political voice. In some variants, it was recommended that parliamentary prerogatives should give way to such functional bodies, and that territorial representation, by geographical constituency, be supplemented or even replaced by functional representation. This movement was dubbed 'liberal corporatism' by its less charitable analysts. It imagined society as corporately organised by sector (labour in its various branches, capital and government) who would adjust their relations by direct political negotiation, bypassing immobilised parliaments. The quality of the relationship between the new formations differed in conception. In America, the relations of capital and labour would be regulated by competition, in Britain by co-operation. In both, however, the purpose of the new organisations was to keep society on an even keel.

Interest groups and the new order

During the 1930s, by which time organised interest groups had clearly emerged as a permanent fixture of the political landscape, the central question among liberal philosophers was their place in the liberal order: the debate was whether such groups could be seen as self-balancing or whether they would, rather, introduce a new form of organised selfish groupism into public life. In 1940, Robert Dahl, to become one of the foremost theorists of liberal democracy in America, sanctioned the existence of the new interest groups and legitimated their entry into the political arena as a form of 'new pluralism', maintaining that, so long as the political process remained open, such groups would balance one another, preventing any from seizing the policy process on a permanent basis. His work was to be carried forward during the early 1950s by David Truman, who recommended analysing modern political processes in terms of the interaction of groups.

A briefly held vision, the new pluralism saw government as a form of neutral body holding the ring, whose purpose was to represent the public interest. But during subsequent decades, further new doubts would emerge about the validity of this picture. Theodore Lowi would be at the forefront of a revived attack on the new pluralism, on the grounds that the 'public interest' would be evacuated by the licensing of serial plural conflict.[23]

The new liberalism and the new nationalism

Since they often used class language, spoke of social betterment and supported widened governmental functions, the new liberals were often confused with socialists, particularly during the first decades of the century. Nor was this simply a popular view. Political historians of the time frequently presented the historical development of the new liberalism in terms of socialist influences invading the liberal movement. But the more accurate appraisal would stress the connections between the new liberalism and the new nationalism. Herbert Croly, one of the architects of America's new liberalism, entitled his treatise *The Promise of American Life* (New York: Macmillan, 1909), and based the new progressivism on a revised sense of political and cultural 'Americanism'. In 1914, the *New Republic* magazine was founded, which argued that America was a new republic: not the status-oriented and particularistic republic of the ancient world, but an inclusivist republic in which all the citizenry would participate equally. One of its aims was to forge a new sense of American nationality which would unite all its immigrant groupings and give them a common identity. In Britain, both Alfred Zimmern in *War and Democracy* (London: Macmillan, 1915) and Arnold Toynbee in *Nationality and the War* (London: Dent, 1915) imagined nationalism as transforming itself into a greater patriotism, but without disappearing.

None saw their new nationalism as contradicting the old liberal internationalism. The new 'federalism', as the new internationalism in Britain was sometimes called, generally portrayed the reordered functional bodies of the state developing towards increased functional international co-operation, and laying the foundations for it. L.T. Hobhouse, in a series of lectures on social and moral progress during the 1910s, graphed the process in moral terms. He presented social progress as an aspect of moral progress and theorised both in terms of a developing social taxonomy, whereby an increasing social differentiation between individuals and groups would be accompanied by an increased co-operation and integration among them. He predicted that this process would continue ad infinitum, linking societies increasingly across boundaries.[24] Frequently among the new liberals, international co-operation was taken as a visible sign that society was, in fact, progressing.

Graham Wallas would give a name to the aggregation of progressive societies, all co-operating with one another. He would call it the 'Great Society' (the title of his irenic vision of the future after the Great War). The great society was an organic whole in which each particular society had a place and a role to perform.

The new liberals and war

As far as war was concerned, most of the new liberals had followed the old liberals in the belief that war was an instrument of the old order: it was outdated, and modern social conditions would militate against it. In a famous argument of 1909, Norman Angell had analysed the interdependence of states in the modern economic condition, an interdependence which, he claimed, made war difficult to entertain and impossible to fight without unacceptable costs.[25] His analysis was adopted wholesale by H.N. Brailsford in his 1914 *The War of Steel and Gold*. Brailsford castigated the militarist spirit of the warmongers and demonstrated the links between weapons industrialisation and the state, but he expressed the same confidence that in the 'modern condition', war was outmoded. Both concluded that, given the modern condition, war was much less likely to occur.

As actual war approached, therefore, the new liberals had to adjust their ideas. They had to account for the persistence of war, despite their theories, and they had to change their theories to account for it. More importantly, they had to evaluate the dangers it posed for the progressive programme. Many also set themselves the task of seeing how, and in what way, war might be directed to serve liberal purposes.

America and 'drift'

Generally opposed to war, Americans were generally united in opposing entrance to it. Accordingly, the old liberals could congratulate themselves on their contribution to America's reluctance to take up arms. It was, however, not so simple for the new liberals. John Dewey, the pre-eminent philosopher of the new American spirit, believed that neither the pacifism of the traditional pacifist nor a willing obedience to follow government were sufficient moral responses to the coming European war. Dewey interpreted the coming war as 'not a war of armies, but a war of peoples', and this made it different from all other wars.

Dewey also believed that there was no aspect of the national life which did not touch the lives of individual people. In the context of such beliefs, to stay out of the war seemed to be yet another example of what Lippmann had castigated as the tendency of American public policy to drift.

Walter Lippmann joined Dewey in his doubts. Traditional neutrality was no longer an appropriate American response; it was an abdication of responsibility and 'an acquiescence in the balancing out that cancels all things'. It was not a positive policy undertaken out of an understanding of what America needed.[26]

The ethnic question was important in comprehending the new liberal agony about America's war participation. The last decade of the nineteenth century and the first of the twentieth had been intense periods of migration. In 1914, one-third of all Americans had been born abroad. The new liberals identified this ethnic brew as one of the major contributing factors to the tendency to drift. Woodrow Wilson, in a speech to become famous as preparing the ground for America's entry into the war, would declare that the 'hyphenated American' had 'not come over entirely'. Moreover, if it were the case that the large number of hyphenated Americans were preventing American entry, this was a sign that 'America had not yet become itself'.[27] Dewey would adopt a similar argument, presenting entry as a sign that 'we are no longer a colony of any European nation nor of them all collectively but ... a new spirit in the world'. Dewey was also convinced that the Allies would win the war, and that the war would therefore present a great opportunity 'to further our democracy and civilisation', were America to enter it. But he also feared that the aims of American entry would not be realised. 'Not until the almost impossible happens, not until the Allies are fighting on our terms for our democracy and civilization, will that happen.'[28]

Increasingly, during the course of 1916 and 1917, the New Republic progressives saw entry into the war as the test of their new philosophy of the new America, a stand against drift and a sign that America was becoming itself. War participation would demonstrate that government was at last leading, and that Americans had ceased being hyphenated. Indeed, they increasingly saw the war as the forge of the new nationalism, the anvil on which it would be wrought. Croly's editorial in *New Republic* which finally committed the journal and the coalition it led, represented participation as bringing together America's disparate social, ethnic and political forces and forging a new realisation of 'the kind of America we are'.[29]

Others were not so sanguine. Jane Addams, an influential progressive and initiator of the Hill House Movement, wrote a long letter to Wilson in 1914 expressing the fear that the war would distort America's objectives and imperil its social reform programme.

Britain and the 'warmongers'

For British liberals, the question was not whether to fight. Britain was emphatically 'drifting to war'. The question was the significance and meaning of this drift. In contrast to the American debate, no heroic interpretation of the undertaking emerged. Rather, war was seen as proof of the distortions of industrialisation. It was also a sign of the inability of political institutions to deal with those distortions.

The most popular analysis of the problem in Britain, which would reappear with regularity during the century, was formulated during this period: that wars were caused by the 'merchants of death', the arms industrialists. One radical organ of 1913 spoke of the helpless condition of European civilisation in face of the war spectre 'manipulated and stage-managed by Krupp ... capable of transmuting the generous blood of heroes into the sordid gold of the safe and snug'.[30] In 1914, when H.N. Brailsford published *The War of Steel and Gold*, he not only popularised the argument but carried it forward to an attack on the Liberal Party, 'hardly less dependent than its rival on the great contractors and bankers who maintain the modern connection of diplomacy and finance',[31] an argument which implied deep structural weakness in British society. When liberal Englishmen spoke of 'secret diplomacy', widely credited with causing the war, they meant generally the anti-democratic nature of the European orders, their plutocratic and oligarchic organisation, and the absence of a sense of fellowship, not only between leaders and led but also between capital and labour.

If war was a capitalist instrument, it seemed to some that a common front of the workers in their new organisations might stem it. Accordingly, the idea grew that powerful demonstrations by a united working class through their trade unions would prevent war from occurring. The project had been initiated by the continental socialist movement. At the Second Socialist International, the liberal and socialistic Frenchman, Gustaf Hervé, had proposed that any declared outbreak of war should be met by the workers with an immediate call for a general strike.[32]

But the new liberalism was too rooted in nationalism and social organicism to allow the majority of British liberals to support any such thing. Jaures spoke for many British new liberals when he wrote in 1911 that 'wherever there are countries, that is historical groups having a consciousness of their continuity and their unity, any attack on the freedom and integrity of those countries is an attack against civilisation, a relapse into barbarism'.[33] Brailsford significantly concluded his argument, which was an argument against war, by defending 'the right of every nationality to defend its liberty and its identity', arguing that any general adoption of Hervé's theories by the more advanced nations would be merely an invitation to the less advanced to conquer and enslave them: 'The country which had the most socialists would be the first to be devoured and exploited by its neighbours.'[34]

An alternative way of resolving the tension inherent in any liberal support of war was to see Germany as a special kind of enemy, and a special enemy of liberalism. Thus, it became a popular argument that Germany represented a form of new barbarism particularly antithetical to liberalism. Alternatively, but in the same spirit, Germany was not backward but the most advanced of the new aberrant and dangerous forms of mass democracy. In September 1914, the

British liberal organ the *Daily News* wrote that however mistaken the policies which had preceded the war, 'being in ... we must win' and, several days later, that barbarism 'is fighting its last battle'. At the end of September, it printed the editorial by the leading liberal journalist, A.G. Gardiner, announcing that Britain now stood for 'the spirit of light against the spirit of darkness'. About the same time, H.G. Wells coined the significant phrase, which would return to haunt liberals, that the coming war would be 'the war to end war'.[35] The *Guardian* would argue to the effect that, whatever was implied by the new Germany, it had to be defeated. By the end of 1914, British new liberals had determined that fighting the war was integral to the defence of, indeed the survival of, the liberal programme.

The liberal pact with war

If this was to be a war against war, however, this also implied certain courses of action. Within a few days of the outbreak of the war, E.D. Morel, Norman Angell and some others in Britain met to set up the Union of Democratic Control, to preserve clarity of thought about foreign policy and to ensure that the war would be fought, and concluded, in accordance with their ideals. The result was *The Morrow of War*, the first statement of what was to be known as the new diplomacy and which enshrined the terms of the liberal pact with war. In it, there was a clear and courageous distinction between Germany and her people; it was the former against which war was aimed, not the latter. There were to be no colonial conquests, no secret diplomacy, and no attempt to reinstitutionalise a balance of power. Jane Addams received a copy from E.D. Morel and forwarded it to Woodrow Wilson, where it formed the basis of Wilsonian rhetoric about America's war aims.

In America, more openly tied to the idea that the war was a 'war to end wars', Wilson would eventually convene the Inquiry, a set of studies to rally popular support for war aims. The Inquiry would involve a broader public in their determination, and would, accordingly, wed the general public more closely to the war effort. Its conclusion would be drafted largely by Walter Lippmann. In it, autocracy was to be brought to an end; diplomacy was to be open; and government was to be carried out with the consent of the governed.[36]

The liberals disappointed

But the war did not follow their expectations. Its course alarmed and its conclusion deeply disappointed them. In the United States, Woodrow Wilson's progressive government had set up a committee of public safety to censor anti-war propaganda and to scrutinise political movements which opposed the war effort. Its targets were anti-war socialists and the IWW, the International Workers of the World, whose leaders languished in prison for its duration, scarcely a liberal development. The strong sense of nationalism inspired by the war also frightened them: Norman Angell, coming to America in 1917 to elicit war support for a beleaguered Allied cause, found a population 'uniformly fanatical'. Each of the terms of the eventual peace directly conflicted with their aims: colonial possessions were redistributed, the peace against Germany was punitive, and empires remained intact. Croly, the editor of the *New Republic*, wrote from Versailles that Allied diplomacy had been a 'disgusting sight'. It has been a dupe, declared another *New Republic* journalist; 'How can we look them in the face?' Croly wailed, referring to those he and his joint editors had convinced to follow them. Lippmann declared that 'we've got no business taking part in an unauthorized civil war in Russia', as Allied troops moved into Russia to intervene.[37]

There were also other, more serious issues. With the end of the war, the progressive cross-party pact in America broke down; Congress' refusal to ratify Versailles or allow American participation in the League signalled the end of domestic as well as international progressivism. In the United States, a set of fiscally conservative Republican governments would dominate federal policy for the next decade, initiating a protracted period of struggle between progressivist state governments, like that of La Follett in Wisconsin, and the anti-progressivist federal authorities. At the same time, the American economy went through a boom period, a boom which served to confirm to many social reformers the urgency of domestic reform (and also the dangers of their previous support of the war): capital had done well out of the war. The thesis that war must always serve capital gained strength during the 1920s, further shaming those who had sought to make war serve progressive purposes. Thus, it appeared that 'when liberalism shakes hands with war, it is liberalism that is defeated'.[38] In the United States, the new liberals in large measure turned against the League they had themselves so largely supported, seeing in it the domination of capitalist and imperialist interests. Those old liberals who had counselled neutrality appeared to have been correct. In America, the consensus for war broke down over the terms of the peace. Not even the *New Republic* would support America's participation in the League.[39]

In Britain, by contrast, the political alliances cut somewhat differently. In the first place, the League was much more the direct product of British new liberal thinking; Angell had designed its sanctioning instrument and Leonard Woolf and the Fabians had inspired its special agencies. Moreover, the League appeared to be contrary to the spirit of the shameful peace treaty, not its continuity. This proposition was not universally held; Charles Trevelyan, on the socialist end, would regard the League as being no more than an alliance of capitalists. But this was not the majority view among left and right social reformers. J.A. Hobson, still calling for democratic control, saw in the League the best hope for achieving it in the future.[40] In Britain, liberals and progressives strove to ensure that officialdom stuck to the League, eschewing alliances or any return to the evils of balance of power politics. Liberal sentiment in Britain, both on the left and in the centre, aimed therefore at strengthening the collective security aspects of the League, further perfecting it. (The high point of these efforts came in 1924 with the formulation of the Geneva Protocol which defined the terms for triggering collective security, a period to be characterised by its historian, Elmer Bendiner, as *A Time for Angels*.)[41]

Theory and the coming storm

It proved, however, to be only an interlude. During the 1930s, America's new liberal isolationism and British liberals' faith in the League both fell by the wayside in the face of fascism. Isolationism, pacifism and the League appeared not only inadequate but collusive. In the face of fascism, moreover, their programmes strengthened and became more specific. The defining positions for liberal internationalism were achieved between 1935 and 1939. The first would define collective security; the second would define the 'internal' requisites for a secure and permanent peace order; the third added welfare internationalism and rights to the liberal agenda.

The next war and rearmament

While British liberals had kept faith with collective security, the question, increasingly urgent as Germany rearmed, was whether the collective security instrument on which they placed such hopes should include war. The British historian Martin Ceadel has recorded the increasing pacificism of the liberal and left movements during the 1930s, and the growing split in the League of Nations movement between an essentially Christian-based pacifist wing, which rejected all war and which sought to exclude military sanctions from the League's arsenal, and a collective security wing which demanded military action by the League.[42] The pacifists insisted on a disarmed League, while the militant liberals not only permitted but strenuously insisted that the League undertake military action in defence of the public law of Europe. The ghosts of Bright and Gladstone respectively stalked meetings of the League of Nations Association during the 1930s, amid increasingly shrill claims for one position or the other.

Norman Angell, considered the voice of new liberal foreign policy in England during the inter-war period, and who had been the architect of League sanctions, was committed to collective security; and he bent himself to keeping the two wings of the movement together. The confusions among the various parties were well illustrated by Angell's stance: he insisted on calling himself a pacifist while defending military sanctions.[43]

In the event, a growing number of British pacifists declared themselves against war but for collective security. When sanctions failed to materialise against Japan's occupation of Manchuria in 1931, the militant liberals took possession of the League of Nations movement and opposed themselves to the governments who refused to take action. In 1931, it was the liberals who were the militants; it was governments who urged caution. In the 'peace ballot' of 1934, one of the more remarkable examples of the new diplomacy in action, over eleven million people in Britain cast votes on the question, and by then the balance within the peace movement had clearly shifted towards the militants: 90

per cent claimed that the nations should combine to stop aggression by non-military means, but slightly over half also supported 'military measures, if necessary'.[44] It was a fair picture of what would remain the balance of liberal opinion for decades to come.

Gradually convinced that the Western governments were distancing themselves from collective security, British liberals generally opposed 'autonomous rearmament' (Britain's rearming alone). But it, too, was a conditional opposition. In June 1936, the *New Statesman* called upon the Labour Party – and indeed 'everyone' – to refuse support of rearmament 'designed not for genuine collective security but for a balance of power policy which means war'.[45] Collective security had by 1936 become identified with resistance to fascism, while rearmament not tied to a policy of firm support for the League represented 'the old game of "alliances" based on the maintenance of the balance of power ... [which] is leading us straight to the disaster of another World War'.[46] Such a stance implied that a rearmament tied to collective security would win liberal support. By the late 1930s, that link had been forged, and it would prove enduring. For decades to come, liberals would support rearmaments on the condition that they were tied to collective and not individual security efforts.

Fascism and the link between internal and external reform

The gradual eclipse of liberal institutions on the continent during the 1930s heightened the sense of panic among liberals, while their analysis of its causes strengthened the view that there was an integral link between domestic and international reform. During the 1930s, the prevalent analysis for the decay of liberal institutions identified fascism as late capitalism under pressure. Increasingly, not only radicals but also liberals interpreted liberalism's decline as one aspect of the growth of fascism, and they interpreted fascism as a decadent capitalism in disarray. Moreover, they increasingly interpreted their governments' reluctance to engage with fascism as an important contributory factor to fascism's spread. Not all liberals believed their governments were fascist, but the official reluctance to openly engage with fascism was increasingly explained in class terms: their own greater fear of the workers. Clement Attlee wrote, 'It is impossible for government which believes in inequality at home to support effective equality abroad.'[47] Thus, impediments to reform at home, inaction over the Italian adventure in Abyssinia and the refusal to confront Japan in Manchuria appeared to be part of the same web, and international and domestic affairs part and parcel of a singular interwoven fabric of political forces. As socialist parties were either destroyed on the continent or incorporated into state corporatist organisations via fascist organisations, liberals increasingly demanded signs from their governments of resistance, and when they were not forthcoming increasingly interpreted their governments' passivity as complicity with the fascist cause, a complicity which would have consequences for liberalism at home. When the Spanish Civil War began during the course of 1936, and America passed the Neutrality Acts with other governments following suit, this was to liberal as well as radical thought the confirmation of their analysis. 'The struggle in Spain is the world at the crossroads ... democracy and peace, or fascism and war.'[48]

By the late 1930s, the same American liberals who had sternly rejected the League and who had viewed Versailles as the duping of a naive Wilson by a perfidious Albion were urging Britain to hold the line in the defence of freedom, inspiring the somewhat ironic British response that 'they [the Americans] wish us to defend freedom to the last drop of our blood'. Others, who saw no sign that Britain would do so, began to fear a division of the world between a new Nazi and a renewed British Empire, which they feared would presage an eventual drift into fascism within Britain itself. By 1939, American new liberals had swung back behind a positive engagement by the United States in the struggle to defeat fascism; and James Shotwell had resigned as president of the League of Nations movement to form, with Clyde Eagleton, the Committee to Study the Organisation of the Peace.[49]

If American New Dealers saw the future of peace in terms of the Four Freedoms or the New Deal abroad, the continental socialists would come to see international co-operation as the guarantee of freedom and economic reform at home. In the first years of the second German war, continental socialist aims, expressed through the resistance movements, gradually took shape. One by one, European socialist movements formally rejected the doctrine of 'socialism in one country'. In its stead, they demanded an international socialist front (they spoke in terms of 'federations'), which would link progressive states, and within which domestic social reforms would proceed and by which domestic socialisms would be protected.[50]

Economic and political rights and war prevention

If some imputed Nazism to deep cultural roots in the German psyche, others sourced its degrees of popular appeal with depression and unemployment, as well as with laissez-faire liberal policies which had allowed populations to sink into impoverishment rather than to attempt to control or discipline market forces. It came to be believed that, as economic want had been an important spur of fascism among people, some attention to economic conditions as they affected political conditions must be paid in any consideration of lasting peace. In the United States, supporters of the New Deal began to argue that the New Deal must have an international counterpart if war were to be prevented. Roosevelt's Four Freedoms, which set the general terms on which the United States would enter the war, would include freedom from want as well as freedom from fear.

There was also a new emphasis on the traditional liberal rights of free speech and due process of law, as these had been suspended on the continent, and not only rights domestically secured but rights internationally secured. It became a firm belief that if human rights had been protected, and if the powers had made their dealings with Nazism contingent on the restoration and maintenance of rights in Germany and Italy, fascism could not have arisen.[51]

Both rested on a widespread liberal disgust with politics, and an increasing emphasis on a social science which would remove policy from the realm of conflict and consign it to the more neutral realm of administration. The scientific spirit originally embedded within pragmatism, and which Dewey had seen as working in concert with a renewed public spirit, was increasingly to be seen as requiring shielding from a public realm regarded as either irrational or dominated by ideological quarrelling.

Federal approaches versus functional approaches

The question was what form these new international efforts should take. As early as 1923, when the French had re-occupied the Rhineland, liberals had begun to consider reforming the League of Nations, and liberal thinking had developed along two different, and increasingly opposed, directions. On the one hand, there were the federal solutions; on the other hand, there were the functional solutions.

The federal solutions focused on constitutional devices and state sovereignty. Federalists demanded that states should formally abrogate aspects of their sovereignty and consign their rights to new, contractually created multinational juridical and administrative bodies. The areas would vary in emphasis, but most 'world government' enthusiasts, as they came to be known, would stress the area of autonomous defence. Federal movements began to develop in Britain and America during the late 1930s and early 1940s, demanding that states turn over their war rights to international organisations which would have formal and specified powers to intervene in and control international conflicts.[52] These powers included the power to demand and enforce adjudication, the power to raise international armed forces and the power to exercise direct sanctions against offending states.[53]

Some federalisers were admittedly rather loose in their understandings of federalism: the institutional arrangements they proposed varied widely in scope and in the precise derogations of sovereignty. In some federal tracts, they were imagined to be primarily *spiritual unions*, in which like-minded states would simply agree to exercise their war rights in common.[54] Others imagined international secretariats who would be provided with autonomous armed forces which could be activated by a majority of states agreeing on their use. Still others stressed the importance of tight legal procedures that would force states to submit to adjudication. Others took a policy focus and demanded that it was independent foreign policies which were the problem and which should be abrogated, and they demanded treaties which would force states into common foreign policy postures, to which common defence policies would be gradually attached. Debate within the various federal movements ranged over the viability of the various approaches and their adequacy, particularly in the light of the experience with fascism.[55]

The functional solutions were a development of the earlier twentieth-century organicist theories, especially as they had developed in Britain and Europe. They focused not on the legal aspects of the state but on the underlying reality of social developments, which functionalists believed state policies reflected. Functionalists rejected intergovernmental co-operation as the solution to the war problem, and stressed the enhancement and institutionalisation of *social co-operation*. They argued that international unions should be formed around specific social needs, such as the provision of food, energy resources and transport. Such unions should be multiple, particularistic and pluralistic, applying to the particular felt needs of different communities and different regions at different times.[56] Various recommendations were put forward for Nordic fisheries co-operation, or riparian co-operative unions which would set rules for co-operation among states which shared rivers. The functionalists argued that, once a web of such unions was established, peace would either take care of itself, or its institutionalisation would follow in due course. In either case, it would be a natural outcome of an enhanced and internationalised social co-operation.[57]

If considered discussion marked most of the encounters between the various legal constitutionalists, an intense ideological and political conflict developed between constitutionalists and functionalists in the several years immediately following the Second World War. Functionalists claimed that federalists were misguided in their analyses, and that true unions had to start from the bottom up. Federalists claimed that functionalists were disguised nationalists, wishing to preserve the crucial areas of foreign and defence policy for determination by the nation-state. The Council of Europe, set up in 1948 to consider various means of closer co-operation among the European states, became paralysed by the disputes between the various 'federalising' tendencies.[58]

Behind these disputes were different assessments of political possibility, as well as different readings of the relations of state and society. Functionalists believed that functional unions were more politically possible; they also argued that social requirements actually determined constitutional forms. Federalists believed that the months following the Second World War provided an historic moment for the federal agenda, and that the moment should not be lost. They also believed the state form and political processes were prior to social construction.

Of more immediate relevance, however, was the fascist experience and the different ways fascism was read by liberal reformers. On the one hand, the fascist experience had disillusioned many liberals as to the adequacy of a singular focus on social change. It had also revived fears of social movements seizing power from below, hence the revalidation of a traditional concern with rights. Hence also a revived concern with liberal institutionalism and the return to efforts to create legal links between liberal societies, in the form of specified obligations, to protect their liberalism as much as anything else. To others, however, fascism had precisely demonstrated that it was the state that was the problem. According to David Mitrany, the foremost functionalist theorist, fascism was the outcome of a distorted state machinery working on social aspirations which could not be realised within the compass of the state, not even the fascist state. To Mitrany, fascism had also demonstrated that the state could not be attacked directly, at least if war avoidance was what was desired, hence the concern with identifying social needs and specifying the conditions for their satisfaction from below.

What was significant about both schools, however, was that both reflected a belief in the inadequacy of purely internal solutions to the achievement of social reform or to the maintenance of social stability. Both also insisted on the requirement for more formal international institutions which would fix states in long-term postures, however different in scope and compass.

Liberalism and the new internationalism

During the nineteenth century, the liberal movement held that the internal reform of states would lead inexorably to external reform. During the twentieth century, the position was reversed. Most twentieth-century liberals during the period up to and beyond 1945 held that external reform was integral to or a positive precondition for internal reform. They also changed their ideas on the nature of reform and imagined it less in terms of limitations on government than via positive engagements by government. This would include not only political engagement with other governments and other peoples, but positive international policies to encourage wealth creation and social stability.

The First World War initiated this movement, but the advent of the Second World War transformed it beyond anything imagined by the first generation of liberal reformers. For all of its novelty, the League remained a nation-state association; it preserved sovereignty and imagined a co-operative union among sovereigns. But the second generation of institution-builders was able to imagine transfers of state sovereignty, world policemen and international bureaucrats with autonomous powers, able to act against sovereigns.

These plans were also formulated with some precision. In America, Eugene Staley had begun to outline some ideas for the liberal development of poorer parts of the world. In exile in America, Etzioni had begun to theorise international communitarianism. In Britain, Arthur Salter had published *Recovery*, which laid out some concrete ideas for managed currencies and international lending facilities; David Mitrany had outlined the methods and potential subjects of functionalism; and Barbara Ward and Lionel Robbins had begun to theorise the methods of wealth transfer to poorer parts of the world and to lay schemes for liberal economic co-ordination. In Italy, Spinelli had begun to theorise the concrete requirements for a European federation.

Liberalism also developed a strong popular movement in support of such policies. By 1935, the League of Nations Movement, founded in 1919 to rally popular support for the League, had become a mass movement in Britain and an integral part of domestic progressivism. In 1939, with the League in tatters, its membership shifted to the support of more specific federalising strategies. That year, a New Europe movement was founded in Britain which immediately gained ten thousand members, most drawn from the League Movement, with a programme for the permanent establishment of European co-operation. In

America, the World Federal Movement was founded, which aimed to bring to the world the lessons of American federalism.

The new liberalism thus provided not merely a new ideology, but a number of diverse routes for government policy-making, as well as a broad-based movement in their support. It had also developed a cadre of specialists who were ready to be called to government service.

Notes

1 I. Berlin, 'Two concepts of liberty', inaugural lecture, Oxford University (1958).
2 See p. 12 of *Democracy and Reaction* (London: Fisher Unwin, 1904), which was partly a response to G.B. Shaw's *Fabianism and the Empire*, a socialist rationale for the union of national reform and imperialism.
3 *The Defence of the Empire* (London: Hamish Hamilton, 1937).
4 Compare Michael Walzer with David Luban in C. Beitz, M. Cohen, T. Scanlon and A.J. Simmons, *International Ethics* (Princeton: Princeton University Press, 1985).
5 First published in 1900, the lectures were still serving as the basic text for Oxford political theory (and thence to the major Commonwealth universities) in 1948: *Lectures on the Principles of Political Obligation* (London: Longmans, 1941 and 1948).
6 His first systematic political work was *German Philosophy and Politics* (New York: Henry Holt, 1915); the grapplings with America's position in the world are in J. Boydston (ed.), *John Dewey, the Middle Works, 1899–1925*, (Carbondale, Ill.: Southern Illinois University, 1976–83).
7 P. Lassman and R. Speirs (eds), *Weber: Political Writings* (Cambridge: Cambridge University Press, 1994).
8 E.g. Gustave Le Bon, *The Crowd: A Study of the Popular Mind* (London: Fisher Unwin, 1897, second edition) influencing H. Lasswell, *Psychopathology and Politics* (Chicago: University of Chicago, 1930 and 1977).
9 The title of an oft-given speech, in R. Baker and W. Dodds (eds), *The Public Papers of Woodrow Wilson* (New York: Harper and Row, 1925).
10 *Drift and Mastery: An Attempt to Diagnose the Current Unrest* (Englewood Cliffs: Prentice-Hall, 1914 and 1961) p. 118.
11 See e.g. K. Loewenstein, 'Militant Democracy and Fundamental Rights', *American Political Science Review*, 31 (1937), pp. 411–32.
12 'Parliament and Government in Germany Under a New Political Order' in *Weber: Political Writings* (Cambridge: Cambridge University Press, 1994).
13 *Drift and Mastery: An Attempt to Diagnose the Current Unrest* (Englewood Cliffs: Prentice-Hall, 1914 and 1961), p. 21.
14 W. Lippmann, *A Preface to Politics* (New York: Mitchell Kennerly, 1913), p. 286.
15 'Leaderless government' in R. Baker and W. Dodds (eds), *The Public Papers of Woodrow Wilson* (New York: Harper and Row, 1925), p. 339.
16 *Weber: Political Writings* (Cambridge: Cambridge University Press, 1994), pp. 309–69.
17 *Democracy and Education* (New York: Free Press, 1916 and 1966).
18 G. Studdert-Kennedy, 'The Broad Church View of the British State' in C. Navari (ed.) *British Politics and the Spirit of the Age* (Keele: Keele University Press, 1996).
19 *Human Nature in Politics* (London: Constable, 1908).
20 His critique of *Congressional Government* had reached its fifteenth edition by 1900.
21 *Weber: Political Writings* (Cambridge: Cambridge University Press, 1994), pp. 334–50.
22 P. Lassman, 'English Pluralism' in C. Navari (ed.), *British Politics and the Spirit of the Age* (Keele: Keele University Press, 1996).
23 *The End of Liberalism: Ideology, Policy and the Crisis of Public Authority* (New York: W.W. Norton, 1969).

24 L.T. Hobhouse, *Morals in Evolution* (London: Chapman and Hall, 1901, 1951), influential especially to the new welfare state policy-makers.

25 *The Great Illusion* (London, 1909 and 1912).

26 P. Manicas, *War and Democracy* (Cambridge, Mass.: Blackwell, 1989), pp. 339–43.

27 May 1914; R. Baker and W. Dodds (eds), *The Public Papers of Woodrow Wilson* (New York: Harper and Row, 1925) and F. Paxson, *American Democracy and the World War* (New York: Cooper Square, 1966) vol. 1, p. 205.

28 'In Time of National Hesitation', *John Dewey, The Middle Works*, vol. 10, pp. 258–63 in P. Manicas, *War and Democracy* (Cambridge, Mass.: Blackwell, 1989).

29 C. Forcey, *The Crossroads of Liberalism: Croly, Weyl, Lippmann and the Progressive Era, 1900–1925* (New York: Oxford University Press, 1961) Chapter 5.

30 Quoted in M. Howard, *War and the Liberal Conscience* (London: Temple Smith, 1978) p. 64.

31 *The War of Steel and Gold* (London: G. Bell and Sons, 1914), p. 161.

32 Quoted in J. Joll, *The Second International* (London: Weidenfeld and Nicolson, 1955), p. 112.

33 J. Joll, *The Second International* (London: Weidenfeld and Nicolson, 1955).

34 *The War of Steel and Gold* (London: G. Bell and Sons), p. 185.

35 Quotations from *War and the Liberal Conscience* (London: Temple Smith, 1978), p. 74.

36 L. Gelfand, *The Inquiry: American Preparations for Peace 1917–1919* (New Haven: Yale University Press, 1963).

37 P. Manicas, *War and Democracy* (Cambridge, Mass.: Blackwell, 1989) pp. 362–3.

38 *The Nation*, 3 November 1920.

39 S. Adler, *The Isolationist Impulse: Its Twentieth Century Reaction* (London: Abelard-Schuman, 1951).

40 *Democracy After the War* (London: George Allen and Unwin, 1917).

41 *A Time for Angels* (London: Weidenfeld and Nicolson, 1975).

42 *Pacifism in Britain 1914–1945: The Defining of a Faith* (Oxford: Clarendon, 1980).

43 L. Brescia, 'Norman Angell and the Pacifist Muddle', *Bulletin of the Institute of Historical Research*, xlv (1972), pp. 104–21.

44 M. Howard, *War and the Liberal Conscience* (London: Temple Smith, 1978), pp. 87–8.

45 Quoted in M. Howard, *War and the Liberal Conscience* (London: Temple Smith, 1978), p. 98.

46 C.R. Attlee, *The Labour Party in Perspective* (London: Gollancz, 1937) p. 190, quoted in M. Howard, *War and the Liberal Conscience* (London: Temple Smith, 1978).

47 Ibid.

48 Henry Pollit, a former 'pacificist', in K. Watkins, *Britain Divided: The Effect of the Spanish Civil War on British Public Opinion* (London: Greenwood, 1976), p. 148.

49 R. Divine, *Second Chance: The Triumph of Internationalism in America during World War II* (New York: Atheneum, 1967).

50 J. Freymond, also a participant, *Western Europe since the War* (New York: Praeger, 1964) pp. 9–12.

51 R.J. Vincent, *Human Rights and International Relations* (Cambridge: Cambridge University Press, 1986).

52 See A. Spinelli, who held strong views himself, 'The Growth of the European Movement since the Second World War' in M. Hodges (ed.), *European Integration* (Harmondsworth: Penguin, 1972).

53 A. Bosco, *The Federal Idea. Volume II: The History of Federalism since 1945* (London: Lothian, 1992).

54 E.g. C. Streit, *Union Now: A Proposal for a Federal Union of the Democracies of the North Atlantic* (London: Jonathan Cape, 1939).

55 A. Macmahon (ed.), *Federalism: Mature and Emergent* (New York: Doubleday, 1955).

56 C. Pentland, *Integration Theory and European Integration* (London: Faber, 1973).

57 The most important functionalist in the immediate post-war period was Mitrany; C. Navari, 'David Mitrany and International Functionalism' in D. Long and P. Wilson (eds), *Thinkers of the Twenty Years' Crisis* (Oxford: Oxford University Press, 1995).

58 C. Navari, 'Functionalism and Federalism: Alternative Visions of European Unity' in P. Murray and P. Rich (eds), *Visions of European Unity* (Boulder: Westview, 1996).

14 The new diplomacy and the new state

The first hopes of the new liberals had centred on the 'new diplomacy'. This did not imply merely different behaviour on the part of diplomats, but also different goals for foreign policy. Instead of narrow definitions of the national interest, the new liberals argued that there were common interests among states, which policy should seek out, articulate and serve. There was to be a modicum of self-determination: diplomacy should take into account the aspirations of peoples within territories, instead of treating them like so many disposable blocks in the game of power politics. Finally, it was to be directed towards conflict avoidance. The advocates of a 'new diplomacy' frequently contrasted its precepts with coercion or war, rejecting the Clausewitzian idea that war and diplomacy formed a continuum. They saw it as functional to peace and part of its special arts, while they conceived of war as the breakdown of diplomacy and a mark of its failure. Hence the notion that the new diplomacy represented a radical break with the past.

Accordingly, its institutionalisation came to be seen as evidence of an emerging progressive and radicalised international community, and the test of its progress. The diplomatic developments of the age, its new laws and practices, were frequently measured against the programmatic aspirations of the new diplomacy, and a more democratic or liberal diplomacy was often taken as a sign that a new, more orderly and more just international community was being built.

But the new diplomacy was more than an ideological construct. It was also a structural and political resultant. The new technological and bureaucratic developments of the age had as great an effect on diplomatic practice as ideological aspiration, while the Cold War and the struggle against fascism produced more immediate and profound effects upon diplomatic practice than the broader aims of a liberal diplomacy. Accordingly, the term 'new diplomacy' came to encompass more than the aspirations of liberal internationalists. Reviewing the 'diplomatic revolution of our time' to a California audience in 1967, Professor Gilbert Craig would include, among the new techniques of statecraft, propaganda and espionage, which, while in contradiction to liberal aims, also revealed something of the inner nature of twentieth-century diplomatic practice. Finally, the term came to apply to the vast reorganisation of diplomacy occasioned by the development of the bureaucratic state, which also seemed to threaten the aspirations of the new diplomacy and would lead even the most ardent of its promoters to question some of its values.

The roots of the new diplomacy

The new diplomacy was a political manoeuvre as well as an ideological aspiration. At the aspirational level, its precepts had begun to be articulated long before the First World War, in the critiques of nineteenth-century radicals as they surveyed the diplomacy of the *ancien régime*. As a political tool, it emerged from the requirement to secure domestic backing in the two 'new democracies' which confronted one another in 1917, and which vied to set the terms of the peace. It was their ideological and political confrontation which would produce the concrete practice.

The new diplomacy as an aspiration

The requirement for a new diplomacy was first articulated by Albert Sorel, the French radical, in 1885 in an eight-volume work on *Europe and the French Revolution*, the first volume of which was a critical analysis of the diplomacy of the *ancien régime* in its conceptions and methods, as well as in the direction of its endeavours. In it, Sorel denied that old Europe represented a community of states 'in which each directed its conduct by principles recognized by all'. He regarded such co-operative conceptions as 'foreign to the thinking' of the statesmen of the old regime, characterising its diplomacy as nothing more than 'international anarchy'.[1] Its English translator, A. Cobban, echoed Sorel's sentiments in a subsequent volume when he remarked that the history of war hitherto 'can be told almost exclusively in terms of power politics and explained by the traditions of the countries involved and the personalities of their rulers and ministers'.[2]

In both accounts, there had emerged a persuasive contrast between an old diplomacy based on the selfish principles of *raison d'état* and a new diplomacy which supported liberalism, reform and reconstruction. Whereas the old diplomacy was a monarchical construct, reflecting the interests of sovereigns and dedicated to maintaining a sterile balance of power, the new diplomacy would reveal underlying harmonies, and would eschew those practices which required the suppression of nationalist movements and which impeded constitutional reform. In it, state interest would be replaced by a broader view of states' rights as also encompassing duties, and by a true self-determination of citizens.

During the first decade of the twentieth century, these claims had fused with the new holistic and evolutionary mood to form the basis of a set of progressive expectations. In Britain, Hobhouse, Angell and the new liberal internationalists all argued that, as society liberalised in the sense they intended – that is, as it developed towards more co-operative forms – not only its governing practices, but its diplomacy would alter by an almost automatic progression. As societies developed, international society would take on more legalised forms, and display more co-operative tendencies, and the diplomat would automatically become a peacemaker[3] – hence, in part, the absence of any specific diplomatic agenda within the late nineteenth-century liberal reform programme. Nineteenth-century liberals expected diplomatic reform to follow automatically from social reform.

The positive agenda was set following the liberal disillusionment with the progress and aftermath of the Great War. On the one hand, there was the growing application of class analysis to the study of international relations, particularly to the explanation of conflict. After the First World War, J.A. Hobson's analysis of state relations as relations also of contradictory classes was taken up with enthusiasm by the liberal left in Britain, as it appeared to explain why a progressive capitalism had not in fact produced peace.[4] On the other hand, there was the new foreign policy programme of the Democratic Controllers as they confronted the task of peacemaking. First, there should be self-determination and no new colonialism (eventually the idea would grow of a mandates system which would establish international control for the old colonies). Second, there was the demand for policy based on solidaristic, communitarian values and common norms. Finally, there was the move for an explicitly popular control of foreign policy, involving the requirements of publicity and parliamentary ratification of treaties, together with movements to promote both.[5]

This agenda was expected to produce other positive values in its wake. The search for common interests would knit societies more closely together. Attention to the aspirations of peoples would create satisfied and democratic states, ready to enter the new co-operative order. The requirement for ratification would force decision-makers to make the goals of policy explicit, and would create room for the criticism and adjustment of those goals. In Britain, the goal of Leonard Woolf, Hobson, Angell and others in the Union for Democratic Control was to establish accountability and stability in British foreign policy, partly against what some feared would be its dominance by a threatened capitalist class.

The political roots of the new diplomacy

Its political origins lay in the diplomacy of peacemaking as that affected the delicate balance of coalitions backing the war effort in the United States. The abandonment of neutrality had been no easy matter for the progressive and liberal Woodrow Wilson; and Wilson's war policy had depended on the 'war liberals', those progressives who had supported the war effort and who held the balance in Congress. But that support was strictly conditional. That some American progressives had been attracted by war participation there was no gainsaying, but they also insisted that American participation must lead to a progressive peacemaking. Thus, as the war came to a close, they began to press for peace objectives that would make America's struggle, in the words of the *New Republic*, 'worthwhile'. The sign of Wilson's seriousness, and the condition of their continued support, was a commitment to build a new world order, not merely to join with the Allies in continuing policy as before. Wilson had responded with the Inquiry, a set of studies to determine America's war aims, which would define America's contribution, and illustrate Wilson's commitment, to a more democratic and progressive diplomacy.[6]

But the anvil on which Wilson's programme was actually shaped was the various 'decrees on peace' issued by the new Bolshevik government following its seizure of power in November 1917, particularly a fiery speech made by Lenin in early January 1918 setting out the Soviet's vision of a 'new diplomacy'. Lenin had demanded a 'peace without annexations or indemnities', self-determination in the European colonies, and the new Russian government's intention to abolish secret diplomacy and conduct all negotiations 'absolutely openly before the entire people'.[7] On 8 January 1918, Woodrow Wilson responded with the Fourteen Points, setting out America's war aims, of which the first, the fifth and the fourteenth constituted the essence of the new diplomacy.[8] The Fourteen Points were intended to distance Wilson from the imperialist manoeuvrings of America's allies while countering the revolutionary appeal of Lenin's new diplomacy and assuring an increasingly uneasy domestic coalition about the direction of American foreign policy during the peace conference.[9]

The early practice

The requirements of the new diplomacy were not entirely understood by its articulators, while the exigencies of peacemaking determined the specific content of some of its general principles. Lansing wrote to Wilson from Paris during the peace conference inquiring whether open covenants openly arrived at meant that the progress of negotiations, as well as the results, should be made public. In the event, the president assured him this was not the case, stating categorically that it would be impossible for all the details of negotiations to be let known. It was also the case that Wilson conducted the peace negotiations closeted with Lloyd George and Clemenceau; not even his own staff were apprised of many details of his commitments. Harold Nicolson called 'few negotiations so secret'.[10] One popular characterisation of the new diplomacy soon became 'open covenants secretly arrived at'.

More significant was the national question, and the scope of self-determination. At Versailles, a wealth of national groupings looked to changes larger than those intended by the peacemakers. Wilson, confronted with the maze of overlapping national groupings within the Hapsburg empire, soon concluded that not all dissatisfied nations could have their own homeland. At Versailles, the concept of self-determination was defined territorially and limited to groupings existing within recognised territorial entities – it was the self-determination of a state which defined a citizenry, not the aspirations of a national grouping. In practical terms, the old territorial divisions of the former empires became the administrative bases of new states.[11]

On the Russian side, the full-blown ideals of revolutionary diplomacy lived slightly longer, until the failure of the German revolution in 1919, on whose success its precepts had largely depended. Thereafter, it was pretty rapidly dismantled. The pragmatist Chicherin succeeded Trotsky as foreign minister of the new regime, and there was a rapid restoration of the classic elements of Russian diplomacy.[12]

How much even these reduced objectives influenced the behaviour of the other major powers may be doubted. During the course of 1916, Britain and France planned the dismemberment of the Ottoman empire with as little regard for either the nationality principle or open diplomacy as at the height of the *ancien régime*. The independence of the detached segments of the old empire was not their aim. Rather, it was the establishment of new suzerainties in the area. That the Sykes–Picot agreement, the Anglo-French agreement dismembering the Ottoman empire, should be kept secret from the public there was never any question. What was more immediately relevant to their concerns was that it be kept secret from the Sharif of Mecca, who had understood the intention of the Allies to be eventual independence and full sovereignty for the Arab lands.[13] The articulation of nationalist aims on behalf of the Arab cause emerged from the Sharif, influenced by the developing nationalist groupings in Damascus, not from the leaders of the two major European representative democracies. Following the Bolsheviks' seizure of power, the new revolutionary government in Russia made public the Sykes–Picot agreement as an example of the direction and intent of bourgeois capitalist foreign policy.[14] Woodrow Wilson, while eschewing class language, would be no less critical, referring to Anglo-French Ottoman diplomacy over the Ottoman question as 'the whole disgusting scramble'.

The new diplomacy's first effects

Notwithstanding such evidence of the obstacles before it, the new diplomacy rapidly gained adherents. By the time the terms of the Sykes–Picot agreement were made public, its goals had gained sufficient, and sufficiently enthusiastic, public support for the powers involved to be embarrassed by their publication, and to adjust the language in which they spoke of their aims. Increasingly, both Britain and France began to use the terms 'independence' and 'national homelands' to describe the eventual status of the Arab chieftaincies.

But their underlying attitudes remained resilient, demonstrated by their treatment of the rising Turkish nationalist movement under Kemal. Determined initially to repel the dismemberment of the Ottoman state, Kemal had organised a new Turkish army, which was the focus of Anglo-French hostilities until 1921 under the impression that they were still fighting the Ottomans. It did not occur to either government that there might be a distinctively Turkish national, as opposed to Ottoman imperial identity, so vague in the official mind was the inner nature of nationalist claims. It took some time for even the limited nationalities principle defined at Versailles to invade diplomacy.

The new diplomacy's most immediate policy effects lay in the efforts, supported primarily by the Scandinavian and smaller powers at Geneva, to design a more effective collective security instrument for the League. The Geneva Protocols, which were the results of these efforts, aimed to make a refusal to arbitrate the definition of 'aggression' and the signal for the organisation of collective security. There was also a set of new principles on minority rights, combined with a rough approximation to the nationalities principle in drawing the boundaries of the new states in Eastern Europe and the Balkans. Finally, there were the plebiscites, where populations would actually be asked to which sovereignties they wished to belong. (Plebiscites had, however, an older liberal vintage: the Italian unification had been steered finally by virtue of a referendum; they also came to be avoided wherever they could not deliver a clear outcome.) Population exchanges were one of its less attractive outcomes. Once the nationality principle had been accepted, the first instinct of liberal policy was simply to move peoples around to achieve the desired uniformity. What was to become 'ethnic cleansing' by the end of the century had enjoyed liberal support – indeed, it was a liberal device at its onset.

Second thoughts on the new diplomacy

If governments took some time to adapt to the new diplomatic canon, this was partly because its precepts were questioned by the diplomatic professionals who had to implement it. In Britain, the old Foreign Office had been reformed in the middle of the nineteenth century to provide a permanent semi-professional cadre which, while still drawn from the leisurely upper orders of society, increasingly considered itself in possession of specialist skills. During subsequent decades it developed what the British diplomatic historian D. Cameron Watt described as a 'contempt of both amateurism and intellectualism'; and it considered the new liberals to be distinctly amateurish in their approach to foreign policy questions.[15] That voice was to be articulated by Harold Nicolson in what would become a standard commentary on the new diplomacy, to be read by successive generations throughout the century.[16] In it, Nicolson, while supporting the idea of the diplomat as a servant of a wider public, especially deplored the new idea of ratification, seeing it as the end of professionalism in diplomacy and the opening of complex questions to the considerations of an ill-informed public opinion, not equipped to understand either the intricacies of the negotiating task or the need to compromise on behalf of the stability of the system as a whole. For Nicolson, the ideal diplomat stayed aloof from publics.

Nicolson's doubts would come to be shared by significant segments of the liberal movement itself. By public, the liberal generation of 1914 had meant primarily the readers of the latest political journals. By popular control, they meant accountability to that public, and the bringing to bear of informed judgement on policy-making. Of the broader public, one of no less firm liberal credentials than Arnold Toynbee would remark that 'though they had heart, they had no head'.[17]

Liberal doubts would be reinforced by the rapid development of the popular press (and its special, and sensationalist, treatment of foreign news), and by the increasingly ideological tone of the political parties. Most of the 'democratic controllers' feared the power of the popular press over an untutored general public; and they rejected the idea that political parties should become the major articulators of foreign policy goals, out of a fear that domestic policy positions and domestic quarrels would invade foreign policy questions, to the detriment of good diplomacy. The liberal creed with regard to political parties and foreign policy would become 'bipartisanship', which meant abstention by political parties from treating foreign policy questions as matters of inter-party rivalry. Their early hopes lay not with the public at large, nor with the press, nor with political parties, but with specialist institutes such as Chatham House and the Council on Foreign Relations, which would tutor both governments and publics in the broader requirements of diplomacy in the modern age.[18] It was, and remained, a distinctly elitist agenda.

As diplomacy moved into the age of mass communication, and discussion of foreign affairs before the public became more extensive, these doubts became much more vocal. Much as they vaunted the public voice, and much as they depended on that voice to hold governments accountable for their foreign policies, yet liberals would continuously deplore the easy sway of television reporting over hearts and minds, the summary treatment of complicated policy questions, and instant and sentimental judgements on complicated foreign questions.[19]

The new propaganda

Their difficulties were mirrored in their attitudes to official propaganda. The educational institutes they had founded, such as Chatham House, proclaimed independence from governments and promised detached analysis of controversial foreign policy questions. But it was also a liberal group in Britain which had prepared the propaganda that had been a major feature of the First World War, while their own education programmes were clear forms of propaganda, albeit for liberal causes. Liberals also became increasingly dependent on (indeed, they relied upon) liberal governments to hold firm in defence of causes of which they approved, and often against recalcitrant publics. (The withdrawal of the United States from the League of Nations was widely adduced to populist isolationism, not to governmental choice; more serious for liberal stances was the apparently popular support for fascist foreign policies during the 1930s.) Most acquiesced to the careful control of news which was to be a feature of the Second World War; and *The March of Time*, a government-sponsored series of short films on the problems of post-war reconstruction, shown widely in American cinemas in the several years following the Second World War, was welcomed by most American liberals as a progressive development.

At the same time, they began to fear that unaccountable executives were setting the terms of foreign policy debates, and that parliaments were writing a series of blank cheques for actions more directed to gaining re-election than securing liberal aims. J. Tulis, an American academic, would coin the term the *rhetorical presidency* to characterise the expanded post-war role of the American president in the foreign policy process and its connections to electoral cycles.[20]

But where most liberals would eventually draw a line was in the scope and direction of the rapidly developing espionage services. Even here, however, they would face perplexing choices.

Espionage and liberal opinion

While spies may be traced back to the earliest political societies, their relationship to official diplomacy varied from age to age, and nowhere bore the marks of the emerging twentieth-century special agent. In Renaissance Italy, where the modern practice of diplomacy was born, the spy was unknown as a special species: all Renaissance diplomats were considered to some degree spies. Hence, 'espionage' had no special meaning. By the time of the eighteenth century, by contrast, diplomats had come to enjoy all the honours accorded to their kings and princes, and were welcomed as part of elaborate courtesies and court rituals. For that very reason, however, eighteenth-century spies belonged to a quite separate and distinctly lower order. That the eighteenth-century diplomat transmitted intelligence was known, but the often close relationship between spies and diplomats was seldom acknowledged. As part of this practice, and consistent with it, the eighteenth-century spy did not serve the state directly. Except for the 'black rooms', where dispatches were intercepted and decoded and whose personnel were permanent servants of the state, the usual field spy was a freelance agent, hired by diplomats out of their own purses to gain information, and paid piece rates. Indeed, it was because they were freelance agents that they often sold the same information two or three times over. Espionage as a modern practice became a permanent, and distinct, office of state only at the end of the nineteenth century, more specifically after the Franco-Prussian War. (Prussia's unexpected victory over France was popularly credited to Frederick's agents in the field; he boasted that he had thirty thousand spies reporting on French field emplacements.)

In their first incarnation as state agents, these new bureaucrats were parts of military services, directed by military officers to serve general staffs and to inform military decision-making. Espionage, like propaganda, formally entered the state apparatus as part of the arts of war. During the first two decades of the century, the regular diplomatic service continued to buy political intelligence in the same haphazard fashion it had done for the previous two centuries. And so it generally remained until the end of the Second World War, the major exception being Soviet intelligence which evolved from the Tsar's internal security service.

But their tasks rapidly outstripped any purely military definition. Agents of military intelligence played prominent roles in the diplomacy of the powers with regard to the new revolutionary regime in Russia. (Robin Lockhart, the British agent, wrote extensively of his own experiences as well as popularising those of

Sydney Reilly, the 'ace of spies', both of whom were heavily involved in conspiring against the new Soviet regime.)[21] At the same time, there was the expansion of military intelligence to include weapons production and long-term strategic planning, information concerning which was as much political and economic as strictly military in nature.

Partly in consequence, spy services gradually gained *de facto* autonomy from the military services in which they were embedded during the inter-war period, often operating in a confused situation with developing internal security services. It was only after the Second World War that military and political intelligence, and internal and external security, were differentiated and a clear separation between the various services was established. The creation of the Central Intelligence Agency in 1947, and its separation from both military intelligence and the Federal Bureau of Investigation, was only a more rationalised instance of a general trend, and among both liberal and non-liberal states.[22]

Espionage does not seem to have been a universal practice, even during the Cold War (although, by its very nature, this was rather difficult to determine). The main spy states were the Great Powers including Japan and East and West Germany. There were also the 'pariah' states and states in particularly sensitive areas: Spain under Franco, Cuba, Egypt, Iran, Iraq, Syria, Israel and South Africa were all states with developed espionage services. Nor in all of these cases was the main task of espionage to serve diplomacy. In Spain, Cuba, South Africa, Iran and Egypt, its main purpose was rather to spy out internal enemies of the regime: the majority of the new intelligence agencies were, in fact, primarily internal security agencies. (In Egypt, it was military intelligence which continued to carry the diplomatic role of reporting foreign intelligence.)

Some of the newer agencies were satellites of older agencies. The Cuban DGI was formed on advice from the KGB; and a Russian was the director of its operations during the 1960s. Iraq organised its intelligence service on KGB lines after 1973, as part of a trade deal in which the newly formed service would assist the KGB and undertake local missions on its behalf.

Most liberals accepted the necessity of espionage in securing the defeat of fascism; and they positively welcomed both counter-intelligence and special operations in that context. (British special operations agents, working behind enemy lines in Greece and the Balkans during the Second World War, were often liberal amateurs who conceived of themselves as supporting sturdy defenders of the home front.) But the Cold War divided them. Indeed, it became one of the significant schisms between the 'right' and 'left' liberals during the post-war period. In general, left liberals regarded those of their compatriots caught spying for the Soviet Union in the immediate aftermath of the Second World War with some sympathy, while right liberals did not.

If parts of the liberal community accepted espionage as a political necessity, there could be no argument that the techniques of espionage were consistent with a liberal diplomacy, much less its broader aims of securing the liberal state. There was not only systematic lying and subversion, but also the intervention it implied into the domestic affairs of other countries. Intervention by secret means was difficult to justify by any liberal creed. More importantly, there was the constant fear that governmental powers were being enhanced through the systematic practice of espionage, and that such practices were escaping the accountability of liberal democratic institutions.[23] Liberals constantly attacked the unaccountability of the espionage services. Finally, there was the fear that the developing espionage facilities could, and would, be turned against the home population on grounds of internal subversion, to the detriment of liberal causes.

The new bureaucracy and the new diplomacy

But more subtle in its effects, and perhaps more far-reaching, was the bureaucratic development of the modern state, which qualified the ability of states to direct their diplomacy towards any single purpose, be it democratic or otherwise. There was also the growing phenomenon of interest groups and private foreign policies on the part of increasingly powerful non-state actors.

Administration and the new diplomacy

In the first place, there was the simple numerical increase in the size of the diplomatic corps. France had only ten ambassadors of class and Britain nine in 1914. There were, of course, also a good many consuls to aid traders and to help travellers who had fallen foul of local ordinances, but even these probably nowhere exceeded some hundred or so persons. By the late 1960s, in contrast, France had some sixty ambassadors of class, each responsible for an embassy in which there also served cultural attachés, political attachés and defence attachés. By 1990, Britain had 130. There were also the diplomatic offices at the newly formed international organisations. In Brussels, state members of the Nato and the European Community would eventually be required to support three delegations, one serving the kingdom of Belgium, one the European Community and one the Nato Alliance. By 1980, the average-sized European state had about 1,500–2,000 officers serving abroad.

There was a parallel increase in the number of diplomatic personnel in the home service, as states' tasks expanded and international economic relations grew. Health, culture, aid, credits, were all tasks that had to be overseen by the domestic side of foreign offices, which led to concomitant increases in the size of home agencies. Canning's foreign office of 1820 had thirty-six people in the home branch managing all the business of dealing with Britain's ambassadors abroad; Britain's home side grew to some three thousand people during the post-war period.

These swollen services came to be bureaucratically structured in differing orders of hierarchy, serving a variety of masters and reflecting different administrative and political traditions. By the 1960s, the French foreign office was structured into three great divisions of the political, the economic and the cultural, each of which served different interests of the state under different long-serving permanent secretaries. Germany had a simpler structure, consisting of only two branches, the political and the economic, but each was a baronial construction whose officers were directly recruited and who remained in the relevant section for their entire careers. Each branch conceived its role in different ways; and they seldom co-ordinated their activities or approaches.[24]

Other agencies of state also entered into diplomatic business. Treasuries set financial limits, gave credits for loans and established convertibility commitments. Commerce and trade departments negotiated trade deals and determined foreign trade strategies. Defence departments decided basings abroad, logistics and mobility requisites. Agriculture departments, especially in agricultural exporting countries, provided specifications for the amount and quality of raw material imports and exports, worked out delivery conditions, and set terms of sales and storage. Aid agencies set long-term aid policies.

Nor were these merely junior or ancillary services. Partly because of their expertise in specific areas and partly because of their power to determine domestic policies and direct domestic lobbies, treasuries and commerce departments became powerful foreign policy agencies in their own right. During the 1920s, Hoover's Commerce Department set up its own offices in industrial and commercial centres abroad which were linked with Commerce offices in numerous American cities, allowing direct communication both from the domestic regions of America to Washington and from country-site specialists to America's regions.[25] It became so powerful a determiner of American foreign policy during the inter-war period that its foreign activities were disallowed in 1941 and its 'foreign offices' absorbed into the State Department, when the administration began preparing for the peace. It retained power, however, because the best-informed agency of government on the Soviet Union in the United States was its Russian section, which had hired practically all the trained Russian speakers in the civil service before the war.

The development of bureaucracy troubled the hopes of the new diplomacy in a variety of ways. The existence of a wide variety of official institutions with foreign policy interests, each of which bore special responsibility for some specific function, increasingly made policy formulation opaque. Diplomacy also became a competitive process characterised by inter-agency bargaining and compromise. Indeed, a whole new literature developed during the 1960s and 1970s called 'bureaucratic analysis' which stressed the short-term, agency-orientation of such competitiveness.[26] If the hope was for a more rational and community-centred foreign policy, bureaucratic rivalries made this difficult to achieve. Inter-service bargaining was, moreover, a relatively secret and closed affair, conducted far from the public view. It scarcely made the policy process more open or accountable.

Interest groups and the new diplomacy

A relatively small matter in 1910, interest groups had grown in both number and size by the 1930s, particularly under the press of the Great Depression; and their invasion of foreign policy began to be felt during the late 1920s and 1930s, with organised agricultural interests and industrial interests clamouring for protection. Some, especially large industrial organisations strategically crucial to the state, gained the ability to act outside of normal diplomatic routes, via commerce departments and directly through chief executives.

They also began to act outside of the state entirely. Increasingly after the Second World War, the large aircraft and engineering firms such as Boeing, Rolls-Royce and their European counterparts, which developed in the post-war period, negotiated directly with one another as well as with foreign governments on large aircraft and weapons projects, bypassing their own respective governments. Banks were another prominent actor whose behaviour governments found difficult to control and whose activities had unintended consequences. Their interest rates and credit policies, particularly during the post-war period when credit facilities became increasingly internationalised, could have large implications for foreign policy.

But the real difficulty of special interests from the liberal perspective lay in their relations with different sections of the bureaucracy, particularly the large economic organisations on which much of any developed nation's wealth depended. The modern denomination for private organisations with special relations with government was 'insider groups', and the modern term for the governing habits it generated was 'neo-corporatism'. Here, foreign policy might come to represent a sectoral group's 'private' interests, or a trade-off between statist and economic concerns, as each swapped conditions with the other. Liberals became divided over whether the problem was the serial seizure of foreign policy by some interest group in a revolving circus of competition or, alternatively, a continuous bias on the part of the state towards some interest which had become embedded in it. Another concern, generally shared, was the openness of democratic processes to retrograde social forces, and their invasion of foreign policy formulation to the detriment of international understanding.

Such close relationships also created involuntary structures harmful to liberal diplomacy's wider purposes. The interpenetration of the US Commerce Department and economic interest groups during the inter-war period had created a groundswell of support for a new more restrictive trade policy in the United States, resulting in the Hawley–Smoot tariff of 1929, at a time when official United States policy was to encourage free trade. In each case, the liberal hopes for a new liberal diplomacy were qualified.

State responses to bureaucrats and private foreign policies

The first noticeable effect of the growing power and organisation of interest groups was felt during the 1920s in the form of enhanced secrecy, as foreign offices tried to shield their policies from public and interest group scrutiny. Thereafter, states took action to control the rampant growth of the formal agencies concerned with foreign policy and to co-ordinate their activities, often with implications for governing structures more generally.

These control devices took different forms. Britain saw the institution of cabinet committees in the early 1960s, a major influence on whose development was the increasing diversity of agencies with foreign policy interests and their reluctance to leave co-ordination with the Foreign Office or Treasury. In France, as part of the constitutional revisions of the Fifth Republic, the new directly elected French president was given a pivotal role in the formulation of external policy, with the result that, since the late 1950s, French presidents have had almost sole power to set its grand lines. Following Germany's division, inner German questions became a reserved domain of the federal chancellor, while other questions of high policy salience, such as federal security affairs, came to be serially handled by specially convened chancellors' committees. In the United States, successive presidents tended to work through one or other of the major agencies dealing with foreign policy questions, either the National Security Council, the Central Intelligence Agency or the State Department, each of which would become the *de facto* co-ordinating agency for the administration in power.

These co-ordinating efforts tended to enhance the role of the chief executive in the diplomatic process. Chancellors, presidents, and prime ministers all came to perform crucial link roles in diplomacy, often bypassing foreign ministers. Indeed, they began to meet regularly, leading large staffs of personal advisors who were served by the home sections of concerned agencies. (The technical term for this type of diplomacy was 'summitry'.)[27] Although this was a far cry from democratic diplomacy, liberals often found themselves in the invidious position of having to approve 'summitry' on the grounds that it enhanced accountability, which threatened to be lost in the bureaucratic maze. But it also enhanced the 'caesarism' which Weber had predicted would become the mark of the modern state.

Countries tried to centralise the work of various departments under the ambassador of place, and sometimes in particular embassies. (This varied from country to country: the London embassy of the United States became the central embassy for relations with Europe, while the Paris embassy served that function for Britain. The degree of centralisation achieved varied according to different national practices: in the case of both the United States and the Soviet Union, different agencies based in various embassies represented their home agencies directly, and resisted even minimal co-ordination by the ambassador of place, while British ambassadors had much more say over the activities of the various agencies sited in their embassies.)

The new diplomat

These developments affected the formal structures of diplomacy in a variety of ways. Increasingly, ambassadors came to carry out representative, not negotiating, functions, while the embassy, formerly the external representation of the 'sovereign power', often served as little more than the site or home for various outreaches of domestic departments. In addition, all diplomats would require the special skills of public presentation, as diplomacy became a permanent and on-going activity. Ambassadors discovered that they had to explain policy to the host public at large through the host's own, sometimes hostile, media. (Indeed, news management became one of their major functions.)

The diplomat had also to deal with quite different settings for diplomacy and different modalities of it. Increasingly, diplomacy came to be multilateral, as international institutions set up after the Second World War proliferated. There was also the continuous convening of special negotiating fora, within the GATT initially for trade matters, and by special conferences for a variety of international legal innovations. (During the post-war period, large conferences were convened to consider a new international law of the sea, for example, on humanitarian warfare and on the drug traffic.) These large conferences required special teams which were sent out from the home country, bypassing official diplomats entirely.

In their original form, however, conferences had developed as an attribute of heads of state diplomacy. Increasingly common following the Versailles Conference, diplomacy by conference owed a lot to Lloyd George and was his response to the demand for a new diplomacy; what was more relevant, he did not want interference from the Foreign Office.[28] The result was that foreign offices had to deal with, and often pick up the pieces of, the ill-regulated efforts of prime ministers to be their own diplomats.

Less attractive in the life of the diplomat, and in complete antipathy to liberal aims, was the increasing focus of the embassy for political protest, rising to terrorist activities. During the course of the 1970s, the United States diplomatic corps lost over three hundred serving officers to murder and kidnapping in Latin America.

The new diplomatic conventions

By the late 1950s, the collection of these changes was deemed sufficiently thoroughgoing to require a full review of diplomatic practice. During 1959, a series of international conferences was convened to consider what new understandings in the law of treaties were required by diplomatic developments, and which new practices should be agreed. The results, codified in the three Vienna Conventions of 1961, represented the first major revision of diplomatic practice since 1815, and reflected what the political authorities of the day conceived as the role of the modern diplomat.

In terms of fundamental principles, the conventions demonstrated an emerging new philosophy of diplomatic practice, and established several new principles. When the Vienna Conferences scrutinised practice, the participants deliberately adopted a new 'functional principle' to evaluate it. All privileges and immunities tended to be considered, in the words of Satow's new diplomatic handbook, 'in terms of the facilitation of the diplomatic task' as opposed to the more traditional concern with the person of the diplomat or the honours of the state. The new conventions also demonstrated a new concern for the security of the embassy. Indeed, concern for the premises of the embassy surpassed concern for the person of the ambassador – and embassy security came to include the right to be free of eavesdropping devices as well as an obligation on the part of the host country to protect premises. Privileges were also standardised, including the usages of the diplomatic bag (which had become so large as to include the transport of household items for diplomats serving abroad).

Immunity of persons and, in particular, immunity from criminal acts were more difficult to conceptualise. Formerly, the diplomat had been exempted from civil as well as criminal jurisdiction, in part to shield him from political pressure. But in the expanded age of mass diplomacy, it became a legitimate matter of doubt whether all who enjoyed diplomatic status should be exempted from the civil laws of the host country, concerning debt, for example, as well as prosecution for 'private' crimes. There were also doubts as to whether the category of the exempted should include entire families as well as casual labour, secretaries, cleaners and drivers, the latter of whom were in fact usually natives of the host country.

The result of these deliberations was a liberal compromise. In essence, the new code separated crime and punishment. It declared that all diplomats, including families and ancillaries, were expected to live by the legal conventions of the host country, and could be expelled for derogations of its civil laws. However, they could not be brought to trial for such derogations. On the other hand, citizens and permanent residents of the host state were only accorded immunity for 'official acts'. Thus, immunity was clarified, and illegal acts became grounds for the expulsion of the person, and on the demand of the host government. Modern diplomats were expected to live within the civil code of the host country. But they were exempted from the hosts' courts for derogations: the only punishment was justified expulsion.

Some of these newly codified practices were quite conformable to the aims of the new diplomacy, but others were not quite so encouraging. On the positive side, when Butterfield's publishing house revised *Satow's Diplomatic Practice*, the bible of the nineteenth-century diplomat, to take account of the new codifications, the new issue included a section of practical advice to the diplomat assigned to the United Nations, pointing out that his duty was to facilitate and to serve the organisation as a whole, not merely the aims of his country, and that, accordingly, his immunity was more conditional than that of an ordinary diplomat.[29] In this respect, Vienna went some way to satisfying host countries (in this case, the United States) as to the limits of immunity, since under the cover of UN immunity some UN missions were engaging in practices which the United States would not have ordinarily permitted to a foreign diplomat serving in Washington. Accordingly, the new convention strengthened ideas of good diplomatic behaviour and of wider community service. What Vienna could not agree, however, was whether *persona* individually *non grata* to the United States could enter the country, either as state representatives to the UN or as non-governmental UN appellants. The United States insisted on reserving the right to deny visa entry to individual foreign nationals, irrespective of status, and routinely stopped representatives of what it considered terrorist organisations from speaking at the UN, much less to the wider American public, effectively limiting their ability to appeal to the world community organ. According to Hardy, such acts were to be 'regretted', but the organisation could do little more than protest.[30]

The new diplomacy and international community

On the wider question of whether diplomacy served the state or whether, rather, it should be evaluated by reference to a wider sense of international community, the Vienna Conventions were unclear and, indeed, could be read in a variety of ways. On the one hand, the protection of the person of the diplomat and the sanctity of the embassy, now secured through a new positive international law, seemed to imply that diplomats were the skeins of a true international institution which had to be protected as such. Vienna supported the notion that diplomacy *per se* was an international institution. But it was silent on the pacific aims of the diplomat, and in no way challenged the notion that diplomats represented governments. In effect, the new code stressed greater security for state representatives, and gave states rights to secure premises. States had also gained increased rights with regard to the diplomatic bag, which there was no longer a right to challenge.

In 1991, Christopher Hill, to become Professor of International Relations at London University, placed the state and the diplomatic system in an uneasy relationship with one another. Reflecting on its conception as a central institution of international society, he observed that diplomacy was also intended to further 'hopes for the state as a vehicle for prosperity, safety and self-realisation', and that the tension between the two might be irreconcilable.[31] He also concluded that the diplomat was better viewed as a 'plain negotiator', working to a specific mandate from his government, and stranded between constituencies, than as an agent of a new world order

In a set of lectures at the London School of Economics in 1951 on the subject of modern diplomacy, Charles Webster, Britain's Official Historian, had expressed himself sceptical of Nicolson's account of the ideal diplomat, and by implication sceptical of the idea that the diplomat should be seen as serving some wider international community interest or purpose.[32] He succinctly defined the purposes of the diplomat as securing the 'maximum of national interest with a minimum of friction and resentment of others', a nineteenth-century professional cabinet interpretation. Most writers on diplomacy in the period following the Second World War would demonstrate a similar lowering of sights.

Notes

1 *Europe and the French Revolution*, translated and edited A. Cobban and J. Hunt (London: Collins, 1969), p. 35.

2 *Aspects of the French Revolution* (London: Paladin, 1971), p. 10.

3 E.g. L. Hobhouse, *Social Evolution and Political Theory* (New York: Columbia University, 1911) and N. Angell, *The Great Illusion* (London, 1912).

4 *Imperialism* (London: James Nisbet, 1902) and *Democracy After the War* (London: George Allen and Unwin, 1917).

5 See U.D.C. Morel, *The Morrow of the War* (London, 1914) and M. Swartz, *The Union of Democratic Control in British Politics during the First World War* (Oxford: Clarendon, 1971).

6 See L. Gelfand, *The Inquiry: American Preparations for Peace* (New Haven: Yale University Press, 1963).

7 It was Trotsky, the new People's Commissar for Foreign Affairs, who declared, 'I will issue a few revolutionary proclamations to the peoples of the world and then shut up shop.' E.H. Carr, *The Bolshevik Revolution*, vol. 3 (New York: Macmillan, 1961) p. 16.

8 Point 1: 'Open covenants of peace openly arrived at, after which there shall be no private undertakings of any kind'; Point 5: 'A free, open-minded and absolute impartial adjustment of colonial claims [in which] the interest of the populations concerned must have equal weight with the equitable claims of the Government whose title is to be determined'; Point 14: A general association of nations to be formed 'for the purpose of affording mutual guarantees of political independence and territorial integrity'.

9 A. Mayer, *Political Origins of the New Diplomacy, 1917–1918* (New Haven: Yale University Press, 1959).

10 *Diplomacy*, third edition (London: Oxford University Press, 1969) p. 83.

11 J. Crawford (ed.), *The Rights of Peoples* (Oxford: Clarendon, 1988).

12 T.H. von Laue, 'Soviet Diplomacy' in G. Craig and F. Gilbert (eds), *The Diplomats 1919–1939* vol. 1, (Princeton: Princeton University Press, 1953).

13 A. Klieman, *Foundation of British Policy in the Arab World* (Baltimore: Johns Hopkins University, 1970).

14 The *Manchester Guardian* published the texts from 12 December 1917.

15 *Diplomacy* (London: Butterworth, 1939).

16 Gordon Martel, 'From Round Table to New Europe' in P. Bosch and C. Navari (eds) *Chatham House and British Foreign Policy 1919–1945* (London: Lothian, 1994), p. 22.

17 D.C. Watt, *Personalities and Politics* (London: Longmans, 1975) p. 27.

18 Walter Lippmann, in the most significant work on democracy in the early part of the century, called representatives 'a group of blind men in a vast unknown world', while experts were the 'entering wedge' which would allow knowledge to be joined to power; *Public Opinion* (New York: Macmillan, 1927, 1954) pp. 288 and 370.

19 See, e.g. W. Dorman, 'Playing the Government's Game: The Mass Media and American Foreign Policy' in C. Kegley and E. Wittkop (eds), *The Domestic Sources of American Foreign Policy* (New York: St Martin's, 1988).

20 See e.g. T. Franck and E. Weisband (eds), *Secrecy and Foreign Policy* (New York: Oxford University Press, 1973).

21 *Memoirs of a British Agent* (London: Putnam, 1932).

22 C. Andrew, *The Missing Dimension: Governments and the Intelligence Community in the Twentieth Century* (London: Macmillan, 1984).

23 See e.g. W. Blum, *The CIA: A Forgotten History* (London: ZED, 1986).

24 See H. Wallace, *National Governments and the European Communities* (London: Chatham House/PEP, 1973).

25 J. Brandes, *Herbert Hoover and Economic Diplomacy, Department of Commerce Policy, 1921–1928* (Westport: Greenwood, 1975).

26 Largely inspired by G. Allison, *Essence of Decision* (Boston: Little Brown, 1971).

27 See D. Dunn, *Diplomacy at the Highest Level: The Evolution of International Summitry* (Basingstoke: Macmillan, 1996).

28 G. Craig and F. Gilbert (eds), *The Diplomats 1919–1939* (Princeton: Princeton University Press, 1953).

29 Lord Gore-Booth and D. Pakenham (eds), *Satow's Guide to Diplomatic Practice* (London: Longmans, 1979).

30 M. Hardy, *Modern Diplomatic Law* (Manchester: Manchester University Press, 1968) p. 119.

31 C. Hill, 'Diplomacy and the Modern State' in C. Navari (ed.), *The Condition of States* (Milton Keynes: Open University Press, 1991).

32 Published as *The Art and Practice of Diplomacy* (London: Chatto and Windus, 1961).

15 The modern law of nations

During the twentieth century, international law expanded in scope and became more legal in nature. Drugs, social welfare, raw materials, health matters, travel, even nationality, came to be regulated in some of their aspects by international law. By the second half of the twentieth century, scarcely a single area of social life remained untouched by international legal codes. The new codes were, moreover, increasingly specific. They established criteria of sufficient precision to allow a judge or an implementing body to determine when a particular law was being broken. Traditional international law had been largely prescriptive in nature, and it was often couched in terms so general that derogation was difficult to determine. Major areas of twentieth-century international law were capable of being applied to a specific case in question. So revolutionary did these changes appear that twentieth-century international law was often described as the 'new' international law.

The 'new' international law seemed to imply a developing international community. A prominent idea of 'community' centred on social relationships which were regulated by law and considerations of justice, and whose identity as a community was defined by its legal corpus and its conceptions of justice. Accordingly, as international law grew, there also grew the idea of an international legal community of, in this case, states whose relations were regulated by laws and which had its own legal personality, as defined by the corpus of laws applying to it.

But it was not so simple. The determination of a true international legal community turned on considerations of the substance of international law, its methods and its subjects. One important question concerned the degree to which the new law chained the state, or rather merely reflected a new articulation of the state. A second question was whether international legal development implied a greater readiness on the part of governments to abide by juridical procedures in the resolution of disputes. These became a constant matter of concern, to test the empirical existence of the putative community. On these two questions, however, the empirical record could be read in quite different and somewhat contradictory ways.

The outlines of the new international law

There were different characterisations of the new law. Philip Jessup identified it in terms of a transition from an international to a 'transnational' law, primarily on the grounds that the new law regulated not only state behaviour but potentially all actions or events that transcended national frontiers, whether of states, individuals, international organisations, corporations or other groups. Wilfred Jenks, in the same vein, referred to a 'growing common law of mankind', while Clark and Sohn observed the change from an international to a 'world law'.[1] Others pointed to its changing functions. One eminent 'realist' scholar called it a shift from what had been, essentially, a law of reciprocity to a law of co-ordination.[2]

Central to the idea of a new international law were its subjects or persona, those on whom it was binding and to whom it applied. The nineteenth-century legal theorist could declare with some confidence that the only proper subjects of international law were states, and that international law applied only to them. But twentieth-century international law concerned also the cross-frontier relationships of individuals, business organisations and other non-state corporate bodies; and it applied to them directly. The 'new subjects' of international law were confronted with legal guidelines and rules to which they were now required to conform as subjects of that law, not merely as citizens or subjects of states.[3] The most obvious cases were persons liable to international crimes such as seizing aircraft, or crimes against humanity.

Whether new subjects implied a new sort of law was, however, questionable. States remained the jurisdictional units of the international legal system and the possessors of the right to trial and punishment. International crimes were, in fact, incorporated into the legal systems of states, and international criminals were tried in national courts. Even the Nuremberg court, which tried German war criminals, was not clearly an international court; it might equally have been understood as a German court, established under the occupation statute by the four powers who 'held' the German sovereign authority. Only towards the end of the century was a genuinely international tribunal convened, within the legal framework of a new law of humanitarian warfare, to try war crimes in the successor states to Yugoslavia. Its extraordinary status was reflected in the efforts, still in progress at the century's end, to establish a genuine international criminal court on a permanent basis.

A more promising development was codification. Not only did new laws with new subjects develop, but entire new legal codes were drafted which absorbed previous legislation. Slavery, for example, and the trade in women became absorbed into more general legal codes on illegal traffic in persons, and these in turn were subsumed into general declarations on human rights. The laws of war were codified and elaborated. The various scattered provisions of sea law were amalgamated into a comprehensive international maritime code. (It was in part due to this process that general principles were supplemented by detailed and specific understandings.)

These codifications were accompanied by the development of the concept of a legal 'regime'. Instead of considering particular conventions and treaties in isolation, commentators brought them together, identifying bodies of international law on a relevant subject and treating them as a single regulatory order or 'regime'. A regime was deemed to include a prescriptive foundation, a shared body of social concerns and some attention to implementation.[4] On this basis, commentators identified a human rights regime, a trade regime and, at the end of the twentieth century, a developing environmental regime. The various agreements included in such regimes tended to be treated as though they were parts of coherent wholes.[5] It became possible thereby to 'fill in gaps'. Twentieth-century legal development was frequently justified in terms of the needs of the regime in question, on sanctions with regard to the trade regime, for example, or on children in respect of the human rights regime.

Accompanying codification was the development of a genuine international case law. In part, this was due to the establishment of the international courts. Between 1920, when it was founded, and its demise in 1946, the Permanent Court of Justice had issued seventy-seven arbitral judgements, while the International Court which succeeded it had, by 1986, issued some fifty important judgements. International case law was supplemented by an enormous number of municipal law cases with international implications, cases which were not formally part of international law but which set precedents and became sources of international legal argument. Important contributions to international law were made by the Supreme Court of the United States and Britain's Law Lords.

With a growing number of cases from which lawyers could cite precedent, international law became more legal in character. Arguing from precedent made the law more convincing and gave it a greater resemblance to harder domestic law. Partly in consequence, the practice of international law became a serious branch of the legal profession. Formal training developed, and international lawyers came to share equal status with civil or criminal lawyers. Moreover, they specialised in different branches of international law. Large law firms offered special services in trade law, for example, or in the law of human rights.

The development of legal method

Since the eighteenth century, writers had generally identified and codified international law by simply listing what states did. The major example was Emmerich de Vatel's influential and enduring *Droit des Gens*, which had based law on practice and consent. The consensual approach produced an extended observation of contemporary practice with the minimum of theoretical elaboration. The development of nineteenth-century legal positivism did not change, but rather confirmed this same tendency and took it to its logical conclusion. According to legal positivism, the law was what legal agencies declared it to be. Accordingly, law and practice came to be considered virtually identical, and there were no grounds for deciding whose practice was more truly law. In the context of a divergent state practice, this approach tended to produce particularly anecdotal descriptions of the law.

Twentieth-century practice was quite different. It began, in fact, to more closely resemble seventeenth-century practice: it argued from juristic principles, and only used cases as examples. Practice remained important to the twentieth-century jurist, but it was used to deduce principles. Twentieth-century legal writers were, moreover, concerned to rationalise the principles they identified. In the process, twentieth-century legal writing began to employ what was often quite abstract juristic logic, sometimes barely mentioning practice at all.[6] Such methods created an analogy between international law and English common law. The common law had evolved from instance to instance and case to case, as judges and jurists developed general principles in relation to circumstances.

State growth and international law

These changes reflected, in part, the growing complexity and range of international exchange. The volume of human migration, of exchange of goods, the greediness for capital and labour, all threw up complex problems of health regulation, of standards of work, of equity in exchange. In consequence, governments were drawn to engage in close parallel or even co-ordinated legal regulation, as their courts become increasingly involved in legal disputes on cross-state matters. There were also the concerns of the new post-colonial states and their demands for equity of treatment. To redraft international law for new users required rethinking the basis of that law. Above all, they reflected changes in the state itself and the growing control over all manifestations of social and political life which the twentieth-century state claimed. Indeed, the two were functions of one another. The more the state had in its control, the more it could 'internationalise'; and the more capacity states had to govern, the more could be made subject to international legal codes.

The two most immediately obvious cases were the economy and migration. As states seized control over exchange and payments provisions, these could only be 'freed' by reference to international legislation or agreement among states. Thus must an international economic law grow. When they began to regulate immigration and to control entry into their territories, international agreements on entry and exit began to appear, to prevent waves of migrants shifting from one state to another.[7]

If an expanded state sovereignty allowed international law to grow, it was also true that international law tended to confirm an expanded state sovereignty. The international legal developments of the twentieth century may have made governments the bearers of many more legal duties than previously, but they also tended to expand the legal orbit of the state. And with few exceptions, twentieth-century international legal development gave more to the state than it took away. Indeed, it was via international legislation that the twentieth-century state achieved many of its enhanced powers over the domestic social fabric.

The law of the skies

The treatment of airspace was an early, and characteristic, example. A potential subject for international regulation from the moment of the invention of aircraft, discussion began in the first decade of the century as to the method of its incorporation, at which point there was advocacy for complete freedom of the skies. Immediately after the First World War, however, and because of the use of planes as weapons of war, the issue was decided in favour of the state. Article I of the 1919 International Convention for the Regulation of Air Carriage adopted the concept of air sovereignty, stating that 'every power has complete and exclusive sovereignty over the airspace above its territory'. This extended to the right to force planes to land, and even to shoot them down if they refused to comply.

The principle of a state's control of its airspace was considerably expanded by the Chicago Convention of 1944 when it was extended to commercial carriers.[8] The Chicago Convention gave states the right to refuse civilian transit as well as landing. This meant that each state was, in effect, licensed to control all commercial flights over, as well as landings on, its territory; moreover, the right of commercial landing came to be granted essentially by bilateral agreement between states. (Hence the pattern familiar to twentieth-century air travel, where the two most important carriers between any two points were the carriers of the respective nationalities, since each was forced to concede landing rights in order to land in the corresponding state's territory.) These provisions turned the state into the licenser of commercial as well as military aircraft. And they were supplemented by rights of cabotage – the right to monopolise carriage on routes wholly within a country. Even aircraft were nationalised; each aircraft bore the nationality of the country of registration so that crimes on planes, for example, fell within the legal jurisdiction of the country of registration, irrespective of where the aircraft was, a provision extended to terrorist activities by the Tokyo Convention of 1963.

The use of airwaves was another example of the state's growing compass. Deriving initially from concern over the use of radio for propaganda purposes, a Convention Concerning the Use of Broadcasting in the Cause of Peace was signed by twenty-five states in 1936 (OJLN 1936, p. 1437) who agreed to stop transmissions 'detrimental to good international understanding'; Article 6 instructed states to provide appropriate guidelines for any autonomous broadcasting organs. Radio proved such an important instrument of foreign policy that all new states wanted airwaves, and a new airwave law began to develop during the late 1960s and 1970s, in the wake of decolonisation, ensuring parity of access to airwaves (but which also reserved bands for international shipping and air transport). In the process, the more powerful older broadcasters had to restrict their band usage. All were confirmed, however, in the right to control domestic broadcasting by whatever method they chose. In 1964, Britain backed a successful proposal at the International Telecommunications Union allowing for the legal boarding of vessels, even if outside territorial waters, which were engaged in unlicensed broadcasting.

The decline of **mare liberum**

So, too, did the sea come progressively under state control. The traditional doctrine of *mare liberum*, clearly established by the beginning of the eighteenth century, by which the sea was a resource to all (and to all as individuals), became seriously eroded during the twentieth century. The first to be affected were territorial waters, which many states extended from the traditional 3 miles to 12, and some to 150. (The old 3-mile limit was dethroned in 1930 and customary law came increasingly to accept 12.) There further developed two new international legal concepts which extended governmental regulation by contiguous sea powers far into coastal waters: the concepts of 'continental shelf' and the 'exclusive economic zone'.

The continental shelf was originally a geographical concept, referring to that area of land mass along coasts (generally to a depth of 200 metres underwater) which generally precedes the falling away into deeper ocean depths. Varying from a few hundred yards in some instances to many miles in others (the United States' continental shelf was estimated to be about 29,000 square miles, equal to the size of the Louisiana Purchase), it became a subject of interest to governments soon after the Second World War, primarily on account of potential oil resources. Between 1945 and 1949, as the technology of oil exploitation developed, some maritime state authorities began to claim exclusive jurisdiction and control, and some complete sovereignty, of their continental shelves, claims formally raised at the first UN Conference on the Law of the Sea.

The first conference confirmed legalisation, and in favour of the state. In 1958, partly because of the uniform pressure of such claims on the part of the major powers and partly because of their ability to enforce them, a convention was signed which went far to establish unlimited jurisdiction by a coastal state over shelf waters. Though sovereignty was not conceded, Article 2 granted 'sovereign rights' for the exploration and exploitation of natural resources, and it granted them *ipso jure*: such rights were automatic, depending neither on effective occupation nor on formal claim (the latter at the behest of the new states who did not wish title to depend on ability to exploit or protect, in which ability many were lacking). Natural resources included not only minerals but 'sedentary organisms', pearl, oyster and other sedentary fisheries which had generally evaded free fishing and which had belonged by tradition to particular communities. These now came under state control, without regard to the acquired rights of local communities or the communities of other, non-coastal states. Also, to create equity for states without a true continental shelf, the notion of the shelf lost its geographical meaning in favour of the criterion of exploitability. States were allowed jurisdiction to 200 miles or where depth 'admits of exploitation'. In 1967, J.G. Starke called this convention 'one of the most influential instruments of international law yet concluded'.[9] The notion that jurisdiction followed exploitation would begin to affect even the high seas, as some state authorities claimed mining rights on the deep sea bed, where a rich store of minerals potentially lay waiting to be harvested.

In the early 1960s, new claims began to appear for extending ocean surface rights. In this case, it was a growing conflict between states whose livelihood depended on fishing and who did not have the sophisticated equipment to engage in long-distance deep-water fishing, and those who did. The former began to claim rights over zones as much as 200 miles beyond their territorial sea. In 1974, in adjudicating a conflict between Britain and Iceland, the so-called 'Cod War', the International Court of Justice held that, since 1960, a customary law had developed which provided at least 12 miles of 'exclusive zone' to fishing states. It further held that a coastal state had a preferential right over fish in adjacent areas, if (like Iceland) it were economically dependent on local fisheries. The decision encouraged numerous further claims and, by 1979, out of 133 coastal states, 92 were claiming exclusive fishing rights for 200 miles and/or exclusive rights of exploitation. (Indeed, 14 states claimed a territorial sea of 200 miles.) Moreover, among the states so claiming were the US, Japan, the USSR and Britain, states which had traditionally opposed restricted fishing zones. With the emergence of agreement between major powers, small states and new states, the outcome was inevitable. In 1982, at a third UN Conference on Sea Law, the largest and most finite of the great twentieth-century sea conferences, states agreed a territorial sea of 12 miles (finally settling in law that knotty question) and an 'exclusive economic zone' of a further 188 miles. Within these zones, states could not interfere with 'freedom of navigation', but they could license fishing, control pollution and regulate scientific research. By this law, some areas of free sea disappeared completely, and states had to fight hard to avoid being deprived of access to traditional international straits and waterways.

The non-territoriality of outer space

The major exception to the gradual expansion of the territorial compass of the state was outer space, and it was not conceded gracefully. During the two decades after the Second World War, as aircraft capability expanded, the limits of airspace were raised continuously, and the initial tendency was to proceed ad infinitum. (Not without some confusion, since the principle of effective physical control had, since the end of the nineteenth century, been the main basis for recognising territorial claims; beyond 30,000 feet, no such control was initially possible.) With the development of missile capability and manned space flight, however, it appeared possible that the concept of state jurisdiction, and hence territoriality, might be applied, if not to the entirety of space, certainly to celestial bodies. While, moreover, it was possible to establish a distinction between airspace and space – there was a clear physical distinction, for example, between the troposphere, the stratosphere and the ionosphere – it was not easy to relate such distinctions to the height at which planes flew or might be expected to fly in future. But in 1961, the General Assembly foreclosed some of these possibilities, resolving that international law, including the Charter of the United Nations, applied to 'outer space and celestial bodies', notwithstanding the difficulties of defining the former, and that these were 'free for exploration and use by all States' (Res. 1721 XVI). In 1963, it established two further legal principles governing the activities of states in outer space: that neither space nor celestial bodies were subject to national appropriation, and that state activities in space must conform to the interests of international peace and security (Res. 1962 XVIII). By reference to these principles, astronauts, for example, had to be licensed, the licensing state was held responsible for their actions and they were to be considered 'emissaries of mankind', entitled to help in case of accident. Both pointed to the concept, formally enunciated by the General Assembly in 1967, that outer space was a form of common space. This, however, occurred during the idealistic early phase of space travel. Some writers doubted it would hold if access to space were to become the norm.

There were more immediate difficulties associated with the rapid development of communications satellites, commercial as well as spy satellites. It was not clear, for example, that spy satellites conformed to 'peaceful uses' (although international law did not ban spying). And by the end of the century, Third World governments were beginning to demonstrate a reluctance to allow unregulated transmissions from Western commercial television satellites into their domestic space.

The state as a subject of international law

Traditionally, a good deal of international law had concerned the definitions, powers and competencies of the state, and this did not change during the twentieth century. Indeed, twentieth-century legal developments rather confirmed it. Since a great many new states were created, part of the new development was especially concerned with defining the state, in order to establish what sorts of entities should be deemed capable of exercising the duties, and enjoying the rights, of statehood.

During the later part of the nineteenth century, with the increasingly frequent encounters between European and extra-European political orders, the most commonly employed regulating concept was the distinction between advanced and backward or civilised and uncivilised states, the latter of which were disqualified from enjoying states' rights on the grounds that they could not comprehend the duties enjoined in European legal codes. (Hall's *International Law* of 1880 termed international law the 'product of the special civilisation of modern Europe', and claimed it formed 'a highly artificial system by which the principles cannot be supposed to be understood or recognised by countries differently civilised'; p. 47.) On such grounds, the principles of state sovereignty were not extended to Japan or Thailand, despite their being entirely coherent and independent legal orders (whereupon Japan rather wisely began to educate its population in Western notions of reciprocity). These regulating concepts, together with their imperial overtones, continued to prevail well into the late 1920s. Sir Thomas Barclay, vice-president of the International Law Association, who contributed the entry on international law to the 1929 edition of the *Encyclopaedia Britannica* would note that the test in the distinction between civilized and uncivilized which is regarded as warranting exclusion from ... admission to the community of the civilized world is in practice the possession of a regular government sufficient to ensure to Europeans who settle among them safety of life and property.[10]

Post-colonial governments increasingly eschewed the use of such language, but some continued to wish for a legal discriminator of good and bad states. The United States, in particular, which had refused to recognise the new revolutionary government in Mexico in 1911, sought legal grounds to withhold recognition in the event of further unwelcome political developments, initially in Latin America. The Latin American states, not surprisingly, were in the forefront of efforts to resist such impulses; and they would find allies among the new states following the onset of decolonisation. Both proffered and defended empirical definitions of statehood, such as *de facto* control by a government of a territory, or the ability to maintain order and conduct diplomacy. Nor could the 'civilised' agree among themselves on the qualifying criteria for statehood. In consequence, definitions of the state, and of the right- and duty-bearing subjects of international law, tended towards the neutral, relying essentially on formal characteristics. The Montevideo Convention on the Rights and Duties of States 1933 became a popular starting point for such definitions, recommending a permanent population, a defined territory, a government and an ability to engage in diplomatic exchange.

State succession and the recognition of new states

Of these duty-bearing entities, more than 130 were created during the course of the century. Not all were entirely new jurisdictional units. New states were generally formed from the administrative units of empires where, moreover, local authorities had often held important powers; some like Algeria, Libya and Morocco had been jurisdictional entities before their incorporation into the French and Italian empires. Nonetheless, their recasting as states on the European model raised important questions concerning the principles of state succession. Was the new state to be considered a product of self-determination, and was recognition to be conceded thereby on demand? Was it to be conceived in contractual terms, as the dissolution of a previously existing contract, whereupon a negotiation should then proceed between the new entity and various members of the international community? Or was state succession to be conceived as a legal handing over from an old authority to a new authority which would then enjoy the privileges formerly accorded to the previous authority? A variant on this question concerned recognition; should states, or governments, be deemed legally to exist on the grounds of recognition by the international community, sometimes called the constitutive theory, or could they be deemed legally to exist as a matter of fact, when they conformed to the legal definition of a state, called the declaratory theory?

Several sets of principles were established to regulate recognition. First, though recognition was deemed to apply to states and governments equally, state succession and government change did imply somewhat different principles. Most lawyers conceded the inherently political nature of recognition and its use to withhold approval from specific regimes.[11] Equally, however, it was widely accepted that recognition of new governments only became a question when regime change came about through non-constitutional methods, such as civil wars or wars of independence and/or intervention. It was also generally agreed that there was no duty in international law to recognise a new government so created. Practice varied: states were generally identified as inclining towards either the declaratory or the constitutive theory. (The British government inclined towards the former, and the United States towards the latter.) But the increasing tendency in practice was towards the Estrada Doctrine, which avoided express recognition altogether, lest this imply approval, while entering into diplomatic relations with new governments for a range of practical and diplomatic purposes.[12]

The recognition of a new state was a somewhat different matter. Despite efforts on the part of new states to declare that they should be recognised as a matter of fact, some form of legal handing over became the general practice. New states generally came into being via a ceremony in which the former colonial master formally handed power to the new authorities, declaring it recognised the new state at that moment. (It also recommended membership of the new state to the United Nations.) This practice, which entailed an element of sponsorship, represented a form of acquiesced secession.

The rights and duties of states

Of the new rights accorded to states during the twentieth century, the most persistently pursued was the right to non-intervention. The London Convention of 1933, concerned to define aggression, noted that no act of aggression could be justified by the internal condition of a state. In 1936, signatories to the Treaty of Buenos Aires foreswore interventions by any one of them in the 'internal or external affairs' of any of the other parties. Article 2 (7) of the UN Charter forbade the organisation 'to intervene in matters which are essentially within the domestic jurisdiction of any State'.[13] On 17 July 1946, the UN General Assembly passed a Resolution on the Draft Declaration of the Rights and Duties of States which pronounced intervention as inadmissible, a proposition which it resolved again in 1965.

Definitions of intervention were, however, as illusive as definitions of aggression. One contemporary commentator criticised the term as covering 'anything from a speech of Lord Palmerston's in the House of Commons to the partition of Poland'. Resolution 2131 (XX) of 1965, after the usual denunciations, defined intervention as 'armed intervention and all other forms of interference or attempted threats against the personality of the State or against its political, economic or cultural elements'. But this was scarcely helpful as a guide to legal practice, particularly since self-defence might authorise armed intervention. Moreover, legal opinion generally upheld the right of a state to go to the aid of a *de jure* government struggling against rebellion, clearly a form of intervention. Where international lawyers seemed to agree was in condemning acts 'calculated to impair the authority of another sovereign',[14] confirmed in GA RES 290 (IV) which called upon every nation 'to refrain from any threats or acts, direct or indirect, aimed at impairing the freedom, independence or integrity of any State, or at fomenting civil strife and subverting the will of the people in any State'. (Both the UK and the US treated as a form of international crime the organisation of rebellion in a friendly state.)

On efforts to expand sovereignty to include 'economic sovereignty', there remained no such formal category in international law, despite the efforts of many new states to claim sole jurisdiction over the use of resources within their territories. The Brussels Conference on Russia in 1921, following the Soviet confiscations, resolved that 'forcible expropriations and nationalisations without any compensation or remuneration of property in which foreigners are interested is totally at variance with the practice of civilised states'. But the principle of nationalisation was gradually conceded. In 1926, in a landmark decision in the Upper Silesia case, the PCIJ declared that 'expropriation for reasons of public utility, judicial liquidation and similar measures' was lawful. But the major powers insisted, and gained the point, that there was a duty to indemnify. (The PCIJ in the Chorzow Factory case, 1928, defined the quantum of compensation as 'the value of the undertaking at the moment of dispossession plus interest to the day of payment'.) The demand of public utility continued to be strongly defended by the major powers, many of whom held plant and economic investments in new states, as well as equity of treatment between nationals and foreigners, and the criterion of public utility was held to exclude 'appropriations essentially arbitrary in character'.

Of their duties, the five principles of Bandung, agreed in 1955 by the first meeting of what were to become the non-aligned states, became the standard formulation the same year. The Bandung Declaration demanded mutual respect for territorial integrity and sovereignty, non-aggression, non-interference in others' internal affairs, equality (including mutual benefit) and peaceful co-existence. But these were, like injunctions against intervention, more political than legal in nature.

The new personalities of the new law

The tendency well into the twentieth century was to concede international personality only to states; certainly, colonies and mandates had no such personality. Gradually, however, international organisations, including the European Community, gained elements of international personality. These entities did not enjoy the rights and duties of states: their 'personalities' were defined by the specific rights granted to them in their founding charters. Thus, the Security Council had an international personality constituted by those rights and duties assigned to it in the Charter, while, by Article 113 (3) of the Treaty of Rome, the European Community was empowered to negotiate tariff and trade agreements with third countries. In each instance, however, these were generally conceded to be non-legislative powers; treaty-making remained the domain of states.

Minority national and religious groups were a variable case of legal personality. The peace settlement following the First World War had made a wide range of religious and ethnic groups subject to international protection, primarily in the new and successor states which were created following the dissolution of the Austrian, Russian and Ottoman empires. Rights were bestowed on special groups of Germans, Moravians and Poles, including rights to citizenship, to education and to language use. Most importantly with regard to legal personality, rights were granted such groups to petition the League if their rights were abused. In 1920, a Minorities Committee was created to whom such groups might apply directly, and the named minorities, as well as others, were not slow to take advantage of the provision. Almost every League Council session was called upon to deal with some issue of racial, linguistic or religious protection. However, during the 1930s, the Nazi and fascist governments in Germany and Italy began using the existence of minorities with unfulfilled rights to make territorial claims against the new states of Eastern Europe, most notoriously on behalf of the Sudeten Germans in the case of Czechoslovakia and the Danzig Germans in the case of Poland. This experience turned opinion against the protection of minority rights, and such rights were subsumed into the General Declarations of Human Rights eventually produced from within the General Assembly. Accordingly, minorities no longer had specific rights, at least none they could exercise directly.

Neither, however, did anyone else. Several general declarations on human rights were produced during the two decades following the Second World War, most notably the International Covenant on Civil and Political Rights and the International Covenant on Economic, Social and Cultural Rights, both opened for signature in 1966. Both contained lists of individual and some collective rights which inferred obligations, but to no specified donors. Moreover, such rights were only enforceable in national courts. Human beings gained rights, but only as 'objects' of international law, not as subjects. The only exception was the European Convention on Human Rights, and in particular the statute of the European Court of Human Rights, opened for signature in 1950 and 1963 respectively, where seventeen signatories allowed their citizens to petition the European Court directly.

The growing category of international crime created several new classes of international subject. The nineteenth century had seen the creation of one new class of crime (to join piracy, termed a crime *humani generis*): that of slaver, according to the General Act of the Berlin Conference on Central Africa 1885 which confirmed that 'trading in slaves is forbidden in conformity with the principles of international law'. But after the atrocities committed during the Second World War, a Convention for the Prevention and Punishment of the

Crime of Genocide was open for signature in 1948, by which year the murder of groups of civilians or soldiers in captivity, committed in times of war or peace, was declared an international crime. In the same spirit, other conventions and declarations named crimes against peace, crimes against humanity and war crimes, and created as many new categories of criminal subject. Finally, there were hijacking and associated acts, commonly thought of as terrorist crimes. Modern international law imposed a direct duty on individuals to refrain from any of these practices.

But while these crimes took their definition and status from international agreements and conventions, the juridical authority remained generally the state in whose jurisdiction such crimes occurred.[15] As previously mentioned, the case was not determinate; a Law of Humanitarian Warfare, concluded in the 1970s, allowed international tribunals to be convened for the punishing of war crimes, and a tribunal was established at The Hague in 1995 to try individual Bosnians, Croats and Serbs who were accused of carrying out war crimes during the dissolution of Yugoslavia. But when crimes against humanity, and to a lesser degree genocide, applied to state leaders, these could effectively be tried only when the major states agreed. Accordingly, the eventuality of bringing important classes of war criminals to trial was determined primarily by political and not legal criteria.

The laws of peace and the laws of war

It had been customary in the traditional manuals of international law to distinguish between the laws of peace and the laws of war. In the twentieth century, this distinction became confused, and not only because of the Cold War, which appeared to be neither. In part, such a distinction had depended on a legal conception of war, in which war was understood as a legal condition to which certain rules applied, and which was signalled by a declaration of war. Given the increasing injunctions against war practice, together with an increasing reluctance, or inability, to adhere to the rules of war, states became hesitant to declare war when initiating small hostilities, or even great ones. The range of hostile practice was such that it also became difficult to determine a state of war on any purely empirical grounds. Nonetheless, jurists were capable of distinguishing a normal intercourse of states on the one hand and a law applying to hostilities on the other.

Developments in the law of peace

In the area of the laws of peace, international economic law was the most striking development in the twentieth century. Previous regulation of economic affairs had fallen under traditional authority, impervious even to the state. Of course, states had worked economic arrangements for their traders (often as parts of general peace settlements) but these were few in number and generally bilateral only. With the establishment of an IMF and the GATT and the so-called Bretton Woods institutions, however, the foundations were laid for a genuine international economic law. The various founding agreements were also sufficiently large and specific to create a substantial international legal regime.

In philosophy, the Bretton Woods regime was economically liberal. Its foundation principles were non-discrimination, the gradual reduction of tariffs, free monetary exchange and free establishment. It was also a multilateral system. Once states had adhered to the agreements, they were committed to treating all other signatories (and the economic enterprises of all signatories) on the same basis. The regime was directed to the creation of a large international market of relatively free trade and payments, and it laid down principles of domestic state regulation which would encourage and protect such a market. (Although, as one of its historians has noted, a free-trade principle was often followed immediately by an exception authorising a trade restriction.)[16]

States also accepted a somewhat non-specified duty to help other states achieve the conditions laid down in the agreements. In 1961, B.V.A. Roling discerned a movement from an old 'international law of liberty' to a new 'international law of welfare' on the basis of many declarations, written into international economic agreements, on the 'right' of developing countries to special consideration. Accordingly, some Third World commentators carried this forward to a claim of substantive economic sovereignty.[17] But the general preference schemes established during the 1970s provided for no more than an imperfect right on the part of poorer states to lay claims for special conditions, of a transitory nature, which would allow them to eventually adhere to the rules.

Protection of national economies was not, however, neglected. In the newly established trade regime, states were allowed to protect themselves from dumping as well as, more ambiguously, from 'economic harm', and to put up temporary barriers when either threatened. The monetary agreements allowed for the temporary suspension of exchanges in times of crisis and the temporary raising of duties to redress a sudden deterioration in a balance of payments position, provisions which were incorporated into the Rome Treaty which established the European Economic Community.

The allowance of such temporary measures gradually began to influence diplomatic practice and, eventually, customary international law. In the early 1970s, when a world economic recession threatened, major traders began to employ temporary suspensions of trade access or the imposition of temporary tariff levels, in order to alter a trade relationship (a form of coercive diplomacy). Such diplomatic devices affected claims to economic sovereignty: they implied that residual rights over the economy did, in fact, belong to the state, which could use access to its domestic economy to force partner states into negotiations.

A second major area of development in the law of peace was in the area of environmental law. Between 1972, following a major international conference in Stockholm, and 1995, more than 160 conventions had appeared, most of them multilateral, which dealt with endangered species, with clean water and with the atmosphere. Some thirty environmental treaties had also genuine regulatory provisions, notably the agreements on ozone depletion and the transboundary movement of air pollutants.

Environmental law endorsed several new legal prescriptions of a genuinely cosmopolitan nature. It supported the notion that the environment was a common heritage of mankind and that states had a duty of prudence in allowing the usage of the environment to sub-state enterprises. It also supported the idea that there was a collective responsibility on the part of states to manage the environment for future generations. Finally, a precautionary principle was widely endorsed concerning abstention from acts with foreseeable conse-quences.[18] But it did not succeed in justifying the idea of the international management of resources that were wholly owned or located within a single state, such as the Brazilian rain forests or rare and endangered timbers. States holding such resources resolutely refused to countenance their management by the international community. Some of the new environmental law also removed resources from 'ownership' by local indigenous groups and gave authority over them to the state.

Jus ad bello

Traditionally the international law of war had distinguished between the *jus ad bello* and the *jus in bello*, just cause and just means. But by the eighteenth century, just cause had come to be confined to state war and war conducted by an authorised agency (the main distinction of the time being the distinction between public 'just' war and private 'illegal' war). The distinction tended to legitimise all wars fought by authorised agencies, irrespective of their causes. With the growth of liberal ideas in the nineteenth century, however, recourse to war came to be seen, increasingly, as the mark of a backward or illiberal society. Liberal thought held that 'proper' states should not use force in relation to one another except in clear cases of torts or wrongs.[19] This belief was enhanced during the First World War by the charge that Germany was a criminal state, on the grounds of its resort to aggression. (The association was created largely for propaganda purposes, but it also corresponded to the liberal view of the relation between force and diplomacy.) By its end, to be a proper state appeared to be contingent on renouncing the use of force. In the famous Kellogg–Briand Pact of 1928, a large number of states renounced the use of force to achieve political, economic or social ends, and it was only the first of a large number of self-denying ordinances. Ian Brownlie has noted that, between 1928 and 1939, 'nearly every government in existence had at some time stopped itself from denying the illegality of resort to force, except in self-defence ... [and] a large number of states had entered into obligations in relation to the use of force on several occasions'.[20] Modern international jurists could point to over three hundred bilateral agreements in which states renounced use of force amongst themselves, evidence sufficiently compelling to imply that force was no longer a normal tool of diplomacy. These renunciations became so general as to affect the jurisprudence of both international and municipal courts. In the Corfu

Channel case, 1949, where Britain sought to justify minesweeping operations in Albanian territorial waters, the ICJ condemned the 'manifestation of a politics of force'.

The injunctions against war affected many other common understandings. One example was no gain of territory, first laid down in the Anti-War Treaty of Rio of 1933. Rio signatories agreed that territorial questions could not be settled by violence, and that there could be no recognition of territorial arrangements not obtained by pacific means. Rio also rejected the validity of occupation or acquisition brought about by force of arms. The Rio Pact was replaced by the Bogota Pact of 1948, which substantially reiterated these provisions. While Lithuanians and Palestinians might have viewed such injunctions with scepticism, they held to a surprising extent. (Lithuania gained recognition quickly after the Soviet Union relinquished control, largely on the grounds that Soviet control had been gained by force.)

Not all resort to force was banned. All such declarations excluded self-defence. Moreover, the League of Nations had sought for a legal definition of self-defence as part of its efforts to define aggression (generally agreed to be a reaction to some resort to force, or evidence of an intention to resort to force, on the part of another state), giving self-defence legal status. More importantly, there was the emerging idea of collective security. By 1942, 'the war against Germany and her allies was regarded as a war of collective defence and a sanction against a source of aggression and lawlessness which constituted a common danger'.[21] Accordingly, the *jus ad bello* came to be increasingly defined in terms of either self-defence or collective security. Indeed, several writers noted the tendency to regard collective security (and recourse to arms in respect of collective security) as a duty, requiring to be undertaken.

The definition of collective security became, moreover, increasingly loose during subsequent decades. In 1945, properly speaking, collective security could only be authorised by the Security Council. In the case of the Korean War, the General Assembly, under the Uniting For Peace Resolution, declared itself an authorised agency; and the Nato alliance was also declared an instrument of collective security upon its founding in 1949. In subsequent decades, the term came to be applied to any resort to hostilities undertaken with a declaration of a public purpose and with the support of a number of legitimate states.

The issue of what constituted a *jus ad bello* was also confused by the national-ity principle, and the high value given to self-determination. Many ordinary citizens came to feel that wars of national liberation were also, and some would argue that they were the only, just wars; and political theory supported their claims. In a widely read and influential argument, the American political philosopher Michael Walzer defended the rights of liberation as well as self-defence of a cultural community, including pre-emptive attack, and argued that last resort, albeit uncommon, might very well justify the suspension of the traditional limitations of the *jus in bello*.[22]

Jus in bello

The rules of the *jus in bello* were first codified by the Hague conventions on the laws of war of 1899 and 1907.[23] (This was the first codification of any body of international law, and it caused great excitement on that account; it was also largely because of this codification that high expectations for a 'new' international law emerged during the first decade of the twentieth century.) In a condition of war, the newly codified rules demanded protection of civilians, allowed diplomatic relations to cease and treaties to be annulled (though it was expected that they would be back in effect when the war relation ceased), the control of subject contacts, the seizure of public property and the protection of private property (which could only be sequestered if for a military purpose and which forbade, for example, art seizures). The rules on the treatment of prisoners were codified, and such rules were to be applied to collective security operations and wars of self-defence: justice of cause was not meant to imply any laxity in justice of means. Accordingly, even those who fought unjust wars could claim the protection of the international law of war fighting.

Government reluctance to declare war, however, caused many problems for the application of the laws of warfare. When war was not declared (and when it was conducted in some cases in secret), neither belligerents nor their soldiers had any clear legal status. For example, during the 1980s, the United States both armed and encouraged a guerrilla campaign against the duly elected government of Nicaragua, and was arguably in a condition of hostilities against Nicaragua; yet it never declared that it was so. During the course of the hostilities, the official government of Nicaragua continued to have an ambassador in Washington, and the two governments continued to treat one another, albeit somewhat coolly, as if they were at peace. In the circumstances, it was not possible for either side to invoke the laws of war with regard to the actions of the other.

The new techniques of war, particularly guerrilla warfare and the requirements of air bombardment, also threatened to erode the *jus in bello*, particularly when combined with the ideological character of much twentieth-century warfare. In its early phases, aerial bombardment was highly undiscriminating, and commanders were led to be rather careless about civilian casualties on that account. Increasingly, the practice was also to make them direct targets, particularly as notions of collective guilt seemed to justify civilian targeting. Guerrilla war theory, as well as practice, confused the status distinction between civilians and soldiers, making them difficult to distinguish in the field.[24] Mercenaries were quite another problem: when captured, some states refused to accord them the dignity of disarmed soldiers to whom the Geneva Conventions on Treatment of War Prisoners should apply; instead, they were declared enemies of the state and put on trial.

It was for such reasons that one commentator would note that 'in the twentieth century the law moved forward only in the sphere of peaceful relations; in the law of war, heavily retrogressive tendencies came to prevail'.[25]

Partly to guard against this state of affairs, some jurists began to develop the concept of 'non-war armed conflict', and to develop a law of non-war hostilities, generally by adapting the laws of war to unconventional warfare.[26] An extension to the Geneva Conventions, often referred to as the 'law of humanitarian warfare', was opened for signature in 1974 and recognised guerrillas as war fighters, capable of the protection of the laws of war, if they were commanded, wore emblems, carried arms openly and conducted operations which respected the laws of war. Such criteria served, for example, to distinguish guerrillas from terrorists.

Weaknesses of the new international law

Despite the considerable advances in the scope and clarity of international law, legal theorists did not view twentieth-century developments with unmixed feelings or see in all of them progress. One source of concern was bad law: some notable developments in international law were made at the cost of legal clarity. A related concern was the explicit politicisation of international law. General declarations on non-intervention or the protection of human rights were more political than legal in character, threatening to deprive areas of international law of legal definition, providing no real standards to which states should conform or from which judges and lawyers could deduce general principles. Other commentators protested at the willingness of certain classes of states, particularly new states, to rewrite international law codes on the grounds that existing international law was a Western code, hence not universal and not binding. In this respect, the new nations followed the Latin American nations which

> developed for a hundred years a series of 'doctrines' all destined to weaken the norms and institutions of general international law as a protest and defense of the weaker states against the powerful ones, first of Europe, later of the United States.[27]

This tendency undercut any basis for international law but a purely contractual one, and weakened the notion that law *per se* should obtain between states, an idea which was, paradoxically, noticeably stronger at the beginning of the century than at its end.

Less referred to but no less serious was the problem of conflicts of law. International law grew during the century, but it also absorbed without rationalising many conflicting principles. Practice continued to be valued, as well as principle; and non-intervention continued to be cited as a basic norm, along with the many new laws which, in fact, endorsed intervention.

Some of the most important conflicts concerned the state itself. Within the human rights regime, the state appeared on the one hand as the protector of rights and on the other hand as the potential chief transgressor of rights. Within the various collective security regimes, it appeared as the guarantor of peace and stability and also as the chief threat to peace and stability.

Moreover, in one area at least, international law had changed very little. Despite a number of ingenious theories to the contrary, it remained primarily a self-imposed law. With the notable exception of Security Council resolutions, to which state signatories of the Charter of the United Nations were bound without exception, and perhaps the statute of the European Court, it was a law which still bound only so long as its subjects agreed to be bound, and its subjects remained its legislators. Moreover, there were noticeably few areas where states were bound to accept interpretations of the law which they themselves had not agreed. If the new international law could be likened to the English common law, it also suffered the limitations of any pure common law system: changeable in its interpretation from instance to instance and invaded by different principles and different interests at different times.

Natural law versus positivism

Several efforts were made to provide the developing international law of the twentieth century with the sanction of 'higher authority'. One such effort drew from the natural law revival that was the Catholic Church's response to nineteenth-century sociological positivism. The Catholic law schools in the United States, such as Notre Dame, and theologians such as Jacques Maritain and Heinrich Rommen, often referred to as neo-thomists, were in the forefront of the Catholic attack on a purely state-centred utilitarian and declaratory law. Integral to this effort, some neo-thomists sought to rest international law on natural law foundations, locating its sources in human sentiment or conscience, and providing an ethical foundation for its validity. In the process, natural law concepts were developed to provide international law with an evaluative standpoint and a point of further development through the criteria of ethical practice. Certain judges of the ICJ, such as Judge Alejandro Alvarez, adopted a neo-thomist perspective, and its influence spread far. Brierly, Huber and Hartmann, generally considered sociological jurists, nonetheless detected and defended a strong normative element in modern international law. Both Lauterpacht and Oppenheim noted the natural law influences behind the idea of an international bill of rights of man.[28] A second direction, growing in influence during the second half of the century, was referred to as the solidarist school. Influenced by communitarianism, the solidarist jurists derived and judged precepts and practices according to the needs of the whole body of states and by their contribution to social co-operation among them. Alfred Vedross, an early solidarist, went so far as to declare that 'states do not have any interests of their own'.[29]

But the values of legal positivism were not thereby vanquished, and positivism continued to guide many twentieth-century jurists in judging and evaluating international law. J. Kunz, reviewing the debate, noted with approval the growing readiness of twentieth-century natural lawyers to concede the essentially ethical and non-legal nature of natural law precepts.[30] Georg Schwarzenberger, one of the most influential of modern British jurists, introduced a strong realist as well as positivist tone to his international law.[31] And Percy Corbett identified a growing world law essentially by positivist criteria, on the grounds that it was states who were legislating such 'world laws'.[32]

Moreover, ordinary people generally judged international law by what were essentially positivist criteria. These were the existence of regularised sanctions and a court authorised to adjudicate whether the law had been broken; and both continued to be applied to international law with relentless regularity. They were, moreover, the most persuasive with the general public. By such criteria, international law would continue to appear seriously deficient.

International law and international community

The major problem with assessing twentieth-century international legal developments lay in the radical differences which prevailed among legal theorists concerning the nature of law and the work that it was expected to perform. On the one hand, there was the 'real law' approach, which demanded a clear definition of law, a resolution of conflicts, and above all adjudication of the law through procedures which paralleled the domestic procedures of states. This approach demanded evidence of subordination and the development of instruments of regularised adjudication. On the other hand, there were those, some from the natural law tradition and some sociological jurists, who saw law in terms of a developing customary law which regulated social relations and whose force derived from its conformability to social needs and to changing social conditions. These tended to judge developments according to which the law became more elaborate and its norms more widespread.

To those who held that law was the command of a superior to an inferior, it could not be said that twentieth-century international legal developments changed much in the traditional conception. During the twentieth century, states were as resolute in the defence of their legal prerogatives as they had been in previous centuries. Moreover, few legal theorists could realistically defend the new international law in terms of the emergence of a hierarchy of laws by which the state was controlled from above. Kunz began his 1968 treatise on the changing law with the warning that 'notwithstanding all new tendencies ... international law, even today, is still basically the law of a community of sovereign states'.[33] From this point of view, those legal realists were definitionally quite correct who argued that international law was not 'real' law, however developed.

If, however, one held the view that law was a social instrument whose purpose was to facilitate social life and whose forms allowed for the application of ethical and legal principles to the regulation of social and political life, then there could be little doubt that twentieth-century international law evinced a progressive development over that of the nineteenth century. The new modes of legal argument, from first principles and regime needs, allowed for a dynamic development of the law, while its codifications encouraged more extensive application. Both movements allowed the developing international law to penetrate more thoroughly into the political debates of the time and to influence their course. It also became increasingly domesticated, reflected not only in the emergence of more uniform practices among states but, what was more important from the viewpoint of international community, in a growing habit of arguing from principles that could be universally defended.

Notes

1 Jessup's *Transnational Law* appeared in 1956, Jenks' *Common Law of Mankind* in 1958, and Clark and Sohn's *World Peace Through World Law* in 1960.

2 G. Schwarzenberger, *Frontiers of International Law* (London: Stevens, 1962).

3 H. Lauterpacht, 'The Subjects of the Law of Nations', LQR, Vol. 63 (1947) was an early and influential treatment.

4 The idea was given a formal definition in S. Krasner, *International Regimes*, a special issue of *International Organization*, vol. 36 (1982).

5 This was particularly evident in the trade and financial area, where references to a trade regime or the financial regime had become common in the literature by the last decade of the century, and it flourished in treatments of human rights where it was encouraged by official publications; in 1973, the United Nations issued *Human Rights: A Compilation of International Instruments of the United Nations* (New York: United Nations, 1973), bringing together a number of diverse covenants, treaties and resolutions and treating them as part of an emerging order, inspiring such works as Paul Sieghart's *The Lawful Rights of Mankind* (Oxford: Oxford University Press, 1985).

6 An influential instance was Hans Kelsen, a German legal theorist who emigrated to the United States and who derived the obligatory nature of international law from a logical requirement for any legal system to exist; *Pure Theory of Law* (Berkeley: University of California, 1967).

7 The process was attended by many conceptual confusions: compare W. Freidmann, 'The Growth of States Control over the Individual, and its Effects upon the Rules of International Responsibility', *The British Yearbook of International Law* (Oxford: Clarendon, 1938), with W. Freidmann, 'The Changing Structure of International Law' in R. Falk and C. Black (eds), *The Future of the International Legal Order*, vol. 1 (Princeton: Princeton University Press, 1967).

8 M. Akehurst, *Introduction to International Law* (London: Allen and Unwin, 1982).

9 *Introduction to International Law*, sixth edition (London: Butterworth, 1967) p. 200.

10 Vol. 12, p. 527.

11 Sir Hersch Lauterpacht, *Recognition in International Law* (Cambridge: Cambridge University Press, 1947).

12 D.P. O'Connell summarises the practices in *International Law for Students* (London: Stevens, 1971) p. 62.

13 But United Nations activities also weakened the non-intervention principle, particularly the activities of the Committees on Apartheid and Colonialism, as well as resolutions which imposed specific obligations.

14 O'Connell, *International Law for Students* (London: Stevens, 1971), p. 130.

15 G. Von Glahn, *Law Among Nations*, fifth edition (London: Macmillan, 1986), p. 194; Akehurst appears to concur; see M. Akehurst, *A Modern Introduction to International Law* (London: Allen and Unwin, 1982), p. 67.

16 K.W. Dam, *The GATT Law and International Economic Organization* (Chicago: University of Chicago, 1970) p. 12.

17 B. Roling, *International Law in an Expanded World* (Amsterdam: Djambatan, 1961) and K. Khan, 'International law of development and the law of the Gatt' in F. Snyder and P. Slinn (eds), *International Law of Development* (Abingdon: Professional Books, 1987).

18 P. Birnie and A. Boyle, *International Law and the Environment* (Oxford: Oxford University Press, 1992), pp. 96–8.

19 Michael Howard, *War and the Liberal Conscience* (London: Temple Smith, 1978).

20 *International Law and the Use of Force by States* (Oxford: Oxford University Press, 1963).

21 Brownlie, *International Law and the Use of Force by States*, p. 109.

22 *Just and Unjust Wars* (London: Allen Lane, 1978).

23 M. Howard (ed.), *Restraints on War* (Oxford: Oxford University Press, 1979).

24 G. Best, *Humanity in Warfare* (London: Methuen, 1980) pp. 216–86.

25 Arthur Nussbaum, *A Concise History of the Law of Nations* (New York: Macmillan, 1947).

26 E.g. J.G. Starke, *International Law*, sixth edition (London: Butterworth, 1967).

27 Josef Kunz, *The Changing Law of Nations* (Columbus: Ohio State University , 1968).

28 Elihu (Sir Hersch) Lauterpacht (ed.), *Individual Rights and the State in Foreign Affairs* (New York: Praeger, 1977) and *Oppenheim's International Law* (Harlow: Longman, 1992), first published as L.F.L. Oppenheim, *International Law* (London: Longman, 1955).

29 '*Jus Dispotivum* and *Jus Cogens* in International Law', *American Journal of International Law*, 60 (1966), pp. 55–63.

30 J. Kunz, 'Natural law thinking in the modern science of international law', *American Journal of International Law*, 55 (1961), pp. 951–8.

31 *Power Politics: An Introduction to the Study of International Relations and Post-War Planning* (London: Jonathan Cape, 1941).

32 *The Growth of World Law* (Princeton: Princeton University Press, 1971).

33 Josef Kunz, *The Changing Law of Nations* (Columbus: Ohio State University, 1968).

16 Public international organisation

Support grew rapidly during the twentieth century for public international organisation which would link states into permanent commitments. There were also significant alterations in organisational philosophy and in organisational principle, which contributed in large part to the growth of numbers. By the middle of the century, sentiment had shifted from the idea of a single, universal organisation expressing a unified international order to the idea of segmented and partial organisations expressing a diversity of situations and problematics. There was also an initial attempt to distinguish political from social and economic power, and to prevent the latter from impinging upon the former. As the 'holistic' view receded, accordingly, a set of great organisational baronies ensued.

The multiplicity became the subject of different judgements according to whether pluralism and a diversity of interests was genuinely valued. Initially, differentiation was generally understood as a positive development, since it seemed to many mid-century commentators that the institutional complexity of the new range of pragmatic international organisations reflected a growing incorporation of a wider range of interests into international co-operation. But the incorporation of new interests also brought into play conflicts of interests; accordingly, the view would shift, and the single order following a single value would again be sought.[1]

It was also the case that the new organisations could not be shielded from the effect of major power initiatives concerning their purposes and scope, or from the conflicts between them and smaller powers. Not only in their origins, but also in their development, Great Power influence was often the final determinant of their scope of operations and their freedom of action – accordingly, their political import varied, depending on the willingness of the Great Powers to act through them – while weaker powers often sought to use them to limit Great Power freedom of action. The result was an international institutional order of tenuous interlinkages and considerable inter-institutional rivalry.

Public and private organisations in the nineteenth century

Nineteenth-century public international organisation was scarce and of fairly late vintage. There were only three significant inter-governmental organisations formed before the end of the nineteenth century: the International Telegraph Union (established at Paris in 1865), the Universal Postal Union (initiated at Berne in 1874) and a Conference on Health and Disease (first established at Paris in 1863).[2] The first two were of old liberal inspiration in that they were designed to support the movement of peoples and ideas inherent in the liberal programme. The third was intended to guard against some of liberalism's unwanted effects. The plague had begun to appear in Paris in 1847, after more than two centuries of extirpation, brought by travellers from the east. The offices of the future World Health Organisation moved to Cairo in 1893 and to Istanbul in 1905, the main sources of plague, to allow its officials to oversee more directly the governments chiefly involved and their policies for its control. Of the three, it was the health organisation which was the most significant portent for the future.

The Concert of Europe, that rather contested instrument for Great Power co-ordination which had emerged after the Napoleonic Wars, was not an organisation, having neither locus, constitution, rules of procedure nor permanence. Its basis was provided by the three Notes and Protocol of 15 November 1818 guaranteeing the provisions of the Vienna Treaty, which the powers determined at the conference of Aix-La-Chapelle, called as their military occupation of France was coming to an end. At Aix, Great Britain, Austria, Prussia and Russia invited the king of France to take part in their 'present and future deliberations, consecrated to the maintenance of the peace; the treaties on which it is founded'. Concerting was originally intended to secure the Vienna Treaty, and the conferences and concert treaties which appeared sporadically though the rest of the century were those which blessed changes to the arrangements of 1815. Despite efforts on several sides, it never surpassed its original compass, fading finally after 1870, when the unification of Germany made the Metternichean system redundant.[3]

Of private international organisation, by contrast, the nineteenth century witnessed a rapid development. As the peace movement began and as communication developed, more than a hundred American and European peace movements were formed, most of them on an international basis. There was also a growing number of organisations of scientists and an International Law Association, besides numerous commercial and trade groups. F.S.L. Lyon, who plotted their growth, notes the existence of some three hundred private international organisations devoted to a variety of international causes at the end of the century.[4] But it was against the thinking of the time to engage governments and foreign offices in such private enterprises. Except for the Anti-Slavery League, which deliberately sought to involve government in its activities, and the International Law Association, which promoted the establishment of a permanent court of arbitration, most of these groups were either non-political or saw themselves as bringing pressure to bear on recalcitrant governments. In any event, nineteenth-century liberals were generally suspicious of state action in the area of international affairs. 'Concerting' seemed to demand the suppression of nationalist and liberal movements and to require the support of absolutist monarchies, particularly in their efforts to retain their respective segments of Poland, Italy and the Balkans. Nor, for their part, was the idea of fixed obligations popular with governments.

In several senses, therefore, the League of Nations represented not so much a continuation of the past as a distinct break with it, first in its permanence, second in its binding states to specific and large political aims, and third in its being at once a darling of liberal sentiment and an organisation of states.

The new League

Its origins lay with a wartime coalition, anticipating the development of the great public international organisations of the later part of the twentieth century and what were expected to be substantial political and economic problems in the transition to peace. France initiated the discussions that would produce the League with a proposal in the middle of 1916 – by which time Germany's defeat appeared likely – that the Allied coalition remain together following the formal cessation of hostilities. (France was particularly anxious that the wartime economic agreements allowing for the suspension of currency convertibility and the cheap delivery of foodstuffs be continued into the peace.) Woodrow Wilson would be a prime force in carrying the idea forward, partly out of concern to avoid the usual Great Power scramble that followed war (and which would be augmented by such a great war), and partly out of his analysis of the inadequacy of American institutions to meet the challenge of what he saw as a new era in American political life. In Wilson's conception, a form of League would allow the world's foremost liberal democracy both to have a Great Power role and to be a liberal political order.

The diplomacy concerning its shape and objectives took place against a background of widespread public discussion concerning the orientation and tasks a new general international organisation should perform. Majority opinion supported the judicial resolution of disputes, while a smaller body supported widened social welfare provision. (Walters highlights the drafts of the US League to Enforce Peace, the British League of Nations Society and that of the Fabian Society, influenced by Woolf's *International Government*.)[5] On the legal side, the generation of 1914, largely influenced by legal positivism, thought of a community in terms of a growing body of law. The same opinion tended to assimilate international relations to domestic relations: civilised states, like individuals within civilised states, should submit their disputes to law and to compulsory arbitration. (Hidemi Suganami would call this tendency the 'domestic analogy'.)[6] Thus, it appeared self-evident that the evolving world community required a judicial organisation to arbitrate disputes. According to this body of thought, the centrepiece of the new organisation should be a court to which states should be required to submit their disputes. Those focusing on social welfare provision were excited by the prospects of carrying the new welfare into the international arena. Between 1916 and 1918, a flood of pamphlets and papers had appeared outlining a new diplomacy which would be concerned with economic and social problems: early proposals included transport co-ordination, international policies to tackle unemployment, raw material supply and monetary co-operation. Accordingly, it appeared that a permanent staff of technically competent individuals should be attached to the new organisation which would give unbiased and technically sound advice on the economic and social problems of the day. By anticipating difficulties, the new organisation would lead governments to avoid recourse to conflict and limit the necessity for judicial arbitration.

If public opinion centred on a judicial body, its chief architects, Wilson, Smuts and Lord Robert Cecil, whatever their other differences, all wished to avoid lawyers and courts.[7] Derogations of sovereignty were in any event ruled out from the start. They also wished to avoid the dissolution of Great Power responsibility which might have been entailed by the establishment of universal legal procedures. Increasingly, they allowed the popular slogan, 'a league of free peoples', to gain currency. If there were to be a court, it would be a court of public opinion, a public court of the peoples, organised in an assembly, which was moreover to be an assembly of sovereign states. The British draft convention submitted to President Wilson, which would serve as the basis of the Anglo-American discussions, centred on three major organs, an assembly, a council and a secretariat, and mentioned the possibility of a court only in passing. Eventually a judicial element was added: a permanent court of arbitration would be established, but there would be no requirement to seek submission. The assembly, for its part, could take on any question it deemed of relevance, including judicial questions.

Within the compass of a universal organisation, each of the planning delegations conceived a special role for the Great Powers. Indeed, Colonel House, Wilson's close adviser, who would be influential in the president's thinking on a League, had initially wanted an organisation confined to the Great Powers alone, a form of institutionalised Concert, while the Phillimore Report commissioned by the British government presented the League as essentially a form of alliance (besides quashing any idea that the League should be a form of federation).

If all had originally intended a special role for the Great Powers, however, it proved very difficult to get agreement on precisely what those responsibilities should be. The circle immediately around Lloyd George and represented by Lord Hankey and Philip Kerr, his private secretary, wished the Great Powers to form a sort of war cabinet, along the model of the imperial war cabinet, whose joint secretariat would provide for the League's administration and to whom all matters of dispute would have to be submitted.[8] But Wilson, under pressure from a recalcitrant Congress, wished to avoid any specific legal responsibilities which would involve the United States in police actions as a permanent undertaking – these were considered French ideas. Besides, the emergence of the

Assembly as its centrepiece, together with the protection of state sovereignty, militated against any special role for the Great Powers. It was also the case that the British dominions, enthused by the prospect of participation, not only insisted on separate representation in the Assembly but resisted the idea of any special body within the League invested with executive powers, and their concerns weighed heavily with Cecil and Smuts. In the event, and as part of a complicated trade-off involving a commitment to disarmament, a collective security instrument and a permanent court with powers to arbitrate, Wilson agreed that the Council should be limited to the major powers and that it could lead discussions, but he remained emphatic that it should have no special powers of enforcement.

The collective security instrument eventually to be proposed by Wilson went through several drafts, one of which would include a ban on conscription, but all involved the whole membership of the Assembly acting together under generalised legal norms. Eventually, it came to centre on a guarantee of territorial integrity, together with an obligation upon all members to participate in collective resistance to aggression. In the final conception, a move against any state's territorial integrity on the part of any other state would constitute a new international legal crime of aggression, which would trigger a collective response; and since these provisions became part of the Covenant, a condition of membership was a commitment to abide by the relevant articles so stating, Articles 10 and 16.

But from the time of the Assembly's first meeting, states began to request revisions of 'collective security' articles, particularly the automaticity clauses, and by its second session the revisionist movement had prevailed. In 1921, the Assembly resolved, first, that each state could decide for itself whether an act constituted a breach of the Covenant and, second, that an ostensible act of war on the part of a defaulting member did not automatically imply a state of war between the defaulter and the League membership as a whole. These resolutions, paradoxically among the few unanimous resolutions on matters of substance the League ever achieved, would effectively destroy the collective security instrument. Moreover, other more well-meaning efforts to define aggression in alternative legal terms, and to signal thereby a League action on a different basis, never reached any fruition.

Finally, there was the League secretariat, the first genuinely international public body. Eric Drummond, its first secretary-general, determined to mould a true international secretariat, which he designed on British civil service principles. There were to be a number of sections, each led by a section deputy who was to work to the mandate of the organisation as expressed in the Covenant and in strict independence from member-states. Liberal opinion succeeded in bringing a wealth of matters into the new organisation's compass, and a number of experts were attached to the secretariat in Geneva with competencies in economics and finance, transit and communications, and social problems such as the drugs transit and traffic in women. Accordingly, the scope of the new secretariat grew to encompass most matters covered by the widening diplomacy of the time.

Contemporary analysis of its deficiencies

The deficiencies of the structure became immediately obvious. At Williamsburg in 1921, Philip Kerr, closely associated with the original discussions, observed that the League unwittingly afforded protection to an unbridled state sovereignty, which became a common charge in subsequent decades.[9] Kerr argued that more rigorous legal constraints were required, and that state sovereignty had to be limited. Others argued, on the contrary, that the new organisation did constrain states, but in the wrong sorts of ways. James Shotwell's Committee of Inquiry, hoping to overcome isolationist opinion in the United States, commissioned a study of the League's sanctioning instrument which revealed, among other things, the difficulties for economically dependent states in contemplating economic sanctions.[10]

The various arguments would be efficiently summarised by Professor Harry Hinsley in an important book read by several generations of students during the 1960s, *Power and the Pursuit of Peace* (Cambridge: Cambridge University Press, 1967). There, he identified a fatal contradiction in the League's design between its expanded role and its loosened structure. At Geneva, the powers had created a vast omnicompetent body, but with no specified, differentiated or located powers. The single unwieldy organisation encouraged unilateral and bilateral action, yet also delegitimated such action; it was everywhere and nowhere. Unanimity was required for every serious action, while its thirty-six member-states were quite sufficient, and quite sufficiently diverse in their interests and conceptions, to make unanimity on such issues extremely improbable. But the most fatal flaw, accordingly to Hinsley, was a confusion concerning the relations of peace and war: that many states wished the organisation to have the capability for police actions and yet also wished to avoid becoming embroiled in hostilities.

During the 1930s, analysis shifted from organisational deficiencies to the role of the Great Powers and their hesitancy and opportunism. The three great threats to the peace of the 1930s were the Japanese invasion of Manchuria in 1931, the Italian aggression against Ethiopia (from 1933) and the German rearmament in 1935; and in each case the League failed to act (or, in the case of Ethiopia, to act effectively), primarily because the Great Powers hesitated to act. But since the Council was the effective cornerstone of the edifice, these could not but be blows for the League as well.[11] Nor did it help the League to point to the fact that none had any special legal responsibility to act within the Covenant, besides recommending courses of action to the Assembly. There was also the problem that the commitments to disarmament and the Assembly's ability to impede, via the unanimity requirement, Great Power action, were scarcely helpful to any state contemplating action outside its framework, since the League's collective security provisions faced any single state or combination of states who did choose to act autonomously with the prospect either of sanctions or, what was more alarming, that they might in the end have to face the German threat alone.

One less canvassed but no less relevant problem was the role of the 'specialised agencies', as they eventually came to be known. The older public bodies were joined by an international labour organisation, formed in 1919, and all were incorporated into the League's framework. This meant, however, that their work could be supervised and overseen by the Assembly. It also meant they would be affected by the political quarrels which invaded it. Several world trade congresses were convened in the late 1920s and early 1930s with a view to lifting the restrictions left over from the war, circumventing depression and regenerating trade and production, but they were politicised by the various quarrels which dominated the Assembly, with detrimental consequences for a more open international trading order.

By the late 1930s, there remained a few who still clung to the original conception of the League. Alfred Zimmern, a leading British idealist, would as late as 1939 laud its central conception as a universal forum, and the grand collective endeavour it implied.[12] But he was in the minority. The general view was that not only had the League failed, but that it had been one of the least successful security organisations in history. Its inadequacies were such that it seemed to some actually complicitous in the rise of fascism, the depression and the eventual drag to war. By 1942, when the Allied powers began again the road to peacemaking, there was some question as to whether a new organisation should be created at all.

Negotiating the new organisation: the Assembly disarmed

The idea for some form of replacement organisation developed slowly, and largely in response to Roosevelt's insistence that, at the end of the second German war, the Great Powers should act alone to ensure a permanent disarmament of the aggressors. In the first draft of the Atlantic Charter which laid out British and American war aims, Roosevelt actually struck out reference to the establishment of 'an effective international organisation', lest this should be taken to imply a resuscitation of an Assembly which might, in turn, impede the ability of the Great Powers to act on their own recognisance. By March 1942, when he met with Molotov in Washington, Roosevelt's thinking had developed to the point where he had identified the problem of the League as a diffusion of responsibilities and a lack of concentrated police power.[13] The two allies declared that their 'present enemies' would not only be disarmed but kept disarmed, and that the Allied powers should act together to guarantee 'peace in our time'. At the time, they envisaged a coalition of the three major Allies to supervise their former enemies for twenty-five years at least, providing the first idea of a security council, albeit for a limited duration and with limited scope. Churchill, essentially concerned with the attitude of the Dominions in the context of efforts to reform the Empire, pressed Roosevelt to restore some reference to a general organisation, but got no further than a commitment to 'disarming all nations who might threaten the peace pending the establishment of a wider and permanent system of general security'.

The problem was such an authority's basis in legitimacy. In Washington in March, 1943, the British foreign secretary, Anthony Eden, produced what proved to be a persuasive argument that it was only by establishing a general organisation, from which its powers could be conceived as derived, that a permanent and authorised Great Power police agency could be instituted. At Dumbarton Oaks, the American president was brought to agree a general organisation, essentially on those grounds. That a universal organisation was recreated at all was due to the perceived necessity of creating a legitimating instrument for an enhanced Great Power role.

The deficiencies of the League were kept well to the fore during the planning of the new organisation and invaded its structure at every point. Instead of attempting to define aggression, the Security Council was given definitional rights to declare a 'threat to the peace', a reflection on the failed attempts to define aggression which had dominated many League sessions during the early 1920s. (In the future, what the new Security Council named as a threat to the peace would become *ipso facto* an aggression.) It was given powers to raise armies and to carry these into the field. Where economics and politics had become mixed in the League Assembly, these were divided, to ensure that political quarrels did not invade economic discussions. Where unanimity had been the rule in the League Assembly, a two-thirds majority would be required for most resolutions in the General Assembly. The specialised agencies were also shielded from constant interference by the Assembly, essentially through the establishment of individual plenaries to whom each secretariat was responsible.[14]

A multiplicity of agencies

The final organisation represented a series of intricate functional differentiations and divided responsibilities. There were three quite separate Councils, each with its own duties: the Security Council with the duty to act against 'threats to the peace', a Trusteeship Council responsible for colonial questions, and an Economic and Social Council responsible for a plethora of economic and social matters. The latter would be handed on to a number of specialised agencies, each of which would have differing memberships and distinct compasses. The areas of money and trade were shielded from the 'political' questions with which the UN might have to deal. The Bretton Woods system, constituted by the World Bank and the IMF and often treated as part of the UN system, was in fact no such thing. It was made up of separate organisations dealing with monetary affairs, trade and reconstruction respectively, to ensure separate treatment of each of these issues; and each was a constitutionally self-standing organisation with no formal links to the United Nations organisation at all. Within the UN organisation, there was a strict division between the organ with war powers, the Security Council and organs with other concerns, while the permanent members of the Security Council also had specified responsibilities and legal powers to carry out those responsibilities. The Assembly was left as the 'conscience and goad' of the Security Council.[15]

The arenas of high politics and low politics were not only defined and separated from one another, but also divided *intra se*. Within the arena of high politics, there was a clear distinction between the Court of Justice and the Security Council: the latter was intended for arbitral and police action; the former to evolve case law and define juristic principles. The various issue areas which were thought of as low politics were distributed among a variety of committees and specialised agencies, notwithstanding the special role of the General Assembly in this area. The United Nations organisation was generally graphed as six parallel organs: the General Assembly, the Court of Justice, the Security Council, the Trusteeship Council, the Economic and Social Council and the Secretariat. But the Economic and Social Council would come to oversee twenty-five specialised agencies, each with its own constitution and with differing participation according to the varied interests of the member-states.[16] It was these ancillary agencies, moreover, that would carry out the bulk of the work that would be commonly associated with the UN system.

There were few formal links between these various bodies. The Security Council was required to report to, but not to seek advice from, the General Assembly. The ECOSOC was to report to and receive general direction from the General Assembly, but the Assembly had no power to command the activities of its agencies. States could use the General Assembly to pass resolutions in support of their individual and collective aims, and they might press these resolutions through their representatives on to the specialised agencies, but the agencies were not required to accept them: the resolution passed by the General Assembly during the 1980s that 'Zionism is a form of racism' was never accepted by any of the special agencies, each of which formed a mini UN in itself. In general, the specialised agencies worked quite independently of the General Assembly in legal and often also in political terms.

In effect, this left the General Assembly as a body of limited influence and powers. It could, of course, roam freely over any question of interest to its members, and it could pass resolutions on any matter on which two-thirds of its members could concur. But it could not impede the work of the other organisations, nor invade their legal competencies, unlike the powerful Assembly of the League. Its main power was to express what was often referred to as 'the moral and ethical sentiments' of its members. What it did more often was to formulate a variety of political consensuses, expressing the various immediate political concerns of the majority. It would become more or less powerful, depending on the willingness of the major powers to work within it.

The UN's changing constituency

Its first membership numbered fifty-one, generally long-standing states with developed political, economic and social systems and substantial populations.

Because of their historical links with the United States and the European powers, the initial membership was generally pro-Western within the evolving context of the Cold War. After cavilling at support for Franco, the Assembly revoked its call for suspension of diplomatic relations with Madrid; it created a special committee to report on the Balkans, which sent observers to check on any efforts on the part of its communist neighbours to support Greek communist guerrillas in northern Greece; also, it voted for the partition of Palestine.

With decolonisation, however, this began to change. By 1959, the membership had grown to 83 states, by 1972 there were 132, and by 1985 this had risen to 159, all of increasingly varied political and economic complexion. In 1955, 16 states were admitted at once, 4 of which were communist states and 6 African and Asian. By 1985, there were 92 African and Asian states in the organisation, some with small populations of under 5 million (and a few with only 1 million), and all anxious to develop and to modernise.

The issues that dominated the General Assembly reflected this changing constituency. The assemblies of the late 1950s pursued de-alignment and decolonisation, as the new states sought to avoid involvement in Cold War politics and to protect themselves from continued interference on the part of former colonial powers. The great issue from the middle 1960s was economic development: much of the activity of the General Assembly during the subsequent decade was directed to changing the rules of international exchange to achieve either redistribution or special statuses, such as non-reciprocal trade preferences. It was during this time that the declarations on economic sovereignty were issued, as well as the principles of peaceful relations between states, all concerned with protecting the economic and political rights of new states and enhancing their rather limited powers. During the 1970s, in addition, coalitions were formed to isolate 'pariah states' such as South Africa, which continued to practise racial discrimination, and attention turned to the issues of neo-colonialism and especially cultural colonialism.[17] The 1970s were a particularly successful era for 'new states'. A fund for agricultural development (the IFAD) was established in 1976; the World Bank established structural adjustment loans; Nairobi became the site for the new environmental agency, UNEP; the UNCTAD held the great shipping conferences; and the Generalised System of Preferences was established.[18]

Following the large 1955 entry, a committee system began to develop within the Assembly. A familiar feature of parliamentary systems, committees were special bodies representing the whole Assembly but with limited memberships and limited remits: each focused on particular topics and members were appointed on a regional basis. They adopted resolutions on a two-thirds majority and then recommended them to the Assembly at large. It became a special technique of committee politics to associate one or other of the leading powers with their work, in order to enhance the legitimacy and status of their recommendations. The Trusteeship Committee was an especially successful example; it speeded along decolonisation, aided by alliances with both the United States and the Soviet Union.

The specialised agencies

The development of the specialised agencies followed a clear historical path. There were the venerable organisations, the transformed WHO, the ITU and the Postal Union which represented the original impulses of nineteenth-century liberal thought. There was then the ILO, the labour organisation, created after the First World War, which represented the new liberal thinking on the need to integrate the masses into the political order. The raft of new creations produced at the end of the Second World War was engendered by what were conceived to be the major problems of post-war reconstruction. Thus, a food and agriculture organisation (the FAO) was established to expand the world's food supply during what was expected to be a period of shortage, and a refugee administration, under a high commissioner, was formed to dispense relief and to organise both relocation and resettlement, as well as camp administration. (It should also be recalled that the World Bank was intended initially to finance post-war reconstruction while a new Trusteeship Council reflected the increasingly contested colonial question.) Finally, there were the technical bodies of the new industrial age: a world meteorological organisation, a maritime consultative organisation, a civil aviation agency and the atomic energy agency.

Both the nineteenth-century specialised agencies and the agencies attached to the League had been deeply imbued with a 'functional' philosophy which directed them to administrative competence, to fulfilling the task at hand and to resisting political influence; and this was carried over into some of the newer organisations created immediately following the Second World War. The new food organisation's officials saw themselves as technical specialists working out empirically defined world food needs, and they isolated the work of the organisation from interest groups and political pressures.

Increasingly, however, the newer agencies became politicised, reflecting the new constituencies, with implications for the organisation as a whole. UNCTAD, the Commission on Trade and Development, and UNESCO, the Educational and Scientific Organisation, became outrightly partisan on behalf of developing and post-colonial states, and their secretariats tended to adopt overtly political roles, providing institutional and informational support to poor countries who did not have expertise of their own in these areas.[19]

By the mid-1970s, a certain backwash from the political activities of these more 'political' unions had begun to be felt in the more technical organisations. In the ITU, a hard-fought campaign was mounted by new states for a revision of airwave allocation, and UNESCO became the cultural spearhead of a sustained campaign against neo-colonialism. UNCTAD gradually lost the appearance of a general commission and became more like an interest group of the developing nations pressing for change, although important conferences continued to be mounted under UNCTAD auspices (notably, the liner conferences which considered international shipping regulations).[20] Increasingly, it came to be argued that the 'functional' separation of political from economic, scientific and cultural questions implied a classical liberal political philosophy, and that such a standpoint supported the status quo and favoured the powers, generally the developed states, who benefited from the status quo.

The reality of 'redistributive justice'

If the policies of the new organs became increasingly radicalised, however, there was little real pressure for any major redistributive policies. The UNCTAD secretariat, staunch in support of the claims of the Third World, was also deeply imbued with political liberalism, and its efforts on behalf of Third World states were largely directed at opposing the closed market habits that had tended to grow among the large enterprises of the industrialised world. The UNCTAD conferences on the organisation of international shipping, for example, were aimed against market monopoly and the high wage policies of the industrialised states, which dominated shipping, and not at any sustained efforts at developing a Third World shipping industry by shifting resources from the shipping 'haves'. This tendency was encouraged by President Reagan's neo-liberal agenda of the 1980s, which concentrated attention on the needs of the 'free market' rather than to the disadvantages of those who had to operate in such a market.[21]

Peacemaking and peacekeeping

Membership of the Security Council had originally been confined to the three wartime Allies plus France and China, both expected to be major powers in the post-war period. Initially, six non-permanent members were added to enhance the democratic credentials of the body, selected on a regional basis. (Two were from Latin America, and one each from Western Europe, Eastern Europe and the Commonwealth.) With the rapid growth in membership after 1955, however, the number of non-permanent members rose to ten, five from Asia and Africa, two from Latin America, two from Western Europe and one from Eastern Europe, constituting fifteen members in all. Action required a 'concurrence' among the permanent members. Their tasks were to identify threats to the peace, to propose conciliation between contending parties and to undertake military action if conciliation were rejected (and if the situation so required). Besides its peacemaking powers, the Security Council also had powers over the general membership, since it had to recommend new members before the General Assembly could accept them.

The UN Charter provided for a military staff committee, structured like a joint command, which indeed met and worked for a year to produce a preliminary report. (No action was taken thereafter to provide the Security Council with its own military forces.) The Charter also outlined the voting provisions which were required to initiate peacemaking. Out of fifteen votes, nine were required for a positive action (including the five permanent members). Originally this was taken to mean that all must agree. Within a short period of time, however, the Soviet delegate had introduced the idea of the abstention. This allowed permanent members not to exercise their veto rights, but merely to abstain, without affecting the outcome of the vote. The Council could determine procedural matters by a vote of nine overall, that is without the 'concurrence' of the permanent members, which allowed questions to be brought before the Security Council even if one of the permanent members was opposed.

During most of its duration, the activities of the Security Council were frustrated by the political divisions among the major powers. Between 1948 and 1963, it met with decreasing frequency; the Soviet Union exercised its veto right a hundred times during that period; and at the height of the Cold War, in 1959, the Council met only four times.[22] The only region concerning which the powers were able to locate substantive agreements, and they were limited, was the Middle East. They all supported the founding of the state of Israel (although for eventually incompatible reasons), the return of and some compensation for refugees, and they united on Resolution 242 demanding Israel withdraw from the territories she had occupied following the 1967 Arab–Israeli war. For most of the period, its members collectively abandoned any efforts in the area of disarmament, leaving activism in this field to the Assembly and to bilateral and multilateral talks among themselves.

The argument for 'majority rule'

During the 1950s, it became fashionable to blame the veto for this state of affairs and to argue that majority rule would have produced a more effective peacekeeping instrument. Some proposed simple majorities, others proposed two-thirds majorities. The argument was that this would allow for a mobilisation of the latent will of the world community, blocked by Great Power dissidence.

While a laudable sentiment, however, this argument ignored the kind of body the Security Council was. The UN, even more than the League, was conceived as the carapace for a wartime coalition. Membership of the UN was initially confined to those powers who had declared war on the Axis powers by 1 August 1945. The provisions for the Security Council were negotiated by the wartime powers at Teheran and Yalta while they were still fighting, and the requirements of the fighting alliance were in the forefront as they were negotiating. The veto right accorded to each an assurance that none would break ranks during the delicate period of war's ending. As the Security Council was conceived as a continuation of the wartime coalition, the veto was incorporated into the permanent arrangements: in a coalition, a disagreement over a major question is a condition for the end of that coalition. The veto was, accordingly, the legal recognition of a *de facto* state of affairs, and the condition of its existence. It was expressive, not problematic.

The problem in the post-war period was the absence of any broad consensus on the central issues of the time among the Security Council powers. They could not agree on how to treat Germany; they could not agree on modes of change in the international order or on political liberty and its definition.

Equally, however, this conception assured that should the situation between the permanent members change, should there emerge areas of agreement among them, the power it would be capable of mobilising would be impressive. Moreover, Security Council resolutions were directly enforcing; that is, they approached the status of 'real' law.

From peacemaking to peacekeeping

During the first four decades of its existence, UN forces were deployed only once in an active fighting role to punish and reverse an aggression, and that during 1950 and 1951, following North Korea's invasion of South Korea. It was an experience, in the words of one of its historians 'so fraught with difficulties' that the United States, for one, foreswore such combined actions. Subsequent to it, blue berets were to be seen in deployments around the globe. But they were deployed not in fighting roles but to interpose themselves between antagonists, to supervise ceasefires and to aid good offices. The historian of its early period judged its supervision of truces open to low-level violations generally successful in impeding escalation.[23]

The fifteen major peacekeeping operations between 1947 and 1987 had a distinct geo-political aspect. They were emplaced in areas of potential major power contestation, but where the Cold War antagonists essentially wished either to avoid contrary entanglements or to stabilise the status quo. The majority were in the Eastern Mediterranean and Middle East, notably Cyprus, Yemen, Lebanon, the Golan Heights and Suez.[24] The India–Pakistan dispute, essentially over contested border questions and the status of Kashmir, produced two long-standing observer missions, one undertaken in 1947 and still in existence in 1990, and the other in 1965. There was also a post-colonial aspect to UN peacekeeping, particularly in Africa where the withdrawal of the metropolitan power had left a disputed situation on the ground: the rapid evacuation of Portugal from Angola and Mozambique led each situation to descend into civil war, both of which had stalemated by 1989, allowing for the entry of UN observer and peacekeeping missions.

The pattern of Cold War peacekeeping followed a standard form. There was a ban on the use of force except in self-defence. Negotiations between the parties, often using the good offices function of the UN secretary-general, would produce a ceasefire; and UN troops, raised from national contributions, would supervise the ceasefire. The organisation was reluctant to intervene in domestic quarrels, not merely because of Article 2 (7) of the Charter outlawing intervention in matters essentially within the domestic jurisdiction of states, but because of the problems of dealing with irregular forces who would not respect the non-forceful nature of traditional peacekeeping. The prime purpose of traditional peacekeeping was to establish a neutral buffer zone between antagonists.[25]

Following the end of the Cold War, the peacekeeping function of the UN was called upon to deal with ethnic and intra-state conflict and the prevalent features of such conflicts, including breakdowns of authority and violence against civilians. It was called upon with increasing frequency; there were sixteen missions authorised between 1989 and 1995, more than in the previous forty years. These missions also demonstrated a widened scope. The peacekeepers were called upon to supervise elections, disarm warring internal factions and provide aid and humanitarian relief for victims of civil atrocities and transport and protection for refugees.

The demand for UN action in ethnic and intra-state conflict began to produce the idea of a third category of military operations, between 'threats to the peace' and peacekeeping. In 'third category' operations, it was envisaged that UN forces would put an end to random and uncontrolled violence and provide a reasonable degree of peace and order so that humanitarian relief could go forward and conciliation and dispute settlement be undertaken.[26] Under this scenario, UN forces would operate more like policemen, and would be prepared to shoot. This depended, however, on increasing the availability of funding for UN operations and placing funding on a regular basis, instead of relying, as was the case, on state willingness to pay their subscriptions. It also depended on establishing a genuine fighting force which would serve the organisation (particularly as, with the crises in the former Yugoslavia, Nato was emerging as a competitor organisation in the collective security area).

The United Nations as a collective will

Analysts would long ponder the question of whether the United Nations was 'more than the sum of its parts'. One issue was whether the United Nations had a legal personality of its own, and the nature and extent of that 'legal persona'. Another was whether it expressed the genuine will of a collective, which its creation either reflected or had brought into being. But above all, there was the central question of whether the United Nations had a will of its own which could be imposed on the will of its members.

Certainly, it had a legal existence, in the simple sense that it could own property and be sued. Accordingly, it was a bearer of legal responsibility within the legal orders in which it operated. It could also receive ambassadors, and its officials swore oaths of loyalty to its purposes: accordingly, its officials belonged to something called the United Nations Organisation.

There were also the aggregation effects of its institutional presence. In its political aspect, the developing practices of parliamentary diplomacy gave member-states the power to combine and to create a collective voice. In the language of systems analysis, it became an important aggregator of opinion and a source of pressure. In terms of empirical outcome, we may also note that states did not welcome being made subjects of General Assembly, much less Security Council, resolutions; and that both sorts of resolutions, as well as the recommendations of the specialised agencies, became focuses for processes of change (in human rights and the environment, to name but two issue areas). Smaller states, moreover, who could not afford diplomatic representation across the globe, tended to concentrate their diplomatic efforts at the UN headquarters where their representatives underwent marked processes of socialisation. They learnt from one another and relied upon one another. They also built diplomatic coalitions from within the various bodies of the organisation which they employed in other contexts. Moreover, United Nations declarations, resolutions and conferences became objects of attention for a growing number of non-state movements and organisations who sought to harness world opinion to their causes; and its various bodies became a focus for the political activities of such groups. In all of these political senses, it had a genuine corporate existence, which produced effects.

The United Nations also changed through the first fifty years of its existence in ways that could be legitimately interpreted in terms of an organic evolution. The secretary-general's position developed rapidly in the area of good offices, while the General Assembly's potential for a security role, through being able to pass resolutions on any matter, also developed. These two gradually formed an alliance which underpinned the continuous development of an increasingly institutionalised and adaptable peacekeeping role.

As a legal body, its persona was limited, however. General Assembly resolutions, as well as the recommendations of the specialised agencies, had no more status in international law than any resolution of any great conference of states. Legally, there was nothing special about the UN except in the degree to which its regular meetings gave rise to more frequent multilateral treaties, and speeded the process of law-making. Moreover, there was a decided inclination to define the legal status of such resolutions more closely. One of the leading legal theorists of the second half of the twentieth century, E.L. Hart, identified them as forms of primary legislation, or first principles, which he would distinguish from secondary, detailed or case legislation, which was law in the more usual sense.[27] Also, they were not binding, which meant that no legal consequences ensued from them. Finally, there was no easy way its institutional structure could be deployed to build a corpus of secondary legislation. There was no seat within the organisation that could define or interpret any of the institution's general goals in any definitive sense, nor build upon its various resolutions. The exception was the Court of Justice. But it was free to apply whatever juristic principles it wished to the cases that came before it. The Court was in no sense limited either to the principles of the Charter or to the subsequent utterances of the various UN organs.

The United Nations was, moreover, a consent organisation and it relied upon the consent of its member-states. Leland M. Goodrich, in a popular text of the period, argued that the UN did not derive its consent from peoples directly, observing that it was established by the legal form, 'our respective Governments ... have agreed'.[28] Neither could it be derived from a common sense of mankind, each of which theories would have separated the organisation from its immediate membership and made it 'more than the sum of its parts'. Governments themselves would have objected to such a reading. In a political as well as legal sense, therefore, it remained an association of existing governments.

The common values of mankind?

At the conclusion to his argument, Goodrich saw the importance of the organisation, finally, in terms of a moral dynamic. In a form of argument frequently posed during the first two decades of its existence, he maintained that the United Nations articulated common values of mankind, values which had a 'popular appeal' and which could be identified by its pursuits: peace and security, the evils of colonialism, human rights and the economic and social well-being of peoples. He also argued that the existence of an organisation with rules of procedure provided a forum for articulating and acting upon those common values and, hence, the means to mobilise the 'will of a nascent world community'.

But the argument that the United Nations represented a common will was problematic. It was possible to argue that governments represented nations (though not always), and that for each nation there should be equality of representation. It was also possible to argue that equality of representation protected small and weak states (and small states were particularly anxious to defend equality of representation). But states differed very greatly in size, in the numbers their governments represented and in the resources they could commit to the organisation. They also differed in the degree to which they could offer convincing liberal democratic credentials. That small undemocratic states aspired to enforce decisions against large, in some cases more democratic, states could not seriously be taken as evidence of an emergent common will of mankind.

The United Nations also suffered a growing problem of accountability, particularly in the light of the very uneven charges levied upon states to support the organisation financially. By the late 1970s, there was evidence of a growing exasperation on the part of the major contributing states that they were committing resources to bodies whose members did not have to take responsibility for their individual and collective decisions and who could not be held to account, even by their own populations. Such considerations limited the validity not only of General Assembly resolutions but also of the recommendations of the specialised agencies, particularly when they strayed from technical recommendations and entered upon political activism.[29] (In some of the specialised agencies, in response, pressure for unequal voting began to grow, whereby votes were weighted to represent shares of budgetary contribution, and which related voice more closely to responsibility for carrying out policy.)

The Security Council did not suffer these problems to the same degree. The binding nature of Security Council resolutions, together with the power inherent in their united action, gave them much more of a legal character. In the degree to which law is understood in terms of command and compliance, Security Council resolutions had the quality of a 'harder' form of law. The Security Council was also so constructed in the balance of votes as to require any single power or combination of powers intent upon an action to explain to its Council cohorts, and hence to the international community at large, the question at issue, to justify its actions and to make them conformable to international opinion.

Even when permanent members began to use the veto sparingly and developed the habit of simple abstention, partly to evade responsibility for Security Council decisions, this did not render them any less publicly accountable for the actions of the Council. Paradoxically, the Security Council was the most accountable among the many UN bodies.

But representation and accountability were not the only marks of a proper political organisation in the twentieth century. The activism of the age also directed attention to effectiveness; and the United Nations, in all its parts, suffered in its collective identity from the slow pace of change and from the limited ability of the organisation to institute processes of change, particularly over high policy questions. There could be little doubt, for example, that the Security Council, even more than the General Assembly, was invaded by the norms of the Cold War, to its detriment, without being capable, as a collective organisation, of ameliorating or ending the Cold War. In the language of contemporary social science, it was the dependent variable: the acted upon, not the actor.

Moreover, the organisation as a whole, while it took value from the impressive functional and technical activities performed by its many agencies, was still largely identified with its peacemaking role. Many of the hopes for the organisation centred on its role as a doer of justice and a righter of wrongs. Accordingly, its political status suffered when the Security Council failed to maintain peace or to stop wars. At the same time, the United Nations had neither the ability nor the right to conscript. It was entirely dependent on the permanent members of the Security Council for mobilising power and for creating a relationship between power and right-doing. In fact, the force the organisation deployed, and accordingly the source of its legitimacy, was the force and the willingness to pursue justice of its member-states.

At the end of the Cold War, the United States, acting through the Security Council, mobilised a large force to expel Iraq from Kuwait, which operation succeeded, the second peacemaking exercise in the organisation's history.[30] Accordingly, hopes began to be expressed that the United Nations might finally realise the main purpose for which it had been founded. But the Allied Coalition which fought the Gulf War was not legally a UN peacekeeping effort, primarily because it was not established by the Security Council and was not under UN command. Partly for this reason, there began to appear proposals for its reform, many of which centred on the make-up of the Security Council. Some aimed to make it more representative, primarily by introducing a wider range of states into Council deliberations. Others sought to make it more closely correspond to empirical power potential – primarily by bringing Germany and Japan, by now leading powers, into the Council as permanent members.[31] Both proposals rested on the assumption that there was an international common will among states which, in the first case, should be more representative and, in the second case, more effective. But no such will existed independently of its being mobilised.

If the crucial issue was mobilisation, this reflected on the kind of organisation the United Nations was. At best a union of states, it remained dependent on leadership by engaged governments. Accordingly, the proper questions to ask in considering the reform of the United Nations were who were the powers best placed to mobilise effective force on behalf of universalisable norms, and who were the powers most willing to act at the behest of collective undertakings; that is, in accordance with Charter rules. And it remained the case, at the end of the century no less than at its beginning, that no small and few large states were capable of undertaking such tasks and, of those who were capable, none demonstrated willingness to perform them in a consistent and accountable manner.

Notes

1 Compare I. Claude, *Swords into Plowshares* (New York: Random House, 1964) with B. Urquhart and E. Childers, *A World in Need of Leadership: Tomorrow's United Nations* (Uppsala: Dag Hammarskjöld Foundation, 1990).

2 R. Jordan, *International Administration, Its Evolution and Contemporary Applications* (New York and London: Oxford University Press, 1971).

3 The *conference system*, the hoped-for regularised meetings of the foreign secretaries of the Vienna Powers, ended after the 1822 Conference at Verona; H. Nicolson, *The Congress of Vienna* (London: Constable, 1946). The sense of historical continuity was, however, strong: Nicolson dedicated it to Anthony Eden, one of the political architects of the United Nations.

4 *Internationalism in Europe, 1815–1914* (Loyden: A.W. Sythoff, 1963).

5 *A History of the League of Nations* (London: Oxford University Press, 1952).

6 H. Suganami, *The Domestic Analogy and World Order Proposals* (Cambridge: Cambridge University Press, 1989).

7 G.W. Egerton, *Great Britain and the Creation of the League of Nations* (Chapel Hill: University of North Carolina, 1978) especially pp. 100–15.

8 S. Roskill, *Hankey*, 3 vols (London: Collins, 1970–74) vol. 1; Kerr used *The Round Table* to publicise his views, especially vols 8 and 9 (March and September 1918).

9 Published, with L. Curtis, as *The Prevention of War* (New Haven: Yale University Press, 1923).

10 The author was D. Mitrany, *The Problem of International Sanctions* (Oxford: Oxford University Press, 1925).

11 Walters assigned to Manchuria the loss of Council authority, and to Ethiopia the decisive blow; *A History of the League of Nations* (London: Oxford University Press, 1952), pp. 499 and 623.

12 *The League of Nations and the Rule of Law* (Oxford: Oxford University Press, 1939).

13 H. Feis, *Churchill, Roosevelt, Stalin* (Princeton: Princeton University Press, 1957, 1967).

14 C. Eichelberger, *Organizing for Peace* (New York: Harper and Row, 1977).

15 H. Nicholas, *The United Nations as a Political Institution* (Oxford: Oxford University Press, 1975).

16 R. Feltham, *Diplomatic Handbook*, sixth edition (London: Longman, 1993) contains a recent list.

17 M.J. Peterson, *The General Assembly in World Politics* (Boston: Allen and Unwin, 1986).

18 P. Taylor and J. Groom (eds), *Global Issues in the United Nations Framework* (London: Macmillan, 1988),

19 M. Imber, *The USA, ILO, UNESCO and IAEA: Politicization and Withdrawal in the Specialized Agencies* (London: Macmillan, 1989).

20 T. Weiss, *Multilateral Development Diplomacy in UNCTAD* (London: Macmillan, 1986).

21 See *Report by the Secretary-General of UNCTAD to the Eighth Session of the Conference* (New York: United Nations, 1992) Part 2, Chapter 1, 'Market forces, public policy and good management'.

22 A. Boyd, *Fifteen Men on a Powder Keg* (London: Methuen, 1971).

23 A. James, *The Politics of Peacekeeping* (London: Chatto and Windus, 1969).

24 United Nations, *The Blue Helmets: A Review of United Nations Peacekeeping*, second edition (New York: United Nations, 1990).

25 S. Morphet, 'UN peacekeeping and election monitoring' in A. Roberts and B. Kingsbury (eds), *United Nations, Divided World* (Oxford: Oxford University Press, 1993).

26 B. Urquhart, 'Security after the Cold War' in A. Roberts and B. Kingsbury (eds), *United Nations, Divided World* (Oxford: Oxford University Press, 1993).

27 *The Concept of Law* (Oxford: Oxford University Press, 1961).

28 *The United Nations in a Changing World* (New York: Columbia University Press, 1974) pp. 23–4.

29 D. Williams, *The Specialized Agencies and the United Nations: The System in Crisis* (London: C. Hurst and Co., 1987).

30 See L. Freedman, *The Gulf Conflict 1990–91* (London: Faber and Faber, 1993).

31 Reviewed in P. Wilenski, 'The structure of the UN in the post-Cold War period' in A. Roberts and B. Kingsbury (eds), *United Nations, Divided World* (Oxford: Oxford University Press, 1993); a major reformist tract was B. Urquhart and E. Childers, *Towards a More Effective United Nations* (Uppsala: Dag Hammarskjöld Foundation, 1992).

17 Allies and alliances

Traditionally, alliances were regarded as the major structuring element to international relationships, a legacy of nineteenth-century diplomatic history, where the making and breaking of alliances was held to represent the dynamic element in the historical time flow, changing relationships and producing new configurations in their wake. In contemporary historical accounts, the Nazi–Soviet Pact of 1939 earned special attention from this perspective: it was frequently identified as the turning point in the German decision for war and the basis from which British and American as well as French policy had henceforth to be conducted. The struggles of the Allies to maintain the anti-Nazi alliance during the Second World War also focused the historical imagination, since that alliance was arguably the single most important strategic factor in Nazi Germany's eventual defeat. For their part, international relationists spent a great deal of time analysing the durability of the Cold War alliances and their consequences not only for peace and war but for state relations more generally.

The concern with alliances was not misplaced, particularly considering the role they played during the century's second half. Out of the Anglo-American alliance, forged during the Second World War, grew the general frameworks for the major international institutions of the post-war period, while the second half of the twentieth century was dominated by the great alliance systems built as part of containment. It was also the case that alliance membership placed considerable constraints on the foreign policies of the member-states during the post-war period. Indeed, it was the close co-ordination demanded by the Cold War alliances, as much as anything else, that conditioned and gave definition to twentieth-century internationalism. Accordingly, the general attitude to alliances, their nature and their cement, became important questions in gauging the nature, strength and durability of internationalist sentiment.

Alliances and alignments

As the term came to be used, 'alliance' served as a general portmanteau for both short- and long-term unions, as well as for both formal and informal unions. The effect was to confuse the status of the relationships intended. More useful was the traditional distinction between alliances and alignments. In the traditional classification, alliances were based on bilateral or multilateral treaties in which defined obligations were undertaken, and which were intended to be of some duration. Alignments, by contrast, were coincidences of interest whereby states acted together, sometimes for long periods of time, but with no formal exchange of obligation.

Alliance phobia in the period up to 1945

Given the significance of formal alliances in the second half of the twentieth century, it may be something of a paradox to observe that, for much of the previous century, alliances were the exception, not the rule. Between 1818, following the Napoleonic Wars, and 1876 there were no formal alliances in Europe at all, not excepting the so-called Holy Alliance of Austria, Prussia and Russia. The soubriquet was a misnomer, since the Three Emperors undertook few obligations in respect of one another and only agreed to concert when specific shared interests appeared threatened.[1] The only significant alliance before the rapid evolution of the alignments which fought the Great War was the 1879 alliance between Germany and the Austro-Hungarian Empire, initiated by Bismarck and intended to preserve the weakening imperial edifice.

The First World War did not change the disinclination to ally; on the contrary, it enhanced it. Following the war, alliances were not merely avoided, they were held in poor repute, as it was believed that alliance commitments had dragged countries into a war which they might otherwise have avoided, besides increasing its ferocity and extending its duration.[2] The smaller European states in particular decried alliances, preferring neutralism or non-alignment as their major provision for security. The only inter-war alliance system worthy of the name, and it was created *faut de mieux*, was the French system of alliances with the countries of Central Europe, including Poland, Czechoslovakia, Hungary and Romania, directed to constraining German power in the wake of Versailles which, the French government believed, provided insufficient guarantees against a revived German threat.

The other alliances of the inter-war period were generally preparation-for-war alliances, and they were achieved only immediately before the outbreak of hostilities or even during them. Germany, Japan and Italy had formed what was arguably a peacetime anti-Comintern Pact in 1937, but the substantial alliance between Germany and Italy was only signed in May 1939, while that between Japan and Germany was only finally agreed in August of 1940, preparing the way for Japan's attack on Pearl Harbor. Japan joined Germany and Italy in a genuine tripartite alliance in September 1941, but it was not a fighting alliance; rather it was a division-of-spoils alliance, outlining what would fall to the Greater East Asia Co-Prosperity Sphere when, as it expected, Germany would win the war in the west. France had signed a form of alliance with the Soviet Union in 1936, in reaction to the Nazi ascendance to power in Germany, but it was never acted upon, and it was nullified by the Ribbentrop–Molotov Pact of 1939. Britain and France did not sign a formal alliance at all in response to the resumption of hostilities with Germany. Instead, they declared a form of union in 1940, a union which implied (but did not specify) that Britain would go to France's aid in case of attack.[3] In the end, Britain declared war on the issue of Germany's invasion of Poland, not as a matter of aid to its French ally.

The prevalent alignments

There were important coincidences of interest where states acted together, in some cases for quite long periods of time. The nineteenth-century Holy Alliance was a form of alignment: it was their shared interests over Poland, to keep it divided among them, which brought the Three Emperors together most reliably, not their commitment to act together against the liberal revolutions of the time. They did act in concert to put down the Spanish revolution of 1821, and again in Belgium in 1830, to maintain the Metternichean system; but Bismarck broke with the defence of the status quo when he began to reorder the German confederation, and the Tsar deduced it would not hold after 1856, after which he supported the revolution which led to Italian unification.

Equally noteworthy was the liberal alignment between Britain and France which gradually emerged after 1848 to seek peaceful changes to the Vienna settlement, to make the Crimean War and to liberate Italy, an alignment which re-emerged in 1904 in the form of the Entente Cordiale, whereby both recognised each other's sphere of influence in the Mediterranean, and which constituted the first step to their alliance against Germany during the Great War. It re-emerged again during the 1920s in the context of the League of Nations, where Britain supported many French initiatives; and it was the break-up of that alignment, due mainly to the coming into power of the British Labour Party, that contributed to Germany's political domination of the European continent.

The major European alignment during the period following the Second World War was an emerging Franco-German relationship, something of a diplomatic revolution. The first steps in its construction had been initiated by France during the late 1920s, when the French foreign minister, Briand, tried to construct a co-operative relationship with Germany within a proto-European community, a project Germany had then viewed as inimical to its aim of overthrowing Versailles. Following the Second World War, however, and the suspension of German sovereignty, the basis of German foreign policy changed. Thereafter, the restructured federal quasi-state began to view co-operation with France and the sharing of political authority within a permanent European entity as one key to the restoration of German sovereignty. France, for its part, came to view the joint exercise of control over the German economy, and the Europeanisation of its economic space, as one key to peace. Both provided the foundations for the construction of the European Economic Community and the eventual creation of the zone of peace among the states of Western Europe.[4]

The Anglo-American alignment

But by far the most important twentieth-century alignment was the Anglo-American alignment. Joint agreement between Britain and the United States determined the basic structures of both the League of Nations and the United Nations. The two powers laid out the economic agreements at Bretton Woods which would establish the post-war international economic order, and they determined the Allies' war aims against Nazi Germany, declared in the Atlantic Charter. Their relationship became the basis of the alliance which finally defeated Germany, and the central element of the Nato alliance thereafter.

The alignment took various forms. In the periods before each world war, first Woodrow Wilson and then Franklin Roosevelt had each loosely interpreted Congress's insistence on neutrality and had quietly helped Britain to prepare for hostilities against Germany.[5] There was also monetary co-operation, begun in 1936 with a tripartite agreement including France, directed against competitive and unregulated devaluations; and a division of labour in the maintenance of open seas, as Britain gradually left to the US the task of guaranteeing free access to Latin America after 1920. During the post-war period, the two powers developed a special nuclear relationship in which Britain received help in developing its nuclear arsenal, partly in return for favourable interventions on behalf of the United States in the evolving Europe situation and partly in return for providing the Americans with basing facilities on British soil.[6] The two powers also enjoyed a special intelligence relationship during the Cold War, dividing surveillance of the Soviet Union and its satellites and sharing information and monitoring equipment. The United States also rendered Britain monetary support for a weakening pound in the 1970s in return for political support during the Vietnam War.

But there were important limitations to the relationship. The United States was hostile to the British policy of appeasement, undertaken after 1936, largely because American political elites feared a division of spheres between Britain and Germany that would leave the British Empire intact. Moreover, the imperial question remained a source of potent division at least until the mid-1950s, since a declared and often determined objective of American policy was decolonisation; this put Churchill and other Conservative defenders of empire in a firm position of opposition to aspects of the American reconstruction programme. Even after British policy gradually turned to decolonisation, the pace and timing of decolonisation, as well as the eventual form of the post-imperial relationship, was often in contention. The two states had also had very different approaches to the question of war aims, and largely because of Britain's imperial links. The 'special relationship', as it came to be known, emerged only gradually during the post-war period, not least because of the situation of mutual dependence in which the management of their two zones in Germany had placed them, and their common opposition to France's European policy and its initial objection to Germany's economic and political reconstruction.

Because of the importance of their alignment to the shape of international relations after 1945, well recognised in the political writing of the time, a substantial theoretical effort was directed to explaining it. The most frequent explanation sourced it in the common cultural and political features shared by the two countries, their common language and similar political institutions. Churchill, who first used the term 'special relationship', called it 'a fraternal association of the English-speaking peoples'[7] (though this theory fitted ill with the various periods during which the two governments were at odds). Others, more impressed with the way in which great wars were related to a rising and declining hegemon and the obsession of American strategic planners with the British Empire after the First World War, related it to Britain's rapid decline, Germany's equally rapid rise and the advantages each offered to the other in terms of countering that rise. Hans Morgenthau, in a variant of the theory, located it in the fact that each was a maritime power seeking to stabilise a continental balance, observing that it was first the German and then the Soviet threat to Europe which served as the central strategic orientation to both powers during the twentieth century. Still others stressed the common economic and political interests of the two leading liberal powers, including open seas, free access to raw materials and an open international trading order. Certainly, during the inter-war period, both powers shared an opposition to corporate forms of state economic regulation and state support for large national enterprises.

The pattern of the post-war alliances

By contrast with the pre-war pattern, the post-war alliances were numerous, wide in scope and intended for the duration of the Cold War conflict and beyond. Each major power became committed across the globe to both multilateral and bilateral arrangements which involved them in rendering what was often extensive financial as well as military and political support, to states in every region of the globe (with the exception of France in Asia). Indeed, John Foster Dulles, the American secretary of state during the 1950s, was accused of 'pacto-mania', as America contracted formal treaty relations with almost one hundred states and became the chief lynchpin of at least three multilateral alliance systems during the 1950s, all of which were expected to be of some duration.[8]

At the same time, small and medium-sized states had few alliances with one another. Their alliance efforts were directed towards one or other Great Power. Alliances were often, moreover, mutually exclusive. It was not merely that few states had alliances with more than one major power, it was also that no major power would entertain an alliance with a partner who had extensive relations with the other side.

The post-war alliances had a clear geographical aspect. Many of the new states of Africa avoided Cold War commitments, while the United States' local alliances were concentrated in areas open to Cuban influence, notably Central America. As for the major alliance systems built after the Second World War, these were all concentrated around the Chinese and Russian littorals. Thus, there was the Nato alliance to Russia's west, America's alliances with Greece and Turkey to its southwest, and with Iran, Pakistan and Thailand to its south. China was hemmed in by the American alliance with South Korea and the Philippines to its south and Japan to its east, as well as by the ANZUS and ANZUK arrangements. The Cold War alliances were thus in a sense also 'preparation-for-war' alliances.

But they also had a clear economic aspect. Within the general framework of the North Atlantic alliance, the United States had worked a series of bilateral alliances with its various Nato allies which acted as conduits for American military aid and political assistance. That aid, moreover, played an important part in solving the dollar shortage with which the countries of Western Europe were faced at the end of the war and in financing reconstruction, necessary before they could undertake liberal foreign economic policies.[9] Military aid to less developed recipients also freed resources for development plans, and often fed the capital accumulation of indigenous elites (although in other cases 'economic assistance' was a disguised cover for military aid).[10] Equally, in the Soviet system, there was a division of labour, as various countries were directed to particular forms of production. Part of the cement of the Soviet alliance system was preferential pricing, especially for energy supplies, and guaranteed markets for industrial goods.[11]

The four-power structure

Four major powers stood at the apex of the post-war alliance system: the United States, Britain, France and the Soviet Union. These powers often set the parameters to the domestic as well as foreign policies of the smaller powers; and they often formed the only link between the various countries with which they were respectively allied. They also provided the link between the individual countries with whom they had special arrangements and the multilateral alliance systems. (Most members of the multilateral alliances gained the military equipment or training to play their part in the alliance system from a 'special partner', usually in return for donating to that power the base facilities or surveillance plant required to carry out the collective task.)

Thus, the four powers formed the hubs of complex systems of linked capabilities. They were the communications links; they were also the main donors of money, arms and political guarantees with each of their respective sets of allies. It was for good reasons that the alliance system of the second half of the twentieth century came to be characterised as one of security donors and security receivers.

Their bilateral alliances differed in mode. America's alliances were primarily military alliances, sometimes in the form of declarations to defend, more often as guarantees of military aid, training and support. The Soviet alliances were, by contrast, mostly mutual aid and friendship alliances. They offered support to an approved government, but without any firm guarantees of direct involvement in cases of war, outside of the European area.

The total alliances

These numerous alliances served distinctly identifiable, albeit not mutually exclusive, purposes. Some were clearly intended to enhance strategic mobility (notably, America's alliance with the Philippines, Britain's reconstructed relationship with an independent Singapore and the Trucial States of the Gulf, and the Soviet Union's relationship with Vietnam). Others were intended to lock groups of countries together into common political and military stances, such as ANZAC, SEATO and CENTO. Still others are better understood as stabilisation alliances, intended to secure certain political groups in power in the receiver state. Alliance membership had internal legitimising effects and established a party or political movement in a position of decided advantage over its internal rivals: politicians who could offer evidence of support from a major power often took precedence among other domestic rivals for power.

Alliance membership became, partly in consequence, a signal to an internal domestic political orientation. The Italian Communist Party signalled its intention to behave as a legitimate party within the ordinary forms of Western parliamentary democracy during the 1970s, in part by its announced intention not to break with the Nato alliance if it came to power. The alliances of the second part of the century were exclusionary alliances, aimed to set governments on certain paths, to prevent entry by left-socialist or other anti free-market forces into the political arenas of the liberal-allied states, and liberal forces from disturbing the political controls established in the Soviet allied states. Indeed, they were originally concerned primarily with internal threats.

The Soviet alliances often entailed close relationships with individual personnel and implied support for fraternal communist parties, if a communist party were in power, and for specific personnel within those parties. Otherwise, they signalled that the Soviet Union would not support political forces inimical to the government of the ally in question, not even communist parties, which was one of their major benefits from the non-communist government's point of view. (The Soviet relations with Iraq and Syria implied not merely limited support for communist parties in those areas but a positive curbing of their activities.) They were also 'aid' alliances, and became the transmission belts for a wealth of arms and military equipment, supplied essentially by Soviet or Comecon arms industries. They were thus an aspect of economic planning within the Soviet system.

Multilateral or concealed bilateral?

Within Nato, individual partners had a variety of relations with one another and often negotiated bilaterally to establish joint positions in alliance councils. In other cases, Nato was a multilateral cover for what was essentially a bilateral relationship. Greece and Turkey joined Nato in 1952, but their special relationships with the United States were much more important than their Nato memberships, diplomatically as well as militarily. Moreover, neither developed extensive bilateral relationships with other alliance members, at least not until after the collapse of a United States-supported military junta, which ruled Greece between 1967 and 1974. (Thereafter, successive Greek governments took care to widen Greece's diplomatic ties.) The substance of the Warsaw Pact was in fact a series of bilateral alliances between the Soviet Union and the states of Central and Eastern Europe through the first two decades of its existence.

The multilateral alliance systems were, nonetheless, unlike any previous form of alliance. They had large, in some cases self-serving, bureaucracies. (In the case of Nato, the secretariat formed a cadre independent of the individual member-states.) They came to have infrastructure assigned to them on a permanent basis, and permanent Councils and committees which were assigned often sensitive and central political and economic tasks, tasks which had significant implications for the domestic as well as foreign policies of the member-states. So developed were they to become that some analysts preferred to think of them as forms of international organisation; that is, as general organisations of shared purpose. But their closest equivalents were the twentieth century's liberal war fighting alliances, on which they were in fact modelled. (Both anti-German fighting alliances had featured joint defence forces, common commanders and the creation of specialised agencies for the carrying out of joint tasks, such as transport and supply.) Their only other equivalent, and that limited to the ideological aspect, was the religious alliances formed during the Reformation and the break-up of Christianity. The Western alliance established the model for other containment efforts on the part of the West. The mutual guarantee alliances of CENTO and SEATO, formed during the 1950s, were structured along the Nato pattern, with rudimentary common defence structures and alliance councils. Both featured permanent decision-making centres, were spoken of as security communities and took on a variety of tasks. But they never maintained the durability of the Nato alliance, falling apart and reforming into bilateral relationships and diplomatic coalitions when the Cold War passed its peak and the super-powers began their first detente.

The new model alliance

When the Nato alliance was first established in 1949, it consisted of little more than a joint military committee charged with co-ordinating national defence plans. As Germany was gradually integrated into Nato, however, its military structure became more complex, developing a unified command structure and the permanent assignment of troops, until it eventually formed a single military organisation under the command of single commander in chief.[12] It was German rearmament which was the efficient cause of the 'new model' Nato.

On the political side, the various representatives on the military committee had initially reported to their respective home defence departments and foreign offices to clear common decisions, a time-consuming procedure. In 1951, however, a Nato Council was established which met biannually, with deputies in permanent session at the first Nato headquarters in Paris. The deputies (later ambassadors to Nato) were empowered to agree uncontentious decisions without first clearing them with their home governments. It was the creation of the Council which gave the organisation its corporate existence.[13]

That corporate personality was supplemented by the creation of a permanent secretariat. Both the military and civilian sides were served by an autonomous staff which belonged to the organisation as a whole and whose chief administrator, the Nato secretary-general, chaired meetings, set agendas and prepared discussion papers. The Council was empowered to establish sub-committees on an ad hoc or more permanent basis, making the structure both flexible and adaptable.

The common threat

The alliance did more than contain the Soviet Union. It served as the security framework for the new Germany and provided it with its only general staff. Germany's integration into Nato also provided security for the surrounding states in the event of a renewed German threat (even the Soviet Union appeared to welcome this aspect of the alliance's existence). The alliance also served as a diplomatic front, ensuring political solidarity in the face of changing Soviet or Chinese initiatives, and it became a clearing house for the various national policies of the member-states when their major antagonists launched new initiatives.

The dynamic of the Nato alliance, and its day-to-day organisation, centred around tabulating the Soviet force posture. The annual accounts of Soviet military preparedness set the main agenda of the alliance; and the activities of its committees, whether in expenditure, in exercise planning, weapons procurement or the disposition and use of the various forces, were all centred around the force posture analyses. Various war-fighting scenarios were periodically agreed, and became the bases of the annual and semi-annual exercises which kept the troops in a state of readiness. The alliance was on permanent military alert throughout the first forty years of its existence.

The alliance, however, owned few weapons, the major exception after 1967 being some nuclear weaponry that the supreme allied commander could deploy directly, together with an early warning aircraft, known as the AWACS. Its base facilities, communications networks and pipelines, as well as its forces, were either owned by the governments on whose land they were located, or they were 'leased' under special agreement between the country in question and, generally, the United States (for example, the special air bases in Britain, Germany and Greece, and the British ports that were used by the United States for basing and refuelling its nuclear submarines). Designated cadres of brigades, air squadrons and mobile units were 'loaned' on a semi-permanent basis to the supreme allied commander, which meant that they could be called upon in times of crisis; and the various Nato commanders commanded them in the annual and biannual exercises which became a permanent feature of the organisation. But since Nato troops never came under fire, the system never operated in a war situation, and the degree of autonomous command the supreme allied commander *de facto* enjoyed was never put to the test.

The 'common threat' as a source of divergence

Agreeing the strategy of the alliance generally involved a political struggle between the United States and the Europeans, a struggle which centred on the balance between conventional and nuclear responses to any putative Soviet attack. The United States favoured strategies which tended to rely on the use of ground troops in large numbers to fight an actual war; the Europeans favoured an early reliance on nuclear weaponry, with the hope of avoiding war.[14]

These respective preferences related to the likelihood of the form of attack and the damage each partner was likely to suffer in the event of such an attack. If the alliance determined on a nuclear or early use strategy, the United States would be much more likely to be made the subject of an early surprise attack, to wipe out its nuclear arsenal; in late use, or more conventional strategies, the Europeans would be likely to suffer the effects of attrition, considered to be grave given the high fire-power predicted for any future ground war. Thus, each strove for that form of strategy with the least immediate risk to its own population and its physical, economic and cultural plant.

The different interests tended to be resolved by 'splitting the difference'. The official strategy of the alliance from 1967 onwards was 'flexible response', a force posture which envisaged meeting the Soviet Union at the presenting level, thus satisfying the United States. Equally, however, it held open the possibility of the early use of nuclear weapons if Nato troops were overrun, reassuring the Europeans that they would not have to fight a ground war alone. But such paper formulae often concealed considerable differences of interpretation and in intention to use.[15]

The most difficult political question that confronted the alliance during its existence was the command and control of its members' nuclear forces. The three Western nuclear powers were each opposed to any multilateral control of their respective nuclear forces. Equally, however, both major and minor powers feared unilateral use by the others in situations with which they would not concur.[16] There was also the fear of mistaken use by ground commanders, driven by military necessity. The alliance had what rose to some 13,000 nuclear warheads on Nato soil, most of American ownership. The dilemma was how to release them without at the same time allowing field commanders a dangerous liberty.

The system which was eventually chosen favoured the national over the multilateral. Called the 'two-key' system, it involved two codes, one held by the country of origin and one by the field commander, both of which were required to be activated for the weapon to be deployed. This allowed for multilateral use and promoted joint co-ordination in times of crisis, but kept the ultimate decision on nuclear use in the hands of the respective national owner governments.

The 'free rider' problem

The credibility of the alliance would have been enhanced by the adoption of common weaponry: again and again, weapons standardisation became a battle-cry. But the economic demands of their weapons industries made Nato members reluctant to standardise equipment, particularly as their industries were engaged in often ferocious competition with one another. The only form of standardisation which really worked was the joint weapons development project, where a single project was agreed and its production shared out amongst several partners (usually Britain, France and Germany). Such projects were, however, laborious to negotiate and not always efficient as to product, since the weapon had perforce to perform a variety of disparate roles in order to satisfy all potential users. Doubt about joint projects was endemic.[17]

Moreover, the alliance could not coerce its members into agreed force provisions. Again and again, force levels were set, only to fall short of achievement.

The alliance had, in consequence, a serious 'free rider' problem, as it was identified in the rational choice literature which became popular during the 1970s. This was the situation where member-states took advantage of one other's commitments to evade burden while enjoying the benefits of the alliance's existence, whether in enhanced security or in reduced force levels, because they knew the others would maintain the alliance in any case. All the member-states threatened to free ride at different times, but the most consistent were Belgium and Holland, and the most notorious was France. By 1964, the alliance was sufficiently well armed and well deployed to protect Germany on the Elbe, its eastern border, allowing France far more leeway in the expression of dissidence. After 1966, by which time it had withdrawn from the joint military command and had expelled the alliance headquarters from French territory, France still enjoyed such security as the Nato umbrella provided, since all the countries on its eastern borders were well-armed alliance members.

The alliance as a bureaucracy

The alliance organisation developed all the features usually displayed by bureaucracies: a permanent cadre, special committees, delegated tasks, etc.; and it displayed all the usual tendencies of large bureaucracies. Its civil servants strove to have tasks allocated to the organisation and they endeavoured to expand its budget. Some sought to adapt it to changing circumstances to gain it longevity; others resisted change so that its structure would continue to have tasks to perform. In other words, it developed survival instincts. It also developed well-defined bureaucratic interests, and quite early in its existence: its first secretary-generals were able people who not only focused the separate interests of the member-states towards the organisation, but fought against any reallocation of its tasks to potential competitor organisations, such as the Western European Union.

As an *international* bureaucracy, however, it suffered from disadvantages. First, unlike the usual national bureaucracy, it had few autonomous powers: its task was simply to serve the Nato council. Second, it had a divided structure – the military and political wings were quite distinct – and the military wing of the bureaucracy directly served the chief military commander, not the organisation as a whole. Third, and crucially, it did not enjoy a monopoly over the roles it was handed to perform. Each state had its own ministry of defence, besides its foreign office, which continued to serve its own interests. Moreover, the 'Nato interest' seemed, especially during periods of detente, difficult to define. This infected the Nato bureaucracy's sense of purpose, draining it of direction and impetus. Indeed, it became important for alliance heads of state to keep redefining its role, if for no other reason than to provide the organisation with a working focus (a function provided by the biannual meetings of heads of state).

These weaknesses would be revealed when the Soviet system dissolved. During the early 1990s, it became clear that the emerging confederal structure in Russia would not be posing any immediate threat to the Nato area, and the Russian government was seeking to join Western councils. For several years, the alliance bureaucracy went into a form of stasis, demonstrating a lack of ability even to articulate future choices or the problems that the global system would face should the alliance dissolve. This seemed to indicate that a bureaucracy of few autonomous powers, serving many members, was particularly vulnerable to loss of shared purpose. In any event, it did not appear able to generate a role for itself in the absence of political impetus, despite a large amount of bureaucratic theory which maintained that that is what bureaucracies did.

The demands of political co-ordination

There was a constant concern that a disarray among national policies would indicate a weakening of resolve in confronting the Soviet Union. Thus, the alliance not only sought to co-ordinate the various Cold War policies of its member-states, but eventually undertook a detente policy of its own, which became part of the official policy of the alliance with the Harmel Report in 1967, dedicating the organisation to both deterrence and detente. It was also the case, however, that each member of the alliance wanted a definition of detente compatible with its own national policy orientations, with the consequence that negotiating common stances was far from easy. It was only the determination of both France and Germany to proceed with their autonomous detente policies during the 1960s, irrespective of American wishes, that brought the United States finally to agree a common policy for the alliance as a whole; and Henry Kissinger would attack the notion of a Nato detente, primarily because it acted as a restraint upon the United States.[18]

The degree to which member countries had to sacrifice national objectives to the needs of the alliance was a constant concern. During the 1950s, when the countries of Europe were still in a process of reconstruction, they were more inclined to put national differences aside. Even then, however, the burdens of membership proved weighty and sometimes took them by surprise. France and Britain joined in a short-lived military venture against the Egyptians in 1956 when the new nationalist Egyptian leader, Nasser, unilaterally nationalised the Suez Canal, a venture which appeared initially to both Britain and France to fall outside of the remit of the alliance. But when the United States threatened to withdraw support for the venture, it had to be abandoned. Thereafter, a 'Committee of Three Wise Men' recommended that independent initiatives which might involve the alliance in conflict with the Soviet Union would have to be cleared with the other alliance members.[19]

Resolving political disputes among the allies took as much of the organisation's energies as its specific military task. The most intense was the conflict between France and America during the 1960s on the organisation and leadership of the alliance. The most enduring was the Greek–Turkish rivalry over Cyprus, which involved the secretary-general in the additional tasks of mediation and conciliation.

Public opinion and the alliance

Public support for the alliance was variable, and appeared to be conditional on the perception of the Soviet threat, the dangers that alliance membership posed and the prospects for political detente; that is, the degree to which the respective leaders of the alliances appeared willing to sort out their difficulties by negotiation. During the 1950s, when the United States and its allies appeared to be in the stronger position, and when the Soviet threat was perceived to be at its most intense, support for the alliance was strong across all political complexions. Gradually, over the 1960s and 1970s, however, as the nuclear balance appeared to even out, as indeed the Soviet Union appeared capable of threatening the Western alliance directly and as policies of detente were undertaken, that consensus began to erode.

Public opinion surveys undertaken in Germany during the period revealed that the number of those who believed that communism was 'very threatening' had declined from 63 per cent in 1962 to 46 per cent in 1978. During the same period, perceptions of the alliance with the greatest threat potential also altered dramatically: between 1962 and 1978 those who believed Nato was the stronger alliance declined from 37 per cent to 14 per cent, while those who believed the Warsaw Pact the stronger alliance rose from 8 per cent to 35 per cent (47 per cent of those who responded in 1978 believed that both were equal, as opposed to 26 per cent in 1962). These opinions correlated with a definite rise in preferences for non-alignment: by 1973, those who preferred West Germany to be non-aligned had risen to 42 per cent (it had been 32 per cent in 1965), representing a slight majority over those who wished it to remain aligned (41 per cent). By 1980, 51 per cent of British respondents wanted their country to be 'neutral and prosperous'. None of this dictated any obvious groundswell for the alliance's dissolution: 80 per cent of German respondents in 1978 also believed that, if alignment continued, the alliance should not be radically altered.

Moreover, support for the American commitment grew whenever detente appeared to run into trouble. But such results did indicate that the alliance was generally considered in purely instrumental terms, and useful in respect of its service to national interests.

The alliance as a collective will

The alliance constantly threw off broad statements of collective purpose. Initially, the favoured American official usage was the 'free-world alliance'; among Europeans, it was the 'Atlantic community', both indicating a form of affinitive commitment. Both implied that the alliance was more than a mere instrument, and that it was a union with a shared purpose, not a mere coincidence of contingent national interests.

In part, the rhetoric was a reflection of United States preferences for a cosmopolitan justification for external involvements. The United States had entered upon diplomatic engagement in both world wars with broad political purposes in view, not on the basis of mere service to the balance of power. But it was also a general requirement of political support for military undertakings at the time: all the wartime alliances put together during the twentieth century felt it necessary to enunciate broad statements of purpose which pictured their alliance as serving nobler ends than mere power-balancing, ends such as freedom or liberation or protection from aggression. There was also the desire to articulate the relation of the parts to the whole, both for public consumption and for diplomatic purposes – to support the diplomatic efforts, sometimes strenuous, required to gain agreement on common policies.

The portrayal of the alliance's collective identity changed over time, partly in response to changing fashions in communal conceptions, and partly in terms of the particular communal formula that appeared to fit the circumstances of the time. What was notable, however, was that the various portrayals demonstrated a definite progression from the unitary and organic to the federated and more mechanistic.

From the organic to the systemic

Its earliest image was that of the common-value community, based on a form of the spiritual union, probably under the immediate influence of Clarence Streit's *Union Now* (London: Jonathan Cape, 1939). In an instance of a popular genre in the early 1940s, Streit had suggested that a simple *feoderus* was insufficient to keep the peace, and that unions among states must henceforth be built on the basis of a shared spiritual commitment. (He was arguing for a union of the democracies to confront fascism.) During the first years of its existence, therefore, Nato was presented as a union of wills resolved to protect a specific and valuable way of life.

The spiritual union was supplemented by the idea of the socially integrated community. In the 1950s, an eminent political scientist, Karl Deutsch, rooted the alliance in a socio-political North Atlantic area which was constituted by a multiplicity of social links, not merely by state interest. Deutsch's idea was that the alliance was merely the security aspect of a much deeper sociological reality, created by common expectations, similar lifestyles and integrative social institutions.[20]

The idea of a social union was supported by the developing functional theory which saw all organisations, including international organisations, in terms of the functions they performed for society at large. In some variants of functional theory, the union widened as more and more tasks came to be performed on a joint basis, until it achieved something like the shape of a single society. (Jean Monnet's conception of the European Community was also modelled on this idea.) It also influenced the Nato bureaucracy, which strove for the continuous attachment of new functions, partly out of the belief that functional growth expressed a deepening social phenomenon.

Attempts beyond mere rhetoric were made to develop these communal conceptions. Initially, there was the creation of the North Atlantic Parliamentary Union, an annual meeting of parliamentarians from the North Atlantic countries which was intended to demonstrate that Nato was a union of shared political ideals. (It strove to maintain support for the alliance among parliamentary representatives.) Increasingly, as well, there was a tendency to reach down to ordinary citizens, usually via schools and universities, who were invited to visit the headquarters for briefings on the organisation's activities. There was also an effort to demonstrate that the alliance had more than the traditionally conceived security functions. In the 1970s, President Nixon would propose the establishment of a Committee on the Challenges of Modern Society, implying that the alliance could meet internal social challenges as well as external security threats.

During the 1960s, the community idea was succeeded, though never completely replaced, by the idea of a partnership. In this conception, the alliance was pictured as an enterprise of two equal and separate parties, America on the one hand and a rapidly unifying Europe on the other: separate parties with, however, common interests and common goals, who had to work together to achieve those goals.[21] (The partnership conception implied a contract based on interests rather than a union of spirit.) The partnership idea was enunciated by President Kennedy upon his accession to office. The conception of a partnership of equals was problematic, however, and ultimately inconsistent with American objectives, since the United States was at that time trying to avoid nuclear sharing and wished to tighten control over the political direction of the alliance (and it was the period when the American guarantee began to look increasingly conditional). If the idea of a partnership seemed to support de Gaulle's aim of gradually loosening the alliance structure, Gaullism in turn jeopardised any idea of a partnership, as the United States remained opposed to any notion of a genuine two-centre alliance.[22] Partly in consequence, the idea of a partnership never seized the public imagination.

The image which proved more lasting was proposed by Harland Cleveland in 1970 in a book called *The Transatlantic Bargain* (New York: Nato, 1970). Here, the alliance was pictured as a form of mutual benefit society in which individuals, each with varying interests, either paid a price to achieve a common good not otherwise available or actually swapped benefits. This portrayal was clearly meant to draw on the developing sense of individual national interests and diverse policy directions then being displayed among alliance members. Here, states were pictured as bargaining to achieve something of value to each, and things of different respective value. This image portrayed the alliance as the more usual diplomatic device, more in the nature of a traditional alliance than a new form of community.

By the end of the 1980s, the preferred term had become a 'security system' which implied a more or less mechanical set of arrangements providing for individual and collective security.

The Eastern bloc

The Soviet system was constructed on quite different principles. First, it consisted of two separate organisations: the Warsaw Pact and the Comecon. The Comecon was arguably more central to the Soviet security system, since it controlled the shape and direction of the East European economies, creating a buffer zone to its west, from the inside out. Second, the Comecon was originally nothing but a Stalinist extension of Soviet central planning. Each important desk in the allied ministries was shadowed by a Soviet agent, in the nature of a governor-general; and the member-states agreed a centralised economic plan.

Accordingly, the Soviet system conformed more to the imperial model of a union than to the traditional alliance. Certainly, the Soviet Union's relations with the countries of Central Europe during the 1950s and early 1960s were more like imperial relationships than alliance relationships. Even during the late 1960s, when the Soviet Union began to allow greater economic leeway to its allies, Comecon remained the agency for market-sharing agreements, cheap fuel and economic swaps; and it was dominated by the Soviet Union. At that point the closest analogy would have been the Commonwealth economic section of the 1950s.[23]

Compared to the Comecon, the Warsaw Pact was rudimentary. It was built up of the several alliances the Soviet Union had with each of its Eastern and Central European allies, collectivised by a general agreement among them. There was originally no common structure, and the Pact had little substantial collective identity for the first decade of its existence. Its meetings were routine occasions during which the several subordinate allies each voiced agreement with the preferred Soviet military doctrine of the moment. Accordingly, the Pact conformed much more closely to the model of the *coefedoris leonas* (the dominated union), particularly since it was the Soviet military that determined the allocation of such defence tasks as its current strategic doctrine required.[24]

By the late 1960s, however, a more genuine collective presence had developed, largely as a result of Germany's various approaches to the states of Central Europe. Faced with the prospect of a genuine competitor, the Soviet

Union had to woo its partners, and to woo them in terms of substantial benefit, to keep them from breaking socialist solidarity. During the 1970s, in consequence, the Pact evolved into a more substantial locus of genuine diplomatic negotiating and political agreement.

The hegemonial aspect of the alliances

The relationship between hegemony and community solidarity became a substantial issue with regard to both alliance systems, as well as to collective enterprises more generally. The question was, were the alliances merely an expression of the power of the respective alliance leaders or did they have a genuine autonomous existence?

With regard to Nato, the answer was both. Clearly, the United States continuously set the terms of the debate, not only with regard to its strategic tasks but also with regard to broader questions of political orientation, particularly concerning the allies' relationships with the Soviet Union.[25] It was equally clear, however, that it did not always win the debate, and that when countries discovered freedom of movement, they exploited it. It was also clear that if the United States was the pre-eminent power, other alliance members also had power and such powers as the alliance required. It was Germany which provided the troops for flexible response; accordingly, the United States had to respect Germany's situation. A second limitation to the United States' hegemonial position was the existence of independent deterrents. Nato's nuclear posture had to account for three independent nuclear capabilities. Finally, the evident desire for a continuation for some kind of alliance structure after the Cold War had ended: that is, in the absence of an immediate threat, it seemed to indicate that, theoretically at least, the gains on co-ordination were valued apart from and irrespective of American power and influence.[26]

In the case of the Warsaw Pact system, the case for hegemonial control was more evident, varying only in its modalities. Under Stalin, there was little doubt that the Pact represented a simple command system, largely based on the physical ability to coerce, assured by the close proximity of the Soviet army. (Most Warsaw Pact countries had permanent Soviet troops stationed in them.) Increasingly during the 1950s, ideological control replaced physical control, and economic and political controls were increasingly loosened (provided a communist party remained in power).[27] The dissolution of the Pact following the freedom of determination of its allies did indicate, however, that it remained essentially a coercive system, even when, as in 1968 in the Prague crisis, some states did agree to join the Soviet Union in repressing Czechoslovakia.

The end of the alliances?

By 1990, with the onset of glasnost in the Soviet Union, widespread doubts began to be expressed about both the necessity and the durability of the alliance frameworks, at a variety of political levels. Republicans in America, always at the forefront in desiring a more equal burden-sharing, insisted that it was now time for Europeans to provide for their own defence, and indeed George Bush set this as one of the objectives for the 'New World Order'. The French government believed that a single Atlantic framework was no longer required in the light of the changes in Central Europe, and that a continental European system of some sort would be a better alternative. The former Soviet Union, having dissolved into a number of states, the major one of which was dedicated to a more Western-oriented position, waited for a major revision of the Western alliance, and insisted that it should dissolve, just as the Warsaw Pact had done.

Of course, the simple Western commitment of 'a threat to one is a threat to all' was not done away with by these initiatives. But such a commitment did not imply a security community, merely a reinsurance treaty; and its maintenance would scarcely require the elaborate structure of the Nato alliance, with its regular biannual restatements of a common purpose and the constant upgrading of its forces in being.

So widespread was the expectation that the Western alliance would follow the Warsaw Pact into dissolution that political scientists began to draw various scenarios as to how it would dissolve. One pictured a gradual process of withering from the absence of a clear rationale for its existence. Another pictured the cumulative effect of countries simply going their own way. A third drew from the reputed dynamics of hegemonic relationships. By the 1980s, a small but influential literature had appeared relating the well-being of the large organisations of the post-war period to the interests and commitment of a 'hegemon', a major power which had the commitment and power to maintain them. This literature was initially concerned with the durability of the post-war international economic institutions, in the light of a detectable turn in the United States' policy from economic multilateralism to unilateralism, but it was soon extended to the alliance. The prediction was that, in a more peaceful environment without a single threat, the United States would disengage from Europe and the alliance would lose the hegemon upon which its survival depended.[28]

The 'declining hegemon' scenario became particularly influential. During 1992 and 1993, obsessive attention was paid to US policy in regard to its troops in Europe, and much relief expressed at every statement on the part of the United States that it would maintain them.

What was interesting about these sets of ideas was that each rested on a different theory of social cement, from common purposes to cumulative habits to the existence of a central power which dominated and pulled the smaller powers together. (Few, however, would have dignified the latter as a genuine community, irrespective of the existence of common institutions.)

The proposed alternatives

The main proposed alternative to the alliance systems was a dynamised Security Council of the United Nations, enhanced by either a Western European or a Pan European security framework. With regard to the latter, Nato would be converted from an alliance resting on exchanges of obligation into a broader security organisation of common rules and agreed structures including Europe as a whole. It would supplement, or be subsumed into, the Conference on Security and Co-operation in Europe, a standing conference concerned with issues of European arms control, and would operate under the legal framework of the Helsinki Agreements, a set of rules agreed between the two blocs during the 1970s which guaranteed information-sharing and freedom of expression, and which could be developed into a security framework.

These proposals reflected a general tendency to see security in broader terms than mere military security, and they related security to the internal disposition of states as well as to international confidence-building measures and agreed and regulated mutual force postures. They did not go as far as to imply the creation of a new international political authority for a widened Europe. Their root lay in the idea of a more specified European common law of peace, which derived from a degree of shared political objectives and which would be supplemented by some agreed rules of the game.

In the event, however, the proposed European security system became a serious source of contention, and not merely among the West Europeans and the United States. The Soviet Union and its allies all preferred a form of pan-European security system, albeit of different sorts (since its former allies precisely feared the Soviet Union). On the Western side, however, there remained grave doubts about simply incorporating the Eastern European states into a revised Nato, particularly given the continued existence of insecure borders among Russia's newly liberated former clients. When Hungary signalled its interest in joining Nato, the major Western chancelleries objected to the West guaranteeing Hungary's borders, particularly without the prior consent of Russia. The role of the former Soviet Union in such a revised security system was also a subject of debate: most Central Europeans wished it excluded. On the Western side, there were serious disagreements about the future locus of any solely Western defence system. Some agreed with the French and wished to enhance the European defence element of the European Community, but without giving up Nato. Others, notably the British, feared such an enhancement would weaken Nato. These disagreements indicated that collective sentiment alone did not produce substantive agreed collective arrangements.

The reformed alliance and international community

When the Nato alliance announced its intention to extend its borders to the east, there was little inclination to relate this expansion to any vestiges of lingering communal sentiment. Most commentators attributed it to varieties of rational, and often interest-driven, behaviour among a set of independent actors. Some saw it as a desire for stability in a period of rapid change. One eminent theorist saw it as a structural requirement of an international system with only one super-power: Kenneth Waltz, the pre-eminent neo-realist, claimed that the new Nato which began to take shape in the second half of the 1990s was not a 'community' and 'community-building'; and many came to see in the new arrangements the germs of a genuinely federal Europe, if not a unitary European super-state. At the same time, it appeared that there might be lessons in its creation for other international experiments. The European experiment seemed the most thoroughly communal of all the post-war creations. Thus, it seemed particularly vital to uncover the efficient secret of European unity and to distinguish what might be particular to it from what might be general, so that its lessons might be applied to state unions more generally. It also became important to test just how thoroughgoing the union actually was.

The cement of Europe

Deciding the essence of the new Europe was not easy, since the 'union' had domestic liberal aspects as well as system-level 'Cold War' aspects. It also had functional aspects, in that both domestic and system-level institutions buttressed one another, giving it the aspect of a social totality which may have been self-supporting. In essence, three sets of processes stood out as central features.

Europeanism as liberalism

Its liberal aspects were the most apparent, as well as the most central. The emergent common policies of the European system all turned on according greater freedom to people and goods. The European Convention on Human Rights provided for a Bill of Rights which guaranteed rights to all citizens of signatory states equally. The original common market (or European Economic Community, as it was first called) established a 'rule of law' in the area of economic transactions which guaranteed traders and producers equal treatment in all member-states. The Arusha Convention, and later the Lome Agreements, created a single post-colonial framework which allowed private enterprises from Community countries to invest and trade in the reserved domains of former colonial rivals. Freedom to seek work was conceded early (although not the freedom to be unemployed). The Council of Europe continuously reviewed state practice with regard to the role of women and the treatment of political prisoners, among a number of other 'liberal' concerns.

The domestic pattern of liberal institutions was also carried up to inform the common institutions. The European human rights regime not only included a common institutions but a court made up of independently appointed judges, and a court to which citizens could appeal directly, against their own governments. States could also be referred to the Common Market's (separate) court for the abrogation of responsibilities under the various Community treaties, like states in a federal system; and they were held accountable to Community law, just as liberal governments were accountable to constitutional law. Its three central organisations had representative assemblies – the Council of Europe, the Coal and Steel Community and the Common Market – and when the latter two were merged during the 1970s to form the 'European Community' (and later the

---

security system at all, but a new management system by which the single super-power would now seek to influence the European political space.[29] Other (rational choice) theorists saw it in terms of the theory of the 'second best'. According to the theory of the second best, outcomes had to be understood in terms of alternative choices. With regard to the choice of a security system, the alternative models which the twentieth century offered had little to recommend them. Few wished a return to the free-for-all of the inter-war period; none wished to return to the League of Nations (widely nominated the least successful security system in history), which would have been entailed by a simple reliance on the Helsinki framework.

Whatever its immediate causes, however, the reluctance to abandon the Western alliance, and the desire of the Central European states to enter it, demonstrated that an important advance had occurred in the conception of security among the European states at least. It demonstrated that ordinary security, that is, security in the absence of a specified enemy, had become established as a form of collective good. (A 'collective good' was the technical term for a good which could only be achieved by a collectivity acting together.) Moreover, security had come to be conceived in more than purely military terms, and was deemed to require attention to human rights and to confidence-building measures as well as to more traditional concerns of military prepared-ness and arms control. These alone implied some institutional duration, as well as a continuing commitment to the co-ordination of foreign and defence policies.

Viewed from this perspective, the contributions of the alliance systems (and indeed, of the Cold War in which they were embedded) to internationalism were considerable. The alliances had inculcated habits of co-ordination; they had tested the limits of the possibilities for autonomous action; they had also extended the notion of what was politically tolerable for the *longue durée* in state relations. They had not done away with calculations of individual political advantage, to be sure. But they had demonstrated that some meaningful definitions of autonomy were consistent with some conceptions of common political space and co-ordinated authority.

Notes

1 A.J.P. Taylor outlines its terms, and limits, in *The Struggle for Mastery in Europe* (London: Oxford University Press, 1957) p. 2; he also notes that the term meant little more than powers who were on friendly terms.
2 R. Ogley, *The Theory and Practice of Neutrality in the Twentieth Century* (London: Routledge and Kegan Paul, 1970).
3 A. Bosco, *Federal Union and the Origins of the 'Churchill Proposal'* (London: Lothian, 1992).
4 F. Roy Willis, *France, Germany and the New Europe* (London: Oxford University Press, 1968).
5 R. Divine, *The Illusion of Neutrality* (Chicago: University of Chicago, 1962).
6 Coral Bell, *The Debatable Alliance* (London: Oxford University Press, 1964).
7 In his Fulton, Missouri, speech; D. Dimbleby and D. Reynolds, *An Ocean Apart* (London: Hodder and Stoughton, 1988).
8 H. Dagenhardt, *Treaties and Alliances of the World* (London: Longmans, 1981).

9 R.C. Cooper, *The Economics of Interdependence: Economic Policy in the Atlantic Community* (New York: McGraw Hill, 1968).

10 For the intentional versus the consequential in 'aid' donations, political as well as economic, see D. Baldwin, *Economic Statecraft* (Princeton: Princeton University Press, 1985).

11 P. Wiles, *Communist International Economics* (Oxford: Blackwell, 1968).

12 See Timothy Ireland, *Creating the Entangling Alliance* (London: Aldwych, 1981).

13 Lord Ismay, *NATO, The First Five Years* (Brussels: NATO, 1954).

14 H. Kissinger, *The Troubled Partnership* (New York: McGraw Hill, 1965).

15 See H. Kissinger, *The White House Years* (Boston: Little Brown, 1979), for a participant's view.

16 See David Schwartz, *NATO's Nuclear Dilemmas* (Washington: Brookings Institution, 1983) and Daniel Charles, *Nuclear Planning in NATO* (Cambridge, Mass.: Ballinger, 1987).

17 Among the doubters, G. Tucker, *Towards Rationalising Allied Weapons Production* (Paris: Atlantic Institute, 1976).

18 For the incompatibilities of the various detentes, see Philip Windsor, *Germany and the Management of Detente* (London: Chatto and Windus, 1971); also H. Kissinger, 'The Future of NATO' in K. Myers (ed.), *NATO: The Next Thirty Years* (Boulder and London, 1980).

19 R. Osgood, *NATO: The Entangling Alliance* (Chicago: University of Chicago, 1962).

20 K. Deutsch *et al.*, *Political Community and the North Atlantic Area* (Princeton: Princeton University Press, 1957).

21 For example, Pierre Uri, *Partnership for Progress* (New York: Harper, 1963).

22 For the conflict of images, see H. Cleveland, *The Atlantic Idea and Its European Rivals* (New York: McGraw Hill, 1966).

23 M. Kaser, *Comecon: Integration Problems of the Planned Economies* (London: Oxford University Press, 1965).

24 T. Wolfe, *Soviet Power and Europe, 1945–1970* (Baltimore: Johns Hopkins University, 1970).

25 D. Smith, *Pressure: How America Runs Nato* (London: Bloomsbury, 1989).

26 The counter thesis was that, with the relative decline in American power during the 1970s and 1980s, the alliance would loosen; see J. Lepgold, *The Declining Hegemon* (New York and London: Praeger, 1990).

27 Brzezinski traces the move from institutional and ideological uniformity to 'institutional diversity and ideological uniformity'; *The Soviet Bloc* (New York: Praeger, 1962).

28 David Calleo, *Beyond American Hegemony* (New York: Basic Books, 1987) and J. Lepgold, *The Declining Hegemon* (New York and London: Praeger, 1990).

29 K. Waltz, 'The New World Order', *Millennium: Journal of International Studies*, 22 (1993), 2, pp. 187–95.

18 The European system

By the late 1950s, the growing institutional links among the states Europe had begun to alter their diplomatic practice in significant of the usual pattern of bilateral or even multilateral contacts, the m European states were agreeing common stances via supra-nat special executive committees and direct negotiations between rele ministries, often bypassing foreign offices. They had begun to prese face in international fora, bargaining collectively in trade negotia United States, a practice which would grow with regard to organisations more generally. Some would even come to sha representation towards a number of smaller states.

There was also the elaboration of common policies which into the domestic fabric of the states concerned. The new Comm more than a customs union; it involved common social policie patent laws. Its agricultural policy was not merely a set of national policies; it was a single policy of centrally managed pr agricultural modernisation, with its own institutions and, even finance. By the end of the century, there would be commo standards, common food standards and close monetary a ordination. Paralleling the Common Market was the Coune inter-governmental body, but within which a European S Rights was agreed, and a European Court of Justice whic common standards of human rights.

If these features distinguished them from any previous ex distinguished the relations of the states of Western Europe the diplomatic coalitions that emerged in the post-war peric the Association of South East Asian Nations, nor the non nor the emerging institutional experiments in Africa and I cover such a wide range of matters or boast purposes so individual citizens. The only exception was the East Eur lished by the Soviet Union, and it was arguable whether th diplomatic conference or an inter-state union in the usual s

The uniqueness of the European system gradually cam which it was discussed. The new Europe was viewed in

European Union), their assemblies were formed into a single Parliament which became subject to direct elections. In 1979, European citizens elected 576 parliamentarians from specially created European constituencies who were mandated to serve the new European Community directly (and the national governments had no formal and few informal powers to regulate their activities).

The relations between its institutions – their articulation – also followed the standard liberal format. The two economic communities displayed a separation of power between a policy-initiating body (the High Authority and the Commission) and a legislative body (the Council, made up of representatives of member governments). The policy-initiating bodies were, moreover, instructed to seek out and articulate a common European interest, quite separate from state interests, and they were open to direct influence from sub-state interest groups.

There was also a welfare and redistributive aspect to at least some common policies. The Coal and Steel Community provided for the retraining of miners and steel workers, and provided it out of a common budget. The Common Market committed its member-states to common agriculture and commercial policies which involved direct fiscal transfers from one state to another as well as direct support for farmers and agricultural producers. Conditions of labour were equalised, generally to the level of those who had the more generous provisions, on holidays and female and child labour.

The Cold War aspects of the union

It was also clear, however, that intra-European diplomacy was shaped by the international environment and the emerging hostility between East and West. The sixteen states who had signed the European Convention on Human Rights in 1949 and who participated in the Council of Europe were all states which had escaped direct Soviet domination. The founding members of the European Coal and Steel Community and the Common Market – France, Germany, Italy and the Benelux – were core members of the Nato alliance. It was, moreover, the institutionalisation of the alliance for the *longue durée* which provided a central impetus to the European Union.

For their part, the major Cold War protagonists each saw 'Europe-building' as a vital part of the Cold War struggle. The United States committed itself to the process, in part to stabilise and strengthen Western Europe in the face of the Soviet Union's advance westward. Britain linked itself with the original 'Six' via the Western European Union, where common defence discussions were held, partly to ensure that European defence did not take a direction antithetical to the alliance – the WEU was essentially a sub-body of the Nato alliance. Moreover, Britain would eventually be pressed to join the other Nato 'core' states in the Common Market, to achieve greater Western cohesion in the face of Soviet nuclear diplomacy. In response, the Soviet Union treated the emerging Common Market as an aspect of the Western alliance, and for a long period refused to deal with it. Also, the Western states avoided interfering with one another's Eastern policies and never sought to co-ordinate their various *ostpolitiks* because of the differing saliency of Eastern Europe in their respective foreign policies.

When, moreover, the Soviet system collapsed, the various states of the former Warsaw Pact were reincorporated into the international system via incorporation into the West European organisations. The latter were expanded to provide the diplomatic and security framework for the states of Central and Eastern Europe, from which the former Soviet Union was excluded, and to oversee their transition to liberal democracies.

The functional and systemic aspects of the union

The system developed various functional relationships. This was particularly evident with Nato, the Common Market and the European Convention on Human Rights. Nato provided the security framework for the Common Market – the six countries forming the original customs union scarcely would have agreed to integrate their economies so closely had the 'German threat' still existed – and it was Nato which contained that threat. On the other hand, the Common Market anticipated and resolved many potential intra-European quarrels which might have disturbed the Nato relationship, with regard to trade, for example, or competitive industrial advantage. The European Convention on Human Rights, in turn, provided both Nato and the Common Market with a criterion of membership. (The definition was that they be loosely liberal states, with a secure body of law providing citizens with legal and political rights.) These criteria were applied universally to the newly liberated states of Eastern Europe after 1991, when acceptance into the Council of Europe became the first condition for wider international and European acceptance.

The various bodies also formed a unified political and diplomatic field with, moreover, multiple entry points, which tended to sustain the whole. Sub-state political actors, interest groups and large corporate economic enterprises, for example, treated the entire complex in a more or less instrumental manner, applying to the various institutions for redress or for action, depending on where influence might most effectively do its work. Moreover, groups from different countries began to combine their efforts to influence individual state policies, through action at the European level.[1] Governments used their membership of one organisation to support diplomatic initiatives they mounted with regard to others.

The system was also functional with respect to domestic political order. Both German and Italian liberal elites believed that it was membership of the European organisations which helped them to maintain liberalism at home; and when Greece, Spain and Portugal applied for membership, after periods of authoritarian rule, it was on the grounds that their newly founded liberal orders required support from without. (It was, particularly, this feature of external support for internal political forms which committed some observers to the view that the European institutions constituted a unique and vital 'system'.)

The 'holistic' aspects of Europe

Such functional relationships were considered at the time to be characteristic of unitary social orders. According to the late nineteenth-century French social philosopher Emile Durkheim and his American follower Talcott Parsons, both of whose works had continuing resonance throughout the twentieth century, society was nothing more than a functional arrangement of parts such that each supported the whole. Each had also put forward the idea that the parts could be identified by means of the purpose or function they performed in relation to the whole. Since the European arrangements seemed to display such 'systemic' features, and since they were clearly functional in the sense of performing purposes integral to the state-members, they gained the strong appearance of regulative or governing bodies of a single social system.

The European system also appeared to be a dynamic system. It seemed to grow and to develop naturally out of its own internal forces. Thus, when historians began to tell its story, they often portrayed the resistance movement or the small immediate post-war union of the Benelux as the 'germs' of the Coal and Steel Community, and that union as the prototype of the Economic Community.[2] In the social theory of the time, growth and change were considered natural attributes of a natural entity, and what developed in respect of its own internal nature must, accordingly, have a being in its own right.

Explaining integration

Theorising its dynamic features became a major enterprise among international relations scholars during the second half of the century, who sought to identify the major forces pushing the separate states together. They also sought to type the resultant union and to specify its uniqueness. This body of theory became known as 'integration theory', since it viewed separate societies as integrating into a single social order.[3] But integration theorists came to different conclusions as to the major causal factors involved. Theorists disagreed as to whether it was the result of 'deep' social and economic processes or rather the result of contingent political factors.

The 'deep process' theorist saw the development of integration as arising from fundamental changes in society and economy, including the spread of industrialisation, technology and the development of common social forms. They also saw such processes as somewhat inevitable. Their theories were, accordingly, rather deterministic. The 'politicists', by contrast, represented the growing union movement as more historical and accidental, and as the result of often short-term political calculation on the part of states and political elites. The 'politicists' also saw European union as serving the requirements of states and not of societies.

The theorists propounding these respective theories quarrelled with one another, as each sought to defend his or her particular point of view. Nor was this merely a scientific quarrel, since each theory had implications for the nature, durability and permanence of the European creation. Accordingly, each side was driven as much by their ideological as by their scientific aspirations, to see Europe permanently settled into a unified whole, or still amenable to break-up and realignment.

The sociological determinists

On the more deterministic side, the leading theorists were Ernst Haas and Karl Deutsch. Deutsch's early work had focused on the emergence of what he called 'security communities'. His main concern was the North Atlantic Treaty Organisation, whose creation, he maintained, was not the result only of the accidents of the Cold War or the existence of the Soviet threat. He identified a pattern of internal links between the societies surrounding the North Atlantic which, he maintained, had developed autonomously and over a long period, as a result of their distinctive social evolution. These included trade, shared technological innovation, shared cultural experiences and cultural transfers of ideas, management techniques and governing forms.[4] Haas adapted Deutsch's general approach to explaining the particularities of the European experience. He maintained that evolving social forces were particularly close among European states, and that these accounted for its increasingly tight integration and its higher degrees of common policy-making.[5]

The two theorists did not identify the forces producing integration in quite the same way. Deutsch had stressed the communication and knowledge systems which had grown up among transatlantic elites. According to Deutsch, it was the way in which people learned from one another and communicated with one another across the Atlantic that constituted the linkages. Haas, by contrast, emphasised technological developments. He argued that the requirements of modern systems of economic production were pushing the countries of Western Europe into institutionalised co-operation, and that these were perceived commonly by decision-making elites who developed common solutions to common problems. (This variant of integrationism became known as 'functionalism'.)

The dynamic elements were also differently explained. Deutsch maintained that the North Atlantic system was pushed into developing a common defence organisation when the system was threatened, an external motivator. Haas, by contrast, identified an internal dynamic. He related the continuous growth of integration to what he called 'spill-over'. Spill-over was the process by which integration in one area created tension for greater unity in adjacent areas. According to Haas, once started, integration created an impetus for greater integration. He also maintained that spill-over was a semi-automatic process, constantly pushing integration forward.

Leon Lindberg, a student of Haas, added a political dynamic to Haas' technological determinism. According to Lindberg, while technological impulses and spill-over were real and observable phenomena, they did not work alone. There was also political calculation and pressure which translated these impulses into common policies. Lindberg assigned a strategic role not only to sub-state interest groups but also to European bureaucrats, whom he saw as key actors in promoting integration. Far from being mere observers of an autonomous integration process, they constantly intervened in it, actively encouraging common policy formation.[6] In this theory, the European bureaucrats were portrayed as highly conscious political animals with a clear sense of purpose and direction, who politicised integration, producing common policies often against the will of the separate state governments. Lindberg maintained that this political activism was as important a dynamic as social change.

One explanation for these differences in stress may be the political climate of the times during which they were formulated. Haas' 'spill-over' theory was drafted during the early, more trouble-free phase of the union movement, when the development of the first common policies was rapid and relatively free from political quarrels. Lindberg's more political theory was drawn from the middle phase of the integration process when it had begun to inspire resistance, and when Common Market bureaucrats had to work hard and imaginatively to achieve agreed policies. Indeed, following de Gaulle's veto over British entry in 1963, Lindberg enlarged the theory to imagine an equilibrium in which integration itself created tension between the various states, sometimes stalling the process. (By the middle 1970s, by which time the European institutions had passed through several crises, another sort of theory had become popular, in which crisis played a central role. According to 'crisis theory', states would be satisfied with certain levels of political, social or economic integration until political, economic or technological crises required them to go forward, to higher levels.)[7]

Politicist theories of integration

'Politicism' took different forms. One body of thought, sometimes called 'statist', stressed the role of political calculation and choice on the part of state leaders, national bureaucrats and economic elites, and the articulation and reach of state power.[8] According to statism, integration was useful, and encouraged in the degree to which it helped state authorities solve common problems of political management and political change. The 'statists' also stressed the importance of the benefits that accrued to the state from participating in integrating organisations. The British economic historian Alan Milward, in an argument which inspired much protest from 'Europeanists', maintained that the European institutions, rather than surpassing the nation-state, had saved it, allowing the European states to consolidate and strengthen after the destruction of the two world wars. He viewed the various European organisations as instruments in a calculated game of securing national advantage.[9] In this view, integration was neither a technical nor a sociological process. Rather, it was a political strategy, consciously engineered. Nor was it opposed to the modern nation-state. Rather, it was part of its evolution, securing it and allowing it to survive.

Another sort of politicism was federalism. Federal theorists argued that the 'sociological' theories placed a misguided emphasis on 'automaticity'. The growing European federal movement wished to see a genuine federation emerge between European states, of common laws and common decision-making. But federalists believed that a genuine and long-lasting union required a conscious political will, not mere technological or social drives.[10] They maintained that the functional theorists encouraged publics to believe that integration was inevitable, whereas it was not. They also argued that the functional theorists were not only distorting the facts, but blunting the impetus to a genuine federation in Europe. According to federal theory, for a true federation or single community to be built, states and peoples had consciously and willingly to agree a formal transfer of real and substantial political authority to central European institutions. As for the organisations that had emerged, the federalists argued that these were merely administrative, not true political unions.[11] In fact, they agreed with the politicists' view that integration as actually practised was intended to save the nation-state, though they scarcely shared the politicists' satisfaction with that conclusion.

Explanatory problems in both approaches

Both types of theory faced obvious problems. The federal theories suffered from the self-evident fact that no governments and few citizens actually wanted to build a federal Europe. For a theory which depended on volition, this was scarcely a recommendation.

The major problem confronting the social determinists was accounting for the actual arrangements which had emerged. While some level of co-ordination may have been required by advanced industrial countries, it was also true that the same functions might have been carried out in a variety of different ways. Neither Haas nor Deutsch could explain the specifics of the various organisations, nor why they were limited to Western Europe, when other industrial powers and other knowledge-communities also existed.

Moreover, institutional development did not always conform to the theoretical expectation. It became evident, as integration proceeded, that there was nothing automatic about spill-over, a central causal explanator in Haas' theory. The evolution of the Economic Community demonstrated that integration could stall or even reverse, with failure backwashing into agreements already achieved.

What was perhaps more relevant, however, was the emergence of often conflicting criteria by which the integration process was tested. The different theories produced a variety of analytical approaches to the integration process, as well as quite different tests of success.

Testing integration

Functional theory demonstrated a central confusion as to whether it was elites or rather the supra-national agency that was the central factor. According to many functionalists, the greater the powers and scope of the Commission, the more the European system could be considered a genuine political system; and these continuously scrutinised the development of the Commission's powers and competences for signs that the Community was moving forward to a more complete union. By contrast, elite socialisation provided a somewhat different test: according to Haas, it was the degree to which national elites and national interest groups sought redress for sectoral claims at the higher European level that determined the degree of social and political cohesion exhibited by the emerging community. Still other functionalists chose, as a sign of a real community, a significant displacement of functions, from the state to the European level.

For the federalists, by contrast, the characteristic signs of a real community were common law-making, especially in the classic areas of defence and foreign policy. But the emphases were placed differently. According to some federalists, one should look for a gradual enlargement of common European constitutional law. According to others, the real test of federal Europe was, finally, a common foreign policy. Still others stressed increased powers for the European Parliament in the policy process.

Such different criteria led inevitably to different assessments of the European system, and to very different accounts of the depth and nature of the European union.

The depth of functional Europe

From a functional point of view, Europe was somewhat of a mixed bag. In one aspect, the European organisations presented the profile of an impressively growing and expanding union, since the system increasingly covered many of the functions performed by states. But by this criterion it was also incomplete, depending far too much upon state officials and state discretion in the execution of common policies. Moreover, while the functions of the European institutions grew, they did not supplant the functions performed by states. Well into the 1990s, European state-members were continuing to provide the vast majority of social security provision, as well as defence and justice – and out of state, not Community, taxes. The European organisations were sub-system dominant, in the language of systems analysis, in that it was difficult for the whole to be greater than the sum of its parts.

The degree of elite socialisation towards common European and Community norms was also debatable. It was a common observation that bureaucrats underwent a process of 'Europeanisation' during service in Brussels, and would support the goals of union, but it was equally noticeable that they differed on what they meant by union. They also took national orientations and national administrative and political styles, as well as differing values, into the various organisations.[12] The Berlymont Palace, where much of the administration of the European Economic Community occurred, displayed a rather delightful babel of national styles, which were quite identifiable as to source. The distinct national viewpoints, moreover, often influenced policy choices. This feature disconcerted the functionalists, who found it difficult to explain.

It was true that the first Commission, led by Walter Hallstein, was uniformly pro-European. More significantly, its members also shared similar views on both the end-goal of the unity process and the means to achieve it. But this unity did not survive the first serious attack on the Community institutions, mounted by the French president, Charles de Gaulle, during the early 1960s. In response, moreover, the Commission not only divided but it divided along national, not ideological, lines, with the Dutch commissioner Mansholt refusing to proceed with common policies unless Gaullist influence was curtailed, a position which both the Belgian and the German commissioners refused to support.[13] Later, as more states joined the Economic Community, the Commission became even more nationalised, and often there was no sharing of goals between commissioners.

Moreover, while the early officials of the various institutions tended to think of their career patterns in purely European terms, increasingly this changed. By the 1980s, it was noticeable that commissioners tended to regard service in Brussels as a staging post to governmental service. This did not imply that there was not a single system, in this case of bureaucratic rewards. On the contrary, for many continental bureaucrats, European office was incorporated into a hierarchy of bureaucratic and political offices. But increasingly the apogee of that hierarchy was seen to be high *national* office, not European office. The same applied to members of the European Parliament, many of whom saw service in Europe as an apprenticeship for national parliamentary service. Otherwise, they were treated as retirement posts for those whose more active careers were coming to an end. Both implied that the European system was sub-system dominant.

The extent of federal Europe

From the viewpoint of federal theory, the different institutions varied enormously in degrees of federalism. Indeed, in strict federal terms there were at least three distinct types of union in the system. First, there was the culture union of vaguely shared ideological objectives, such as the Council of Europe. Second, there was the 'administrative union' where member-states simply lent their administrative competences to common exercise – notably, the Coal and Steel Community. Finally, there was the formal confederation, a genuine union but where common policies emerged by unanimity among participating states – increasingly, the Common Market.

Even doubtful federalists had to acknowledge, however, that there were genuine federal features throughout the system.

The most notable of these was the division of competence. If not strictly legally, then in policy terms, both administrative unions and the confederation displayed a pattern by which some matters remained with national parliaments and some matters were passed up to the European bodies, as was the common practice in a federation. Also, the various ministerial councils which decided policy were only comprehensible by federal theory: they were all genuine legislators. All had contractually defined policy responsibilities, agreed in a founding document, and they made common policies which, once achieved, became binding on all.

There was also the distinctive character of European law. In 1964, the EEC Court declared in a landmark case that Community law must take precedence over domestic law, the case of *Costa v ENEL*. (Costa was an Italian who refused to pay his electricity bill because, he claimed, the new nationalised Italian electricity industry was contrary to the letter, as well as the spirit, of the Rome Treaty.) Building on this case, some jurists began to argue that Community law was a hybrid form of law, somewhere between international and domestic law, and that the true model of it was federal law. The idea of European law as a form of federal law had important implications for all Community law, since it implied a hierarchy of laws, in which federal law took precedence over national law. Whether, however, the federal metaphor was any more apt than the 'functional' metaphor was a moot point.

The limitations to federal Europe

In the first place, there was a constant quarrel among the early federalists as to the proper direction for the future federal Europe. In the early days, federalists viewed the Common Market with suspicion as being merely an 'economic' union directed essentially at the regulation of European states' foreign economic policies. But a genuine common foreign policy continually eluded the European Union. The famous third pillar, agreed at Maastricht in the early 1990s, allowed for little more than foreign policy co-ordination, and among still autonomous foreign ministries. Moreover, at the end of the Cold War, the states of Western Europe became even more anxious to maintain autonomy over foreign policy, at least for the transitional period. (It was also clear that Nato's survival meant that it would be the more significant locus of foreign policy co-ordination.)

Second, the common institutions, while they had extensive autonomous powers, were also suspiciously centralist from a federal point of view. At the heart of the new Europe was a 'power duopoly' between a political secretariat and an inter-state council. Moreover, within the duopoly, the Commission was given the role of defining the European interest over the entire Community and it could propose policies for the whole, in any matter of its choosing, neither of which would be usual in a true federation. The Commission also tended to guard its prerogatives rather jealously. Only one Commission president, Gaston Thorn, was ever responsive to claims by the European Parliament for an enhanced role, since that development would have undercut the Commission's claim to be the only body which 'represented' Europe. The Commission also, and significantly, acted as a broker of national interests, which enhanced the diplomatic (as opposed to democratic) aspects of the union.[14] (The other part of the duopoly, the Council, represented the member-states, and it was clearly a confederal rather than a federal body, since a veto effectively operated over central areas of decision-making; it was also this confederal body, not the Commission, which made European law.)

Another principle which the most federal of the institutions offended was in the area of division of competence. While federal unions often had an admixture (and some confusion) of responsibilities between 'federal' and state authorities, there generally was a way of establishing who had the final authority in each area. In the case of the European Union, however, no such clear precedence was ever established, even where joint policies had been agreed. Many areas, such as energy policy, aspects of trade policy and monetary policy, were 'mixed' areas, where Europe was given an interest and a right to propose policies but where states did not abandon their own prerogatives. Even in agriculture, the area where European bureaucrats had the clearest and fullest competences, states retained rights to introduce special agricultural provisions, and it was left to other states to argue that such provisions were inconsistent with treaty provisions. In consequence, there was no clear division of competence; and this necessarily qualified the system's federal as well as its confederal aspects.

The question of legal subordination was also confused. On the one hand, it became increasingly accepted within the several European juridical orders that European law, when duly agreed by the various states, took precedence over state law. State after state gradually accepted the ascendancy of European law within its own legal system. But the ability of the juridical system to produce a steady view of that law was lacking, since it was applied by national courts, and those courts had no obligation to send for a European reading or interpretation. Moreover, there was no way contestants at law could appeal directly to a European court on most of the administrative and technical matters with which the various institutions dealt; they had to be content with the readings of their own national courts. This left room for idiosyncratic interpretations of European law, as each local judge was able to decide cases on his own. It also left room for calculations of national advantage. (In cases of public procurement, for example, a foreign contractor could claim disadvantage in a national court, but the national court might well favour the domestic over the foreign contractor, especially if the case were local.) It was also up to national courts to decide upon, and the national authorities to enforce, punishments. This meant variable penalties. Moreover, while European Community law directly passed down into the European state orders, it co-existed alongside a variety of distinct national laws within different national juridical systems; and it was incorporated into those systems in a variety of ways. For this reason alone, it remained unclear that the European legal order really constituted a single legal order.

The European Community as a unique political system

Considered in all its parts, few doubted that the European Community (created by the union of the Coal and Steel Market and the Common Market in the mid-1970s) constituted a political system of some sort. Its weighted majorities, juridical nature and common policies brought states and populations to interact more intensely and to focus more steadily on political developments in one another's countries, particularly those that had implications for their common enterprise, than would otherwise have been the case. Moreover, its institutions became arenas for political activism, and not just of governments, but also directly by groups of citizens as well as by sub-state administrative and political bodies. A political system was such because it directed the activities of its participants and brought them to a single focus: few doubted that the European Community accomplished such a feat. The most popular work on the Community treated it like a national system.[15]

As a political system, however, it was curiously diversified. Influence could be brought to bear from many directions. Moreover, the Commission allowed very different sorts of political animals to move it in the formulation of policy, mixing states and interest groups simultaneously. This alone made it difficult to identify within any recognised political typology. Leon Lindberg, with some exaspera-tion, would eventually refer to it as a 'sui-generis political system of a pluralist type'.[16] Donald Puchala, another American political scientist, in a famous characterisation which became quite popular during the 1970s, called it a *concordance system*, a term which implied, however, a new kind of international relations, not a new kind of super-state.[17]

Behavioural models were frequently applied to the developing European Community to try to characterise it more closely. According to behavioural theory, the degree of community development could be tested by observing the behaviour of interest and cause groups. In a development of pluralism, behaviourists argued that interest groups were rational actors who would focus their efforts at the points where real influence might be brought to bear on policy-making. Accordingly, if such groups acted at a European level and through co-ordinated action, this would tend to suggest a substantially unified political system.

Here, however, the criteria fell short of demonstrating a clear preference for Community over national levels of action.

Originally, the Commission required that all groups who wished to approach it be 'Euro-organised'; that is, they had to form into single European interest groups. Accordingly, around the Commission offices in Brussels grew the offices of various European interest groups which were federations of national groups. How firm these groups were, however, varied. Some were no more than loose co-ordinating bodies; most were small and had only a few officers. Moreover, none could control the activities of constituent members. Local, regional and national interest groups all continued to operate both independently and more or less opportunistically, sometimes acting collectively through their European office, sometimes acting on their own. Nor did they limit their activities to Community institutions. On the contrary, they kept close to their national governments, who increasingly took care to consult with major groups when some contentious piece of European legislation was pending.

Whether such groups truly mobilised their members and influenced policy was also a question. According to the rules, the Commission was to be neutral in policy-formation and accordingly it was to 'receive' views. In fact, however, it used interest groups to mobilise public opinion in support of its policies as much as it sought advice from them. Moreover, an important function of all groups was to process information on Community developments and to pass it down to their members. In other words, they were as much transmission belts for passing policy downwards as generators of political impetus upwards.[18] Moreover, the more important the groups were, and the more power they might have to determine Community policy, the more the various states took care to monitor their activities and influence their views.

The case was somewhat different for the large organised commercial and economic interests. The very largest European firms had increasingly direct access to the Commission, particularly during and after the decision to create a truly single market, taken during the late 1980s. Jacques Delors, the commissioner who initiated the single-market programme, began to convene meetings of the large industrial, commercial and financial interests and listened carefully to their views, many of which influenced the single market legislation.[19] Moreover, part of the intention of the single market was to allow for the creation of very large European firms, through mergers and acquisitions, able to compete on the world market.

In the event, a large number of mergers did occur, but not only among European firms. Many American companies also joined the merger game. Allowing the Commission to deal directly with 'interests' did not necessarily strengthen an independent or self-conscious European presence.

Europe as an object of popular loyalty

If political scientists asked such questions, it was because they were looking for objective signs of the state of the integration process. They wished to determine whether Europe was uniting in fact. But objective elements were only one aspect of community development. There was also the subjective element, the degree to which the institutions, as well as the 'European idea', had worked their way into popular consciousness. Given the democratic ideal, 'elective affinity' was considered an important aspect of any political community. Indeed, federalists such as Altiero Spinelli had insisted that Europe could only be unified, finally, on the basis of a united popular will. Even the functionalists came to accept the importance of what they called 'permissive consensus', the willingness of various national populations generally to support the goals of union.[20]

The testing of popular loyalty to political institutions was a major feature of the new political science, and survey techniques were familiar elements of it. Accordingly, the new technique was also applied to the European system by the Commission via the 'Eurobarometer' surveys, which tested popular attitudes across member-states. In addition, there were numerous national surveys which tested various national opinions at different points.[21] What they revealed, however, was ambiguous and often difficult to interpret.

In the first place, the surveys themselves were decidedly timid. They generally required only positive or negative responses to the question of whether European unity was a good thing, and in all its diverse features, confederal, federal and consensual. They did not enquire whether populations actually desired a federal union, much less amalgamation into a single political community. Moreover, and it was not insignificant from the point of view of popular attitudes, it was taken for granted that populations would answer negatively to such direct questions. Accordingly, it was deemed better to avoid them, if what was desired was a view of popular attitudes to the current state of play. The surveys also tested the opinions of distinct national electorates. They did not, for example, test socialist opinion across Europe or liberal opinion or conservative opinion, to correlate Euro-loyalty with particular cross-European ideologies, nor did they often correlate Euro-loyalty with age or occupation. Such surveys also asked different questions at different times, which made it difficult to read them as constant trend demonstrators.

Some experts went to so far as to doubt any general trend, either for or against European unity. One theory correlated the points at which the British were the most enthusiastic about union (never more than 54 per cent) with the points at which the issue had high saliency within contemporary debate; that is, European issues were most debated, and European sentiment mobilised, when some British interest or policy was being affected. This indicated that, in Britain at least, there was a strongly instrumental view of European unity, and that 'Euro-enthusiasm' correlated with the degree to which greater unity served some British national or sectoral interest. This had important implications for the European construction: it implied that an equal enthusiasm might exist for any international organisation to which Britain belonged, on similar grounds. Accordingly, a favourable opinion towards European union did not imply any transfer of loyalties to a European political body.

In other countries as well, the 'permissive consensus', as Lindberg called it, appeared to relate to the ability of the respective government to link particular national requirements to the progress of union. Popular support was essentially utilitarian.[22]

It also correlated with low levels of politicisation. Popular opinion was most supportive when the organisations appeared to be simple technical or administrative bodies, serving the general well-being within an already agreed political framework. In 1990, the single-market legislation was deemed to require a popular referendum, since it altered the Community considerably. At that time, however, the Europe of blocs was dissolving, and the new provisions became linked to intensely political questions about Europe's future, whether it should expand to the east and the role of a more powerful united Germany within it. The process turned out to be remarkably painful, and generated antithetical attitudes which sent the Eurobarometer surveys to historic low levels of popular support for the European venture.

Europe and the locus of popular sovereignty

But perhaps the most important question which might reasonably be asked of the emerging European system was the locus of the final legitimating authority within it. Here, the relevant question was: Which political community determined, finally, the direction and purpose of the union? Here, at least, there could be little doubt as to where sovereignty lay. This was with the separate political communities that made up the union.

The point was amply demonstrated during the series of referenda to ratify the move towards a single market, undertaken during the course of 1992 and 1993. At that point, despite the fact that the European Community had been in existence for some thirty-five years, there was no question of an open vote being taken across Europe, much less through the mandating of European parliamentary representatives on the basis of the European constituencies. Indeed, neither option appears even to have been considered. Instead, there were a series of national ratifying processes. Moreover, each national community had to agree before the ratification process was completed. None doubted the rights of the smallest political community to express its views on Europe, as well as the largest, despite the fact that this might hold up the progress of the rest.

Accordingly, we may conclude that the sense of political community, the arena within which ultimate public choices were finally determined, had shifted very little during the period of the European Union's existence, despite the enormous weight of the new organisation and its importance for national policy-making.

Notes

1 See Brigid Laffan on 'people's Europe': *Integration and Co-operation in Europe* (London: Routledge, 1992).
2 E.g. Jacques Freymond, *Western Europe Since the War* (New York and London: Praeger, 1964).
3 See C. Pentland, *International Theory and European Integration* (London: Faber, 1973).
4 Karl Deutsch *et al.*, *Political Community and the North Atlantic Area* (Princeton: Princeton University Press, 1957).
5 Ernst Haas, *The Uniting of Europe* (Stanford: Stanford University Press, 1958).
6 *The Political Dynamics of European Economic Integration* (Stanford and Oxford: Oxford University, 1963).
7 Altiero Spinelli's *The European Adventure* (London: Charles Knight, 1972) was an influential account in this vein.
8 Coral Bell's 'The Diplomatic Meanings of Europe' in C. Bell (ed.), *Europe without Britain* (Melbourne: F.W. Cheshire, 1963) was an early instance and Andrew Moravascik's 'Negotiating the Single European Act: national interests and conventional statecraft in the European Community', *International Organization* 1991, pp. 19–56, a famous instance.
9 *The European Rescue of the Nation-State* (London: Routledge, 1992).
10 Spinelli and those of the 'Italian school' were the most determined federalists; see A. Bosco (ed.), *The Federal Idea*, vol. 2 (London: Lothian, 1991).
11 See A. Spinelli, *L'europa non cade dal cielo* (*Europe Will Not Fall from the Sky*) (Bologna: Il Mulino, 1960).
12 J. Sewell, *Functionalism and World Politics* (Princeton: Princeton University Press, 1966).

13 Miriam Camps, *What Kind of Europe?* (London: Oxford University Press, 1965).

14 An early study of the Commission's conflicting roles was David Combes, *Politics and Bureaucracy in the European Community* (London: George Allen and Unwin, 1970).

15 N. Nugent, *The Government and Politics of the European Community* (London: Macmillan, 1989, 1991).

16 L. Lindberg and S. Scheingold, *Europe's Would-Be Polity* (Englewood Cliffs: Prentice Hall, 1970).

17 Puchala, 'Of blind men, elephants and international integration', *Journal of Common Market Studies*, 10 (1971), pp. 732–63.

18 E. Kirchner and K. Schwaiger, *The Role of Interest Groups in the European Community* (Aldershot: Gower, 1981).

19 W. Sandholtz and J. Zysman, '1992: Recasting the European Bargain', *World Politics*, 42 (1989–90), pp. 95–128.

20 L. Lindberg and S. Scheingold, *Europe's Would-Be Polity* (Englewood Cliffs: Prentice Hall, 1970) pp. 45–63.

21 Reviewed in M. Hewstone, *Understanding Attitudes to the European Community, a Socio-Psychological Study in Four Member-states* (Cambridge: Cambridge University Press, 1986).

22 M. Slater, 'Political elites, popular indifference and community building', *Journal of Common Market Studies*, 21 (1982), pp. 69–87.

19 The revolution of internationalism

The persistence of the lineaments of the state through the most thoroughgoing internationalist experiment, together with its continued dominance of diplomacy, law and alliances, raises questions about the nature of the transformation which the twentieth century witnessed. If, even within the European Community, states remained recognisably states, with foreign offices, autonomous armies and independent judicial systems, and if they remained obstinate objects of loyalty, then what meaning can be given to internationalism? What did it add to the corpus of political thought and practice, and what part of the political map did it occupy? Was it merely the rearticulation of the state within a still traditionally conceived diplomacy, or did it specify a new kind of state in a new kind of international order?

Part of the answer may be found in the major political transformation which attended its development: the historical transformation from empire to nation-state. 'Decolonisation' began during the 1920s. With the demise of the Soviet Union after 1989, the process was virtually complete. It was a transformation which involved not merely the creation of a number of separate sovereignties and new states but also the decline of the imperial idea. By the time of Victoria's accession as Empress of India in 1887, imperialism had regained force as a political vision, engulfing all social orders to a greater or lesser degree. Continental Europe also succumbed: even Belgium became involved in colonial ventures. Even after Versailles, when the defeated lost their colonies and the mandate system was established, imperial practices remained the norm. The British and French empires continued to grow, and even America flirted with the idea of becoming an imperial power. Increasingly after 1925, however, under the press of necessity and political circumstances, it gradually ceased to guide policy. Declining numbers in the metropolitan countries would be held by the idea of being citizens of an empire, less and less would it seem the natural orientation of a Great Power, and less would it appear a solution to political and economic problems. After 1945, governments had few lingering political ambitions to administer territories far from their metropolitan centres, except in instances where the imperial game had given them foreign base facilities of immediate strategic advantage.

In this sense, the 'international' represents a fundamental shift and a revolutionary response. It marked the death of the idea that empire was the normal accoutrement of a Great Power, and the assumption that the normal pattern of political development would be the self-responsive political community with a self-determining life of its own. Relations were to be inter-national, between self-determining political groups which decided their own patterns of development, and whose rulers were people identifiably and factually like themselves. There was to be no rule from afar.

A second fundamental change was in ideas concerning the basis of wealth-creation and the balance between endogeny and exogeny, between internally generated growth and externally located resources. During the latter part of the nineteenth century, it was accepted as common wisdom, and had become an integral part of the imperial drive, that 'trade followed the flag' and that wealth, industrial growth and direct administration of foreign territories were mutually related. Countries wanted colonies to secure strategic resources for developing industries and to protect trade and traders. Administrative colonialism was the first response to the demand for 'development', and to the growing belief in the government's power and duty to produce growth. Gradually, however, imperial development was superseded by the idea that industrial growth and national wealth were held back by the administration of poorer parts of the globe, and that an economy with both forward- and backward-looking sections was constrained by the need to deal with declining industries, less efficient traders and poor 'natives'. Growth appeared increasingly dependent on continuous modernisation of advanced 'heartland' industry, and not on 'large spaces' and extended imperial control.

This movement in thought was shortly followed by another: that advanced industry required both competition and foreign markets, and that international competition, within bounds, was an integral part of domestic industrial development. The decline of empire was followed within a remarkably short space of time by the rise and decline of 'self-sufficiency', to be replaced by the idea of the managed or directed domestic economy open to managed foreign competition and to managed trade and monetary exchange. This was not 'globalism' – no self-directing industry was set loose in a fully open global market of few regulations. Twentieth-century industrialisation proceeded within a framework of national planning and national protection, and it operated within a framework of careful international controls and cross-border regulations. It seemed, however, that too much protectionism was growth-inhibiting. Economic internationalism came to signify that particular mix of the national economy open to international competition and international regulation, with government responsibility for ensuring favourable terms in international competitiveness. It signified at one and the same time the abandonment of mid-nineteenth-century ideas of 'free trade', of early twentieth-century ideas of the imperial economic redoubt, and of the fleeting but ever reappearing ideas of national economic self-sufficiency.

Finally, there was the direction of diplomacy among industrial states with regard to questions of peace and war. Up to the First World War, recourse to arms was simply an aspect of policy to be applied to friend and foe alike, to wherever policy demanded. By its second year, however, war had become the confrontation with the radical 'other', with the deviant political community. In time, it would become the reserved domain of liberation movements and confrontations with international outlaws. It was no part of normal relations between normal states. Internationalism signified that movement in thought which consigned war to the extremities of politics, or which saw in it the abandonment of politics altogether. It implied that peace was the normal condition of the relations of states and that war was the abnormal condition.

These developments followed and to some degree depended upon other conceptual and political changes with which internationalism also came to be associated. The first were changes in the concept of sovereignty. The second involved the limits to nationalism and the techniques for its management. Finally, there was the contested idea of pluralism in the conceptualisation of the members of an international community.

The changing concept of sovereignty

The twentieth century had inherited from the nineteenth the idea of the *contrat social* or Jacobin state, in which government held the full plenitude of the sovereign powers. In Britain, the doctrine was associated with the writings of John Austin and implied the absolute sovereignty of parliament. It conceived the state as both a horizontal contract, in which the government represented all interests, and a vertical contract in which the government held all powers and devolved them downward administratively. The sovereign power was conceived to be whole, unitary and total. It could neither be divided, nor could sub-state authorities hold power in their own right; they exercised power, rather, by a form of *lèse-majesté*.

The idea continued to resonate throughout the twentieth century, but with declining force. Under attack during its first decades by various forms of pluralism, the fascist experience seriously dented it. Thereafter, it co-existed with quite different notions of the state – with the corporatist state and the pluralist state – and with quite different notions of state–society relations.

Among the new concepts was the idea that non-state associations were in some sense 'natural', with rights of their own which were, potentially, inalienable and which were exercised independently of the state. The right of free association and the right to redraft contracts, essentially middle-class rights in the nineteenth century, were widened to include trade unions as well as business groups and professional associations, and would eventually be enjoyed even by political dissidents, even when they did not promise to stay within the civil contract. Nor were these rights conceded as a matter of fact. They were regarded also as a matter of legitimacy: free-standing associations came to be seen as a barrier against totalitarianism and integral to good governance. They were deemed to perform beneficial public functions. Indeed, they were provided with public functions, such as charity, interest aggregation and 'voice'.

Second, there was federalism – the idea that sovereignty, or the public power, ought to be 'divided', and that different powers could be reposed with different authorities. At the beginning of the century, the United States seemed the exceptional political order, with its division of powers and with the extensive and inalienable rights that belonged to the separate states. Well into the 1960s, Britons would criticise the United States for the supposed 'inefficiency' of its public order and the often considerable delays in its legislative programme which the federal system was prone to produce. In Europe, federalism was generally seen as the constitutional recipe for imperfect or troubled states, applicable to Germans as a barrier against the resurgence of Nazism or to multi-ethnic post-colonial states whose separate ethnicities could not live in peace.

But the experience of 'Europe-building' brought federalism into the everyday experience of Europeans and established it as a model for other regional and international experiments. The 'new Europe' was not a federal structure along the American model: the *acquis communautaire* was a rather hazy concept which mixed ideas of the *contrat social* with a kind of integral or organic federalism. But it had obvious federal elements, such as a Court of Human Rights, and a body of European law to which citizens could appeal directly. Moreover, the requirement of making Europe more democratic – that is, making it more than a cabal of governments who could bypass their own legislatures (or, equally, more than a business coalition) – raised again and again the question of the powers of the European Parliament and how those powers should be shared with the national parliaments – a classic federal question. Increasingly, the United States would be looked to as a source of experience in how such questions might be resolved.

Finally, there was the idea of 'shared sovereignty' or confederation. The European experiment turned on the joint determination of specified policies, and co-determination implied a division of function between European and national authorities. Moreover, the considerable benefits which seemed to flow from co-determination supported the idea of a sovereignty which expressed itself, not in opposition to another's will, but in joint decision-making, and in negotiating the terms of co-operation.

None of these new ideas conflicted with internationalism. Indeed, they provided the institutional, and some of the conceptual, foundations for it. Internationalism came to be seen in terms of transnational groupings of free associations with rights of their own who petitioned governments and international organisations, and who carried out public functions of reporting, aid and humanitarian relief. International organisations were increasingly conceptualised as parallel bodies to agencies of government, with defined responsibilities in discrete areas and with their own regulatory powers. International co-operation became defined as the willingness of governments to exercise their powers jointly. Internationalism became, in effect, the external expression of the new sovereignty.

The limits of nationalism

Nationalism, by contrast, would seem to have become decidedly anti-international. During the twentieth century, nationalism emerged as the antithesis of the general, stressing particularistic claims and the values of self-consciously parochial groupings, often portrayed as exclusive and mutually antagonist. It justified self-serving foreign policies, and provided a potent source of argument against power-sharing with outsiders. Twentieth-century nationalists would also claim that their nations had rights against any putative law of nations. Moreover, some of the new nationalisms promoted the idea of self-realisation through war, and related war to community progress and self-betterment.

Nor was the tension limited to theory. During the twentieth century, nationalism was drafted, and successfully, in support of economic protectionism and drives for self-sufficiency and autarky. It was deployed to attack disarmament, and it scuttled attempts at the regularised adjudication of conflict. Above all, it was on the doctrines of organic nationalism that fascists drew to win support for aggressive fascism. It is no accident that in searching for the ideological roots of fascism, many historians have settled for nationalism: it limited individualism, subsumed the individual in the group and posited the subjectivity of all claims.

It has also proved to be a persuasive source of claims to limit liberal rights, on which internationalism rose and on which it largely depended. Internationalism is, after all, the foreign policy stance of the liberal state. Nationalism, by contrast, asks for and often gains the subordination of liberal rights to a collective good. Moreover, nationalism has been used to trump rights. It has, for example, been used, and successfully, to trump the universalism of rights.

It is not surprising, in the circumstances, that many contemporary liberals lost faith with nationalism, nor that it began to be seen as the antithesis to internationalism. Certainly in Europe, dedicated Europeans began to speak of the need to transform identity in order to create a new European sense of grouping; and, by its last decade, the argument had become prevalent that identity transformation was the final key to a genuine 'transnational' creation in Europe.

But it was a painful separation. From the first appearance of the nineteenth-century nationalist uprisings, liberals had regarded nationalism as the key to 'identity transformation', to rights and to internationalism. The nineteenth-century nationalist agitations in Poland and in the Balkans appeared to the majority in the liberal movement to signal not merely the death knell of the unreformed, anti-progressive autarchies of Russia, Prussia and Austria, but the active agents of a wide-ranging psychological and social transformation whose end would be the creation of 'new citizens'. The 'New Europe' movement, formed in Britain just before and after the First World War, actively promoted the creation of independent national states in Central Europe as the basis for the extension of liberal constitutionalism to the rest of the European family; and proponents of a Europe of nation-states argued that the recognition of 'new' nations would force the construction of a new, pacific and co-operative international order more generally. Even the 'newer' nationalisms, the Chinese and Arab nationalisms, were seen to presage reform and modernisation, and to be creating the possibilities for a global liberal contract. Up to the 1930s, most liberals relied on nationalism to deliver internationalism.

Nor was the separation ever complete. The liberal parlay was not, in fact, to overthrow nationalism but to surround it with conditions. In 1920, in the framework of the League, there was the condition of equal treatment for minorities. In 1946, there were formulated the international crimes against humanity and peace and the crime of aggressive war. In 1948, there was the Universal Declaration of Human Rights. These new rules were intended to create a normative and quasi-legal framework to curb rather than annihilate nationalism. Moreover, they anchored the critical distinction between 'good' and 'bad' nationalisms. Rather than condemn nationalism wholesale, the prevalent tendency after the 1930s was to identify some nationalisms as special cases – as 'backward' nationalisms or 'immature' nationalisms or 'malignant' nationalisms – and to establish criteria for their identification. The various international rights documents were those criteria.

The crux of the matter was self-determination. Liberals were unable to throw off the impression that self-determination was in some sense the fundamental right, and that a group in search of such a right had a legitimate claim. Nor did liberals reject the idea that self-determination might have to encompass the culture-community as well as the rights-community. Room would be made in liberal theory for groupings whose culture was being threatened with extinction, and for rights of 'voice' on some sort of ethnic ground.

The eventual liberal compromise turned on a conjunction between identity and territoriality. Where a group could demonstrate intra-communal conscious-ness, generally of an historically substantive variety, and where it occupied a more or less defined territory, it was generally conceded that some sort of right to a separate voice existed. Nor was this a mere concession. An identifiable group in possession of a territory and fighting against subordination was generally seen as a movement worthy of support on genuinely liberal grounds and its struggle as integral to the liberal cause. Liberals only turned against those nationalisms which proved to be illiberal.

This method of discrimination was not confined to the academies. On the contrary, it guided mainstream liberal public opinion through the whole course of the twentieth century, and would be demonstrated in the repeated tendency of liberal publics to support nationalist movements when they promised to reform, or endeavoured to escape from, communist or other forms of autocracy, and to deplore such movements when they promised illiberal or aggressive political orders of their own or when they suppressed the ethnic minorities within their midst.

It would seem, therefore, that many liberals made a kind of peace with nationalism, and that they did not cease on that account to be internationalists. The question is, were they wrong?

The limits of 'liberal nationalism'

Liberal nationalism enjoys three defences, of varying solidity. First, there is a – somewhat weak – historical defence, deriving from the historical coincidence of the two doctrines. In the historical time-flow, the most vigorous development of nationalism accompanied the most vigorous development of liberal internationalism. This synchronicity cannot be a mere accident: it must have an explanation, and one, moreover, which relates the two. In the second place, there is an empirical defence related to nationalism's cultural claims: these are not all parochial – some make more universal claims than others. Third, there is a philosophical defence which turns on the relationship between nationalism and rights. It maintains that the language of nationalism is also, and necessarily, the language of rights, but equally of a rather conflictual sense of rights.

The parallel trajectories of nationalism and internationalism relate to their nature as opposed political claims. It was when one pressed that the other appeared. Rights-internationalism was invented when nationalism began to threaten rights. Equally, the various demands of internationalism, including the claim that internationally protected human rights should take precedence over all other claims – even to the extent of justifying intervention – have produced the strong counter-claim that states have rights of their own, connected to the choices of their people. Each movement took part of its drive from the movement of the other.

In this dialectical process, there is a functional differentiation. In it, the international represents a form of general claim, putatively on behalf of mankind or the international community but in reality on behalf of outsiders in the context of nationalist politics, which provides non-nationals with a *locus standi* against the self-determination claims of a national community. It also takes the form of a collective claim, of some international collective body representing some international community against some 'deviant' member of that community. In general, in the dialectic between internationalism and nationalism, internationalism has served, paradoxically, as the collective claim, and nationalism has served as the 'individualist' trump claim: it is used to trump the collective.

We should also observe that internationalism was largely defined in the context of circumscribing nationalism, and that it was the agreed limits of nationalism which created many of the doctrines associated with internationalism. The justification of war in terms of self-defence, a central tenet of internationalism, was formulated out of a regard for what was due to the nation-state in the context of a wide-ranging debate on the war-right. The 'European' was articulated out of a concern for the mutually destructive aspects of European nationalism, and was first shaped with an eye to reducing the availability of the 'national' economy to aggressive nationalist political ambitions. Internationalism in the United States is the opposed doctrine to either unilateralism or isolationism, and implies multilateralism and positive engagement. The two doctrines are related, in that they are mutually self-defining.

The political context of these rhetorical appeals is often characterised in terms of an equal and pervasive interdependence. In fact, it is a world of inequalities, of labour divisions among unequal partners, and of mutual dependencies between sectors which provide different services and which receive different comparative value for those services. It is also a world of separate political authorities which have to manage such inequalities and uncomfortable dependencies. This is *asymmetrical interdependence*; it locks parts of the world together into relations of potential subordination and relative inequality: the genuine interdependence of equal partners exchanging equally valuable goods whose products can be used to purchase other equally valued goods is exceedingly scarce. The growth of asymmetrical interdependence, both in the twentieth century and in the decades immediately before it, produced management needs and engendered policy responses directed to avoiding or mitigating dependency, and to achieving some measure of mutual benefit. It was when asymmetrical interdependence began to demand policy responses that nationalism and internationalism began to appear.

The relevant matter is the way in which each has confined the other. Significantly, while internationalism has limited some rights to parochialism, it has given way to others. It has outlawed autarky but it has justified the optimum tariff. It has limited economic protectionism to the clear demonstration of economic benefit, but benefit understood in terms of equality between identifiable groups. It has demanded co-ordination, policy harmonisation and demonstrable gains for a citizenry. But it has unseated neither independent states with independent foreign policies nor governments who are responsible to self-determining communities, nor has it in any sense reduced the responsibilities of government for the security and economic well-being of those communities.

Nationalism thus appears to be the 'higher' doctrine, but within bounds. Increasingly, the demand has become that the goods nationalism reputedly procures should be demonstrable, and that they should, in Bentham's words, 'do no more harm to others than good to oneself'. Utilitarian or functional nationalism has become, in practice, the approved form. What liberal nationalism demands is that nationalists demonstrate a compatibility between their local aims and some definition of the general good or species humanity.

A second consideration concerns the sorts of cultural claims that nationalism makes. If nationalism was an invention, still it had perforce to draw on local cultural resources. It is also the case that the more successful nationalisms were connected to high and not 'parochial' cultures. Whereas Hungarians and Slavs had to break with the high Latin, Catholic and universal civilisation of their imperial masters and to draw on local, often peasant, practice, Greek nationalism drew on the cultural heritage of Greek civilisation, and connected rural and Ottomanised Greeks to a continuous and universal set of cultural categories. The major European nationalisms all drew upon continuous developments from Roman times, and connected ordinary people, often sunk in local customs, with 'high' cultures which gave them access to more general political and social practices and systems of belief. Chinese nationalism is a civilisation in the guise of a nation. Arab nationalism draws as much on the high culture of twelfth- to fifteenth-century Islam as on the low culture of the Bedu experience.

Their high-culture content may explain why some nationalisms saw little conflict with internationalism, and why some nationalists could argue that their nationalism would lay the foundations for internationalism. If a nationalism connected ordinary citizens to universal concepts, such as citizenship, rights, self-betterment and progress, then the achievement of self-determination on such foundations was itself the preparation for a union, not merely of high-culture elites, but of peoples. It also implied the possibility of a genuinely democratic compact among nation-states. Moreover, there would be material among the compactors for cross-national comprehension. It also meant, however, that other sorts of nationalism would have to be excluded.

The more questionable part of the liberal compromise was the conception of rights it entailed, and the relationship between individual rights and national self-determination. The question some liberal defectors posed was whether a 'nation', or some other identifiable group, such as a territorial group, had to have rights in order for individuals to have rights, and whether this concession endangered the whole concept of rights. Some liberal theorists argued that the idea of national or 'collective' rights placed the group above the individual and threatened the proposition, central to the concept of rights, that individuals were the primary bearers of rights. If this were true, then the attempt to bound nationhood with rights, the central tenet of the liberal compromise, would fail, leaving nations free to define any sort of qualifications for membership of their group, including the most illiberal. In brief, were liberal nationalists being led down the road of denying the primacy of rights by conceding the right of national self-determination?

It is true that national self-determination is an odd form of right. It is a form of collective right: a group makes the claim. Individuals cannot claim a right to political self-determination alone; they must exercise that particular right together with others. It is, however, no less a right, and it only makes sense within a rights-based conceptual framework. When empires broke into their component parts, the operative concept was one of equal rights as against those who did not recognise the fundamental equality of putative rights-holders. It was a right that was being claimed from someone who was denying this right.

Nor should we be misled by its collective nature. The consciousness of nationhood, and most other forms of group identity, lie within the individual. National self-consciousness is not merely ascribed; it must be felt by, or make sense to, the relevant individuals for the identity claim to be substantiated. It then proceeds on the basis of the individual's right to choose by whom to be ruled and to decide what form of rule, reflected in the requirement for national referenda and national elections. Politically, nationalism does little more than explain, or argue, within which group, and together with which relevant others, that right should be exercised, and whose set of interests and self-conceptions it should serve.

The necessary link between rights and nationhood is not merely a political fact, it is a sociological requirement. Nationalism developed where status-linkages were breaking down, and where equality became the only basis for common action. It also became prevalent during the formation of an intricate division of labour, with the result that, sociologically, there are few sufficiently strong similarities among any large national grouping such that a single general claim would satisfy all interests. Nationalism in such circumstances can be little more than a form of null hypothesis: its fundamental and most substantive claim is that, whoever we are, we should all be treated the same. The most effective language of equal treatment is the language of rights. Thus nations were not merely engendered on the basis of rights: their being-as-nations embroils them constantly in claims and counter-claims based on ascribed rights.

The combination of ethnic groups who are rights-seekers affords no easy guide to diplomatic practice. The twentieth-century citizenry may be a group of people whose rights are guaranteed by a constitution, but try as it might the state has not succeeded in throwing off the obligation to defend the rights of a specific people with a particular historical consciousness and particular ways of going on. Few operative theories of political legitimation in the liberal era have rested on abstract rights alone. Most twentieth-century governments, as well as popular movements, have bowed to and drawn upon the historically present values, indeed the historically contingent ideas of rights, derived from being a particular sort of people with a particular historical trajectory. At the same time, rights claims provide the political bases for different sorts of treatment, and they move power around: rights empower different groups at the expense of other groups. The conjunction of the two means that there will be inevitable conflicts between incompatible rights claimants, often on an ethnic basis. Rights-talk is a form of political ideology, not an escape from it.

The result has been a continuous tension in international political theory, reflected not least in the contemporary debate between 'communitarians' and 'cosmopolitans'. The central ethical questions in this debate are whether states represent values *qua* states or whether they are merely the agent of some higher good, and whether nations are legal fictions or whether they are, in some substantive sense, the condition for becoming humans. In it, those who believe the state is a good in itself are accused of 'romancing the nation-state', while they accuse their opponents of neglecting the importance of states-rights in the achievement of individual and human rights. The agenda of this body of theorising is to locate the higher order principle which will finally resolve the two.

But the contrary claims of nations and humans are not the only source of tension in theorising the ethical basis of an international order. Behind the conflict of cosmopolitanism and communitarianism lurks the janus of pluralism, as that relates to our understanding of the ends or purposes of an international political order. The more fundamental question is whether the international order is to be understood as a form of universal order with a single end towards which all parts are moving, or whether it should be understood, rather, as a pluralistic order which has no ends of its own. The conception of nationalism, and the sorts of curbs that should be put upon it, turn upon whether it is seen as a staging post to a single, higher order, or whether it represents the abandonment of any single telos altogether.

Internationalism and pluralism

Pluralism was not much in vogue in thinking about international relations in the twentieth century. To the more radical left, it implied a form of false consciousness concerning the realities of power. The left repudiated pluralism because it (falsely) represented the state as constituted by equal and similar claimants, each with roughly equal access to the sources of power. If they rejected this as an appropriate approach to political processes within the state, still less did it seem an appropriate portrayal of international relationships, where inequality and structured relations of dominance and subordination seemed to prevail.

For the 'new' liberals, by contrast, the problem was not power but *interests*. In the liberal conception, where a multiplicity of states serve diverse populations with no over-arching contract, pluralism signified the inevitability of a diversity of interests, and established the diversity of interests as the chief obstacle to international co-operation. The major agenda for the liberal theorising of international relations has been how to overcome the diversity of interests, generally through an articulation of, and an emphasis on, common or compatible interests, or through the promotion of legalised forms of interest adjudication.

In each case, the tendency has been to produce ethical theories of international relations which emphasise universal experiences and draw from and elaborate concepts of universal ends. On the left, this has generally taken the form of claims to the universality of exploitation and to a stress on the common and universal experience of being oppressed. The concept of exploitation, in turn, identified a single end to which all humans were moving – the end of liberation – and the necessary commonality of liberation. Equally, though in a different key, liberal universalising looked to a common humanity regulated by a common law – a legal community of mankind. It has at times even assumed the existence of a palpable historical movement which would take all humans to such a community, either in the form of a universal recognition of rights or a universal acceptance of reciprocal duties, to be inculcated by education and processes of self and communal development.

But pluralism's meaning is exhausted neither by the conceptual discomforts of a diversity of power nor by the self-evident existence of an unfortunate diversity of interests. It was also the liberal version of an older idea which rejected the *summum bonum* or highest good, and whose proponents doubted the proposition of a single end for all humanity. It moreover validated the pursuit of a diversity of ends. Liberal pluralism is the liberal version of the civic republican ideal of non-domination in the pursuit of a diversity of ends, and civic republican thought posed the possibility of form of political order in which a diverse, and free, citizenry could pursue a diversity of ends together.

The international has, in consequence, become charged with diverse significations and contrary meanings. At one extreme, there is the internationalism of the brotherhood of man where the oppressed march in unity to a single goal. At the other extreme, there is the ideal of the republic of republics which preserves a plurality of ends. Each has, moreover, its own programme of action and emphasises different routes by which the different goals will be reached.

In the brotherhood of mankind, the key notions are liberation and redistribution. Liberation will be reached by throwing off the shackles of power and redistributing resources back to freed subjects. In the brotherhood of mankind, all brothers (and, hopefully, sisters) share equal access to social goods, and all capabilities are equally valued. To this agenda have been joined calls for the liberation of thought, in the form of critiques of the balance of power, of state sovereignty and of the very notion of fixed identities. An early instantiation was the disarmament movement, and disarmament has been a persistent goal; by the 1970s, redistributive justice had become its clarion call; in the 1990s, deep ecology had entered its agenda.

Liberal internationalism has implied, by contrast, the idea of a legal hierarchy, or higher legal order, where the goal would be reached not by disarming power, but rather by harnessing it to a common law based on universal guarantees of rights and/or duties. In this order, power is not distributed back to individuals. Rather, it is collectivised and directed to common ends and communal purposes. This form of internationalism looks to the gradual development of, and widened participation in, international regimes which institutionalise common norms. It emphasises 'prisoners' dilemmas' and the inevitability of the second-best in the absence of co-operation, and it searches for the institutional formula which will allow for the realisation of underlying compatibilities of interests. It advocates collective security directed to the protection of rights and to the defence of commonly agreed norms.

But there is also the third form of a possible international political order: the international civic republic, constituted by republics, where autonomous powers would be balanced, and where nations might co-exist within the bounds of a temporal stability. Here, the means is an enlightened diplomacy where each keeps his powder dry, where the search for advantage is seen as part of the natural order, but where self-interest is prudentially trimmed by a recognised dependence on the moves of historically contingent others.

We do not have to look far to see the conflict among these different internationalisms. They are reproduced in the quarrels about whether distributive justice, or human rights, or alliances and the trimming and hauling of power to maintain international stability, are the foundation principles of diplomacy. They are present when new liberals agonise about whether every nation must have a state and when old liberals observe that universal self-determination would have baleful consequences for international and intra-regional stability. What one can say is that, at the end of the twentieth century, none had gained any clear ideological ascendancy over the others, and that pluralism had, so far, been the victorious doctrine in fact.

Index